RELEASED

BEFORE THE SOCIALISTS

STUDIES IN POLITICAL HISTORY

Editor: Michael Hurst
Fellow of St John's College, Oxford

BEFORE THE SOCIALISTS

Studies in Labour and Politics
1861–1881

by

ROYDEN HARRISON

Senior Lecturer, Department of Extramural Studies,
The University of Sheffield

LONDON: Routledge & Kegan Paul
TORONTO: University of Toronto Press
1965

First published 1965
in Great Britain by
Routledge & Kegan Paul Ltd
and in Canada by
University of Toronto Press

Printed in Great Britain by
Richard Clay & Co. Ltd
Bungay, Suffolk

To Bert Wynn and all my friends and comrades
in the coalfields of Derbyshire and Yorkshire

EDITOR'S NOTE

UNLIKE so many history series this one will not attempt a complete coverage of a specific span of time, with a division of labour for the contributors based on a neat parcelling out of centuries. Nor will it, in the main, be a collection of political monographs. Rather, the aim is to bring out books based on new, or thoroughly reinterpreted material ranging over quite a wide field of chronology and geography. Some will be more general than others, as is to be expected when biography is included alongside of detailed treatment of some comparatively short period of crisis like the appeasement of the Axis Powers. Nevertheless, whatever mode of presentation may have been appropriate, each work should provide an exposition of its subject in context and thus enable the reader to acquire new knowledge amidst things he knows, or could have known.

MICHAEL HURST

St. John's College,
Oxford.

CONTENTS

PORTRAITS

*The portraits of Beesly, Harrison and Crompton are reproduced by courtesy of
the late Alfred Beesly and the Howell portrait by courtesy of the Bishopsgate
Institute.*

ACKNOWLEDGEMENTS

MY greatest debt is to my old friend and teacher, the late
G. D. H. Cole. He acted as my Supervisor while I was an Advanced Student at Oxford preparing my thesis on the English
Positivists and Labour Movements. Like all great teachers, he
gave an unobtrusive guidance which had a value which extended far beyond the limits of my research topic.

Professor Asa Briggs and Mr. John Saville have both read
the greater part of the manuscript. They have been generous
with their time and I am thankful to them for many valuable
criticisms and suggestions. Mr. F. Kool, Editorial Secretary to
the *International Review of Social History*, has, by virtue of his
scholarly regard for detail, saved me from a number of errors.
I am indebted to Chimen Abramsky, Peter Jackson, W. E.
Williams and others (unfortunately too numerous to mention by
name) for help with particular points of fact. My friend,
Stephen Coltham, gave me much assistance particularly during
the earlier stages of my research. Mr. Michael Hurst made a
helpful suggestion about the form which the book should take.
For all errors on points of fact or mistaken judgements which
may remain, I alone am responsible.

None of the material in this book has been published before
in England. However, a large part of three of the following
studies has appeared in foreign periodicals. I therefore wish to
express my thanks to the directors and editors of the following
journals for permission to republish work which appeared in
their pages in an earlier form: *Science and Society* (New York)
Vol. XXV No. 4 for Chapter 11: to the Director of the International Institute of Social History and to the Editorial
Secretary of the *International Review of Social History* (Amsterdam) for permission to use as Chapters III and IV material
which first appeared in the *Review* Vol. VII pt. 3 and Vol. V
pt. 3 continued in Vol. VI pt. 1. A small part of what is now
Chapter V first appeared in the *Bulletin* of the International

Institute for Social History (Amsterdam) 1953 No. 3. Some of the research upon which these articles were based was partly financed by grants from the Sheffield University Research Fund.

I wish to thank all the directors and librarians who allowed me to consult the archives which are listed in the bibliography. They and their staffs showed me the greatest courtesy and consideration. Their learning and their patience made my task easier and more agreeable than it would otherwise have been. I am particularly indebted to Professor Dr. A. J. C. Ruter of the International Institute of Social History and the scholarly and friendly members of his staff. I am under a similar debt to the Director of Le Musée d'Auguste Comte in Paris. The Librarians of the London School of Economics and of University College London were quite exceptionally helpful. Members of the staff of the British Museum Manuscript Room and the Newspaper Library at Colindale endured much on my behalf and I am sincerely grateful to them. I am obliged to the Earl of Wemyss for allowing me to consult the family papers at Gosford House and to Chimen Abramsky for access to his micro-films of the Minutes of the London Trades Council and of the Thomas Larcom Collection in the National Library of Ireland. To all the others, for the keepers of the Richard Congreve Collection at Wadham and the Mundella papers at Sheffield, to the Directors of the Institute of Marxism–Leninism in Moscow and the staff of the Bishopsgate Institute in London, my thanks are also due. (*The abbreviations which have been employed in making references to these archives will be found in the List of Unpublished Sources.*)

I owe a special debt to my friend, Else Hibburd, for helping in checking references, detecting typing errors and suggesting improvement in points of style and to Michael Dunsmore, who prepared the index.

To my wife I am grateful for her generosity in subordinating the claims of crystallography to those of history.

ROYDEN HARRISON

Sheffield.

What happens to a dream deferred?
Does it dry up like a raisin in the sun?
Or fester like a sore and then run?
Does it stink like rotten meat,
Or crust and sugar over like a syrupy sweet?
Maybe it just sags like a heavy load,
Or does it explode?

LANGSTON HUGHES

I

THE SETTING

———◆◆◆———

THIS is a book about working-class politics during the two decades which separated the last of the Chartists from the first of the modern Socialists. If it is not an attempt at a comprehensive or balanced history, neither is it a mere collection of essays. The principal personalities appear in each chapter, the chronological arrangement being designed so as to disclose the development of character as well as of events. The experienced student may manage these studies in any order he pleases, but the general reader will discover a growing dependence of each upon its predecessor. The Republicanism of the early 'seventies, for example, is best understood in terms of the disappointed hopes of 1868. As for the final study of the Intellectuals, this relies heavily for its pursuasiveness upon references to their work made in earlier pages.

With the exception of this opening chapter, nothing has been included for the sake of roundness or completeness. Each study is expected to justify itself in terms of filling a gap or supplying a revision in the received account of the political behaviour of workmen in these two comparatively neglected decades.

There can be little argument about the neglect of the twenty-year interval. Some forty years have passed since Emma Gillespie wrote her pioneering *Labour and Politics in England*[1] and that work did not go beyond 1867. Her fellow countrymen, Slosson and Park, who belonged to the same generation,

[1] F. E. Gillespie, *Labour and Politics in England, 1850–67* (Durham N.C.), 1927.

produced valuable articles and monographs.[1] Subsequently, G. D. H. Cole established the general contours of the period in his *British Working Class Politics*.[2] Since the Second World War these decades have attracted little attention, with the exception of Jeffreys' exciting and judicious volume of documents which dealt with this period without confining itself to political developments.[3] By and large, Labour historians with an interest in politics have been drawn away from the mid-Victorian period by the seemingly greater excitements of Chartism and the birth of the Labour Party. Others, eager to rid themselves of the reproach that Labour history is committed and unacademic, have suggested that too much attention has been devoted to political topics and that the field has been worked so thoroughly by Cole and others that it yields diminishing returns. (Cole himself would have been the first to repudiate such a view.) In deference to Professor Briggs, it is generally conceded that comparative studies of local movements might be rewarding, but apart from this the Labour historian ought to confine himself to economic and social problems. The reader must judge for himself whether or not the present volume demonstrates the possibility of continued useful work in the classic tradition established by the Webbs and the Coles.

The period 1861–1881 belongs to the political, rather than to the socio-economic, chronology of Labour. A few Chartist Associations still existed in the 'sixties and they entered the Reform Movement,[4] but by 1861 Chartism was, to all intents and purposes, a departed force. This was not true of the position in 1851. If Chartism was deprived of mass support in the 'fifties, it still represented a significant tendency in the Labour Movement and it showed its capacity for further theoretical development. As for Socialism, until 1881 it counted its support merely in terms of a few scattered individuals: mostly Owenites or members of the immigration, such as Eccarius, Lessner, Dupont

[1] P. W. Slosson, *The Decline of the Chartist Movement* (New York), 1916; J. H. Park, *The English Reform Bill of 1867* (New York), 1920; J. H. Park, 'The English Workingmen and the American Civil War', *Political Science Quarterly*, Vol. 39, 1924.

[2] G. D. H. Cole, *British Working Class Politics, 1832–1914* (1941).

[3] J. B. Jeffreys, *Labour's Formative Years, 1849–1879* (1948).

[4] M. Dunsmore, 'The Northern Department of the Reform League' (unpublished M.A. thesis, Sheffield, 1962).

and Jung, who belonged in Marx' immediate entourage. Organised Socialism appeared only in the questionable shape of the sect headed by Maurice and Ludlow. Independent working-class politics was not as completely eclipsed as is commonly supposed, but it lacked any clear ideological basis and came into being in relation to much more limited and modest objectives than was the case in earlier or later periods. Apart from Positivism, there was no political philosophy which influenced working men, or won adherents among them by assigning to the working class a distinctive political function or independent role.

The 'sixties and 'seventies therefore represent a tolerably well-defined period in the history of proletarian politics, but this period must itself be seen as comprising three main phases. The first occupied the years 1861–67. The dominant theme was Reform. The extension of New Model Unionism into the building industry, following on the protracted struggles of 1859–61, raised the Labour Question back into a national issue, but under a new form.[1] On all sides fresh assessments were made of

[1] It was in the course of the builders' struggle that George Potter and other labour leaders of the 'sixties first made their reputations. It was also the occasion for the beginning of the long association between the Trade Unionists and the Positivists. The Amalgamated Society of Carpenters and Joiners (ASC&J), the London Trades Council and the Bee-Hive newspaper all owed their foundation, in part at least, to the experience of this conflict. R. W. Postgate, The Builders' History (1923), pp. 167–211, remains the best source despite some minor inaccuracies. The bitterness of the struggle may have owed something to two neglected circumstances of its origin. First, the tragic accident at the site of the Westminster Palace Hotel which occurred on 13 May 1859 when eight men, forced to work overtime against their will, fell to their deaths from an over-loaded scaffold. Second, the success with which the Metropolitan Gas companies locked out their workmen in August 1859, importing German Sugar bakers to take their place and obliging them to sign the 'document'. It was with this example directly before them that the Master Builders locked out their own men and explained to the public that they were being 'cruel only to be kind'.

Other source material which has not been exploited by historians of the London building strike include: M. Nelson, The Nine Hours Movement, Marsh Nelson's Reply to the Master Builders (May 1861, pp. 8); George Potter's own account in Weekly Wages, July 1861, and the critical comments on the full text of his circular of 10 March 1860 which appeared in The Counsellor, 2 April 1860. However, the general significance of the builders' struggle to the working classes of the United Kingdom has been well understood and such new light as might be shed on it falls only on its details.

the characteristic institutions and aims of the working class. In the early 'sixties a new alignment of class and political forces began to emerge. In practice this took place around a number of international issues of which Britain's response to the American Civil War was the most important.

The second phase, 1867–75, is dominated by the politics of the Labour Laws agitation—a subject considered in the concluding chapter. The Trade Union leaders, very much against their will, found themselves forced into conflict with the Government. Soon the associated forward movements of Republicanism and the organisation of the unskilled added to the 'Labour unrest'.

The final phase, 1875–81, saw the consolidation of Lib-Labism. The legal settlement of 1875, concluded under the immediate auspices of a Conservative administration, removed the main obstacle to closer unity between the Labour leadership and the Liberal Party. The onset of the Great Depression contributed to the decline of Republicanism, just as it reversed the tide of militancy and organisation which had swept forward among the unskilled. The programme of the T.U.C. continued to be drafted by the Radical intelligentsia, but it no longer had much political importance. Close working relations between the intellectuals and the Labour leaders ended in 1881. The former brought charges of pedestrianism, subservience to the Liberals and insularity and indifference in relation to colonialism and imperialism.

The chronology of British economic development and of the industrial and social movements of Labour precedes, rather than coincides with these events. It is the socio-economic characteristics of 1850–73 which underpin the political developments of 1861–81. It is the purpose of this introductory chapter to identify those features of the socio-economic background which enter as important elements into the interpretation of the events described in the subsequent studies.

In the first place it is assumed that the whole Labour Movement did indeed undergo a massive transformation, unequalled by any that have occurred before or since, between the second and the third quarters of the nineteenth century. The changes in the quality of working-class politics have to be understood as part of these larger ones which extended into the Trade Union and Co-operative Movement. The temptation to over-draw the contrast has proved irresistible to many historians, but the current reaction against this practice has over-compensated for the earlier emphasis on discontinuity. Never has it been more difficult for the workers of one generation to understand the hopes and experiences of those of another.

Next it is assumed that the basis of this transformation is to be found in the success of British capitalism in overcoming its growing pains and in moving into a position of unquestionable predominance in the world economy. However, references to the 'golden age' of British capitalism are too general to furnish any adequate insight into what was happening in the Labour Movement. If real wages rose, the lion's share went to only a stratum of the working class—the Labour aristocracy.

This notion of a Labour aristocracy is crucial to much of the analysis that follows. If Seton-Watson is right and 'the theory of the labour aristocracy is as artificial as the theory of the class struggle within the peasantry',[1] then the analysis in this volume is faulty at its core. In fact, it will be established that the concept of a Labour aristocracy is not an invention or discovery of Marx and Engels, but almost a commonplace of mid-Victorian socio-economic literature. The distinctive institutions of mid-Victorian Labour become unintelligible without reference to it, and the story of working-class politics in the third quarter of the century is largely about the activities and aspirations of this stratum.

However, it is not a single change in British class structure, but a whole complex of inter-related changes, which lie behind the political developments. The entry of the Labour aristocracy into its classic period coincided with a very marked contraction in the number of domestic producers, the rapid expansion of the professions, and the appearance of a group of new model employers standing at the head of large enterprises possessed of sufficient capital to place them beyond the reach of the everyday dangers of competition. All these changes emphasised in different ways the increasingly polarised character of British society as far as ownership of property was concerned. The absence of a peasantry, and the need for some alternative basis of mass support for property, was more conspicuous than it had ever been

[1] H. Seton-Watson, *The Pattern of Communist Revolution* (1953), p. 341.

before. The paradox of the growth of the proletariat being combined with a decline in revolutionary temper is to be explained, in part, by the industrial and political statesmanship of wealthy men who were profoundly impressed by the exposed position which they had come to occupy.

The rest of this chapter is devoted to the discussion of these propositions. First, the contrast between the Labour Movement in the second and third quarters of the century is pointed up. Objections to the 'simplicities' of this picture are then considered and some of these are accepted, some rejected.

I

The idea that 1850 or thereabouts represents a watershed in the history of the Labour Movement in general—and of the Trade Union Movement in particular—is one which we owe to Sidney and Beatrice Webb. It was taken up and elaborated by their successors who quarrelled, not about whether there had been a vast transformation around the middle of the century, but about how it should be explained and evaluated. Selig Perlman hailed it as marking the discovery of the true philosophy of organic Labour and inaugurating 'perhaps the most notable chapter in world Labour history'.[1] On the other side, Theodore Rothstein treated the emergence of the 'New Model Unionism' under the direction of the 'Junta' as a profoundly reactionary development compared with the militant and revolutionary spirit of the Chartists.[2] In a more recent and less committed discussion of this turning-point, Margaret Cole has gone so far as to assert that 'there have been *two* working-class movements in this country since the Industrial Revolution'.[3]

Ignoring for the moment a whole complex of lapses and anticipations, a stark contrast can be drawn which does bear a recognisable likeness to the developments. Between the second and third quarters of the nineteenth century, the Co-operative Movement did pass from community-building to shop-keeping; the Trade Unions did become less like 'schools of war' and more like the workman's equivalent to the public school;[4] the

---

[1] S. Perlman, *A Theory of the Labour Movement* (New York), 1928, p. 129.
[2] T. Rothstein, *From Chartism to Labourism*, 1929.
[3] M. Cole, *Makers of the Labour Movement*, 1948, p. 1.
[4] A. Briggs, *Victorian People*, 1954, p. 179.

importance of political activity did decline as compared with that attached to promoting social and industrial movements and, as this happened, so did the vigorous insistence upon an independent class basis for such activity diminish; working-class politics became less of a 'knife and fork' and more of a 'collar and tie' question. In the first period the Labour leadership was largely recruited from the crowded ranks of prophets, visionaries and demagogues; by the second it had exchanged these 'outside' enthusiasts for 'great men of business' trained into 'carefulness' through the management of the substantial institutions which they controlled.

The contrast was, above all, one of spirit—as anyone who compares the *Northern Star* with the *Bee-Hive* (even the early *Bee-Hive*) must quickly recognise. In the 'forties, workmen sang the Chartist Hymn on Barebones, or Hartshead Moor. As late as 1850 they could still relish the words of Ernest Jones or of Alfred Fennel.

> Away to the winds with the cant 'moderation!'
> Mercy is not with king, tiger or snake,
> Crush to the dust as they've crush'd each nation
> In the day of our triumph, kings tremble and quake.
> 'Mercy!' yes, *Mercy* such as *they* gave us
> *Such* we'll return, and throneless we'll drag
> From their high places those who enslave us
> To bow—mean and abject—before our Red Flag![1]

Less than twenty years later, not on the moors or in the streets, but in the music halls, they joined in the chorus of 'Don't Stop, Let "Progress" be the Word'.

> For Queen and for Country together we'll stand,
> And you'll find us both loyal and true,
> And if any danger should threaten our land,
> As of old we shall know what to do:—
> We'll follow the plough or we'll follow the drum,
> But don't try to fetter our will,
> For no matter how good the time that has come
> We mean to have a better time still.[2]

---

[1] A. Fennel, *The Red Flag*, in Y. V. Kovalev (editor), *An Anthology of Chartist Literature* (Moscow), 1956, p. 130.

[2] Sung by Miss Nellie Nisbett at the Theatre Royal (1866?), *Reform League Miscellaneous Papers* (H.C.).

The case with the Co-operative Movement is, perhaps, the clearest. The passing of visions of the 'New Moral World', its place being taken by a new pre-occupation with the more tangible advantages of the 'divi', is well documented. 'We have seen enough of Communism,' exclaimed a Co-operator of the early 'sixties, 'enough of the Utopian ridiculous mummery of Socialism . . . We don't want it . . . Let Co-operation be what it is.'[1] What this was conceived to be was well expressed by Henry Pitman's 'Co-operator's Catechism' composed about this time.

What is your name?

Co-operation.

Who gave you this name?

My godfathers and godmothers, the Rochdale Pioneers, by whom I was made prudent, provident, and persevering.

What did your godfathers and godmothers do for you?

They did promise and vow three things in my name: First, that I should renounce 'the public', and all its ways, the pomps and vanities of this wicked world, and all the sinful lusts of the flesh. Secondly, that I should believe my own principles. And, Thirdly, that I should act as if I did, by keeping down expenses, buying in the cheapest market, and giving me credit without ample security.

Dost thou not think that thou art bound to believe and do as the Rochdale Pioneers have promised for thee?

Yes, verily, and by the reciprocal help of the shareholders and other customers I will; and I heartily thank my northern friends that they have called me into this happy condition, through the instrumentality of their principles. And I hope to illustrate those principles by continual practice unto my life's end.

Rehearse the articles of thy belief.

I believe that honesty is the best policy; that 'tis a very good world we live in, to lend, or to spend, or to give in; but to beg, or to borrow, or to get a man's own, 'tis the very worst that ever was known. I believe in good weight and measure, in unadulterated

[1] Cited in S. Pollard, 'Nineteenth Century Co-operation: From Community Building to Shop-Keeping', in K. Briggs and J. Saville (editors), *Essays in Labour History*, 1960, p. 100.

articles, in cash payments, and in small profits and quick returns. I also believe in the maxim 'live and let live', in free trade; and, in short, that my duty towards my neighbour is to love him as myself, and to do to all men as I would they should do unto me.

What does thou chiefly learn in these articles of thy belief?
First, I learn the folly of being a slave, when I may be free. Secondly, I learn to save my money, as well as to earn it. And, Thirdly, I learn how best to spend it.[1]

Co-operation, which had been a system of social justice, was reduced to a few saws worthy of any scrupulous grocer. In place of romantic and reckless experiments in community building, the Co-operators of the 'sixties devoted themselves to the methodical development of retail trading societies and the creation of the C.W.S.

The readiness with which they continued to indulge in expressions of communitarian ideals and to employ an Owenite vocabulary cannot obscure—save from the most superficial observer—the change which had overtaken their purposes. As Pollard has pointed out, the British Co-operative Movement maintained its identity throughout the nineteenth century only with respect to its essentially voluntary character; its reiteration of the virtues of collaboration as against competition, and its avowal of a standpoint felt to be peculiarly working-class.[2]

The development of the Trade Union Movement is generally held to have paralleled that of the Co-operative societies. In fact, discontinuity was much more pronounced in the case of the Co-ops. The relationship between the Rochdale pioneers and this or that society which anticipated their principles is not like the relationship between the Amalgamated Society of Engineers and its precursor, the 'Old Mechanics' or Steam Engine Makers Society. The fact that Rochdale began in the second quarter of the century does not conceal the fact that its importance belonged to the third.

According to the Webbs, the third quarter of the nineteenth century belonged to the New Spirit and the New Model.[3] For the first time it became characteristic of Unions that they had a

[1] F. Harrison, 'Industrial Co-operation', *Fortnightly Review*, 1865, p. 501.
[2] Pollard, op. cit., pp. 110–12.
[3] S. and B. Webb, *History of Trade Unionism* (1912 edition), chapters IV and V.

trained staff of salaried officials and that they discovered how to retain their members. If they paid high benefits, they extracted high contributions and soon attained a position of unprecedented financial strength. The New Model Unionists built on solid foundations, and many a Union, Trades Council and indeed the Trades Union Congress itself could trace back a continuous history to those formative years which saw the establishment of the Amalgamated Society of Engineers. Organisation was nation-wide or even international, and the authority of the centre was insisted upon and re-enforced by the principle of the equalisation of funds between lodges. Instead of attempting to form General Unions, Trade Unionists now set their sights on the national organisation of all those who possessed a common skill. Instead of attempting to secure control over the entire process of production, Trade Unionists aimed at increasing control over the job. Instead of complaining when labour was described as a commodity, 'just like fish', they set out to raise its price by informing themselves about demand and trying to control supply. They tried to encourage emigration, but more important, they sought to shorten the working day, eliminate systematic overtime, limit the number of apprentices and control the size of the task.

The Webbs taught that the New Model was more than an institutional departure: along with this went a New Spirit; a new concern with peace and respectability. The leaders of the New Model taught industry, chastity and sobriety. They advised their members to listen 'to the voice of the lecturer on all subjects connected with our interests', that they might become 'respectful and respected'.[1] In the 'sixties, workmen wrote of the strike as a 'dernier resort': something which was rarely legitimate except in the face of the 'document' or the 'discharge note'. 'Defence not defiance' was the favourite maxim. Instead of trying to crush the employers, the New Model Unionists bent their efforts to securing regular machinery for negotiating with them, and for securing the peaceful settlement of disputes.

The struggle between George Potter on the one side and Robert Applegarth and the Junta on the other was interpreted by the Webbs in terms of a conflict between the old and the new in Trade Unionism. They treated Potter as the spokesman of the

[1] S. Higgenbottam, *Our Society's History* (Manchester), 1939, p. 50.

old-fashioned trade club: of the mindless militancy of the pot-house. An examination of the rules and regulations of Potter's Progressive Society of Carpenters and Joiners brings fresh support to the Webbs' conclusions. The subscription was only 4*d.* a week and there was no thought of expanding beyond London. The constitution enshrined the principles of primitive democracy. For example, the committee was renewed by rotation over a six months cycle. The preamble to the rules harked back to the old panacea of co-operative production as a means of absorbing surplus labour.[1] This Society was a straggler from the 1830s. It survived into the 'sixties because the New Model aroused resentments associated with the unavoidable loss of a democratic experience which had been found valuable in the past.

In 1937, G. D. H. Cole published 'Some Notes on British Trade Unionism in the Third Quarter of the Nineteenth Century'.[2] This article began the work of critically reviewing the Webbs' achievement and introduced a number of serious qualifications into the received account of how the 'pompous trades and proud mechanics' had made over the Trade Union Movement. Cole showed, first, that the New Model Unions differed from some of their precursors with respect to their 'wider effectiveness' rather than in any institutional novelty. Moreover, they organised only a minority of Trade Unionists. The New Model's most spectacular conquests were in the engineering industry, where it extended to cover ironfounders, brass-founders, smiths and patternmakers. It subsequently made substantial headway in building, where it was well represented among the carpenters and bricklayers, and rather less successfully developed among plasterers and painters. In mining, cotton and other textiles, printing, bookbinding, cabinet making, coach building, iron and steel manufacture, glass, pottery, and boot and shoe manufacture, little or no attempt was made to follow the New Model. In this large 'outside' group, Unionism remained either purely local (as in cabinet making), or federal (as in cotton), and often looked upon wider unity as a means to political rather than to industrial action, as with some of the miners. Second, Cole pointed out that the dominance of the Junta in national movements was less complete

[1] *Builders' Salesman and Mechanics Advertiser*, 3 September 1859.
[2] *International Review for Social History*, Vol. 2 (Leiden), 1937, pp. 1–25.

than the Webbs had suggested. George Potter and the 'outside' group were responsible for initiatives, such as the development of the Trades Union Congress, which cannot be dismissed as frivolous or unimportant. Third, he demonstrated that the great amalgamated societies were not so pacifist or capitalist-minded as has sometimes been supposed. He made particular play of Halliday's Amalgamated Association of Miners, as instancing how centralisation of funds might be as readily associated with a militant trade policy as with its opposite. Indeed, militancy did extend to the New Model proper, as was witnessed by the success of the 'nine hours' struggles of the builders and the engineers. (Cole ignored the fact that the latter began as an unofficial dispute). Pacifism, he argued, was a characteristic, not of the New Model as such, but of the policies which these Unions were compelled to pursue after the onset of the Great Depression.

> But for the Great Depression which began in the middle '70s, British Labour would not have waited until 1889 before asserting itself as a movement of the whole Labour class against exploitation . . . It seems to me important [added Cole] that this point should be appreciated, because it is often suggested that, with the decline of Chartism in the later 1840's, the British Labour Movement relapsed suddenly into an acquiescence in capitalist conditions of employment, and even into a belief in the inexorable laws of capitalist Political Economy. That the Trade Union leaders of the 1860's and 1870's were in no sense Socialists I fully agree; but the same may be said of the leaders of Chartism.[1] That they were in no sense revolutionaries I also agree; but it is one thing to abandon revolutionary attempts and quite another to accept the philosophy of capitalism.[2]

Labour historians have been as eager as their colleagues in other fields of historical research to strike blows against 'the fallacious theory of discontinuity'. Consequently, they have seized on Cole's arguments and pushed them further than he was prepared to do. Thus, the New Model is dismissed as a piece of 'historical fiction'.[3] Trade Unionism is held to have exhibited a

[1] It may, but surely not with so much confidence as one realises the moment one thinks of J. F. Bray, Bronterre O'Brien, G. J. Harney or Ernest Jones. The next proposition is also open to question.   [2] Ibid., p. 22.

[3] V. L. Allen, 'Valuations and Historical Interpretation', *British Journal of Sociology*, Vol. 14 (1963), p. 54.

'basic continuity from 1820 to beyond 1870'.[1] Trade Unionists, it is said, had never been much impressed by Chartism or Owenism, and they were no more impressed by the wage fund or any other immutable law of political economy. Since there was no genuine departure, whether in institutions or trade policies, and since Unionists were stolidly indifferent to ideological issues, the quarrel between Potter and the Junta is treated as merely a question of personal antagonisms rationalised in terms of a few differences over tactics.[2]

Whether or not one discerns a basic continuity in Trade Union history during the second and the third quarters of the nineteenth century largely depends on what one is interested in. Perhaps the Webbs paid too little attention to Trade Unionism at the level of local workshop practices. Here the traditional policies with respect to raising wages, reducing hours, enforcing apprenticeship restrictions and imposing the closed shop probably underwent little change. From this standpoint the Webbs devoted too much attention to collective bargaining and too little to the 'unilateral imposition' of craft rules. They allegedly missed the fact that centralised administration was combined with highly decentralised trade policy so as to allow the national leaders to talk sweet reason while the members 'quietly put the screw on the local employers'.[3] Up to a point this is plausible, although it suggests a serious underestimate of the extent to which strike control was attempted by the Centre.[4]

The case for discontinuity has to be made out in terms of changes in national movements rather than with reference to local developments. Whereas in the second quarter of the nineteenth century the craft or 'closed' Unions appeared as laggards in relation to the Trade Union movement as a whole; in the third quarter, they assumed the leading position. The despised

---

[1] See Hugh Clegg's contribution to the symposium on the Webbs as Historians of Trade Unionism, *Bulletin of the Society for the Study of Labour History* (Sheffield), No. 4, Spring 1962, pp. 4–9.

[2] R. V. Clements, 'British Trade Unions and Popular Political Economy, 1850–1875', *Econ. Hist. Rev.*, Vol. 14 (1961), pp. 93–104. See in particular p. 99.

[3] H. Clegg, op. cit.

[4] Consider, for example, Robert Applegarth's intervention in the dispute between the Birmingham carpenters and the local master-builders in 1864–65. R. Postgate, *The Builders' History* (1923), pp. 214–16.

'pukes' and 'exclusives' who had once stood aside from attempts at general union came forward to actively assist the spread of Trade Unionism. However, when they spread Unionism it was cast in their own image. When the A.S.E. gave £1,000 on each of three successive weeks to the strike-fund of the London builders, it signified not only that Unions had attained a new financial strength but that it could be employed on behalf of a new, much more discriminating kind of solidarity. Once a single craft union had attained a position of predominance within its own industry, such that it was no longer endangered by sectionalism or localism, it showed an unsuspected readiness to widen its horizons. The A.S.E. was taken to be something new in the world and its constitution was deliberately copied, not only by English carpenters and bricklayers, but by German and American Unionists. The writ of the New Model might not run beyond the confines of craftsmen's organisations, yet its prestige was such that its spirit, and perhaps even the vocabulary in which it described itself, impressed cotton workers and coal miners. The spinners wrote the word 'Amalgamated' into their title.[1] What is more to the point, the historian of the cotton Unions finds a change of attitude occurring around the mid-century which exactly matches that of the engineers and builders: 'a reconciliation with the new order'.[2] Of the three main sections into which organised Labour was divided between 1850 and 1870 (coal, cotton and craftsmen), it was the last which played the decisive and leading role in most matters which concerned Trade Unionism as a whole. Having substantially solved the problem of how to unify the craftsmen within their industries,[3] the New Model Unions enjoyed the advantage of a national as opposed to a regional membership, so that, from their head offices in London, they could concert and direct policy in quite a new way. The dominion of coal and cotton in Trade Union affairs still lay in the future.

[1] H. A. Turner, *Trade Union Growth Structure and Policy*, (1962), p. 109.
[2] Ibid., p. 119.
[3] Neither Robert Applegarth nor Edwin Coulson were as free from challenges from within and without as Allan of the engineers, but their authority and prestige grew as fast as the membership of the organisation they controlled.

What is new in Trade Unionism between 1850–75 is not so much the changes that occurred in the institutions or trade policies of the craft or closed Unions, but their altered relationship to one another and to the movement as a whole. Craft Unionism, no longer requiring to shelter from storms that had their centre beyond itself, overcame its earlier exclusiveness and generalised its principles. It attained a heightened self-confidence and a wider and more generous purpose which found expression in the 'Junta' and its work in the London Trades Council, the Conference of Amalgamated Trades and—to an extent—in the International. A Trade Unionism concerned with its public image and with its wider mission was encouraged by the continuous association of its leaders with teams of intellectuals. Hitherto, individuals had rendered distinguished service to the Unions in Parliament or in the courts. But it was not until the third quarter of the century that the intellectuals went out to the Unionists in an organised way, seeking to justify Trade Unionism before the public at large, while trying to direct it in accordance with their own social philosophies.

The first of these important intellectual groupings which now entered into close relations with the Trade Union world consisted of the Christian Socialists. In one sense they are ill-described as intellectuals, for they cared more for the heart than for the intellect, and far from aspiring to independent thought they conceived their task to be the revival of Christian influence through a re-statement of Christian principles in terms relevant to contemporary social relations and problems. Despite the fact that the Christians at once attached themselves to the main growing point in the Trade Union Movement, namely, the A.S.E., they maintained their position as principal confidants and spokesmen for the Unions only in the 1850s. From 1861 they were more or less rapidly displaced by the Positivists, a grouping to which the term 'intellectuals' can be applied with much less likelihood of misunderstanding. In relation to several practical issues the two groups worked together, but the Positivists were soon in the ascendant. The Christians were bound to the past by their traumatic experience of 1848, and by their advocacy of Co-operative production in which they saw the alternative to Trade Unionism and industrial warfare. The Positivists on the other hand, treated the Unions as

15

the most fundamental institutions of the modern working class, and neither asked nor expected that they should turn themselves into something else.[1] Taking Trade Unionism as they found it, they became its tireless apologists in the press and its resourceful advisors in the committee room. They tried to supply Unionism with an intellectually-satisfying rationale and defend it in relation to the claims of Liberty; of the State; and of Political Economy. In doing so, they helped to raise craft Unionism to a *movement* dignified with its own *social philosophy*.

To argue that all this relates to the surface of national developments, and that it has no bearing on Trade Unionism in the workshops, is mistaken. In the early 'fifties the engineers had to fight for their existence. So had the builders ten years later. In the late 'sixties and early 'seventies the entire Trade Union Movement was involved in the struggle for a secure legal status. In all these conflicts the intellectuals played a valued and distinguished part. Whatever was the case with the average organised workman on the shop floor, the leaders of Unionism could not afford to be indifferent to public opinion. A picture of stolid indifference to ideology in general and political economy in particular, is misleading.

Trade Unionists in mid-Victorian England took up three attitudes to political economy. Logically these attitudes were mutually exclusive. In practice it was characteristic of many Labour leaders and some of their advisors, that they committed themselves sporadically to two or more of them. First, there were those who openly expressed their hostility. 'If political economy is against the working class, then the working class will be against political economy.'[2] This attitude was supported by the indifference which most workmen displayed to the 'lessons' of political economy when it came to trade disputes. Second, there were a few attempts to champion a Labour political economy independent of, and opposed to, the generally received teachings. This was not merely a question of Marx reading his papers

---

[1] It was largely for this reason that Selig Perlman exempted the Positivists from the censorious judgements that he lavished on other 'intellectuals'. In fact his appreciation of them was one-sided. He missed their 'historicism' and much else besides, as is shown in the final chapter, op. cit.

[2] Report of speech by a bricklayer, *Reynolds' News*, 7 August 1859.

on Wages to the General Council of the International.[1] Occasionally workmen themselves announced that 'they had hit the blot, and urged a fact that would set the working classes all over the country thinking'. Namely, that the working day was divided into two parts, one part going in the shape of wages, the other of profits, the whole case being elaborated (albeit, most imperfectly) in the tradition of Thomas Hodgskin and William Thompson.[2] The third and most distinctive attitude attempted to establish the validity of Trade Unionism within the terms (or the interstices) of orthodox economic theory. Thus, one of the Unions' intellectual counsellors contributed an article to the *Westminster Review* in October 1861 which was the subject of a special letter of thanks by the London Trades Council.[3] According to T. J. Dunning, the respected bookbinder and the school master of London Trades Unionism:

> Previous writers of the same class have written fairly and luminously on the subject of Trade Unions, but this, as far as we know, is the first instance in which the subject, from the working man's point of view is taken, and, from beginning to end, fairly argued in accordance with the stern and inexorable rules of political economy.[4]

This novel article was an attempt to square the trade policies of the New Model with economic theory.[5] The author (E. S. Beesly) set out from the significant assumption that Trade Unionism, although it showed large vision and was generous hearted, was necessarily a minority movement. For a long time to come only a few would exhibit the wisdom and moderation required if the enormous difficulties that faced the formation of an effective organisation were to be overcome. One day with the help of the skilled workmen the agricultural labourers might have a Union, but that day was distant. Moreover, on Beesly's argument, the benefit which Unionism could bring to them was far from clear. He held it

> true that the aggregate wages of the labouring classes cannot be raised except by either an increase of capital or a check to

[1] K. Marx, 'Value, Price and Profit'. (First delivered to the General Council of the International, 20 and 27 June 1865.)

[2] Statement by George Potter, *Reynolds' News*, 13 September 1859.

[3] Minutes of the London Trades Council, 13 November 1861.

[4] *Bookbinders' Trade Circular*, 21 November 1861.

[5] E. S. Beesly, 'Trade Unions', *Westminster Review*, October 1861.

population, neither of which changes do the Trades Unions pretend to effect, at least, directly. But the wages of a particular trade may be, and are continuously from various causes, increased without any increase of the whole fund applicable to wages.

This was possible where the demand for the product was inelastic or 'imperative'. In this case the wage increase would be financed by the consumers. In other cases it might be financed at the expense of the employment or earnings of other groups of workers. If this was so, such behaviour was no more selfish than that of other classes. 'When self-denial becomes the order of the day, it will not be among bricklayers and carpenters that there will be the most room for reformation.'

In its attitude to the unemployed, who were held to be 'usually the worst workmen', and in its high estimate of the non-wage benefits of Unionism, Beesly's article accorded well with the psychology of the New Model Unionist. But he also exhibited their characteristic inconsistencies, for elsewhere he was ready to express sympathy with those who declared their impatience with political economy.[1] In the same article he could speak of wages in general oscillating between the reserve price of labour and the supply price of capital, and refer to this 'debatable ground on which the battle of labour is fought'. It was not so much indifference to theory as confusion on theoretical questions which distinguished the New Model Unionists and their advocates. But the vital limitations which they thought had to be imposed on the scope and usefulness of Trade Unionism showed through this confusion and helped to distinguish it from that which had been characteristic of an earlier time.

Cole was doubtfully correct in holding the Great Depression entirely responsible for the failure of British Labour to assert itself as a class movement against exploitation. The prior predominance of the 'closed' Unions of the engineers and builders within the general movement represented a retarding factor which was not present to the same degree in earlier or later periods.[2] When they could be induced to think about the

[1] E. S. Beesly, 'Mr. Goschen on the Extension of the Franchaise', *Weekly Dispatch*, 8 July 1877.

[2] For some interesting insights into the implications for Trade Union growth within an industry of prior organisation by 'closed' unions, see H. A. Turner, op. cit.

organisation of the labourers at all, the craftsmen always thought in terms of the agricultural labourers and never of their neighbours in the towns.

The changes in working-class politics between the second and the third quarters of the century were more pronounced than in the case of Trade Unionism and rather less pronounced than those which took place in the Co-operative Movement. It is easy, by a selective reading of Chartist literature, to overstress its affinities with revolutionary socialism; to overlook its nostalgia for pre-Industrial society and the persistence and importance of 'knowledge Chartism'. Lovett's concern with the moral, social and educational improvement of the people was of a piece with the leading preoccupations of organised Labour in the third quarter of the nineteenth century. Nor were Labour politics in the 'sixties and 'seventies as 'pedestrian', as remote from all forms of class-consciousness, as given to an opportunist, docile acting-out of roles prescribed for them by the middle class, as has sometimes been supposed. The following chapters will do something to show how complex Labour politics were: how Chartist traditions, far from vanishing without trace, played various and sometimes surprising roles; how the question of class power still intruded and overshadowed political struggles; how the intellectuals exerted an influence very different from that commonly attributed to them.

Yet however much the generally-accepted contrast needs to be refined, it remains a contrast which must be insisted upon. The evidence for the altered mood and the reduced ambitions is compelling. Thomas Cooper's report from Lancashire deserves to be well remembered. On a visit in 1863 he had been depressed by the intellectual and moral decline of the working class. On returning in 1870 his

> sorrowful impressions were confirmed. In our old Chartist time, it is true, Lancashire working men were in rags by thousands; and many of them often lacked food. But their intelligence was demonstrated wherever you went. You would see them in groups discussing the great doctrine of political justice—that every grown-up, sane man ought to have a vote in the election of the men who were to make the laws by which he was to be governed; or they were in earnest dispute concerning the teachings of Socialism. *Now*, you will see no such groups in Lancashire. But you will hear

C 19

well-dressed working men talking, as they walk with their hands in their pockets, of 'Co-ops' (Co-operative Stores), and their shares in them, or in Building Societies. And you will see others, like idiots, leading small greyhound dogs, covered with cloth, in a string![1]

Cooper himself had changed in ways which were scarcely less significant. So had the other Chartists who had held leading positions whether at a national or at a local level. By the 1850s, 'Men who had then (in 1848) been members of the Executive Council of the Charter Association were now directors of a Life Assurance Company.'[2] John Vallance of Barnsley, who had to endure frequent arrests and imprisonments for his political activities, who had spent time in the hulks awaiting transportation and who had even heard the sentence of death pronounced upon him for his association with the Grange Moor insurgents, gradually abandoned politics after the 1840s. Characteristically he devoted himself to social movements. He was one of the first members of the Barnsley Co-operative Flour Milling Society. He took up the 'Water Question' and interested himself in a movement for a public park. He was introduced to the local gentry and although he was not enfranchised by the Reform Act of 1867 'the veteran Radical was not allowed by his wealthy neighbours to want the comforts of life in his last days'.[3] Nearby in Halifax, another member of the Chartist 'Old Guard' told Ernest Jones:

Many of those who were once active Chartists have emigrated. And others, though residing here as usual, have become so thoroughly disgusted at the indifference and utter inattention of the multitude to their best interests that they too are resolved to make no more sacrifices in a public cause.

The writer, John Snowden, sold his services to a local mill-owner, a Whig who had once dismissed him from his employment, but from whom he now received 10s. a week as a kind of retainer. He advised Jones to stop displaying a 'foolish integrity and zeal' and to look in future to his own personal

---

[1] T. Cooper, *The Life of Thomas Cooper*, 1872, p. 393.
[2] T. Frost, *Reminiscences of a Country Journalist*, 1888, pp. 86 and 94.
[3] T. Frost, 'The Life and Times of John Vallance', *Barnsley Times*, 15 April to 29 July 1882.

interests.[1] Jones could never be reproached with having followed this counsel, but he revised his political position during his last years. In 1858 he was coming under heavy fire from the Left, and at the end Engels had to remind himself that Jones' 'bourgeois phrases were only hypocrisy after all'.[2]

In the 1860s, the politically-conscious workman felt closer to the Tolpuddle Martyrs than he did to the Chartists. He was much more likely to meet with imprisonment as a result of a trade dispute, than he was as a result of his political activities. Ernest Jones still had great prestige, and in the North he still carried some real weight, but he won sympathy and respect for his personal sacrifices rather than for his opinions. These were not understood except in terms of some bygone age. George Howell, the Secretary of the Reform League, aspired to be Jones' hagiographer. He saw a continuity between his hero's efforts and his own in terms of the persistent demand for political equality. He hardly grasped that, for Jones, this had meant a bid for class supremacy. Howell himself declared:

> I have never been, and never shall be, an advocate for merely changing our masters. I want neither aristocratic rule, nor the rule of the middle classes, nor the rule of the working classes. I want a government of the entire people—where wealth and intellect will have its fair share of power—no more.[3]

Whereas Jones' old Chartist comrades had appealed to Trade Unionists on the grounds that universal suffrage was an additional means of 'striking property on the head',[4] the Reform League asked them to support it as a dependable means of their 'rising in the social scale'.[5]

Thus, even if the thesis concerning the 'two working-class movements' contains a considerable exaggeration, it is not so extravagant that it can be dismissed out of hand. On the

[1] J. Snowden to E. Jones, 16 October 1859 cited in J. Saville, *Ernest Jones: Chartist*, 1952, p. 74.

[2] F. Engels to K. Marx, 29 January 1869.

[3] G. Howell to J. Morrison, M.P., 30 November 1868 (H.C.).

[4] B. O'Brien in the *Poor Man's Guardian* cited in M. Morris (editor), *From Cobbett to the Chartists* (1948), p. 133.

[5] Reform League, *To the Trade Unionists of the United Kingdom*, n.d.—but in George Howell's hand, 'first issued in June 1865'. In second volume of minutes of the League's General Council (H.C.).

contrary, there was a whole series of inter-related, far-reaching and dramatic changes around the middle of the nineteenth century. The difference in the temper and character of organised Labour in the second and the third quarters of that century are not to be gainsaid: they must be explained.

II

In the Inaugural Address of the International Working Men's Association, Marx argued that 'the misery of the working masses has not diminished from 1848 to 1864'. He would allow only that amidst 'an unheard-of development of industry, and an undreamed-of expansion of imports and exports . . . a minority of the working classes got their real wages somewhat advanced . . .' He declared that commercial and industrial crises were quickening in their return, widening in their compass and deadlier in their effects. Five years later, the Land and Labour League announced that: 'All parties are agreed that the sufferings of the labouring poor were never more intense, and misery so widespread, nor the means of satisfying the wants of man ever so abundant as at present.'[1] If Marx and his supporters could not point to *increasing* 'immiseration', they could still insist that the standard of living of the working class had not risen in a time of unprecedented prosperity. If the real wages of some workmen rose, the share of wages in the national income declined. These conclusions served both as a basis for an appeal to the militancy and revolutionary spirit of the workmen and as an explanation of why such appeals were not responded to. If the working class grew relatively poorer as Capitalism developed, they might be expected to become more class-conscious; but if they suffered no absolute reduction in their standard of life, while a privileged minority actually did better than before, then their theoretic development would be retarded. At the same time Marx believed that the level of theoretic development and of organisation would itself help to determine the worker's standard of life and the distribution of the national income. Thus, the Inaugural Address presented a picture not merely of undiminished misery continuing within unrivalled development, but also an account of the victories of

[1] This Address is reprinted on pp. 246–50.

the political economy of labour over the political economy of property. Co-operative production foreshadowed the end of exploitation and the Ten Hours Act brought 'immense physical, moral, and intellectual benefits'.

There were few who could have quarrelled with Marx' insistence on the unprecedented expansion of British capitalism. The third quarter of the nineteenth century was the Golden Age in which steel and free trade celebrated their triumphs. The annual percentage rate of growth of the industrial economy between 1856 and 1876 was 2–3%. This was 1% down on the earlier period, 1818–55, but the relatively greatest expansion in *output per head* occurred between 1850–80. Output per head rose in the most spectacular way between 1850–70.[1] Similarly, if the British share in world trade declined, its volume grew at an impressive rate, rising from 7% per annum between 1816–42 to 11% per annum between 1842–73.[2] The British economy had reached maturity at a time when problems of political unification still postponed the challenge to its pre-eminence which was to come from North America and Germany.

During this period 'exploitation' (in Marx' sense) may well have increased, since the share of wages in the national income declined after 1850,[3] but real wages (allowing for unemployment) rose substantially. During the 'fifties they showed no upward trend, but from 1863 there was a sharp forward movement which continued for two years until the index reached 120 (1850 = 100). There was a setback at the beginning of the second half of the decade, but real wages began to climb again in 1868 and advanced uninterruptedly until 1875 when they stood at 138. As in the 'sixties, the second half of the 'seventies saw a decline, this time at the rate of 2–4% per annum, and the peak figure of 1875 was not reached again until 1882.[4]

Wood's index of retail prices was avowedly 'experimental',

[1] W. G. Hoffmann, *British Industry 1700–1950* (Oxford), 1955, p. 31. See also D. C. Paige, F. T. Brackaby and S. Freund, 'Economic Growth: The Last Hundred Years', *National Institute Economic Review*, No. 16, July 1961, Table 5, p. 34.
[2] Ibid., p. 40.
[3] Hoffmann, op. cit., p. 54.
[4] B. R. Mitchell and P. Deane, *Abstract of British Historical Statistics* (Cambridge), 1962, pp. 343–4, based on the work of G. H. Wood and A. L. Bowley.

but the trend which the real wage index suggests is confirmed by a study of the *per capita* consumption of coffee, tea, cocoa, beer, sugar and tobacco as illustrated on the accompanying graph. From this it will be seen that in 1880 the consumption of

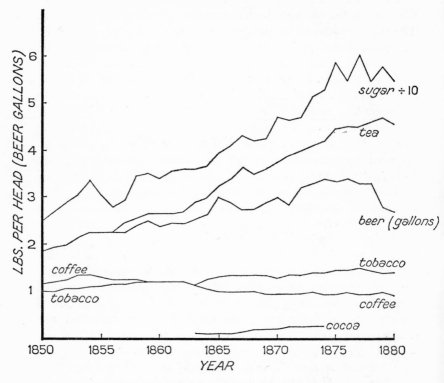

PER CAPITA CONSUMPTION IN LBS. PER HEAD OF COFFEE, TEA, SUGAR AND TOBACCO, 1850–80 AND OF COCOA, 1863–74.

Sources: B. R. Mitchell and P. Deane: *Abstract of British Historical Statistics*, Cambride 1962, p. 356–357 and for cocoa, *Accounts and Papers* (32) 1878, table 18, p. 42–43. Figures for sugar have divided by 10. Beer from W. H. Beveridge, *Unemployment a Problem of Industry* (1930), pp. 42–3.

sugar and of non-alcoholic beverages had more than doubled since 1850 and, as with the 40% increase in the consumption of tobacco, there is a marked upward trend extending across the whole period, interrupted by only minor setbacks. Further evidence is supplied by the increased imports of oranges and lemons. In 1854 the number of bushels imported stood at

814,065. It rose to 1,346,585 in 1863. From that year it rose continually—apart from slight setbacks in 1867 and 1873, until it reached 3,533,781 bushels in 1877.[1]

It seems likely that real wages rose by at least a third between 1850 and 1875. Therefore, if the argument for undiminished misery is to be sustained, it would be necessary to show that there was a worsening of living standards as a result of longer hours, greater intensity of work, inferior housing conditions or other factors which are not taken into account by wage or consumption indices. It is doubtful whether this could be done. Even over-crowding of houses was no worse at the end of the century than it had been at the beginning.[2] If that line of defence is found untenable, it only remains to argue that the entire gains secured by the working class were appropriated by 'the labour aristocracy'. In fact neither the size of this aristocracy nor the extent to which it succeeded in increasing 'differentials' in this period are of the order of magnitude required to account for anything like the whole increase in real wages. However, the presence of this aristocracy and its success in appropriating an increasing share of working-class income, is of cardinal importance. Just as the working class as a whole was raising its standard of life, but at the same time securing a decreasing share of the national income, so within the working class itself the absolute improvement in the standards of the masses took place at the same time as there was a relative worsening of their position *vis-à-vis* the labour aristocracy.

Between 1825 and 1875 a fully-fledged proletariat emerged in England. During the first half of this period the most conspicuous feature of this process was the breaking down of traditional distinctions among the labouring poor; during the second, attention shifted to the building-up, consolidation and sharpening of distinctions within the working class. The domestic outworker was one of the most characteristic figures in the Labour Movement before 1850. Chartism appeared in its most aggressive and determined forms in those small towns in the North where such workers were concentrated. It was the linen handloom weavers of Barnsley and their counterparts in

---

[1] *Accounts and Papers* (32), 1878, Table 18, pp. 42–3.
[2] G. D. H. Cole, *Short History of the British Working Class Movement, 1789–1927* (complete edition in one volume), 1932, Part II, p. 188.

Leicester, Nottingham, and certain districts of Manchester and London who supplied the most devoted following for Feargus O'Connor. It was not the developed proletarian, so much as the workman who was being *proletarianised*, who furnished the best material for those who dared to think of physical force. Although the domestic outworker survived for longer than is often recognised, the rapid erosion of this group continued between 1825 and 1850. In 1832, there were 350,000 handloom weavers. By 1842 there were only 97,000 and by 1848 they had been reduced to 50,000.[1]

To a superficial view, this decline of the pre-industrial craftsmen was bound to lead to the labourers becoming an undifferentiated mass. All who worked with their hands would be known by a single term: 'ouvrier', 'arbeiter' or 'workman'.[2] In fact, the term 'working classes' rather than 'working class' accorded most closely with the linguistic conventions of the mid-Victorians. Politicians, political economists and members of the working classes themselves were at pains to spell out the implications of this distinction. The decline of the domestic producers led to a heightened awareness of the importance of the labour aristocracy. If the one impressed its character on the Labour Movement before 1850, the other did so in the twenty-five years which followed.

Probably the 'aristocracy' grew no bigger, but it certainly became more prominent.[3] Differing from the labourers in the social security which they enjoyed and in their prospects of upward mobility; treated in a markedly different way by the

[1] P. W. Slosson, *The Decline of the Chartist Movement* (New York), 1916, p. 131.

[2] See the lament of Professor Huber who seldom spoke of an 'arbeiter' without 'a certain compunction, and deprecating *reservatio mentalis* or saving clause in favour of the pre-eminent dignity of Handwerk'. *Trans of the Nat. Assoc for the Promotion of Soc. Sci.*, London meeting of 1862, p. 740.

[3] The size of the aristocracy obviously varied greatly from industry to industry. It was large in engineering and in building. According to M. and J. B. Jeffreys ('The Wages, Hours and Trade Customs of the Skilled Engineer in 1861', *Econ. Hist. Rev.*, XVII, 1947, p. 30 n.), 70–75% of the engineering workers were skilled; 15–20% labourers and the balance were semi-skilled. Ignoring men under twenty years of age, L. Levi estimated that in the building industry of the 'sixties there were 447,000 artisans and 250,000 labourers. (*Wages and Earnings of the Working Classes*, 1867, p. 66.)

'boss' and in social relations generally; the privileged position of the labour aristocrats was most evident in the height and regularity of their earnings as compared with those of the plebeians. G. D. H. Cole, using Dudley Baxter's figures, has shown that 14·4% of the wage-earners in the 'sixties had weekly wages at least 40 to 50% higher than those of labourers.[1] Dr. Hobsbawm, who excludes from the labour aristocracy those of the 'highly skilled' who failed to exhibit the second order features that distinguished the true aristocrat, makes a 'plausible guess' that they accounted for 10% of the working class in the third quarter of the century.[2]

Hobsbawm has pointed out that 'the boundaries of the labour aristocracy were fluid on one side of its territory' (where it converged with the lower middle class) but 'they were precise on another. An "artisan" or "craftsman" was not under any circumstances to be confused with a "labourer"!'[3] This was well understood by contemporary observers. Leone Levi admitted that:

> Some are startled with the thought that, in the aggregate, the working classes far outnumber the middle and higher ranks of society. But how many are there who are only a shade below the middle class? Where is the difference between an ill-paid schoolmaster and a foreman in a factory?—between a small tradesman and a mason or a carpenter?[4]

Alfred Marshall was equally alive to the fact that the line that separated 'gentlemen' from the rest lay through—and not above—the working classes. He remarked that

> artisans whose labour is not heavy, who are paid chiefly for their skill and the work of their brains, are as conscious of the superiority of their lot over that of their poorer brethren as is the highest nobleman in the land. And they are right: for their lot does just offer them the opportunity of being gentlemen in spirit and in

[1] G. D. H. Cole, *Studies in Class Structure*, 1955, p. 57.

[2] E. J. Hobsbawm, 'The Labour Aristocracy in Nineteenth Century Britain', in J. Saville (editor), *Democracy and the Labour Movement* (1954), pp. 201–39. The next few pages show the extent of my debt to this admirable essay.

[3] Ibid., pp. 203–4.

[4] L. Levi, *Wages and Earnings of the Working Classes* (1867), p. xxiv.

truth; and to the great honour of the age be it said, many of them are steadily becoming gentlemen.[1]

Frederic Harrison, as a follower of Comte, expected modern society to exhibit a more and more clear-cut division between 'workmen' and 'non-workmen', but, as an astute social investigator, he found it hard to make up his mind whether the most important break occurred along the line that separated the propertied from the propertyless or that which divided the skilled from the unskilled.[2]

As for the precision of the line that divided the 'aristocrats' from the 'plebeians', there is plenty of first-hand testimony.

Between the artisan and the unskilled labourer a gulf is fixed. While the former resents the spirit in which he believes the followers of genteel occupations look down upon him, he in his turn looks down upon the labourer. The artisan creed with regard to the labourers is, that they are an inferior class, and that they should be made to know and kept in their place.[3]

The same point was made with even greater force by another working-class author a few years later.

There is no place in which class distinctions are more sharply defined, or strongly, or, if need be, violently maintained, than in the workshop. Evil would certainly befall any labourer who *acted upon* even a tacit assumption that he was the social equal of the artisan—if, for instance, he added himself unbidden to a group of the skilled hands of the shop who were just chatting about things in general or even put his oar into a conversation that they might be carrying on in his full hearing. Whenever he is admitted upon an apparently equal footing it is the toleration and condescension of the artisan, not the real equality of the labourer, that is to be taken as understood.[4]

[1] A. Marshall, 'The Future of the Working Classes': An Address Delivered on 25 November 1873 in A. C. Pigou (editor), *Memorials of Alfred Marshall*, 1925, p. 105.

[2] F. Harrison, *Order and Progress* (1875). 'There is no greater break in our class hierarchy than that between the lowest of the propertied classes and the highest of the non-propertied classes' (p. 171). 'Perhaps throughout all English society there is no break more marked than that which in cities divided the skilled from the unskilled workmen' (p. 274). The first judgement was originally made in April 1868, the second in March 1874. Harrison reprinted them both without detecting the inconsistency.

[3] T. Wright, *Our New Masters* (1873), pp. 5–6.

[4] 'A Working Man', *Working Men and Women* (1879), pp. 111–12.

That the labourer was a man, 'or at any rate like the murderer in Macbeth, "in the catalogue goes for such", the artisan class would of course be fair to acknowledge; but they would scarcely count him a brother and certainly not an equal'.[1]

As for the labourers, they were grateful enough to be spoken to now and then 'like as if we was the same flesh and blood as other people'.[2] 'The navvies won't go along of the mechanics and the bricklayers. They jeer at us, and calls out, "Oh, here comes an old navvy" and makes game of us: but we reckon we'reselves quite as good as what them is for all that.'[3] A man who had worked as a labourer in 1866 recalled: 'The bricklayers appeared to me, at that time, almost as demigods, the way they shouted for mortar or bricks and the difference between their treatment and ours by the boss.' [4]

The labourers themselves were not wholly without self-respect, or organisation or their own elaborate system of social gradations. Thus, the general labourers working at the docks or coal-portering enjoyed more freedom and displayed more militancy than that 'servant unto servants', the 'attached' labourer who had more security and who tried to bask in the reflected glory of the craftsmen that he worked under.[5] Navvies would insist upon distinguishing between themselves and 'the poor labouring men that happens to be out of work in the neighbourhood'. Moreover, the navvies or 'Ground Men' were subdivided into the 'bankers' or piece-workers (who had an informal version of the artisan's tramping system) and the 'little flannel-backs' and the 'Rodneys'. Each had his distinctive style of dress and a 'banker' would mix socially with a 'little flannel-jacket', but not with a 'Rodney'.[6] The important point to notice, however, is that if the labourers had a system of social stratification it was not joined on to the end of the one which contained the labour aristocracy. Between aristocrats and plebeians there lay a large intermediate group which had as yet neither name nor acknowledged character. It was not until the 'eighties that its presence was remarked upon and it had to wait

[1] 'A Working Man', *Working Men and Women* (1879), p. 105.
[2] E. Eden (editor), *The Autobiography of a Workingman* (1862), p. 49.
[3] Ibid., p. 54.
[4] 'A Working Man', *Reminiscences of a Stonemason* (1908), p. 78.
[5] 'A Working Man', *Working Men and Women* (1879), p. 108.
[6] E. Eden, op. cit., p. 51 et seq.

until the following decade before it was first called 'the semi-skilled'.[1]

If the social distance between the labour aristocracy and the labourers widened during the third quarter of the nineteenth century, it is likely that the differential did also. Cole believed that this happened,[2] and Knowles and Robertson support his opinion.[3] Hobsbawm has assembled much detailed evidence, although it is scattered and incomplete. His figures for the worsted industry, cotton, engineering, mining and ship-building suggest that the wages of the skilled rose more often and sooner than those of the unskilled.[4] The table opposite for building provides further corroboration. It is of interest, not only because of the importance of the builders in the mid-Victorian Labour Movement, but because the differential was probably more rigid in building than in many other industries.

These figures clearly reveal the tendency for the size of the differential to 'hump' up over the period under discussion. In the building industry this can evidently not be explained by technical change. It may have been associated with a situation in which the scarcity of most grades of skilled workers was felt much more acutely than any shortage of their 'attached' labourers. But if market forces assisted the process, the decisive factor was the new readiness of the skilled workmen to discover what the market would bear, instead of allowing custom to go on governing their earnings relative to those of the labourers.[5] As Turner points out: 'Trades Unionism—whatever its effect on the relative shares of workers and employers—has the profoundest impact on the distribution of income among the organised working-class itself.'[6] Thus, the comparative failure

[1] E. J. Hobsbawm, op. cit., p. 213, fn. 1.

[2] G. D. H. Cole, *Studies in Class Structure*, 1955, p. 38.

[3] K. G. J. C. Knowles and D. J. Robertson, 'Differences Between the Wages of Skilled and Unskilled Workers, 1880–1950', *Bulletin of the Oxford Institute of Statistics*, Vol. 13, 1951, pp. 109–27 ('. . . it seems probable that the strong craft unions of the mid-nineteenth century were able to establish a new wage differential in favour of their members . . .', p. 115).

[4] E. J. Hobsbawm, op. cit., particularly pp. 224–5.

[5] E. J. Hobsbawm, 'Custom, Wages and Workload in Nineteenth Century Industry', in *Essays in Labour History*, A. Briggs and J. Saville (editors), 1960.

[6] H. A. Turner, 'Trade Unions, Differentials and the Levelling of Wages', *Manchester School of Economic and Social Studies*, Vol. 20 (1952), p. 282.

of the Manchester plasterers, which is revealed in the Table above, is doubtless associated with the relatively poor standing and low level of organisation of this trade. The trend to widening differentials has to be understood in terms of an 'aristocracy' which looked on organisation as its own exclusive province, and

RATIO OF WAGES OF CRAFTSMEN TO LABOURERS IN THE BUILDING INDUSTRY AROUND THE THIRD QUARTER OF THE NINE-TEENTH CENTURY

	1850	1860	1870	1877	1883
In London (all craftsmen)	1·50	1·65	1·68	1·85	1·58
In Manchester:					
Joiners	1·41	1·58	1·77	1·77	1·56
Bricklayers	1·52	1·66	1·60	1·79	1·56
Masons	1·41	1·50	1·50	1·61	1·65
Plasterers	1·52	1·40	1·45	1·58	1·56

In Southern England:				
1847–52	1853–60 (cs) 1853–65 (ls)	1866–71 (cs) 1867–71 (ls)	1871–73 (cs) 1872 (ls)	1873–92 (cs) 1873–82 (ls)
(All craftsmen):				
1·48	1·58	1·68	1·61	1·56

cs = craftsmen   ls = labourers

Sources: For London, A. L. Bowley, *Wages in the United Kingdom in the Nineteenth Century* (Cambridge), 1900. Chart facing p. 90.
For Manchester, L. Levi, *Wages and Earnings of the Working Classes* (1885), p. 107.
For Southern England, E. H. Phelps Brown and S. V. Hopkins, 'Seven Centuries of Building Wages', *Economica* (N.S.), Vol. XXII (1955). Table on pages 205–6.

took the defining features of a labourer to be that he had neither skill nor a Union to protect him.[1]

Those who did attempt to organise the unskilled in the towns complained that 'strikes had failed in consequence of the aristocracy of mechanics and artisans ignoring the underpaid labourers'.[2] Sometimes they asked the skilled mechanic to help elevate the lowest strata; at others they mocked 'the

[1] 'A Working Man', *Working Men and Women*, 1879, p. 105.
[2] Speech by C. Keen, *Eastern Post*, 22 December 1872.

head-workers, the geniuses of labour' and told them that they were only labourers themselves.[1]

By the third quarter of the century the Labour Movement had become pre-eminently a movement of the Labour Aristocracy. The most distinctive and stable Labour institutions were constituted in such a way as to shut out the vast majority of workmen. The subscriptions to the New Model Unions in building and engineering were never less than 1s. per week and sometimes rose to as much as 2s. per week.[2] The Rochdale principle of no credit without ample security, closed the Co-operative Societies to the great mass of unskilled labourers. Bad weather, strikes by the artisans or the normal fluctuations of trade, could reduce the earnings of such men to 7s. a week and made shopping on credit unavoidable.

This profound gulf between the 'aristocracy' and the 'plebeians', between the organised and the unorganised, did not prevent the spokesmen of the former stratum from presuming to speak on behalf of all the working classes. Socially and industrially the labour aristocracy took care to separate itself from the vast labouring majority, but in politics it sometimes found it convenient to pose as the authentic spokesman of the working classes as a whole. It was encouraged in this by some of its advisors, who began by arguing that the 'best part of the working classes' forms the most fit class to exert political influence; 'the superior order of workmen' possessed higher social sympathies and a more practical knowledge of social misery than other classes. These sympathies and this knowledge 'identified' the labour aristocracy with the vast labouring majority. From these premises the conclusion was drawn that the political opinions of the labour aristocracy could legitimately be treated as if they were the opinions of the masses and were entitled to that reverence which democratic prejudice reserves for the will of majorities.[3] But the Trade Union leaders, who were acquainting the Government and Public Opinion with the needs of Labour, carried on trade policies which hinged on preventing the unskilled from 'creeping into the trade'. The sponsors of

[1] *Republican*, January 1871.
[2] H. J. Fyrth and H. Collins, *The Foundry Workers* (Manchester), 1959, p. 57.
[3] F. Harrison, *Order and Progress*, 1875, pp. 150–1.

Co-operative Society projects might explain that 'the poorest son of toil is not shut out, the shares being £1 each',[1] but these words must have had an equivocal sound in the ears of the millions who earned 15s. or less per week. Speaking of Co-operation in all its forms it was observed that by 1867 it had raised nearly 150,000 of the working classes

> collectively, if not individually, by this means alone, into the position hitherto occupied by the shopkeeping class[2] . . . Thousands of working men in these various establishments (Co-operative production units) are learning to enter into the position and to share the interests of the employer class.[3]

The more discerning members of the governing classes saw through the presumption of working-class spokesmen and were alternately reassured and perturbed by it.

Mostly they were reassured: 'During the last quarter of a century,' wrote Leone Levi, 'the higher strata of the labouring classes have exercised an elevating influence over every branch of British labour.'[4] By the 'sixties, Members of Parliament corrected those of their colleagues who continued to think of the working class in terms of the type of person one saw at the corners of the streets of the Seven Dials: the Irish labourer or the stalwart navvies with red handkerchiefs. These were the symbols of the 'dangerous class'. The working class consisted of men who had distinguished themselves by 'great ingenuity, by great skill, by the most unshaken loyalty to Throne'. With a pardonable exaggeration, one Honourable Member declared that such men were not to be found in 1832.[5]

The political importance of the Labour aristocracy had been recognised even before 1850. Indeed, the saying, 'Only pull down the artisan class of this country to the level of the labourer and the Charter will have to be granted', was held to be a commonplace,[6] but it was not until the 'sixties and 'seventies

---

[1] S. Pollard, op. cit., p. 108.

[2] J. M. Ludlow and Lloyd Jones, *Progress of the Working Class, 1832–1867* (1867), p. 139.

[3] Ibid., p. 146.

[4] L. Levi, *Wages and Earnings of the Working Classes*, 1885, p. 25.

[5] G. Leeman, *Parl Debates 3rd Series*, clxxxii, 26 April 1866, 2127.

[6] R.C. Trade Unions, 1867, 8753.

that a new generation of large employers turned their sense of the Labour aristocracy's importance into a coherent policy.

The New Model employers of mid-Victorian England were impressed by the growing polarisation of society with respect to the ownership of property, and by the opportunities and responsibilities of the large employer of labour.

> In England [one of them wrote] the class of persons is gradually being diminished, who, without large means, enjoy the advantage of holding a position of independence. Theirs is an order essential in a happily constituted society, as the connecting link between the rich and the poor. They are the defenders of the rights of property, while in their modest and frugal households there is nothing which obtrudes itself in painful contrast to the condition of the less independent wage-earners among whom they live.[1]

The French bourgeois, even though he was confronted by an artisan class which was supposed to be thoroughly imbued with socialism, viewed the future with more composure than his English counterpart. He could draw attention to the reassuring circumstance which was absent in England:

> Enfin, entre ces couches extrêmes flotte la couche moyenne, en minorité dans les grandes agglomérations, mais en majorité dans les campagnes et dans les petits centres de population. La plus sensée, la plus attachée à ses devoirs; se mariant et visant a l'épargne; indifférente aux questions politiques qui ne touchent pas directement à ses intérêts; capable cependant, bien qu'elle montre peu de goût pour les utopies socialistes, de se laisser entraîner momentanément par intimidation ou par séduction. Population honnête après tout, et qu'on gagne par de bons procédés.[2]

In France the peasantry and the petit-bourgeoisie brought mass support to the defence of property. Solomon had peace on all sides, although Judah and Israel were many as the sand which is by the sea for multitude, because every man dwelt under his vine and under his fig-tree. If in England the provision of vines and fig-trees even on the basis of co-operative production, presented difficulties, then rich people had to find

---

[1] T. Brassey, 'Co-operative Production', *Contemporary Review*, July 1874, pp. 215–16.

[2] Anon., *Les Classes Moyennes Dans La Démocratie Moderne: Des Causes Qui Menacent Leur Influence: Des Conditions Qui Peuvent La Maintenir* (Paris), 1868.

other ways of convincing the masses that they cared for their welfare. The case was stated with brutal candour: 'rich people, some day, will be so few that they will not be able to make any stand against the many poor'. If the upper classes wanted to have 'the game in their own hands', then they would have to show sympathy with those below them. In that event

> all classes will become united, and the upper class will really be the ruling class. And what is this but a spread of true religious feeling, from the upper class to the lower classes? It means that religion must bind all classes together. And this must begin with the upper classes: for if it begins with the lower classes, these will come to the top and get the upper hand.[1]

But who among the upper classes could be expected to respond to these dire warnings? In the first place, it was the large employer who was seen to have—and frequently felt himself to have—the strongest interest as well as the greatest opportunity. It was Brassey who formulated the law that 'the disposition to be liberal towards workmen is developed, as a general rule, in proportion to the business and capital of the employer . . .'[2] The Positivists, with diminishing assurance, taught workmen to expect this. What was more to the point, the workers' own experience tended to bear it out. Thus, the gifted tailor, J. G. Eccarius, long before he broke with Marx and associated with Brassey, declared that

> the large manufacturer, the interest of whose capital is sufficient to maintain his household in comfort and affluence, is more likely, when profits run low, to enter into partnership with his work-people, than the little exacting, avaricious, busy-bodies, who can scarcely hold their ground against the large capitalist, and yearn to make a fortune.[3]

The experience that the big employer of labour was easier to deal with may have been peculiar to the skilled workman. The unskilled, trying to form industrial or general Unions, found

---

[1] 'A Daughter of the People', *The Working Classes*, 1869, pp. 15 and 27–8.

[2] T. Brassey, op. cit.

[3] J. G. Eccarius, 'A Working Man's Refutation of Some Points of Political Economy Endorsed and Advocated by John Stuart Mill Esq., M.P., XII Property', in *Commonwealth*, 2 March 1867.

the 'great companies' their toughest opponents.[1] Big capital was associated with a special readiness to make concessions to the labour aristocracy organised in craft unions, and a specially determined resistance to the claims of unskilled labour organised in general Unions. The point, however, should not be pushed too far, since employers almost always offer fierce resistance to the *creation* of Unions, whatever policy they may care to adopt towards them subsequently.

Whether there was a tendency between 1850 and 1880 for production and employment to become concentrated in certain large firms is difficult to determine, because of the meagre statistical evidence. However, this does seem to have been true of some branches of industry. For example, while brewing did not proceed towards concentration as rapidly as it did between 1880 and 1900, the tendency was already at work although it proceeded at half the pace which it subsequently attained.[2] In the 'sixties, it was alleged that 20,000 iron miners worked for 10 mine owners.[3] After 1850 'the number of firms engaged in calico printing reached its maximum and all further expansion took place through the extension of these printworks'.[4] The emergence of big producers in the worsted industry was conspicuous even in the early years of the century.[5] In other branches of textiles there were firms which had, by the 'sixties and 'seventies, reached twentieth-century dimensions while retaining the characteristics of the family business and employing, in part, pre-factory productive techniques. This was the case with the great concern of I. and R. Morley, the hosiery manufacturers. In the 'sixties Samuel Morley was the sole head of the business in London and in Nottingham. It employed 3,000 persons in seven factories in the Midland counties. But this business still employed a considerable number of frame-work knitters, and behind men who figured as direct employees of Morley stood the members of their families who were indirectly

---

[1] Speech by T. Venner to 20,000 labourers in Shoreditch; *Eastern Post*, 7 July 1872.

[2] J. A. Hobson, *The Evolution of Modern Capitalism* (Revised Edition 1926), p. 118.

[3] Address of the *Land and Labour League*, 1869. See below p. 247.

[4] G. Turnbull, *A History of the Calico Printing Industry of Great Britain* (Altrincham), 1951, p. 111.

[5] C. Driver, *Tory Radical, The Life of Richard Oastler* (Oxford), 1946, p. 11.

employed by him. If the man made the hose, his wife sewed it and the children had a share in the minor branches of the work. Allowing for this, it is estimated that Morley employed as many as 8,000 persons.[1]

Whether or not the trend to concentration set in rather earlier than economic historians have suggested, there can be no doubt that in the 'sixties and 'seventies a number of large employers adopted a new, positive approach towards the Trade Unions in particular and the Labour Movement in general. The first characteristic of these New Model employers was that they stood at the head of substantial, well-established enterprises. If these businesses were not large enough to confer monopolistic power, they were of a size sufficient to free their owners from the more pressing anxieties of the competitive struggle. Such was the position of the Bass brothers in brewing; of Lord Elcho in coal and iron; of Brassey among railway contractors; and of a whole host of wealthy textile manufacturers, headed by Samuel Morley who was reputed to be one of the wealthiest men in England. The textile manufacturers tended to come from the woollen industry of the West Riding rather than from Lancashire, and were particularly well-represented in and around Bradford where Titus Salt, Alfred Illingworth and the Kell Brothers furnished some of the leading examples. The New Model employer believed in the economy of high wages (like Brassey), and favoured the recognition of Trade Unions, collective bargaining and the orderly settlement of trade disputes through settled machinery for conciliation and arbitration (like A. J. Mundella and Samuel Morley). He was not a mere industrialist. He had wide social interests and a highly developed political sense which was marked by a readiness to engage in political activity which, in so far as it bore a party aspect, was generally—but not always—identified with the cause of Gladstonian Liberalism. Strong, he felt that if he tried his strength he might merely show his weakness. If he inherited the self-confidence of his pioneering forebears, he exhibited less of their arrogance: he was conscious of the exposed position which he had come to occupy.

[1] E. Hodder, *The Life of Samuel Morley*, 1887, pp. 186–9.

Whatever the poor may feel towards the rich, the duty of the rich towards the poor is too plain for misconception. Whether moved by considerations of policy or by the nobler impulses of humanity, it must be the object of our universal solicitude that no class in society should be exposed to the fatal influence of despair.[1]

Just as the Professor of Political Economy at Oxford thought 'it might be convenient in times of trouble, which are perhaps not so far off as many think, that we should be able to work upon the mind of the working classes through teachers and advisors whom they trust',[2] so the New Model employers themselves cultivated the Trade Union leaders. Lord Elcho would have the miners' leader to a champagne breakfast,[3] and A. J. Mundella would congratulate himself on the good effects of wining and dining delegates to the T.U.C.[4] Special relationships grew up between particular employer-politicians and Trade Union-politicians. For example such relationships existed between A. J. Mundella and Robert Applegarth; Lord Elcho and Alexander Macdonald; Samuel Morley and George Howell; Crawshay, the iron-master, and John Kane. Just as Samuel Plimsoll concerned himself with the welfare of the merchant seamen, so his fellow employers, Bass and Morley, actively aided Trade Union organisation among the railwaymen and the agricultural workers. Morley, the Kells, Edmond Potter and others gave financial assistance to working-class papers such as the *Bee-Hive* and the *Commonwealth* at certain critical moments and they made important contributions to the coffers of the Reform League.[5] Samuel Morley even presided at meetings where Ernest Jones or E. S. Beesly delivered speeches which had markedly revolutionary undertones. When sections of the press

[1] T. Brassey, op. cit., p. 235.

[2] *Spectator*, 20 July 1861.

[3] Earl of Wemyss and March, *Memories, 1818–1912* (Vol. I), (1912). Printed for private circulation.

[4] 'The Trade Union Congress falls very heavily on me but I am doing my duty and marvellously good is the apparent result. Much more forbearance and moderation characterise all their proceedings . . . I wish you could have been at the breakfast this morning, given by Morley, myself and the borough members. The kindly tone which prevailed at the gathering was excellent. It is very pleasant to have such evidence of the usefulness of one's labours.' A. J. Mundella to R. Leader, 10 January 1872 (Mundella Collection, Sheffield University Library).

[5] For further discussion see particularly chapters IV and VI.

mocked him for doing this or referred to the irony of it, he replied that

> it is better that large employers of labour should be willing to hear all that can be said by the advocates of the working class, rather than, from over-sensitiveness as to their reputation, or indifference as to the condition of the people, or even fear of 'unconscious irony', shut themselves within their own circle.[1]

Probably it was always the case that the well-established, second-generation employer was less inclined to dedicate himself to grinding the faces of the poor. There had been Fieldens and Woods before there were Morleys. Many of the attitudes and practices of the big employers of the 'sixties had been anticipated by their predecessors, just as Peel anticipated much that went into the making of Gladstonian Liberalism. As with the New Model Unionists so with the New Model employers: what distinguished them was the multiplication of their number, their wider effectiveness; their team work and their heightened self-consciousness and sense of social purpose. Similarly, the example was one which only a prosperous minority might follow: not every British employer could afford to take Morley for his mentor and erect philanthropy into a system of business.[2]

The motives of the New Model employers were varied and complex, but they shared a common awareness of the exposed position of property and of its need to find outside support. Hence the importance of coming to terms with the Labour Aristocracy and playing court to its leaders. If they could offer no encouragement to hopes of the millennium, they could sustain a lively expectation of the half-loaf. The Labour leaders, weary of apocalyptic forecasts and revolutionary movements, rarely asked for more. They preferred a pedestrian success to an heroic failure.

Yet they were not incapable of heroism, nor were all their successes so pedestrian. Sometimes harried from without; sometimes harking back to the past; sometimes given a premonition of the future, the Labour leaders hesitantly advanced into a new formative era. It was in the context of the British response to the American Civil War that the new leaders discovered their identity and established their own character through conflict with some of their predecessors.

[1] E. Hodder, op. cit., p. 251. [2] Samuel Morley, *D.N.B.*

II

BRITISH LABOUR AND
AMERICAN SLAVERY

T HE unanimity with which the British workers condemned the Slave Power was insisted upon by contemporary observers and has been affirmed by historians.[1] Had
not Lincoln himself referred to the stand of the Lancashire
workmen as 'an instance of sublime Chritsian heroism which
has not been surpassed in any age or country'?[2] The perspicacity and courage of these men was repeatedly referred to
by supporters of the Russell–Gladstone Reform Bill of 1866 as
evidence of their political maturity.[3] Not a single member of
the House dared to challenge the view that the working class
had stood by Lincoln and the North from first to last. Historians
as hostile to Labour as Professor Beloff have attempted to revise
traditional estimates of the importance of working-class
opinion, but have referred—without qualification—to 'the
pro-Northern sentiments' of the proletarian press.[4] Academic
historians who would not go as far as P. S. Foner in describing
the heroic efforts of the English workers as 'by far the most
important force' preventing intervention on behalf of the
Confederacy,[5] still acknowledge it to have been a significant

[1] H. Schlüter, *Lincoln, Labour and Slavery* (New York, 1913), pp. 8–9.
[2] Ibid., p. 10.
[3] Hansard, Vol. 182 (3rd Series). See particularly speeches by Villiers
(p. 173), Fawcett (p. 204) and Layard (p. 1444).
[4] M. Beloff, 'Historical Revision CXVIII', *History*, February 1952.
[5] P. S. Foner, *History of the Labour Movement in the United States* (New York,
1947), p. 313.

factor for peace in Anglo-American relations. Thus, it is said that

> the anti-war attitude of the British Labour was a cardinal point in the struggling Labour sheets of the time, such as the *Bee-Hive* and the *Miner and Worker* [*sic*] *Advocate*; the files of these papers portray a threatening protest against those who would support the Confederacy for a bale of cotton . . .[1]

Karl Marx declared on more than one occasion that it was the British workmen who had averted war. He referred to 'the labour kings of London' as the men who had 'prevented Palmerston from declaring *war* upon the United States, as he was on the point of doing, through the monster meeting in St. James's Hall (under Bright's chairmanship)'.[2] E. S. Beesly, who had been a principal participant in the meeting mentioned by Marx, recalled at the end of the Civil War how the workmen and their allies had forced the upper classes to 'keep their hands off when they wanted to break into the ring'.[3] This opinion has been sanctified by a century of tradition in both Britain and the United States.[4] It has been embellished to the point that the International Working Mens' Association is made an important agency for the promotion of support for Lincoln, and Marx himself is described as the author of the great meeting in St. James's Hall.[5]

It has been well said that 'To realise the relative validity of one's convictions and yet stand for them unflinchingly, is what distinguishes a civilised man from a barbarian'. Similarly, to recognise the true proportions of human achievements and yet to preserve them from those who would dismiss them or magnify them, is what distinguishes an historian from a propagandist.

---

[1] M. P. Clausen, 'Peace Factors in Anglo-American Relations', *Mississippi Valley Historical Review*, Vol. 26, No. 4.

[2] Marx to Weydemeyer, 29 November 1864. (Cited in L. E. Mins, *Founding of the First International* (New York, 1937), pp. 51 f.)

[3] E. S. Beesly, 'The Republican Triumph', *Bee-Hive*, 29 April 1865.

[4] For example, speech by Senator George Hoar, *Congressional Globe*, Vol. 64, p. 102. And A. Rothstein, *Peaceful Co-Existence*, 1955, p. 14.

[5] 'The organisers of this meeting were Karl Marx and Frederick Engels.' P. S. Foner, *History of the Labour Movement in the United States* (New York, 1947), p. 316. See also H. Koht, *The American Spirit in Europe*, 1949, p. 138, and R. Greenleaf, 'British Labour Against American Slavery', *Science & Society*, Vol. 17, No. 1, 1953.

The serious student of the Labour Movement knows that internal conflict is as much a law of its development as is the struggle against its enemies. The British working class was profoundly opposed to American slavery, but it had within it influential Trade Union leaders, editors and advisors, whom hatred of the North made friends to the Confederacy. If these men have no place in the mythology of Anglo-American relations during the Civil War, they retain a place in its history.

I

In the Summer of 1863, T. J. Dunning, secretary of the Bookbinders' Society and 'father of London Trades Unionism', wrote three articles for the *Bee-Hive* newspaper on the 'National Character of the Federal States'.[1] The title itself gave a kind of backhanded support to Gladstone's contention that Jefferson Davis had created a nation.

In considering Dunning's opinions, it ought to be borne in mind that not every champion of popular causes in England belonged in that tradition which saw the United States as 'the fairest experiment ever tried in human affairs'. Dunning was a singularly well-read man and it may be presumed that his notes on the Yankees owed something to Dickens' description of them as boors; Carlyle's view of them as bores; and, perhaps, to Ruskin's references to their lust for wealth, their vulgar faith in magnitude and multitude.[2]

Dunning asserted that the peoples of the Northern States were, unlike the Southerners, ethnically heterogeneous. They numbered among them what he termed 'a considerable proportion of the scum of Europe'. The majority of them were not, however, vicious or turbulent. Rather were they timid and apathetic. Timidity and apathy—given republican institutions —led to the ascendency of the truculent and overbearing few.

Whereas the Southerner, in Dunning's opinion, was too proud to care what others thought of him, the Yankee became excessively sore at adverse criticism. He was forever blowing his own trumpet. It was characteristic that Mr. Seward could celebrate the second anniversary of the attack on Fort Sumter

[1] *Bee-Hive*, 16 May, 13 June, 11 July 1863.
[2] H. Pelling, *America and the British Left* (1956), Introduction, pp. 1–6.

by announcing, 'our armies are moving on with a firmer step than those of the Roman Empire or the French Republic ever maintained'.

After egotism and brag, the leading features of the North American character, according to Dunning, were astuteness and credulity. The Yankee was astute about what affected his interests and credulous about all else. Dunning conceded that the Federals were a people of 'great enterprise and ingenuity. But besides the undertaking of arduous and difficult things—a merit they undoubtedly possess—there is another somewhat ironical and perhaps spurious meaning to the word 'enterprising' which the late Mr. Cobbett illustrated by saying "that he never knew an enterprising young man who did not want others to work for him while he looked on and received the benefit of their labour". While they have the benefit of the first sense of the word they are most certainly entitled in a most eminent degree to the merit of the second, as illustrated by Mr. Cobbett. While not altogether refusing to do it themselves, there is among the Americans generally, an invincible desire of getting all their laborious and dangerous work done by others.' In business, they are selfish and grasping; in time of war, they prefer to let the Germans, the Irish and the Negroes do the fighting for them.

If racial considerations were at the root of these weaknesses of the American character, such influences were powerfully seconded—in Dunning's opinion—by the much-vaunted educational system of the Northern States. Certainly, education was much more widely diffused in America than in England, but it would be 'a profound mistake' to think that this would lead to excellent and responsible citizens.

Education should train the mind to suffer as well as to do . . . This teaching, however, seems to be as a rule entirely neglected in America. In England, if a boy does not do as he is told, or mind what is said by his parents, he most commonly gets a good thrashing and, therefore, he is more or less docile and obedient . . . This is not the case in America. Children there, not being made to obey, soon condemn the authority of their parents, and the result is that the boy is only half educated. By having his own way in everything he is well indoctrinated as to his own rights, but has been, by this process, kept in ignorance of the duty of respecting

43

the rights of others . . . As the masses, when children, condemned the authority of their parents, so, when grown up, they condemn the counsel and authority of their superiors in intellect and morals, and will have none of them.

Hence, the corruption and mendacity of public life in the Federal States. Hence, the insubordination and incompetence of Federal armies which convert 'what would otherwise be good soldiers into a ferocious banditti, the derision of the enemy, and the terror only of the peaceful inhabitants whose country they devastated'.

Dunning concluded by dismissing the declared war aims of the Federal Government.

Slavery—though not practically an institution in the North—alas for John Bright and all sincere haters of Negro slavery—was, up to the present quarrel, carefully fostered and protected. North and South conspired to make the whole of the continent under their control one vast slave pen. It is this circumstance and its corresponding results that cause so few heartily to sympathise with the North. Men who exercise their judgement, are not able to see the Northern hatred of slavery, in its intense hatred of the Negro, and of all their race, or in its alacrity to pass the Fugitive Slave Law. It is impossible to conceal the fact that if the South had desired to return to the Union, they would have been gladly received with slavery restored more rampant than it had ever existed before. It is only spoken and acted against as a military measure and because the North see themselves cut off from its profits . . . This feeling against the Negro has abated since they have been enlisted as soldiers in the Federal Army. Two reasons have been given by the American press. First, because it will save the American people from serving in the Army; and, secondly, because it will, to that extent, destroy the Negro.

Dunning sought to add authority to his account of the National character of the Federal States, by allowing qualifications and exceptions. If they boasted, they had some things to boast about. If Seward was 'the prince of wind-bags', Lincoln, 'with all his faults, has too much good-sense and thorough honesty of purpose to be their truly chosen representative'. (His election was a 'fluke'.)

It has been repeated that the North are a heterogeneous people. It may be true, therefore, that some parts of the above are inapplicable to a certain section of the people, exactly as, in a description of their army—the character of the Pennsylvanian Regiment which laid down during the fight, and could not be made to get up, would be wholly inapplicable to the brave Negro regiment, which is said to have lost 400 of 600 men, before it retreated.

Dunning, born in 1799, was the most respected and articulate representative of the older generation of Trade Unionists who were active in London during the Civil War. He had been a Chartist, had worked with Lovett and contributed to the Chartist press. In 1860 he wrote a book entitled *Trades Unions and Strikes: Their Philosophy and Intention* which won public approval from John Stuart Mill.[1] He offered vigorous and continual opposition to every attempt to enlist the sympathies of London workmen on behalf of Lincoln and the Federal Government. With the support of the Compositors, he revived the old 'no politics' cry in the Trade Union movement.[2] When this failed to prevent the famous St. James's Hall meeting, Dunning disciplined one of his members who had been a party to the arrangements and took the Book-binders out of the London Trades Council, on the grounds that that body had allowed the public to imagine that this was a demonstration of the Trade Unions of London. Dunning declared that 'The trades were not consulted at all, much less their authority given.' He told a Lodge Meeting of his own Society that

> the trades of London are dead against slavery, but they have no confidence in Mr. Lincoln either as an opponent to slavery or as a friend to the Negro. His Emancipation Proclamation, which extends only to the disloyal states, they consider less intended to benefit the Negro, than to destroy, if possible, the 'Confederates'. Of course we say nothing as to their correctness, but such are the opinions of nine out of every ten workmen we have heard speak on the matter. Nor have we found one who can see the justice or the neutrality of one of the belligerents being allowed to obtain men, arms and ammunition from this country, while the other is not allowed to obtain ships, or able to see the legal distinction between the two except as so much 'bosh', set up to cover the partiality or the fears of the English Government.[3]

[1] 'Labour Portrait, No. XVIII', *Bee-Hive*, 8 November 1873.
[2] T. J. Dunning, 'On Politics and Trade Unions', *Industrial Magazine*, No. 1, 1862.   [3] *Bookbinders' Trade Circular*, 2 March 1864.

It would not be difficult to show that Dunning's estimate of working-class opinion in 1864 was wide of the mark. Yet there were other Labour leaders in London, at one time or another, who certainly shared his sympathies: Facey of the Bricklayers,[1] Thomas Vize of the Painters, and John Bedford Leno, shoemaker, Chartist and poet who was to be refused membership in the Reform League because of his Southern views.[2] *Reynolds' News*, with its immense circulation and old Chartist associations, spent 'week after week exhaust(ing) its horse-powers of foul language in appeals to the working classes to urge the government, for their own interests, to war with the Union'.[3] Throughout the whole course of the Civil War it strove to reconcile its own advanced democratic programme with bitter hostility to the Federal cause. Then there was the *Bee-Hive*, the paper in which Dunning's own articles appeared and in which his society, along with many others, held shares. Until the end of 1862 it was strongly opposed to Lincoln and there were periods after this in which Confederate propaganda was given great prominence in its pages.

If the working-class press was to be taken as a reliable guide to labour sympathies then Dunning might indeed have claimed the support of nine out of every ten workmen. For an examination of the Labour press fails to support the hitherto accepted belief that it was overwhelmingly against war and staunchly pro-Federal.

During the period of the Civil War there were three types of journals to which the term 'working-class' might be applied. First, there were periodicals which were produced by and for organised bodies of working men. Into this category fall the numerous monthly reports and circulars of the Unions. These were devoted, almost entirely, to trade questions. There were few references to American affairs and some of these were merely incidental to the discussion of more prosaic matters. Thus, a branch of the Stonemasons' Society in commenting

[1] G. Howell, *Reynolds' News*, 29 November 1896.
[2] Reform League Minutes, 21 April 1865 (Howell Collection, Bishopsgate Institute).
[3] K. Marx, 'English Public Opinion', *New York Daily Tribune*, 1 February 1862. (Cited in Marx and Engels, *The Civil War in the United States*, New York, 1937, p. 49.)

upon a dispute with the London Master Builders, suggested that the leadership ought to follow the example of the British Government in dealing with the Yankees over the Trent affair. It paid to adopt a firm stand against wrong-doers. A few months earlier, the newly established Bricklayers' journal had observed that in America 'man is pitted against his brother, without any great principles being involved, except, indeed, that of self-government claimed by the Southerners'. It immediately went on to add that 'the Southerners are only fighting for greater despotic power in relation to slavery'.[1] The fact that this was written by George Howell, who was to become one of the most important Labour leaders of his day, is indicative of the confusion and muddle which characterised working-class opinion in England during the first eighteen months of the War.

We have seen that Dunning wrapped up his hostility to the Northern States in a wider opposition to political commitment and comment by Trade Unions. Whether it masked Confederate sympathies or not, this attitude was widespread. It was argued that if Unions tried to take sides on the American question it would mean that they would be powerless

> to wage any strife whatever against the capitalists in future . . . There could no longer be the unity requisite to protect the rights of labour amongst Trades Unionists . . . Some would no doubt support the North, yet there are also those who would support the South in their desire to preserve their independence.[2]

This argument was felt to have its application to the Co-operative, as well as to the Trade Union, Movement. There was indeed, one journal, the *National Co-operative Leader*, which was decidedly pro-Federal, but its influence was negligible compared to that of its Manchester contemporary, the *Co-operator*. The latter was taking up a representative position when it explained that, 'after the due reflection and consideration', it had decided not to discuss the Civil War. It reached this

[1] *Operative Bricklayers' Society Circular*, October 1861.

[2] *National Co-operative Leader*, No. 1, 18 November 1860. (For pro-Federal articles, see the contributions of C. C. Cosmopolitan, 17 May 1861, et seq.) G. D. H Cole, *A Century of Co-operation*, Manchester (1944), stresses the importance of the *Co-operator*, but does not mention the *National Co-operative Leader*.

decision 'not alone through fear of causing a schism in the co-operative camp . . . but because the topic would be foreign to the object of the *Co-operator*'.[1]

A Friendly Society journal, *The Friends of Labour Association's Monthly Circular of General Information and Working-Man's Advocate*, found space to support the London builders; to lament the death of the Prince Consort; and to run a series on self-made men; but it never uttered a word about the Civil War.

Apart from specialised journals, there were newspapers which were owned and operated by wage-earners. Some of these, like the Manchester *Weekly Wages*, were short-lived; others, like the *Artisan* in Liverpool, have not been preserved. Of general newspapers of this type, the most important was the *Bee-Hive*. It had been intended to make the *Bee-Hive* into the organ of the newly established London Trades Council, and a large part of the share capital of the Trades Newspaper Company which owned the *Bee-Hive* was held by Trade Unions. Although the paper was edited by a professional journalist, George Troup, it was managed by the most famous Trade Unionist of the day, the leader of the London builders' strike of 1859, George Potter.[2] Right up until the end of 1862 the *Bee-Hive* made no secret of its hatred for the Federals. It opposed slavery, but held that Secession would soon bring that institution to an end and pointed to the fact that the Negro was a second-class citizen in the Northern States. It made the most of rumours concerning Seward's 'foreign war panacea', denounced Yankee tariffs, and declared that Britain was entitled to break the blockade of the Southern ports.

Troup cannot be made to bear the entire responsibility for the *Bee-Hive*'s policy. The government and administration of the paper was formally vested in a Board of Directors, working men elected by the shareholders. George Potter found it expedient to ignore, rather than to rebut, the charge that he had been Troup's willing accomplice in making the *Bee-Hive* a Confederate organ.[3]

[1] *Co-operator*, June 1863.

[2] S. Coltham, 'The Bee-Hive Newspaper: Its Origins and Early Struggles', in *Essays in Labour History* (edited by A. Briggs and J. Saville, 1960).

[3] 'Odger v. Potter: Decisions of the Committee', *Bee-Hive*, 24 June and 1 July 1865.

A great struggle for control of the paper occurred at the end of 1862. It was alleged that Confederate agents and a pro-Federal manufacturer were actively involved.[1] Although this resulted in Troup's being dismissed from his editorial office, the Southern sympathisers retained an interest in the journal. The Book-binders were among the largest shareholders and this, no doubt, helps to explain how Dunning's articles came to appear in 1863. Troup himself held a large block of shares. Early in 1864 articles by Troup reappeared in the editorial columns. He and Dunning took exactly the line which had been decided on at this time by the Confederate agents.[2] They tried to arouse alarm at the great increase in emigration to the Northern States. Emigrants would be better off in the colonies, where they would not be slaughtered in the army or used to break strikes. Lincoln was the greatest military bungler since Xerxes. The United States was in the grip of inflation, and peace would be followed by a complete financial collapse. The present misery endured by women workers in New York would soon become the average condition of American labour. Free land in Illinois was not really as cheap as land at £1 an acre near Adelaide.

Troup and his supporters denied that they favoured the South's 'peculiar institution': 'I seek the abolition of the slaughter of Negroes by the North, and the slavery of Negroes in the South.'[3] While they accused Lincoln of destroying every vestige of liberty in the North and of every crime in the calendar—Dunning alleged that his nephew had been kidnapped by the Federals—they took care to deny that they were advocating pro-Southern views 'so far as they may be pro-slavery views'.[4] It was in vain that the friends of the Federal States protested against such hypocrisy. The *Bee-Hive* declared itself in favour of 'free discussion' of the American question.

[1] R. J. Hinton, *English Radical Leaders* (New York, 1875). (See chapter on 'George Odger' for Hinton's rather garbled account.)

[2] E. D. Adams, *Great Britain and the American Civil War* (New York, 1925).

[3] Troup, 'The Editor, Professor Beesly and Mr. Beales', *Bee-Hive*, 5 March 1864.

[4] For the Troup-Beesly polemic see issues of the *Bee-Hive* from 20 February to 2 April 1864. There are pro-Southern contributions from Dunning, the Rev. E. A. Verity, T. Vize and others. Beesly was supported by Tom Hughes, M.A., Edmond Beales, G. Odger, G. Howell and many more.

The episode ended with the retirement from the paper, not of Troup and his allies, but of Professor Beesly—who had been the most prolific and effective exponent of the Northern cause.[1]

A month before the first issue of the *Bee-Hive* appeared, another Labour paper had been established in London. Like the *Bee-Hive*, the *Working Man* was controlled by a board of Trade Unionists. Its chairman was the Socialist and Co-operator, A. C. Cudden.[2] This paper was pro-Federal after May 1862, but before this it had been impartial and therefore bellicose. It allowed that the slave-holders having 'invested their fortune in human stock, should have some reason to complain if, all of a sudden, they were to be dispossessed of their property'. It asked, 'if North and South are the willing accomplices of slavery, what are they fighting for—and with which can we sympathise? Are they not both our enemies. Are they not both tyrants of human labour?' The conclusion was that there could be no moral objection to raising the blockade and getting cotton for starving Lancashire.[3]

There was a second group of journals, although not owned and managed by organised workers, which could fairly be described as 'working-class'. These were papers which were edited by men who had been identified with the Labour Movement; men who were acknowledged friends of Labour in view of the substantial services and sacrifices which they had made in the past. *Reynolds' News*, with its immense circulation of 350,000, obviously belongs in this class. Its founder, proprietor and editor was G. W. M. Reynolds, an old Chartist; a champion of Trades Unionism and an ultra-Radical. The decidedly Confederate sympathies of his paper have already been mentioned.

In Scotland, the *Glasgow Sentinel* was generally regarded as a 'workers' paper'. During most of the Civil War period, the *Sentinel* was edited by Alexander Campbell who had an unrivalled record of service to organised Labour both in Scotland itself and further afield. For more than forty years he was active as an industrial and political leader; as an Owenite

---

[1] R. Harrison, 'Professor Beesly and the Working Class Movement', in *Essays in Labour History* (edited by A. Briggs and J. Saville, 1960).
[2] *Working Man*, 7 September 1861. [3] Ibid., 5 October 1861.

Socialist and as a pioneer of the modern Co-operative Move-ment.[1] Both before and after Campbell became editor, the *Sentinel* was hostile to the North and eager for peace in America at any price. It prepared its readers for British intervention: 'It is quite certain that when the moment for action arrives, our own government must energetically second the efforts of France to stay this bootless strife.'[2] Like Dunning, the *Sentinel* suggested that its opinions were shared by most workmen: 'The idle artisans of the English towns begin to regard the American conflict less in the light of a misfortune to an allied people than as a blameable struggle for supremacy between the two factions of the States in which the North especially seeks to gratify its desire for territorial aggrandisement.'[3] Campbell allowed his old friend and collaborator, Robert Buchanan, to fill the paper with 'Garrisonian' arguments against the Union. Late into the Civil War, Buchanan was still insisting that it was impossible to subdue the Southern States.[4]

The *Glasgow Gazette*, edited by Peter Mackenzie, was virtually the only paper in Scotland which could rival the *Sentinel*'s claim to the loyalty of politically conscious workmen. Mackenzie did much to keep alive the memory of Thomas Muir and other revolutionary martyrs, and he had himself been an advocate of physical force during the Reform agitation of the early thirties.

The *Glasgow Gazette*'s opinions on the Civil War moved in the opposite direction from those of the *Working Man*. Before Bull Run, Mackenzie favoured the North. After that disaster, he dwelt with equal relish on the prospect of a British Regiment settling accounts with 'the scoundrels of New York' and on the Southern Slaveowner perishing in the wreck of his own destruction.[5] Finally he arrived at the conclusion that 'Demo-cracy has been at the root of the whole of the present difficulties in America'.[6] Britain ought to recognise that secession was inevitable and try to bring the war to an end as swiftly as

---

[1] R. Harrison, 'British Labour and the Confederacy', *International Review of Socialist History* (Amsterdam), Vol. 2, 1957, Part I.

[2] *Glasgow Sentinel*, 17 May 1862.   [3] Ibid., 5 July 1862.

[4] 'London Letter', *Glasgow Sentinel* 1863–64. Also obituary of Robert Buchanan, *Glasgow Sentinel*, 17 March 1866.

[5] *Glasgow Sentinel*, 25 January and 28 June 1862.

[6] Ibid., 6 September 1862.

possible. The old revolutionary never tired of lauding the achievements of the Confederate troops. 'There is nothing,' he declared, 'more magnificent in the history of man.'[1]

The *British Miner*—subsequently named the *Miner* and then *Miner and Workman's Advocate*—was almost equally enthusiastic about the glory of Confederate arms. It delighted to contrast the plight of the British mineworker with conditions of slave labour in the old South, where contented Negroes laboured for cultured and philanthropic masters.[2] No doubt, the editor of the *Miner* deserved to be described as an unscrupulous adventurer, but he enjoyed considerable support at pit level. His name was John Towers and he had served as Secretary to the Conference at Wakefield at which the National Association of Miners had been established.[3]

If the Secretary of the Miners' Conference had dubious claim to the confidence of workmen, the same could not be said of Joseph Rayner Stephens who served as Chaplain on that occasion. Stephens' name ranks beside that of Richard Oastler as a leader of the anti-Poor Law agitation. Francis Place had observed that he cared for no opinion but that of the working people. Place complained that Stephens 'domineered, carrying everything he wished with a high hand: he was obeyed, almost adored by multitudes . . .'[4]

During the early 'sixties, Stephens controlled the *Oldham Standard*. He dismissed as a 'ridiculous and contemptible imposture' every attempt to attribute pro-Federal sympathies to the Lancashire working class. Workmen, he alleged, knew that this was a subject which 'they were not called upon to discuss'.[5] When the *Standard* delivered its own judgement on the conflict, it encouraged Southern sympathies. 'The North and their abettors are well aware that the independence of the South means the abolition of slavery; but that the maintenance of the Union signifies its perpetuation . . .'[6]

There remains a third group of journals which—with considerably less assurance—might be described as 'working-class'. These consist of papers which were run exclusively, or mainly,

---

[1] *Glasgow Sentinel*, 9 April 1864.   [2] *British Miner*, 28 February 1863.
[3] *Miner and Workman's Advocate*, 14 November 1863.
[4] G. J. Holyoake, *Life of J. R. Stephens* (1881), p. 76.
[5] *Oldham Standard*, 3 January 1863.   [6] Ibid., 6 June 1863.

as commercial ventures, but which aimed at a proletarian readership. With the exception of the *Weekly Times*, most of these journals were strong in their Confederate sympathies. A single extract from the *Weekly Budget*, which claimed a large circulation among the factory operatives of the North, must serve to illustrate their position and their style:

> Bloody as the war is and inflictive of untold wrongs and mobberies upon virtue and innocence, it will not have been without its compensation in ridding the world, by the bullets of the Southerners, of the human scum, poured out of every country under heaven, which forms the ruck of the mob armies of the tyrant States.[1]

It is notoriously suspect procedure to make inferences from the opinions of newspapers as to those of their readers. But no such inferences are required to disturb the received account of how the British working class responded to the Civil War. That account insisted on the pro-Northern character of the Labour press as evidence of where proletarian sympathies lay. Yet it is a problem to find a single influential working-class paper which consistently favoured Lincoln and opposed British intervention. The predominant tendency was decidedly the other way—and this is scarcely less evident in the later than in the earlier period of the conflict. Famous and respected leaders of the working people sided with the Confederacy. The problem is to explain how this came about and how far their views were shared by the masses.

II

During the early stages of the Civil War, the hostile tone of the English labour press might be explained by the seeming confusion and ambiguity of Federal war aims; the diplomatic blunders of Seward (the rumours of his foreign war panacea followed by the Trent affair); and by the appalling disaster at Bull Run. It must be remembered that the editors of working-class papers had little or no independent sources of news about events in America and that they were completely dependent on the middle-class press. Even the staunchest friends of the

[1] *Weekly Budget*, 22 November 1862.

North were shaken by the evidence of corruption and incompetence. Not only Richard Cobden,[1] but Frederick Engels, had his doubts. Engels told Marx,

> for the present moment I must say that I cannot work up any enthusiasm for a people which on such a colossal issue allows itself to be continually beaten by a fourth of its own population, and which after eighteen months of war has achieved nothing more than the discovery that all its generals are idiots and all its officials rascals and traitors.[2]

So long as 'Emancipation' was not inscribed upon the Union banners, British workmen could be asked to respect the right of the Southern States to independence. While defeat followed upon defeat, it was plausible to suggest that the Federal Cause was lost. If Secession was inevitable, why should Britain not hasten peace by intervention? As *Reynolds'* put it: 'Better fight the Yankees than starve the operatives.'[3]

However, no explanation of Southern sympathies is adequate if it relies entirely upon political and military considerations, which were characteristic only of a limited phase of the hostilities. As has been shown, Southern sympathies were still being entertained by prominent Labour leaders after the Emancipation Proclamation. Indeed, that measure was described by the *Glasgow Sentinel* as 'petty and abortive spite'.[4] Even if it were true of politicians and journalists that they are peculiarly reluctant to acknowledge their own errors, this will hardly suffice as an explanation of the prolonged and passionate hostility to the Federal States.

The explanation which we are looking for will be found, not by discarding the traditional interpretation of British public opinion on the Civil War, but through its further development. The traditional interpretation insisted that British opinion was divided along class lines. As John Morley noted: 'partisanship with the sides there was the veil of a kind of Civil War here. An unspoken instinct revealed to mutually hostile classes in England that their battle also was being fought in the contest

---

[1] J. Morley, *Life of Richard Cobden* (1881), II, pp. 372 f.
[2] Engels to Marx, 5 November 1862, *The Civil War in the United States* (New York, 1937), p. 259.
[3] *Reynolds' News*, 29 September 1861.
[4] *Glasgow Sentinel*, 11 October 1862.

between the free North and the slave-holding South . . .'[1] At first sight the existence of Southern sympathisers within the working class would appear to signify the limitations or even the breakdown of this analysis. However, this is not the case, since the divisions within working-class opinion can be explained, in large part, in terms of rival estimates of where the workers' interests stood in relation to other 'mutually hostile classes'. Throughout the nineteenth century there was no unanimity in the Labour movement on the question as to whether the landed oligarchy or the manufacturing capitalists represented the main enemy of Labour. The veterans of the class struggles of the first half of the nineteenth century were, many of them, still completely unreconciled to Capitalism, and the hostility which they felt for the manufacturers and mill-owners took its point of departure in the old, primitive opposition to modern industry as such, rather than in visions of constituting modern industry on a co-operative instead of a competitive basis. Working-class leaders, journalists and advisors who still thought of the industrial capitalist as the main enemy, or who treated the propertied classes with an impartial and indiscriminate hostility, tended to favour the Confederacy, or took up a 'neutralist' position which, in practice, favoured the South . . .

The relation between the American War and domestic political conflict was recognised on all sides. The trials of American democracy became a test of the viability of the creed of the English Radicals. The name of Bright was everywhere linked with that of Lincoln, so that there was nothing unusual in a representative of the English oligarchy remarking: 'If I had my way, I would blow President Lincoln from a mortar with a bombshell, and, if there wasn't wadding enough, I'd ram John Bright down in after him.'[2] Those Labour leaders and advisors who remained unreconciled to Capitalism and who shared vivid recollections of the competition of Bright and Cobden with the Chartist and factory reform movements, were the mainstay of the Confederacy in the Labour movement.

It was the older generations of Labour leaders who—out of hatred of the Federals—came to befriend the Confederates.

[1] *Fortnightly Review*, October 1870.
[2] H. Solly, *These Eighty Years*, II, 1893, p. 247.

Men like Dunning, Buchanan and Campbell, who had seen millennialist hopes go down before the triumph of free trade; old militants such as Mackenzie and Reynolds, soured by defeat and disappointment. Patrick Matthew, who had represented Perthshire and Fife at the first Chartist Convention of 1839, and Mortimer Grimshaw, one of Preston's delegates at the People's Parliament of 1854, were both Southern sympathisers.[1] The failure of Chartism led the former into increasing eccentricity; the latter into complete political corruption. But if Owenism and Chartism figured in the background of some Confederate sympathisers, it was the Tory Democrats who were most uniformly pro-South. Men like the Reverends Stephens and Verity, along with Charles Kingsley, were justly suspected of trying to work up discontent with the middle-class relief committees in the cotton districts, with the object of discrediting the stand taken by Bright, Cobden and the Radical manufacturers on the Civil War.[2] Stephens' *Oldham Standard* made Bright the author of every demonstration of working-class support for the North, and the *Weekly Budget* called for recognition of the Confederacy by explaining: 'We have no desire to see the government of this country Bright-ridden.'[3]

It was enough for men reared in the hard school of the anti-Poor Law agitation, the factory reform movement and Chartism, that John Bright and his friends identified themselves with the Federal cause, for that cause to stand condemned in their eyes. If the North American Republic represented his ideal, it could not be theirs. If there was one argument to which Dunning and Troup and Vize and Verity returned again and again in the pages of the *Bee-Hive*, it was that E. S. Beesly, Edmond Beales and other supporters of Lincoln wanted to

[1] For Matthew see below. Grimshaw was used by Dickens as the model for his portrait of a Trade Union leader in *Hard Times*, but he was regarded as a traitor and a scoundrel by the weavers of Lancashire who repeatedly defeated him at public meetings and threatened him with physical assault. No one had a good word for him except the Confederate organ, the *Index*. R. Sharpe France (editor), 'The Diary of John Ward of Clitheroe, Weaver, 1860–64', *Transactions of the Historic Society of Lancashire and Cheshire*, 1953, Vol. 105 (Liverpool, 1954). Also *Index*, 8 December 1864, and J. Saville, *Ernest Jones: Chartist*, 1952, p. 272.

[2] E. S. Beesly, 'The Cotton Famine and the London Relief Committee', *Bee-Hive*, 6 December 1862.

[3] *Weekly Budget*, 22 November 1862.

make that paper 'on the American question, a Manchester School and Federal paper, similar in these respects to the *Morning Star*'.[1] They pressed the point so insistently that the Federal sympathisers were compelled to indicate precisely where they stood in relation to Bright and his friends. Beesly, who had been charged with 'treachery' in 'bringing back John Bright and the Manchester School . . . into the Society of Trade Unionists',[2] made an energetic disavowal of any sympathy with 'Manchester's' views on industrial questions.[3] George Odger, William Dell and others 'writing on behalf of a large body of our fellow-workmen, the friends of the Federal States of America', cheerfully admitted that they found much merit in the Manchester School which had cheapened the people's bread.[4] One of Beesly's fellow Positivists, Frederic Harrison, asserted that working men would not readily forget how 'on the great common ground of sympathy with Freedom and Republicanism, the leaders of the manufacturing party have frankly offered them their hands'.[5]

Thus, partisanship with the sides in America was, in truth, a 'veil' for social and political antagonism in Britain. Those who would be for Lincoln could not escape the fact that they would be allied with Bright. This consideration did not deter the rising generation of Trade Union leaders who had experienced little or no commitment in the great struggle of the first half of the century. They were favourably disposed to conciliation in industry and collaboration with middle-class Radicalism in politics. They asked no more than an increasing 'stake in the country', and to be brought within 'the pale of the constitution'. They were the representatives of skilled workmen who were coming to terms with capitalist industry. To such men it was meaningless and absurd to talk, as some Confederate sympathisers did, of cotton as 'the great seducer that has deluded our active population from the labour of the fields'. They did not share the view that 'since, unfortunately,

---

[1] T. J. Dunning, letter, *Bee-Hive*, 5 March 1864.

[2] E. A. Verity, 'The Secularists and the East Lancashire Relief Fund', *Bee-Hive*, 28 March 1863.

[3] E. S. Beesly, 'The Colonies and the States', *Bee-Hive*, 12 March 1864.

[4] *Bee-Hive*, 12 March 1864.

[5] F. Harrison, 'The Political Action of Working Men', *Bee-Hive*, 30 January 1864.

cotton has become our bread . . . (we should) insist on the raising of this blockade'; any more than they thought that working in 'the pure air', instead of accumulating 'great fortunes for the high priests of Mammon', led to a 'sounder wealth'.[1] This was the language of Cobbett used in the age of the 'Junta'. To the leaders of a growing and increasingly prosperous Labour aristocracy, it was mere rhetoric to suggest that slavery and wage labour differed only in form or that North and South were equally tyrants over human labour. Such sentiments were possible only to some of the old guard in the Labour leadership.

Schlüter, in discussing the attitude of *American* Labour to slavery, shows an awareness of the complexity of the question which is wholly absent from his account of English Labour and the Civil War. Schlüter knew that there were many influential working-class leaders in the States who were far from 'clear' on Negro emancipation. Their 'confusions' help to throw some light on the source of Confederate sympathies in England. Thus, he cites William West's remark that the American workers 'do not hate chattel slavery less, but they hate wage slavery more';[2] Hermann Kriege's contention that Abolition would 'throw the Republic into a state of anarchy . . . extend the competition of "free workingmen" beyond all measure, and . . . depress labour itself to the last extremity';[3] and Wilhelm Weitling's contempt for the Abolitionists, and failure, in his New York paper of the eighteen-fifties, to make an explicit condemnation of slavery.[4] In particular, Schlüter showed how George H. Evans declared himself against emancipation on the grounds that the Negroes' lot would be worse still as wage labourers. Evans complained that Garrison's *Liberator* never allowed its English correspondents to say a word against 'the worse slavery of the plundered landless of England'. In his detailed account of Evans' opinions, Schlüter observes that 'his hatred of the white slavery of the wage labourers came near turning into a defence of Negro slavery'.[5] This bears a decided resemblance to the situation in Britain. To a superficial judgement, it would appear that it was in Britain, as in America, precisely the most militant and class-

[1] *Working Man*, 5 October 1861.   [2] H. Schlüter, op cit., p. 61.
[3] Ibid., p. 72.   [4] Ibid., p. 73.   [5] Ibid., p. 62 ff.

conscious leaders, those most ready to insist upon the subjection and exploitation inherent in a wages system, who kept company with the slaveholders. It was not that they defended slavery, but that they detested the hypocrisy of its leading opponents. They remembered Wilberforce and they could recognise his successors when they saw them. They would not hold the ring while Americans decided whether the Negro was to be a slave or a wage labourer; a chattel or a leper. What interest had English workmen in a struggle for mastery in America between slave-owners and enterprising capitalists who wanted foreign labour to help break strikes[1] and who worshipped nothing but the 'all-mighty dollar'? Seeing no great principle at stake in the Civil War, some of the older militants felt free to urge British intervention. Others half persuaded themselves that the real issue was the South's right to independence, and that the Confederates were therefore entitled to the support which British workers traditionally accorded to subject peoples. If Bright led the opposition to war, this was but another instance of his devotion to the interests of the money-lords; of his pacifism and indifference to aggression.

Of course, old Owenists and Chartists had behind them a tradition of sympathy for the North American Republic and of opposition to slavery. In 1837 the London Working Men's Association had sent fraternal greetings to the workers of America. Workers had been prominent in the anti-slavery league which had been founded in 1846 under the presidency of the Chartist, George Thompson. Seven years later G. J. Holyoake had sent an anti-slavery address to America signed by 1,800 workers. But one must beware of oversimplified interpretations of this tradition. The most perfunctory examination of it will show that it exhibited precisely the sort of contradictions which furnished the basis for the kind of Confederate sympathies to which attention is being drawn.

> When one listens to an Abolitionist one might think that outside of the blacks there was no slave under British rule [wrote Bronterre O'Brien]. If these scoundrels entertained a sincere hatred against slavery they would begin by abolishing it at home . . . How is it that we never hear the Buxtons or the Wilberforces complain

[1] G. Troup, 'Conspiracy Against the Trade Societies of the Federal States', *Bee-Hive*, 26 March 1864.

59

about slavery here at home? Listen, Buxton, and we will tell you; it is because you know, you smooth-tongued rogue, that English slavery is indispensable for our highly civilized state.'

O'Brien explained that under English wages slavery 'the master employs and supports his slave only when he needs him; in the other (form of slavery) he supports him whether he has work for him or not . . . Emancipation enables the master to get more labour and to pay less for it.'[1]

Other Chartist leaders were far from being uncritical admirers of the United States. Feargus O'Connor in an article entitled 'Abuses of American Republicanism' declared that 'the people of the United States have much to answer for at the bar of mankind'. By tolerating slavery, and by indifference to Chartism, they 'caused the republicans of Europe to weep for very shame and mortification'.[2] Reynolds and Mackenzie developed these opinions, albeit in a sour and one-sided manner. Similarly, such prominent Owenists as Campbell and Buchanan were presumably acquainted with their Master's opinions on slavery. At a meeting of the New England Anti-Slavery Society, Owen said that

> from an early period he was opposed to Negro slavery, and also to slavery of all kinds. At home in England he had seen by far worse slavery than any he had witnessed among the coloured population —all should look to the *great causes* of slavery. They could be traced to the spirit of inequality in and under all governments—all we wanted was the establishment of equal rights over all lands and countries. The black man proclaimed liberty for his colour—but he stood there to contend for liberty to the white man, who was bound to the most arrant slavery of all.[3]

The Southern sympathisers were—as has been shown—men whose class-consciousness was far more developed than that of the Trade Union leaders who joined forces with Bright on behalf of emancipation and reform, but it was by no means the case that every veteran of Chartism opposed the North. Ernest Jones was one of the most passionate and active supporters of the Federal cause.[4] George Julian Harney resigned his editor-

---

[1] H. Schlüter, op. cit., p. 104 f.
[2] Ibid., p. 62 f.   [3] Ibid., p. 49.
[4] J. Saville, *Ernest Jones: Chartist*, 1952, p. 77 f.

ship of the *Jersey Independent* rather than submit to the wishes of the proprietors who sympathised with the Confederacy.[1] Lloyd Jones, who worked for the *Glasgow Sentinel*, preferred to break with his old friends, Campbell and Buchanan, rather than lend his pen to the Slave Power.[2] What distinguished these men from some of their old compatriots was that they had no desire to undo the work of the industrial revolution. Because they had, in varying degrees, a sense of the historical development and 'destiny' of labour; because they conceived of exploitation historically and not merely as an abstraction, an 'essence', subject to almost irrelevant changes of form, they were able to acknowledge that wage labour was an 'advance' upon slavery without, thereby, offering anything in extenuation of it. The point is as well illustrated by the contrast between the attitude to slavery of Evans and Weydemeyer in America, as it is by that between Stephens and Harney in England.

Not all the Southern sympathies expressed in the British labour press can be explained in terms of the long memories of Tory Democrats and soured Chartists. George Troup, the most influential and informed journalist, who sided with the Confederacy in the working-class press, belonged in neither of these categories. His motives were religious and imperialist.

Troup was a devout evangelical and a member of the Free Church of Scotland.[3] That Church had attempted to surmount its financial difficulties by despatching a mission to the United States in 1844. The response in the Southern States had far surpassed that in the Northern and, when this became known, the Anti-Slavery Societies raised a cry about accepting 'blood-stained slave money'. Troup and his co-religionists had to face 'a full-scale onslaught from the abolitionists'. No doubt this experience helped to dispose him favourably towards the munificent Southerners.

Troup's association with the shipping interest—he edited important papers in Liverpool, Glasgow, Belfast—encouraged an active jealousy and hatred of the North American Republic.

[1] *Jersey Independent and Daily Telegraph*, 29 November 1862.

[2] J. M. Ludlow, 'Some of the Christian Socialists of 1848 and the Following Years', *Economic Review*, January 1894.

[3] For Troup, see G. E. Troup, *George Troup: Journalist* (Edinburgh, 1881); W. H. Marwick, 'George Troup', *Scottish Educational Journal*, 16 March 1934.

As early as 1844 a Liverpool owner had said that it was only possible to compete in the North Atlantic trade by 'having North American ships . . . We could not send British ships in that trade.' And when it came to the Australian passenger services, Liverpool shipowners preferred to place their orders in Massachusetts. British ship-building suffered a further blow in 1857 when, following upon the commercial collapse in the United States, there were important purchases of American clippers from bankrupt American firms. Yet by 1860 American shipping employed in the foreign and the whale fisheries alone, was more than half that of the United Kingdom. In this year the North American Republic stood at the summit of its naval strength and this was associated with a decline in Britain's share of the world's carrying trade.[1]

When Alexander Alison, a great iron-master and proprietor of the first provincial daily newspaper in Britain, had been faced with ruin in consequence of the financial crises of 1847, his editor, George Troup, had been saved from dismissal by the support of Glasgow ship-owners. It is scarcely surprising that five years later Troup appeared as a foundation member of a remarkable body known as 'The West of Scotland Reciprocity Association', which anticipated, in its programme and general character, the Liberal Unionism of thirty years later. While Troup had once discoursed on the 'Anti-Christian Character of the Corn Laws', he now championed imperial preference, and urged the government to abandon free trade in favour of the principle that no concession should be given to the foreigner without extracting a similar concession in return. The West of Scotland Reciprocity Association brought Troup into contact with the great Birkenhead ship-builder, W. S. Lindsay, M.A., who subsequently became one of the most prominent English supporters of the Confederacy.

Ideological factors, rather than the direct operation of economic considerations, governed British opinion in relation to the Civil War. If, as a result of that conflict, Yorkshire and Dundee gained much of what Lancashire and Glasgow lost, there is little evidence to show that this had any appreciable effect on opinion about the rights and wrongs of the American

[1] J. H. Clapham, *An Economic History of Modern Britain*, II (Cambridge, 1932), pp. 65 ff.

struggle. But shipping does provide an exception. Men who had felt the pinch of American competition, and were presently employed on war work for the Confederacy, could hardly fail to have Southern sympathies. As Schoyen points out, Gladstone's interventionist *gaffe* of October 1862 was 'cheered by a crowd of Jarrow ship-workers'.[1]

Troup's enthusiasm for British emigration to the colonies was shared by some other Labour sympathisers with the South. It fitted in naturally with his imperialist opinions. It provided an additional reason for enmity towards the Americans. The colonial policy of the British Government was based upon the ideas of E. G. Wakefield and his doctrine of 'the sufficient price' for land. This was one of the main obstacles to securing increased emigration to the Empire, and helps to explain why British emigrants showed such a decided preference for the United States.[2]

When George Potter first met Troup, the latter was editing *Tait's Magazine* in Edinburgh. He used the pages of that journal to lend some support to Potter's activities with the building workers, but most of his powder and shot was employed in attacks upon America. We ought to get our cotton from the Empire; the colonials were our friends; the Yankees viewed us with suspicion; they thought of us as one vast Emancipation Society hell-bent on crusading for freedom in the Carolinas; we had more important interests; we ought to buy less from America; they spent the bullion which they earned here in France and Switzerland. (In 1861, gold actually went West instead of East.)[3] The only answer was Empire free trade.[4]

When he became editor of the *Bee-Hive*, Troup developed these opinions. He fulminated against American tariffs and told his readers about American designs against Canada. He foretold disaster for the American economy at the end of the war and contrasted this grim prospect with a picture of the ever-expanding British Empire. Anticipating Rhodes, he dreamt of British dominion in Africa extending up from the Cape to the sources of the Nile.

[1] A. R. Schoyen, *The Chartist Challenge*, 1958, p. 259.
[2] B. Thomas, *Migration and Economic Growth* (Cambridge, 1954), p. 202.
[3] Clapham, op. cit., p. 373.
[4] *Tait's Edinburgh Magazine*, August 1859.

There is a striking similarity between Troup's Southern sympathies and those of Patrick Matthew.[1] Both were Scots; they shared a keen interest in shipping and in emigration to the colonies; they saw the United States as the main challenger to the hegemony of the British Empire. Matthew was a Scottish Nationalist and if Scotsmen were prominent among Confederate sympathisers it may have been due, in part, to a disposition to favour any movement which could be construed as asserting the right of national self-determination. But this was certainly a subordinate consideration in Matthew's case, as was the view, which he shared with Peter Mackenzie, that a vast Republic was unworkable. An opponent of Negro slavery, Matthew argued that the British ruling class had tried to bring our working population into a state of 'indirect slavery' and had therefore no right to condemn American slave owners: the familiar equation of all forms of exploitation. His support for Secession was related to his belief that 'the pertinacity of opposition in the Northern States to division of the United States is from the hope of a great American Republic being able to dominate over the whole earth'.[2] It has been pointed out that Matthew had important associations with Chartism. Thus, he supplies a link between the two main sources of Confederate sympathies in the British Labour movement: the stunted class-consciousness of the older generation of leaders and the new imperialism whose spirit was, as yet, expressed only by a few pioneers. For either tendency John Bright, his ideals, his friends, and all his works, were anathema.

III

How far is it still correct to speak of the pro-Federal sentiments of the British working class? Given the Confederate sympathies of a large fraction of the Labour press, is it plausible to maintain that the working class played an important part in preserving

[1] W. H. Marwick, 'Patrick Matthew', *Scottish Adult Education*, No. 23, August 1958.

[2] P. Matthew, *Schleswig-Holstein*, 1864, p. 62. (In this pamphlet, Matthew styled himself: 'Author of "Emigration Fields", "Naval Timber and Arboriculture"; Solver of the problem of species; first proposer of Steam Rams; metallic cover; Sloping Sides; Heavy Gun Boats, etc.' His claim to have anticipated Darwin was not without some warrant.)

peace? Is it true that working-class support for Lincoln was big with consequences for the subsequent progress of democratic reform in Britain?

From the end of 1862 there is overwhelming evidence to support the view that the great majority of politically conscious workmen were pro-Federal and firmly resolved to oppose war. As soon as the feelings of the masses were tested at public meetings they showed where they stood. The argument from democratic principle; the absence of a politically privileged class in the Northern States; the argument from the principle of the solidarity of labour interests everywhere; and the ties of family that bound many British workers to their relatives in North America, all told decisively against the South. Basing himself on official reports sent to Seward and on the files of the *Liberator*, E. D. Adams showed that British workers organised five pro-Federal meetings in 1862, fifty-six such meetings in 1863 and eleven more in 1864. Workmen also attended numerous meetings arranged by middle-class sympathisers with the North. As Adams himself points out, these figures understate the amount of working-class activity.[1]

Southern sympathisers alleged that these meetings were got up by Federal agents. To some extent this was certainly the case,[2] but that does not alter the fact that Beesly could taunt his opponents with their unwillingness to try their strength at meetings of their own.[3] If the Southerners failed to take up the challenge, this was not due entirely to the fact that they believed that 'King Cotton' would do their work for them, nor can it be explained by their preference for devoting funds to the press.[4] It was because they knew of the humiliation which almost certainly awaited them. Thus, in September 1862, they had got up a meeting at Stalybridge in favour of intervention in America. Despite the fact that this was the place where J. R. Stephens had the greatest influence, the workers carried an amendment by an immense majority, 'something like a hundred to one', '"That in the opinion of the meeting, the distress

---

[1] E. D. Adams, op cit., p. 223.

[2] M. P. Clausen, 'Peace Factors in Anglo-American Relations', *Mississippi Historical Review*, Vol. XXVI, No. 4.

[3] E. S. Beesly, 'The Colonies and the States', *Bee-Hive*, 12 March 1864.

[4] J. F. Jameson, 'The London Expenditure of the Confederate Secret Service', *American Historical Review*, July 1930.

prevailing in the manufacturing districts is mainly owing to the rebellion of the Southern States against the American constitution." [1] Similarly, when Mortimer Grimshaw tried to get the workers of Blackburn to support British mediation in America, his platform was taken by the Secretary of the local Weavers' Association. Grimshaw lost in a vote which was estimated at four to five thousand against twelve. The meeting went on to carry a vote of no confidence in Grimshaw and declared itself in favour of the policies of Abraham Lincoln. [2] The Sheffield workmen told Roebuck—who wanted to recognise the South—'Never! We should have a civil war in England.' [3]

It is the record of public meetings which provides the most convincing support for the traditional account of working-class opinion on the Civil War. The celebrated silence in Lancashire is of far less importance. Politically conscious people are rarely able to acknowledge the apathy of the masses. They read into their quiescence a significance which it often lacks. Thus, in relation to the demand for intervention, Marx found in silent Lancashire, 'A new, brilliant proof of the indestructible excellence of the English popular masses.' [4] But within the same year, in relation to the silence of these same masses with respect to the abuses and inadequacies of the relief committees, he complained of their 'sheep's attitude' and 'their christian slave nature'. [5]

It was not its inactivity, but its deeds, which established the predominantly pro-Federal opinion of British Labour during the greater part of the Civil War. While aristocracy was overwhelmingly for the Confederates and while investing England, with the help of France, found three million pounds sterling for the South, [6] the working class stood by the North American Republic. The existence of a small group of influential Southern sympathisers within the Labour movement, the decidedly

---

[1] 'Meeting at Stalybridge on Intervention in America', *Bee-Hive*, 4 October 1862.

[2] 'Mediation in the American Quarrel: Meeting of the Operatives', *Blackburn Patriot*, 5 July 1862.

[3] L. Blanc, *Letters on England* (1867), p. 185.

[4] *Die Presse*, 2 February 1862.

[5] Marx to Engels, 17 November 1862.

[6] Clapham, op cit., p. 238.

Confederate tendency of the Labour press, enhances, rather than diminishes, the achievement. Little known figures like the Weavers' President in Clitheroe, who steadfastly supported Lincoln while he received three shillings a week in relief,[1] and John Donald and the sturdy handloom weavers of New Milns [2] deserve to be remembered. So too do the leaders of the 'New Model Unions in London' who—in conjunction with Beesly and a few others—fought to regain control of the *Bee-Hive*; to bring the Unions into the political arenas; to break down the blind prejudice against any collaboration with Bright.

Whether the workers' efforts averted war is another matter. As has been noted, Marx held that the St. James's Hall meeting prevented Palmerston from declaring war upon the United States and this story enjoyed some currency at the time. (Dunning went out of his way to ridicule it in the *Bookbinders' Trade Circular*).[3] In fact there would appear to have been only one period, the Autumn of 1862, in which immediate intervention by Britain and France was being seriously contemplated.[4] It was not until six months after this that the working class had given conclusive proof of where its sympathies lay. What apparently restrained Palmerston in October 1862 was not that intervention would be unpopular, but that its advantages could not be clearly demonstrated to outweigh its risks. The subsequent progress of opinion in Britain would certainly have made war a most hazardous enterprise had any government been insane enough to undertake it.

Marx was fond of affirming that: 'As in the 18th century, the American war of Independence sounded the tocsin for the European middle class, so in the 19th century, the American Civil War sounded it for the European working class.' [5] And so, in a sense, it did. It gave an immense impetus to the demand for democratic government throughout Europe and in Britain

---

[1] R. Sharpe France, op. cit.

[2] R. M. Paterson, 'Newmilns Weavers and the American Civil War', *Ayrshire Archaeological and Natural History Society, Collections*, 1947–49. Second Series, Vol. I (Kilmarnock, 1950).

[3] *Bookbinders' Trade Circular*, 2 March 1864.

[4] E. D. Adams, op. cit., p. 103. Also J. Morley, *Life of Gladstone* (1903), II, pp. 84 ff.; P. Guedalla, ed., *Gladstone and Palmerston* (1928), p. 245.

[5] K. Marx, *Capital*, Vol. II (1938 edition), p. xviii. See also the *Address of the International to the People of the U.S.A.*, sent in September 1865.

in particular. In England, the demand for reform was made in direct association with declarations in support of Lincoln. As the demand for democratic rights was stimulated by involvement in the American struggle, so were the organisational conditions and class alignments necessary to a successful Reform agitation brought into existence. As the Secretary of the Reform League told Bright: 'Your presence with us on the American question . . . gave a great impetus to the political tendencies of the Unions, and aided us in our endeavours to bring them into the political arena.'[1]

It would, indeed, be difficult to over-estimate the importance of the Civil War for the subsequent history of the British Labour movement. Scarcely any of the political developments of the 1860s are intelligible without reference to it. Thus, the bitter quarrel between Potter and the 'Junta' was, in part, the result of the former's Southern sympathies and his alleged efforts to keep Troup as editor of the *Bee-Hive*. The close association between the Positivists and the 'New Model Unionists', which had been inaugurated during the builders' strike of 1859–61, was consolidated by their collaboration on behalf of the Federal cause. Justin McCarthy was one of the few contemporary observers who recognised the importance of the Positivists and their role in the Labour movement. He wrote of their work during the Civil War:

> I am bound to say that the admirable knowledge of the realities of the subject; the clear, quick, and penetrating judgement; and the patient, unswerving hope and confidence which were so signally displayed by the London working-men from first to last of that great struggle, were in no slight degree the result of the teaching and the labour of men like Professor Beesly and Frederic Harrison.[2]

It is worth noting that Dr. J. H. Bridges did not share Beesly's and Harrison's enthusiasm for the North. He was on close terms with J. R. Stephens and opened the eyes of his fellow Positivists to the oppressive conduct of some of the relief committees in the cotton districts. Bridges had spent some time in

[1] G. Howell to J. Bright, 7 October 1867 (Bishopsgate Institute).
[2] J. McCarthy, 'The English Positivists', *Galaxy* (New York), March 1869.

Australia and—like Troup—he admired Wakefield's plans for Colonisation.[1]

Even more than the Polish and Italian national movements, the Civil War helped to widen the horizons of the British Workers, and prepared their leaders for participation in the I.W.M.A. Indeed, its influence could be traced at the end of the decade in the rise of British Republicanism. Beesly had foretold its coming in an article which he contributed to the *Bee-Hive* in the hour of Federal victory.

> America [he wrote] is a standing rebuke to England. Her free institutions, her prosperity, the education of her people, the absence of a privileged class, are in too glaring a contrast with our own position to be forgiven ... Our opponents told us that Republicanism was on its trial. They insisted on us watching what they called its breakdown. They told us plainly that it was forever discredited in England. Well, we accepted the challenge. We forced them to keep their hands off when they wanted to break into the ring ... it is now we who call upon the privileged classes to mark the result. They may rely upon it that a vast impetus has been given to Republican sentiments in England, and that they will have to reckon with it before long.[2]

APPENDIX

'THE FREE INHERITANCE OF US ALL'

Beesly's Speech in St. James' Hall, London, 26 March 1863

The Right to take up a good cause, thank Heaven,
is the free inheritance of us all

Bee-Hive, 28 March 1863

Several references have been made to the great meeting which was held in St. James' Hall, London, on 26 March 1863. This meeting has been described as the most notable in support of the North held

[1] S. Liveing, *A Nineteenth Century Teacher; J. H. Bridges*, 1926, pp. 75, 95 et seq.

[2] E. S. Beesly, 'The Republican Triumph', *Bee-Hive*, 29 April 1865.

throughout the course of the war.[1] The description is just. The proceedings of that night over-shadowed the foreign affairs debate which took place in the Commons on the following day. *The Times* acknowledged that the speeches had to be regarded as expressing the general standpoint of British Workmen on the Civil War, while the *Bee-Hive* concluded that Southern sympathies had become confined to 'a very small section of the least thinking of the working millions'.[2]

The *Bee-Hive*'s manager, George Potter, is alleged to have tried to dissuade Trade Unionists from speaking at St. James' Hall. But after the meeting he changed sides and joined a deputation which called on the American Ambassador. Potter now assured the Ambassador that 'should our Government be forced into a war with America by the pressure of the Southern sympathisers in Parliament, the whole power of the masses would be brought to bear against such a war'.[3]

John Bright headed this deputation. It was of the highest significance for the subsequent development of the Reform question in England that he had taken the chair at St. James' Hall. For this meeting was avowedly a working-class gathering at which all the speakers, with the exception of Professor Beesly and Bright himself, were leading London Trade Unionists. All who took part in the proceedings understood that it portended a new alignment of social and political forces.

Karl Marx was present at St. James' Hall and came as near as he ever did to expressing admiration for Bright—'He looked quite like an Independent'.[4] Bright's incomparable gifts as an orator were certainly rarely displayed to greater advantage than on this occasion. However, the story that Marx was responsible for the meeting has little or no evidence to support it.[5] First, even in the interests of checking the War Party, it is doubtful whether Marx would have favoured anything resembling a *rapprochement* between Bright and the Labour leaders. Second, there is no evidence that he possessed the means for bringing the two sides into association with each other. He was not acquainted with Bright and he was not yet keeping company with the new Trade Union leaders. More than a year after the St. James' Hall meeting, at the time of the formation of the International, Marx made mistakes in his correspondence about the posi-

---

[1] E. D. Adams, *Great Britain and the American Civil War* (New York, 1925), p. 292.

[2] *Bee-Hive*, 11 April 1863.

[3] Ibid., 9 May 1863.

[4] K. Marx to F. Engels, 9 April 1963.

[5] R. Greenleaf, 'British Labour Against American Slavery', *Science & Society*, Vol. 17, No. 1, 1953. This is the fullest account of Marx' alleged part in getting up the meeting.

tion and occupation of W. R. Cremer who had shared the platform with Bright.[1]

All the available evidence points to the fact that it was not Marx, but Edward Spencer Beesly who deserves the credit for organising the meeting in St. James' Hall. Beesly was acquainted with Bright and was being encouraged by his fellow-Positivist, Frederic Harrison, to collaborate with him in politics.[2] As a result of his activities during the great struggle in the London Building trades, Beesly came to be on close terms with the Labour leaders, but he had not yet begun his friendly association with Marx.

Beesly announced the project of the meeting in the *Bee-Hive*. When it was over, he drew the moral: 'If you had supported Mr. Bright when he tried to get the suffrage for you a few years ago, you would not now be so helpless.'[3] On 6 February 1863 he attended a meeting of the London Trades Council which took the first steps in preparation for a meeting to endorse the policy of Negro emancipation.[4] A few days later the Council heard a letter from Beesly proposing a Trade Union protest against the South.[5] It was well received and Beesly was profusely thanked for his advice. He spoke at St. James' Hall; he went on the deputation that followed it; he audited the meeting's accounts and sent the balance to the Emancipation Society.[6] Ambassador Adams wrote to Secretary of State Seward 'of the pressure put on him by Professor Beesly, of the University of London, to send a representative of the American Ministry, Beesly expanding upon the importance and high standing of the Trades Unions'.[7] The Ambassador told Beesly:

> The suggestions made in your note on the 25th instant, seemed to me so valuable that I immediately adopted measures to carry them out. As a consequence I have sent to my government by this day's steamer a report

[1] Marx to Engels, 4 November 1864. Marx describes Cremer as a mason and secretary of the Masons Union, whereas he was a carpenter and a member of the Amalgamated Society of Carpenters and Joiners. Marx would hardly have made this mistake had he been collaborating with him before this date. In this letter Marx identifies Cremer and Odger as the organisers of the St. James' Hall meeting. He makes no claim to have played any part himself. Cremer certainly played an organisational role as well as speaking, but he did so with the guidance and encouragement of E. S. Beesly.

[2] See p. 257 *et seq* below.

[3] E. S. Beesly, 'Working Men's Emancipation Meeting', *Bee-Hive*, 14 March 1863.

[4] E. S. Beesly, 'The Meeting in St. James' Hall', *Bee-Hive*, 4 April 1863.

[5] 'Trades Intelligence', *Bee-Hive*, 28 February 1863.

[6] E. S. Beesly, 'Trades Emancipation Meeting', *Bee-Hive*, 9 May 1863.

[7] E. D. Adams, op. cit., p. 292.

of the facts attending the call of the meeting on Thursday as given by yourself, as well as another made to me by a confidential person (in pencil Beesly wrote against this, 'his son') who attended it . . .[1]

Marx was present at St. James' Hall, although unlike Beesly, John Stuart Mill, Henry Fawcett and Frederic Harrison, he was not on the platform. The story that he organised the meeting has no support beyond the statement, made many years after the event, by Henry Adams, that he had always believed that Marx was responsible.[2] Adams, and others after him, overlooked the fact that at the time it was reported to the State Department that the meeting was the result of 'the patient efforts' of Professor Beesly.

Beesly's speech in St. James' Hall has not, to my knowledge, been printed since it first appeared in the *Bee-Hive* nearly a hundred years ago. It was received almost as rapturously as Bright's own oration and it admirably conveys the spirit of one of Abraham Lincoln's most vigorous supporters. The fact that Marx made no comment on this speech suggests that he left the Hall before the end of the proceedings. (Beesly was the last speaker.) Had he stayed to the end, he would assuredly have joined in the cheering with which Beesly's address was received.

The Bee-Hive: Saturday, March 28th, 1863
Great Meeting of Trade Unionists
Negro Emancipation: Professor Beesly's Speech

The speakers who have preceded me have proved so conclusively on which side the right is, in this American War, that I think I should be wasting the few minutes allotted to me, if I dwelt any longer on that aspect of the question. I shall therefore confine my remarks to that part of the resolution which affirms that the cause of labour is one all over the world. I shall ask you to look at this question as one affecting your interests, and considering the proportion which the labouring class bears to the rest of the community, here and everywhere else, I don't think such a mode of looking at the question can fairly be stigmatised as narrow or one-sided. I say then, that whatever conflicting views or interests may be imported into this question, you, as working men, have a very simple criterion by which to test it. You will say we are accustomed over here to test a policy by the bearing it will have on the interests of labour, and we shall apply the same tests to the other side of the Atlantic. Political economists tell

---

[1] Charles Francis Adams to E. S. Beesly, 28 March 1863 (B.Coll.U.C.).
[2] E. D. Adams, op. cit., p. 292 for 1.

us that labour is a commodity, and like other commodities, if it is very cheap in one place it will have a tendency in the long run to sink in value in other places also. It is not our interest that labour should be cheap here or anywhere else, much less that it should be absolutely unpaid. We made a great outcry when sappers and miners were employed to do the work of Mr Higgs at the Chelsea Barracks.[1] Now if the unpaid labour of forty or fifty sappers and miners interfered with the fair price here, surely the unpaid labour of four or five millions of negroes must interfere with the fair price of the labour market in the world, and it's very easy to see why. No one ever emigrates from England to a slave state, and if the Northern States of America had been accursed by slavery, like the Southern, where would have been the outlet for our surplus population during the last twenty years? In other words, what would have been the rate of wages in England at the present moment? Now, there may be some who may feel a little shocked at the idea of being classed with slaves, under the general term of labourers. They may feel loth to believe that their interests are the same, that they are fellow soldiers in the same cause, that the struggle over there is but another version of the struggle with which you are but too familiar here. And yet, I think that the conception of the solidarity of labour is one which must have dawned on many of you of late years. I am persuaded that you have thought of the working men of France, for instance, as bound to you by sympathies and interests, which overlap material and geographical demarcations. But you must go further. There are two classes of workmen, both infinitely below you in intelligence, in organisation, and in social position, but still workmen, and therefore irrevocably bound up with you, I mean the agricultural workers of England and the negro slaves of America. I might of course mention other classes, but I select these two because they co-operate closely with you and are, so to speak, working for the same employers as you. If this was the proper occasion, I would give you my reasons for believing that your efforts to organise labour in England will never be thoroughly successful, until you have taken the agricultural workers as it were, into partnership, until they, like you, have begun to reflect seriously on the relation of labour and capital. But what I want to insist upon now is, the cause of the enslaved labourer in England. The slaveholding aristocracy of the South understand this perfectly. They maintain in the most open manner that slavery is the natural condition of labour, that society is divided normally into slave-owners and slaves. You might have hesitated to give that language its full literal interpretation; but the passages quoted from their own writings by the speaker who

[1] See R. W. Postgate, *The Builders' History*, 1923, p. 211.

preceded me, leave no doubt as to their meaning. I saw the thrill of horror and indignation, which ran through this vast assemblage, as he read those infamous words. Why, the white labourers of the South must be a little better than slaves already, if such words can be used among them with impunity. The editor of *The Times* has not got quite so far as that yet. I should not like to walk down Fleet Street in his shoes if he had. Now of course my friend Mr. Cremer was not trying to persuade you that there was any danger, even the remotest, of your being reduced to slavery. But just as you can tell a plant better when it is in full leaf and blossom, than when you merely see a root or a seed, so the full-blown significance of these doctrines and their real bearing on your interests, stands confessed in these imprudent avowals of some extreme partisans. Again I am far from imputing to our upper classes the design or desire to buy or sell you like cattle. But I think the greater part of them even of those calling themselves Liberals, are of the opinion that you have got a great deal more independence and freedom of action than is good for you. I don't pretend to say what modicum of freedom they think ought to be conceded to you, but from what we know of human nature I think we may safely say that if they could fix it now at what they pleased, the next generation of them would discover that even that modicum ought to be still further curtailed and so on, until at length you would differ from negro slaves in nothing except the colour of your skins. (Hear!) That model Tory, George III, could not bear the idea of emancipating our West Indian slaves because it savoured of the Rights of Man. He was a particularly stupid man; but even the brutes have instinct, and his instinct told him that if the black labourers got their rights, the next thing would be that the white labourers would be wanting theirs, and you may depend upon it, that that feeling is at the bottom of all the hostility to emancipation which we see now in England. Where was it that the attempts to abolish the slave trade met with the fiercest opposition? Why, in the House of Lords. Mind, no slavery, but the slave trade. Nay, even the attempt to impose some sanitary regulations on slave ships, the sort of thing they apply now to emigrant ships, though it passed the Commons with only some half dozen votes against it, met with the fiercest opposition in the House of Lords. Now you may think that a very harmless measure, nothing very dangerous or revolutionary. Trust the House of Lords for knowing what they are about. They can detect the thin end of the wedge as soon as most people. Even when the abolition of the slave trade was carried in the House of Commons, it was rejected in the House of Lords. As for emancipation, that was carried in the first favour of a reformed parliament and a good job too. For I am very certain if it was still to do, that

Mr. Gregory, the member for Galway, and Mr. Bentinck, the Protectionist, and Mr. Beresford Hope, the Puseyite, and Mr. Walter of *The Times* would find a great many excellent reasons why we should be in no hurry about it. Why, these people are getting so insolent that they are forgetting even common prudence and decency. They assign openly as their reason for supporting the South, that the slave-owners are gentlemen. They are passing the word round to stand by their order. Well, you stand by yours. (Cheers.) You won't have so low to stoop as they have. Your allies may be humble but they are not infamous. We know what these people mean by gentlemen. With them it is equivalent to idlers, the ornamental class that haven't got to work for their living. All workers they look on as dangerous—a class to be kept down—to be schemed against—their natural enemies. Amongst themselves they have made up their differences. They still call themselves Whigs and Tories, but they have borrowed the motto of your societies, 'Union is Strength'. For they have found one grand cardinal principle on which they can agree. It is the key to the whole political situation, to our foreign policy no less than to our domestic, to every measure of the government, to every manoeuvre of the opposition. Shall I tell you what this all-absorbing sentiment is? It is the fear of you. (Hear!) When Lord Derby came into power in 1852 he announced that his mission was to make a stand against democracy. It was the builders' strike in 1859 that settled the fate of the Reform Bill. They were thrown into a state of crazy terror by the glimpses they then caught of your unanimity and organisation. Over and over again have I heard it alleged as a proof of the danger of entrusting you with the franchise. Now, fellow citizens, when you are seriously bent on having the franchise and tell them so plainly, of course they will have to give way. If the Reform Bill failed, it was not because of their firmness, as they are silly enough to suppose; but because there were other things just then which you cared about a good deal more. Still it was not pleasant to have the door slammed in your face even though you did not care about going in. And I imagine your temper will not be improved by seeing them parade their sympathy and their admiration for these Southern gentlemen, while they keep you at arm's length like so many wild beasts. To come now to the practical question, what can working men do? I am rejoiced to think that there is not the slightest doubt on which side your sympathies are. But what is wanted is that you should express them in an imposing, unmistakable manner. Such meetings as these, genuine gatherings of working men, will have a good effect in two quarters, in America and in the House of Commons. In America it will do something to remedy the mischief that has been done by a wicked press. I don't for a moment

mean to excuse the foul-mouthed and idiotic bluster that many
American papers have used towards us. Newspaper writers are the
plague and curse of both countries. But I most fully excuse the grief
and indignation felt by most respectable Americans. They only hear
what *The Times* says to please the upper classes. How are they to
know that you, the real people of this country, wish them well, when
you have not made yourselves heard? Never has a poor country been
so ungraciously and cruelly treated. For years we have been taunting
them with slavery. They make a move to get rid of it. We turn round
and class them exterminators. When they seemed reluctant to draw
the sword they were cowards; when they drew it they were bullies.
First their battles were sneered at as bloodless and now they are
denounced as murderous. There is a story of an Italian poet who had
tried a great many ways of getting his living, but with such uniform
bad success that at last he said that he believed if he had been a
hatter, people would have been born without heads. Really I think
the Americans may fairly say that there is no possible policy they
could adopt that would satisfy some people over here. But it is no
trifling matter that a bitter feeling should grow up against us in a
country which in a few years will be able to do us more harm than all
Europe put together. If you allow the upper classes to pass themselves off as the people of England, you will have only yourselves to
blame for the consequences. Let America see that there is a mass of
honest, friendly sympathy over here among people who don't read
The Times. Cheer her in her sore trial by an expression of your good
will. A few kind words go a long way at such a season. Long and
anxiously has she listened for them. Shame on us that the manly
voice of the people has not long since swelled into a roar to drown
the malignant taunts of those who are not the people. *The Times* tells
us that there is no genuine movement for Emancipation or we should
see the hereditary champions of the cause in our van. Well we know
where Mr. Buxton is, and more shame for him; and as for the Bishop
of Oxford, if they mean him, I think we had rather be without him.
They might as well say that our respected chairman[1] had no right
to bring forward a Reform Bill, unless he could prove his descent
from some Baron of Magna Carta. No! there are a great many rights
and privileges hereditary in England: more perhaps than you
approve of. (Hear! hear!) But the right to take up a good cause, thank
Heaven, is the free inheritance of us all. (Loud cheers.) But the
popular voice must make itself heard not only in America but at
Westminster. We have had attempts made to get the South recognised and we shall have them again. I believe the Government will
defer it as long as they can. But it is not at all clear to me that the

[1] John Bright.

76

Tories won't get a majority on it. Now are you going to stand that? (Loud shouts of 'No!') Speak out loud and it won't be done. Our governing classes may refuse to enfranchise you. They may shut the door of the House of Commons in your face and value themselves on their cleverness. But when there is need you know how to make your voice heard. You would sweep away like so many cobwebs, were it necessary, the flimsy constitutional handcuffs in which they think they have you fast. But at present you don't care to stir. If, by coming here and quietly expressing your wishes, you can determine the policy of the country, it is much the same to you whether you do it here or at Westminster. So long as your interests are not flagrantly outraged, you allow your rulers to play their little game, and quarrel with one another for places and profit. But if they so far forget their weakness and your strength, as to trifle with you on matters of this kind, you will shake it all down some fine day like a house of cards. (Cheers.) But it won't come to that this time. They won't risk our precious constitution for their slave-holding friends. Tell them that you won't have quarrels picked with any country, but least of all with a republic, to please the gentlemen, (Cheers) that private ships shall not be sent out from Liverpool by members of parliament to embroil us with a friendly people,[1] and that whether the slave-owners' mutiny succeeded or not in America, noblemen and gentlemen had better not try to take the bit in their teeth over here. (Loud cheers.) Gentlemen, I have touched on other subjects besides Emancipation, but I don't think you will charge me with introducing irrelevant matter. Let them make politics a forbidden subject at other Emancipation meetings. We are met here tonight, we say it openly, not merely as friends of Emancipation, but as friends of Reform. (Loud cheers.) This is the first time, I believe, that the Trade Unionists of London have met together to pronounce on a political question, but I am sure it will not be the last, and the importance of such a question is not to be measured by counting heads. I hail it as a proof that you will no longer, in the absorbing interests of industrial questions, lose sight of those political questions which concern your class most vitally, though they may seem not to come home so palpably to each one of you. There is no danger of your Unions being degraded into electioneering agencies or mere political debating clubs, but there is as little danger, I am sure, that intelligent working men will ever meet together in any place or on any subject without encouraging one another in the sacred cause of political progress. (Loud cheering.)

[1] W. S. Lindsay, M.P.

III

THE TENTH APRIL OF
SPENCER WALPOLE: THE
PROBLEM OF REVOLUTION
IN RELATION TO REFORM,
1865-67

———————————<>———————————

THE tenth April 1848 is one of the most famous days in the
history of the nineteenth century. The Chartists of London had reputedly screwed themselves up for a decisive trial of
strength with the ruling classes. They found themselves out-
numbered by the combined resources of the civil and military
powers. They shrank back before the prospect of a collision with
the vast forces of law and order and property commanded by
the Duke of Wellington and Richard Mayne. What was to have
been a triumphant demonstration of the overwhelming power
and determination of the people, ended in the anything but
triumphal progress of a few hired hackney coaches carrying a
dubious petition.

> The 10th April, 1848, will long be remembered as a great field
> day of the British Constitution [announced *The Times*]. The signal
> of unconstitutional menace, of violence, of insurrection, of revolu-
> tion, was yesterday given in our streets, and happily despised by a
> peaceful, prudent, and loyal metropolis. That is the triumph we
> claim . . . This settles the question. In common fairness it ought to
> be regarded as a settled question for years to come. The Chartists
> and Confederates made the challenge, and chose the field and

78

trial of strength. They must stand by their choice. They chose to disturb the metropolis for the chance of something coming of it. They fished for a revolution and have caught a snub. We congratulate them on their booty, which we hope they will divide with their partners in Dublin. It is, perhaps, a fortunate circumstance that so momentous a question as the *free action of the British Legislature* should be settled thus decisively . . .[1]

Chartism was not extinguished by the events of the tenth April and had the economic and social conditions which characterised the late 'thirties and 'forties continued into the succeeding decade it would, no doubt, have revived. Yet on the Kennington Common it suffered a blow to its prestige from which it never fully recovered. The Government had the initiative, and the arrest and imprisonment of Chartist leaders became the order of the day. 'Respectable society' could henceforth indulge in the agreeable reflection that Revolution might sweep across Europe and leave England 'sound'. Quite as much as the great Exhibition of 1851, the tenth April 1848 contributed to the popularity of Mr. Podsnap's interpretation of history.

Yet the victory of tenth April was of a different order from that suggested by *The Times*. The Chartists had not 'raised the signal of revolution' nor had they 'made the challenge'. The Government had not foiled a bid for revolution, but had skilfully manoeuvred the Chartists into a position in which it could represent itself as having done so. The workmen's party paid the penalty which any party is likely to pay if it organises for peaceful purposes while talking academically about the right to make a revolution in the last resort. Instead of this being a threat which the Government anticipated with dread, the Government took the initiative and anticipated the threat. It used the threat to push its opponents into a false position from which they could extricate themselves only by acting up to the intentions which had been ascribed to them or by going through the humiliating experience of climbing down without ever having climbed up. This was a situation from which the leaders of the British working class proved unable to disengage themselves in 1848 or again in 1926. The Government's victories were not less real for being cheaply bought or theatrically managed. By giving a form to the conflict which outstripped its real content, the

[1] *The Times*, 11 April 1848.

79

Government disabled the working class from ever occupying the position which had been officially ascribed to it. Perhaps on the continent, History, as Hegel said, repeats itself first as tragedy and then as farce. But the English governing classes found ways of omitting the first style of performance. But in these unripe crises, these conflicts, in which the appearance of a decisive confrontation arrives well ahead of its substance, it was not always the governing classes which came off best.[1]

I

It took twenty years for the British working class to raise once again the question of its political rights into a great national issue. It did so, not upon the basis of the Charter as a whole, but by agitating for only two of the six points: universal manhood suffrage and vote by ballot. Although the Reform League of the 1860s was a predominantly working-class body, it never insisted as emphatically as the Chartists had done upon its independence. Indeed it was conceived as a result of negotiations between a group of Labour leaders and a number of 'influential gentlemen', advanced Liberals, who promised to raise £5,000 to work up an earnest agitation.[2] The rivalry between the League and the middle-class Reform Union was always limited and contained by the dual membership of wealthy manufacturers, upon whom both bodies were largely dependent for financial support.

The Reformers of the 1860s were not above references to Revolution. As early as 1865 one Labour paper could observe: 'The granting of Manhood Suffrage', they say, 'would effect a Revolution. Well let us be plain and say that it would be of small value if it did not.'[3] But the occasional blasé reference of this kind ought not to conceal the distance which had been travelled since the 'thirties and 'forties. Behind Chartism lay

---

[1] G. J. Holyoake, *Bygones Worth Remembering*, Vol. 1 (1905), pp. 73–83, understood the 10th April, at least negatively. He knew that there was no immediate intention of mounting a revolutionary challenge. Mr. John Saville in 'Chartism in the Year of Revolutions', *Modern Quarterly*, Vol. 8, No. 1, 1952–53, pp. 23–33, has called the received interpretation into question.

[2] *The Times*, 21 February and 24 February 1865.

[3] *Miner and Workman's Advocate*, 19 August 1865.

boundless, if inchoate, dreams of social reconstruction; behind the Reform League lay little more than the expectation of 'rising in the social scale'.[1] Yet the limited demands and modest ambitions of the League did not prevent it from being drawn into a direct confrontation with the ruling powers. In 1867 the scene at Kennington Common was re-enacted with some of the principal actors still playing their old roles, but this time there was to be a very different *dénouement*. Essentially the same kind of double bluff occurred again. London, which had disappointed the hopes of the Chartists, was the main bastion of the Reform League. In establishing its headquarters in London, the League was not repeating the old error of separating the leadership from the main body of its supporters.

During the early months of 1866, while the Russell–Gladstone Reform Bill was being debated in Parliament, there was little agitation in the country. Tories and Adullamites taunted the Government with its failure to interest the public in its measure. Horsman declared that Bright had tried to use 'all the machinery of uproar', but 'the agitation has failed—failed ridiculously, failed ignominiously'.[2] Lowe mocked the Gladstonians' attempt to frighten the House with the spectre of the serious unrest which would follow a rejection of the Bill. He observed that, in the speeches of Government supporters, the working men came in like lambs and went out like lions.[3]

The Government's difficulty had been correctly anticipated by E. S. Beesly before the terms of the Bill became known. He foresaw that every £ off the qualification for the electoral register would increase the number of the old Palmerstonians who would be ready to join forces with the Tories. 'A strong popular enthusiasm might encourage him (Russell) to risk these desertions, but no strong enthusiasm can be got up for anything less

---

[1] 'Let us once be able to maintain by the force of intellect and truth our rights as workmen in that House, and depend upon it we shall rise in the social scale . . .' Address by the Reform League 'To the Trades Unionists of the United Kingdom', no date—but in George Howell's hand, 'first issued in June 1865 a few weeks before the General Election'. This 'Address' is pasted into the front of the second volume of Minutes of the General Council of the Reform League, Howell Collection, Bishopsgate Institute, London. Herein after referred to as H.C.

[2] Parl. Debates, 3rd Series, cxxxii (12 March 1866), 107 and 109.

[3] Ibid. (26 April 1866), 2104.

than manhood suffrage, which Lord Russell would resist as firmly as Lord Derby.'[1] The Government's measure not only split its own supporters, but divided the League. Beesly, out of regard for Bright, supported the Bill, others followed Ernest Jones in his bitter denunciations of it.[2]

The resignation of the Government healed the breach in the League and opened the way to months of intense agitational activity. Frederic Harrison, who with his colleague and fellow Positivist, Beesly, was one of the most trusted and influential advisors to the Labour Movement, announced: 'Compromise has been carried to the last point, but it is now over.' He explained that workmen could and ought, 'to make Government after Government impossible—to oppose everything, to accept nothing, and to force to its extreme point this palpable mockery of popular government. Let them from this moment declare themselves in permanent opposition to every Government and to every Government measure.'[3]

Following immense demonstrations in Trafalgar Square at the beginning of July, the League resolved to meet in Hyde Park. The chief of Metropolitan Police, Sir Richard Mayne, was charged with preventing any entry into the Park. The events which followed are sufficiently familiar. Edmond Beales, the President of the League, having demanded and been denied admission departed with his immediate followers and supporters to the Square. The crowd, possibly incensed by this and by the arbitrary manner in which the police allowed well-dressed and well-spoken people to go through the gates,[4] burst down the dilapidated railings and three days and nights of intermittent skirmishing followed. The Home Secretary in the new Conservative government, Mr. Spencer Walpole, received a deputation from the League which offered to go back to the Park and attempt to restore order, on condition that a halt was called to

[1] E. S. Beesly, 'The Liberal Majority', *Workman's Advocate*, 27 January 1866.

[2] For this split see, for example, 'A Word in Reply to Mr. Ernest Jones on the Reform Bill', *Commonwealth*, 21 April 1866. Also Jones' letter in same issue.

[3] F. Harrison, 'The Government Defeat', *Bee-Hive*, 23 June 1866.

[4] This was recalled as the occasion of the riots, *Daily News*, 6 May 1867.

all further exercises by the police and the military. The Home Secretary was 'much affected'[1] by this offer—popular tradition had it that he actually wept—and he gratefully accepted it. It was believed by the League leaders that he had also agreed to the holding of a meeting, not for the purpose of clearing the Park, but for the advocacy of manhood suffrage. G. J. Holyoake—'the thin voiced, intrusive, consequential Holyoake', as Marx was to call him in consequence[2]—supported Walpole's denial that he had ever entered into such an agreement.[3]

Although Sir Stafford Northcote told his wife on 23 July, 'We are expecting to have all our heads broken tonight, as the mob are now trying it on in Hyde Park, and perhaps if they are defeated there, they will come on here (the House of Commons)',[4] the moment of greatest danger came after the Reform League had restored order. 'After the riot very dangerous elements really apeared. There was complete preparation for a grand street fight. I know,' wrote Frederic Harrison, 'of men of good position who travelled up to London from the North to fight, and that clerks in business houses had their rifles beside their desks.'[5] It is clear, from more than one source, that '*political* forces of a fighting kind came on to the scene or rather behind the scenes'.[6] Gustave-Paul Cluseret, soon to be chief of staff of the Paris Commune, appears to have been at work trying to promote a Fenian–Reform League alliance.[7] Beyond doubt, a number of working-class leaders were bent on defying the Government and holding their meeting in the Park. It was at this point that a Conference was called between the Council of the League and a number of Radical M.P.s. It was at this conference that J. S. Mill had recourse to what he described as 'les grands moyens'.

---

[1] *The Times*, 25 July 1866.

[2] K. Marx to F. Engels, 27 June 1866. (*Marx and Engels on Britain* [1954], p. 496.)

[3] G. J. Holyoake, *Sixty Years of an Agitator's Life*, Vol. 2 (1893), pp. 186–90. But as to Holyoake's reliability see A. R. Schoyen, *The Chartist Challenge* (1958), p. 296, fn. 2.

[4] A. Lang, *Life of the Earl of Iddesleigh* (1891), p. 161.

[5] F. Harrison, *Order and Progress* (1875), p. 184, fn.

[6] Ibid.

[7] J. B. Leno, *Aftermath* (1892), p. 71.

I told them that a proceeding which would certainly produce a collision with the military, could only be justifiable on two conditions: if the position of affairs had become such that a revolution was desirable, and if they thought themselves able to accomplish one. To this argument, after considerable discussion, they at last yielded: and I was able to inform Mr. Walpole that their intention was given up.[1]

But it was only given up for a time. On both sides feeling was running high. Walpole and the Government had only barely scraped home and there was much indignation that he had, by treating with the League, made it appear that he was dependent on its good will for the preservation of order. Beales was able to assert that

> Hyde Park was handed over to myself and the other members of the Reform League for the express purpose of our maintaining that order in it which the police could not maintain, and we completely accomplished our object ... by the Reform League alone was not only the Park but all London preserved that night from most disasterous scenes of violence and bloodshed.[2]

Emily Eden expressed her sense of anger and humiliation to the Earl of Clarendon:

> I attempted a drive round the park and am so indignant at the sight that I feel boiling and bloodthirsty. As for Beales, I suppose the meekest of babies would hang that man as soon as look at him, and also I do not see how we are to die peacefully in our beds without having exterminated that wretched coward Bright ... Poor dear Walpole! there never was anybody so little up to the *hauteur des circonstances*. How could he *cry* to Beales? However, it seems to have answered.
>
> 'Twas too convincing—dangerously dear—
> In Walpole's eye the unanswerable tear,'[3]

Disraeli assured the Queen that the discussion in the House on the riots in the Park was 'highly and unexpectedly satisfactory'. The Queen thanked her Chancellor for his reports, but most of all for carrying the vote for the gun-metal for 'her dear great

---

[1] J. S. Mill, *Autobiography* (1873), pp. 290–1.
[2] E. Beales, letter in *The Times*, 28 July 1866.
[3] H. Maxwell, *The Earl of Clarendon*, Vol. i (1913), pp. 321–2.

husband's memorial'.[1] As for the rest of 'respectable society', its feelings were somewhat mollified by the fact that Beales was deprived of his appointment as one of the revising barristers for Middlesex, and by the severe sentences which were passed on those who were alleged to have been involved in the disturbances. The magistrate told a bystander who had been injured by the police, that he ought not to complain about the constable but about 'those who turned loose the scum and refuse of the town on the peaceable inhabitants'.[2] Marx observed that while 'the old ass Beales' went in for 'peacefulness and dissoluteness', the 'cur Knox, the police magistrate of Marylebone, snaps out summary judgement in a way that shows what would happen if London were Jamaica'.[3] In the months which followed the July days there were men on both sides who began to think and talk as if London might well become Jamaica.

The end of 1866 and the beginning of the following year were marked by an economic depression and tens of thousands were thrown out of work. The cholera, which was ever the companion of political disturbance, made its appearance. Like the depressed state of trade, it was felt with particular severity in London. Meanwhile, there was a growing preoccupation with political violence as a result of the Jamaica Committee's attempt to prosecute Governor Eyre, the activities of the Fenians, and cases of 'rattening' and murder in Sheffield. The ruling classes viewed with the greatest apprehension the prospect of an amalgamation between the Reformers on the one side and either the Irish or the Trade Unionists on the other. In the Workers' press, Beesly and others linked up martial law abroad and police violence at home. 'The impunity accorded to Eyre is part of a system recently introduced and steadily carried out. Public servants are to be uniformly screened from the consequences of any illegal act, provided that the act was done in the interests of wealth and respectability.'[4] 'Every policeman now understands that when he is acting in defence of the swells he may use his

[1] W. F. Monypenny and G. E. Buckle, *Life of Benjamin Disraeli*, Vol. 2 (1929), pp. 183–5.
[2] Cited by P. A. Taylor M.P., Parl. Debates, 3rd series, clxxxiv (7 August 1867), 2134.
[3] K. Marx to F. Engels, 27 July 1866.
[4] E. S. Beesly, 'The Trial of Mr. Eyre', *Bee-Hive*, 18 August 1866.

truncheon just as he pleases, without any fear of the consequences.'[1] 'The Eyre Committee recently published in the *Standard*, and thereby endorsed, a letter which openly threatened "Reform Leaguers and Trade Unions" with the treatment of Gordon. Nothing is commoner than to hear the wish expressed that Mr. Bright may find his way to the gallows.'[2] By the end of 1866, the *Commonwealth*, 'The Organ of the Reform Movement', reached the conclusion that 'we have slightly overdone "moral force" here lately' and added, 'like "lovely woman", moral force may stoop to folly, and when she does it is invariably discovered too late that "men betray".'[3]

Meanwhile, Bright had placed himself at the head of a series of impressive Reform demonstrations in the North. Behind bands and banners the working men of Glasgow, Leeds, Birmingham and Manchester showed that, no less than the men of London, they cared for political equality. But in the winter of 1866–67 the Reformers began to discuss forms of direct action which made John Bright himself extremely uneasy. Sir Richard Mayne had declined to accept responsibility for the preservation of the peace at a great meeting and demonstration to be called by the London Working Men's Association in December.[4] Beesly declared that this left the workers no choice but to organise themselves on physical force lines and establish a Reform constabulary.[5] The League resolved 'that each London Branch be requested to furnish a number of men as "peace protectors", in consequence of the refusal of Sir Richard Mayne to provide proper police constables'.[6] Bright saw that: 'If the thing goes off well and in great force, it will help the Derby Conspiracy in their deliberations, and Walpole's tears will be shed amid the sighs of his colleagues.' But he was also alarmed: 'It would be easy to induce many scores of thousands of men to provide themselves with arms—to form something like a great

[1] E. S. Beesly, 'The Trial of Mr. Eyre', *Bee-Hive*, 18 August 1866.

[2] E. S. Beesly, 'The Prosecution of Governor Eyre', *Commonwealth*, 20 October 1866.

[3] 'Physical Force', *Commonwealth*, 15 December 1866.

[4] Alfred Austin's reply, on behalf of the First Commissioner, to R. Hartwell's letter of 17 November 1866.

[5] E. S. Beesly, 'Reform Constables', *Bee-Hive*, 25 November 1866.

[6] Minutes Executive Committee, Reform League, 23 November 1866 (H.C.).

national volunteer force, which, without breaking the law, would place the peace of the country on a soil hot with volcanic fire.'[1]

Bright always insisted that 1832 had demonstrated the possibility of peaceful constitutional change. Yet it was not just a threat, but a genuine expression of anxiety, when he told a great Reform Banquet in September 1866:

> These great meetings, as Mr. Mill very justly said, were not meetings so much for discussion, as they were meetings for the demonstration of opinion, and, if you like, I will add for exhibition of force. Such exhibitions, if they are despised and disregarded, may become exhibitions of another kind of force . . .[2]

When the working-class reformers copied this sort of language and warned that their mightiest demonstrations of the autumn of 1866 were but 'dress-rehearsals', they were told that they were attempting to over-awe Parliament, a thing which could scarcely be distinguished from rebellion.

> We cannot believe that (such attempts) will be tolerated. We trust and believe that if attempted they will be immediately put down. All the respectability of London turned out when the capital was threatened some years ago with an invasion of Chartists, headed by Mr. Fergus O'Connor. All the respectability of London will turn out again, and disperse whatever mob Mr. Beales and Mr. Potter, with Mr. Hartwell's combination, may collect. We are not friendly to letting loose troops against any portion of Her Majety's subjects, however unlawfully engaged. And in the event of the threatened outrage on Parliament taking place, we are confident that the civil power will prove strong enough to hold its own, and to put down the disturbers of the public peace . . .[3]

This confidence was not entirely shared by the Government. It was thought expedient to prepare a confidential memorandum on the aid which could lawfully be given to the civil power by the Regular and Auxiliary Forces.[4] General Peel told the Home Secretary that

> numerous applications have been received from Lords Lieutenant of Counties, and officers commanding Volunteer Corps, for

[1] G. M. Trevelyan, *Life of John Bright* (1913), p. 364.
[2] H. Jephson, *The Platform: Its Rise and Progress*, Vol. 2 (1892), p. 451.
[3] *Blackwood's*, January 1867, p. 132.
[4] Charles M. Clode's confidential memorandum of 20 December 1866 (Home Office stamp, 2 February 1867), H.O. 45. O.S. 8060.

instructions for their guidance in cases of civil commotion; and as to the liability or the competence of the Volunteers to act as a Military Body under Arms in aid of the Civil Power.[1]

The Minister of War drafted a 'Reserve Force Bill' which, in its eighth clause, sought to strengthen and clarify the position.[2]

In 1867 the Government introduced its resolutions. The suspicion that it had come by the 'Hyde Park Rail-Way' to Reform was expressed by *Punch*:

> In framing our scheme, let's enlist the whole House,
> So Reform's Bill won't be Revolution's;
> And as Walpole had got no resolution to move,
> Let's get Walpole to move resolutions.[3]

The League held an impressive meeting to coincide with Disraeli's speech in Parliament, but it was not content with this. In its search for new ways of twisting the Government's arm, it hit upon a plan for a day of Individual Petitions in Favour of Reform. This was a dodge for staging something like a march on Parliament without (it was thought) risking arrest. At intervals of a few minutes, parties of not more than ten men were to set off from the Reform League's Offices and walk to the House of Commons carrying petitions. Walpole wanted to prevent it, but the Law Officers advised him that, although it was illegal, he could not have those taking part arrested on the spot and that it would be difficult to use force.[4]

Encouraged by their own successes and the evident weakness and hesitancy of the Government, the leaders of the workmen grew bolder. Voices from the past had for long been calling for a 'People's Parliament' chosen by the non-electors and a 'Grand National Holiday'.[5] Although these voices were never too distinct, they became more audible and menacing.

[1] General Peel to S. H. Walpole, 20 February 1867 (H.O. ibid.).

[2] Reserve Force Bill, war office solicitors, 23 February 1867 (H.O. ibid.).

[3] *Punch*, 16 February 1867.

[4] Opinion of Law Officers of the Crown, 28 January 1867 on 'Individual Petitions in Favour of Reform'. (H.O. 45. O.S. 7854.)

[5] A proposal for a 'People's Parliament' had been discussed as early as 29 September 1865. It was raised again and rejected on 12 October 1866 (Minutes of General Council, Reform League [H.C.]). With respect to a General Strike, at a delegate meeting on 27 February 1867 it was resolved that 'Unless a satisfactory prospect is held out in Parliament of the working

By the end of February 1867 they were loud enough for Mill to complain to W. R. Cremer of 'a readiness to proceed at once to a trial of physical force if any opposition is made either to your demands or to the particular mode, even though illegal, which you may select for the expression of them'. He found in one speech evidence that Reformers asserted the 'superiority of physical force as constituting right, and as justifying the people in "riding down the ministers of the law" '.[1] On the same day as Mill expressed these anxieties, Beesly told his friend, Frederic Harrison:

> I think old Beales is getting out of his depth. Dickson and Bradlaugh are panting for a row and there is really no excuse for it at present. They defy the police when no one has talked of police interference. They are trailing their coats before the Government. As long as meetings and processions are admitted by Lord Derby to be legal what call is there to talk of force? The worst of it is that they will not be backed. There is no widespread sense of wrong. Nothing has occurred yet to put up people's blood. Dickson kept saying all kinds of nonsense to me at Islington. His mind was evidently running on barricades. I dare say it may come to that very shortly if some accident should occur such as Nap's death. But as we are at present—it is too ridiculous.[2]

It was against this background, in which force was both ridiculous and yet an item to be reached further down the agenda: this situation in which Bradlaugh, Dickson and the

[1] J. S. Mill to W. R. Cremer, 1 March 1867, in: H. S. R. Elliot, *The Letters of John Stuart Mill*, Vol. 2 (1910), 77–9.
[2] Beesly to Harrison, 1 March 1867 (B. Coll. U.C.L.).

---

classes being universally enfranchised upon the principles of the Reform League, it will be necessary to consider the propriety of these classes adopting a universal cessation from labour until their political rights are conceded'. (Minutes of General Council, Reform League [H.C.].) George Potter, leader of the London Working Men's Association and manager of the *Bee-Hive*, took up this threat in a speech in Trafalgar Square. He posed the issue as either household suffrage [*sic*] with a lodger franchise or else a week's cessation from labour aiming at a complete stop being put to all traffic and all business. (*The Times*, 4 March 1867.) The far fiercer temper which the Reformers were displaying at the beginning of 1867 is evidenced by the need for appeals to avoid all expressions 'involving in the slightest degree any indication of physical force'. Minutes, General Council of the Reform League, 20 April 1867 (H.C.).

Left within the League were forcing Beales' hand: that it was resolved to trail coats still more provocatively and to try, once again, the right of public meeting in Hyde Park. With the help of 40 billboard men, hundreds of posters, and 35,000 handbills, they announced that they would hold a Reform Meeting in the Park at half past six o'clock; Edmond Beales, Esq., M.A., presiding.[1]

To this challenge, the Government replied by issuing a proclamation:

> Whereas it has been publicly announced that a meeting will be held in Hyde Park on Monday the 6th of May, for the purpose of political discussion: And whereas the use of the Park for the purpose of holding such meeting is not permitted, and interferes with the object for which Her Majesty has been pleased to open the Park for the general enjoyment of Her People: Now, all persons are hereby warned and admonished to abstain from attending, aiding, or taking part in any such meeting, or from entering the Park with a view to attend, and, or take part in such a meeting. S. H. Walpole. Home Office, Whitehall, May 1st 1867.[2]

On the evening of 1 May, three superintendents of police attended a full delegate meeting of the Council of the League and informed them of the Government's decision. A majority of those present resolved that they would not yield.

> The Government [declared Charles Bradlaugh] had invited a contest and upon it depended the question whether they would have a real Reform Bill or not. If they all bore themselves like men through all this—if they took care there was no disorder, if they took care they were not the first to strike, if they took care to go upon their legal right, they might depend upon it, if the Government attacked them, out of this Monday's meeting would come more than out of months of Parliamentary debating. (Loud and prolonged cheers.)

He concluded by moving a resolution to the effect that the meeting should be held, and that 'the crime of interfering to prevent it must rest upon those wicked enough to pursue such an infatuated course'.[3]

[1] Minutes of the Hyde Park sub-Committee of the Executive Committee of the Reform League, 20 April 1867. (In E.C. Minute Book [H.C.].)

[2] *The Times*, 2 May 1867.

[3] Minutes General Council of Reform League, 1 May 1867 (H.C.).

On Friday, 3 May, the Commons had one of the most un-nerving days it had experienced for twenty years. First, a num-ber of Honourable and Gallant Members took the most unusual step of dividing the House on the question of whether a petition should be allowed to lie upon the table. This petition had been drawn up by Beesly and his friends and been introduced by John Bright. After rehearsing the crimes of the British Army from 1789 to the Jamaica Outrages, it expressed understanding for Fenians and prayed that the Fenian prisoners should be treated in a humane and civilised fashion.[1] Having reminded itself that there were English sympathisers with Fenianism who were ready to question the honour of British officers, the House went on to debate the Government's preparations for meeting the challenge to its authority in the Park. Many Members re-called that they had served as special constables in 1848 and demanded assurances that Beales and Bradlaugh would be arrested if they dared to address their supporters on Monday.[2] Beales had made it quite plain that this time he would not con-fine himself to demanding admission to the Park, but would, in his words, 'enforce that admittance if required'.[3] The Home Secretary observed that such language was of a kind which 'no Government could submit to with due regard to the interests of the country'.[4]

The following day the *Times* reported that

> Nearly all the proclamations issued by Mr. Walpole and posted all over London have been either torn down or defaced. In some cases they have been completely covered by what is called 'the yellow placard' . . . it calls on the people to disregard Mr. Walpole's pro-clamation . . . this placard has been more extensively posted throughout the metropolis even than the proclamation itself. The credit of the agitation party is thus staked on holding the meeting and the Government and the authorities are as firmly resolved to prevent it by all means in their power.[5]

[1] Parl. Debates 3rd series, clxxxvi (3 May 1867), 1929–33 and also debate of 14 June 1867, clxxxvii, 1886–1906.

[2] Parl. Debates, 3rd series, clxxxvi (3 May 1867). See particularly speeches by Denman (1982–3), Selwyn (1981–2), and Neate (1964–6).

[3] *Working Man*, 4 May 1867.

[4] Parl. Debates 3rd series, clxxxvi (3 May 1867), 1972.

[5] *The Times*, 4 May 1867.

The Government decided to strengthen the hand of Sir Richard Mayne, who twenty years earlier had helped subdue Fergus O'Connor, by recruiting 12,000 to 15,000 special constables, while troops, including cavalry, were sent into London from Aldershot and elsewhere. Rumour had it that several batteries of Armstrong guns were being brought to the Metropolis. All Sunday, 5 May, men at the Woolwich Arsenal worked overtime producing staves for the special constables.[1]

In the face of these massive preparations some of the Reformers began to lose heart. From the beginning, Connolly, a stonemason and one of the most powerful orators in the League, had warned his colleagues against talking as if they were generals commanding a well-disciplined army. 'The whole question was not worth shedding blood for, or resorting to physical force in any way.'[2] Joseph Collet, who edited the journal of Bronterre O'Brien's old 'National Reform League', generally criticised Beales for being too soft and compliant, but on this occasion he cautioned the Reformers against behaving like 'bombastic children'. He told Beales:

> It would appear that you, with the Executive, are determined to call forth a demonstration similar to that of July last and that if the authorities adopt the same course they did then, either an appeal to force must be the result, or Reformers would have once more to retire. I believe that it would be, not only impolitic but criminal to bring the question to such an issue as this, and I will give you my reasons:—If the people of this country are really prepared to join issue with the government, then they have something better to do than fight their fellow men of the army and the police about a question of admittance into the park.
>
> However important the question of the right of meeting may be, if to settle it force must be resorted to and blood spilt, then the people must be prepared either to submit or to destroy the present political fabric. I think they are not yet ripe for such an issue . . . Suppose that the Reformers were even to force their way into the park, what then? Do you think that the Government would stop there?[3]

But there had been a curious reversal of roles; while the old Chartist League urged caution, the new one was intransigent

---

[1] *The Times*, 6 May 1867.   [2] *The Times*, 2 May 1867.
[3] *Working Man*, 4 May 1867.

and defiant. 'Let but a single drop of blood (be) shed on Monday next,' wrote the *Commonwealth*, 'and, if we are not mistaken, the word will go forth that such blood must be avenged. We at least will be prepared to admit that the reign of terror has commenced and must be played out.'[1] Although Gladstone and others expressed their solidarity with the Government in the interests of order, and Tom Hughes and other influential friends urged them to abandon the meeting,[2] the League appeared to be settled upon what the Tory press referred to as its 'madly wicked purpose'. 'We gather on the green sward,' wrote Bradlaugh, 'we shall have to gather there as a People's Parliament, denying that you (the Commons) are the parliament of the nation; and we will gather there with or without your permission for it is our right.'[3]

On the morning of 6 May one of the leading Conservative newspapers wrote:

> Today, more than on any other occasion since the pitiable episode of 1848, the working men of London are on trial. They are invited to band themselves together and offer a public defiance to the constitutional authorities, to violate the law, and the plainly defined rights of the Crown, to insult the House of Commons, to annoy and outrage the upper and middle classes, and to jeopardise the peace of the Metropolis.

If necessary, the military would have to teach the Reform League that 'sedition is a dangerous game to play in England'.[4]

Meanwhile, the civil and military forces were taking up their positions.

> A part of a regiment of Hussars, having been brought in from Hounslow, was stationed near the Park and in the Royal Mews. A strong detachment of Life Guards was at Knightsbridge, while another was under cover at the end of Park Lane. The Horse Guards (Blue) were in readiness to move at a moment's notice from Regents Park, and the Guards were kept to their barracks in anticipation of any emergency. Behind the police barrack in the

---

[1] *Commonwealth*, 4 May 1867.
[2] Minutes of the Executive Committee of the Reform League, 6 May 1867 (H.C.).
[3] C. Bradlaugh, *Reform or Revolution*, n.d. (1867?; 8 pp.).
[4] *Standard*, 6 May 1867.

park itself is a very pretty enclosure known as the Wood-yard . . . Here a regiment of the Guards were placed, under the Command of the Hon. Colonel Keppel . . . Here too were mounted orderlies, superintendents of police on horseback, officers passing continually to and fro. This spot was . . . the headquarters, and though from the outside scarcely more than a dozen sentries and police were to be seen; yet all within this quiet looking enclosure was war-like in its every aspect. Altogether more than 10,000 men, police and military, were kept ready to move and close in upon the park within half an hour's notice . . .[1]

At about 6.00 p.m. the Clerkenwell Branch of the Reform League appeared at the Gates of the Park carrying a red flag surmounted with a cap of liberty. Half an hour later there were between 100,000 and 150,000 people in the park.[2] The leaders of the League entered to the sound of great cheering and proceeded to address the crowd from no fewer than ten separate platforms. They tried to avoid giving full expression to their sense of triumph, but every reference to Beales and the League was saluted by prolonged applause while mention of Walpole or the police was the signal for hisses and groans. From one platform the call was given for a great national convention to prepare a Reform Bill. If their demands were rejected 300,000 men should be brought into London from the North and no man return until either the Commons passed the Bill or 'until England had found its new Cromwell to turn out the men who had misrepresented the people in St. Stephens'.[3] Those who could not get near enough to hear the speeches listened to 'ballad singers without number' tell of the defeat of Walpole and the coming victory of Reform.[4] The police were hissed and a few stones were thrown, but crime was confined to a couple of pick-pockets and three cases of thimblerigging.[5]

The working-class press was exultant: '. . . the triumph of the working men was complete and bloodless. They had everything their own way. The enemy, notwithstanding his insulting defiances and incessant vapourings during the last six weeks had

[1] *The Times*, 7 May 1867.

[2] *Daily News*, 7 May 1867. (There was as usual, an enormous difference in the estimates made of the numbers present. The top figure was 250,000–500,000, the lowest 20,000.)

[3] Rev. Sharman of Bradford reported in *National Reformer*, 12 May 1867.

[4] *The Times*, 7 May 1867.   [5] *Bee-Hive*, 11 May 1867.

not the courage to show his face.'[1] Beales, who reported that as late as 5.00 p.m. on 6 May the Government had served further notices on all the leaders in the League's premises, summed the issue up:

> The Government gave them all to understand that they had an enormous array of military force—infantry, cavalry, and artillery (laughter)—yes, artillery at the railway stations—cutlasses without end at Scotland-Yard, batons fabricated at Woolwich, and special constables—(great laughter)—ridiculous and absurd as they were, sworn in in all directions . . . Supposing he had flinched for one instant, what would have been irreparably damaged. Supposing he had given way and issued an address requesting the men of London, in consequence of the powerful appeal of Mr. Gladstone on Friday, not to go to the Park. Many of them would not have gone, but many would, in bad temper, under the impression that they had been dealt doubly with, and that there had been something in the shape of treachery, and riot and tumult would have inevitably occurred . . .
>
> It was impossible to conceive a more marked contrast than was presented last Monday between the feebly, insulting conduct of the Government and the ruling classes, and the admirable, orderly, peaceable, self-possessed, and dignified conduct of the people. (Loud cheers.) It was a great moral triumph—a triumph greater than any language of his could express.[2]

Beyond question, it had been a much more clear-cut victory than the one which had been claimed in the July Days. Then the League had shown that the Government could not preserve order without its help; now it had demonstrated that it was able to impose its will upon the Government.

The lesson could not be escaped. In the House of Lords, Earl Cowper declared that the Executive had brought itself into contempt. 'No greater blow could, in his opinion, have been struck against all respect for law and authority.'[3] Earl Granville said:

> He knew nothing more powerful in this country, as was shown in 1848, than the power of calling out special constables to aid the regularly organised police. But if the Government called out

[1] *Reynolds' News*, 12 May 1867.

[2] Minutes of the General Council of the Reform League, 8 May 1867 (H.C.).

[3] Parl. Debates, 3rd series, clxxxvii (9 May 1867), 217.

special constables when there was no need for them there was a danger of their crying out 'Wolf' once too often, and thus diminishing the readiness with which these classes had hitherto responded to the call of the Government. He had sometimes heard it said in that House, with regard to foreign Powers, that you should never menace them unless you were prepared to carry out that menace . . . If it were true with respect to foreign nations, it was still more true that a Government should not threaten any portion of their own countrymen unless they were strong in the power to carry out those threats, and strong in the justice of the course of action they adopted.[1]

The Prime Minister admitted that the Government had been 'humiliated' or, as he chose to express it, had 'suffered some slight humiliation in the public mind'.[2] He announced that he had received and had accepted the resignation of the Home Secretary, Mr. Spencer Walpole. The Leader of the Opposition, Lord Russell, declared that the course pursued by the Government had 'exposed the authority of the law and the dignity of the Crown to a degree of contempt that I hardly ever remember before'.[3] Challenged to explain what he would have done had he been in office, he replied in a single sentence: 'I would recommend the course which was taken in 1848.'[4]

Thus, 6 May 1867 became the 10 April of Spencer Walpole. But just as O'Connor's disgrace had, in a measure, to be shared by all his followers, so with Walpole it was not merely that unfortunate Minister and the Government of the day who shared the defeat. It went much further than that. 'What is lost is, not honour only, but the cause of Society.'[5] The Times, which had received advance notice of the Government's capitulation, led the way in sackcloth and ashes. Beales and his colleagues, it declared, reigned not only in Hyde Park, but might be considered 'the actual Government of the country'. 'We have reached what may be called the very bottom of this question, and cannot fall lower.'[6] The Saturday Review observed that if the tulips and

[1] Parl. Debates, 3rd series, clxxxvii (9 May 1867), 250–1.
[2] Ibid., 227.
[3] Parl. Debates, 3rd series, clxxxvii (9 May 1867) 228.
[4] Ibid., 233.
[5] Saturday Review, 11 May 1867.
[6] The Times, 6 May 1867.

hyacinths escaped, something much more important had been trampled under foot on 6 May.

Perhaps no more disgraceful day has ever marked the political history of this country. The dangerous classes in their most dangerous aspect, have been formally assured by authority that authority is impotent to preserve the peace and order of society whenever it suits illegal violence openly to defy and challenge the law . . . It is, as they say, an era, and may as well be marked with the blackest charcoal. We now date constitutional history from the WALPOLE period.[1]

The *Saturday* was not alone in sensing a profound historic and constitutional significance behind the events in the Park. Carlyle, looking at the whole period of Walpole's tenure of the Home Office, wrote: 'When Beales says, "I will see that the Queen's Peace is kept", Queen (by her Walpole) answers: "Will you then, Glod bless *you*" and bursts into tears. These tears are certainly an epoch in England: nothing seen, or dreamt of, like them in the History of poor England till now.' It was, he thought, 'Nigger philanthropy', condemnations of Governor Eyre, and strictures against martial law that had brought everyone down to tremble before 'Beales and his Roughs'.[2]

Four or five weeks after the events of 6 May a further episode occurred in the Park which seemed to confirm that the guardians of order were, indeed, trembling before the 'roughs'. While the Colonel of the City of London Militia led his men to Hyde Park, a large number of bystanders were openly set upon and robbed. The worthy Colonel explained that he had made no attempt to interfere since his men might have been overpowered and their rifles taken from them. This incident made a profound impression upon Matthew Arnold and led him to recall, for the benefit of the trembling hands of 'Barbarian Home Secretaries' and the feeble knees of 'Philistine Alderman-Colonels', the words of his father: ' "As for rioting, the old Roman way of dealing with *that* is always the right one; flog the rank and file, and fling the ringleaders from the Tarpeian

---

[1] *Saturday Review*, 11 May 1867.
[2] T. Carlyle, 'Shooting Niagara', *Macmillan's Magazine*, August 1867, p. 324.

Rock!" ' Until Odger gave more evidence of light, and Brad-laugh of sweetness, the author of *Culture and Anarchy* was not prepared to welcome the apparent readiness of the working class to take upon itself the functions of government.[1]

But what had been gained on 6 May? What were to be the characteristics of this new era?

> A 'famous victory' has been achieved over a gentleman already well known for a certain 'alacrity at sinking' . . . Mr. Walpole has once more found himself unequal to a Fabian policy. But there remains to be asked the question which has been asked of a thousand other victories, and which it has sometimes taken the whole world many centuries to answer. What is the worth of the victory? In what cause has it been gained?[2]

The first and most certain consequence of the events of 6 May was the enormously enhanced prestige of the League and its increasing independence of its parliamentary and middle-class patrons. It was soon receiving graciously worded communications from Prince Bismarck and Garibaldi, as if in acknowledgement that it was 'itself a power'.[3] It now referred to its own class character with a new sharpness and pride. 'The movement of the League had been eminently a working-man's movement. They had great cause of complaint against the middle classes for not having given the League either personal or pecuniary assistance.'[4] The repeated attempts of the Government to introduce a new Park's Bill which would enable the authorities to enforce the alleged rights of the Crown, were met by promises of an unrestrained class struggle. Beales said that the right to meet in the Park was not to be 'sacrificed to the fastidious and insolent whims of Rotten Row. If there was to be a war of

[1] M. Arnold, *Culture and Anarchy*, first paperback edition (Cambridge), 1960, pp. 92–3 and pp. 203–5.

[2] *The Times*, 8 May 1867.

[3] Prince Bismarck replied to a resolution of congratulations to the people of North Germany on securing vote by ballot and full representation: Minutes of the General Council of the Reform League, 22 May 1867. At the next meeting, 29 May, it was recorded that Garibaldi had accepted the office of Honorary President of the League (H.C.).

[4] Minutes of the General Council of the Reform League, 22 May 1867 (H.C.).

classes, which we have anxiously endeavoured to avoid, let it come. To the Park we shall go more determinedly than ever.'[1] In its efforts to introduce a Park's Bill, the Government met with repeated, complete and unquestionable failure.[2] It was peculiarly appropriate that upon the very day on which the Reform Bill was passed the Royal Park's Bill was finally withdrawn.

In July 1866, *The Times* had declared: 'It is against all reason and all justice that motley crowds from all parts of the metropolis should take possession of Hyde Park, and interfere with the enjoyments of those to whom the Park more particularly belongs.' After 6 May it discovered that the Park really belonged 'to the whole British family' and that it was this family over whom the League had gained its victory.[3]

It was not until 6 May that Gladstone discovered the importance of the Lodger franchise and 'the immense anxiety of the working men of London to obtain it'.[4] Within a fortnight Hodgkinson's amendment had been accepted by Disraeli. This was the amendment which extended the franchise 'almost four times as much as was originally contemplated. The character of the Bill was so materially altered that for all practical purposes it became a new measure.'[5] In the Commons, Disraeli denied that in accepting this amendment, he was in the least influenced by the presence or prospect of agitation. But Gladstone in recommending it stressed the agitation out of doors. This had to be extinguished or it 'may become to us a source of public danger, involving, possibly, much that has not yet been drawn into the vortex of political controversy'.[6] Some of the Government's own supporters confessed: 'We cannot pretend that it is a matter of option with us whether we will undertake this question or not.' Successive governments had raised the question of Reform till they were obliged to ask themselves, 'is it a more

[1] Minutes of the General Council of the Reform League, 23 July 1867 (H.C.).

[2] Jephson, op. cit., pp. 467–9.

[3] *The Times*, 24 July 1866 and 8 May 1867

[4] Parl. Debates, 3rd series clxxxvii (6 May 1867), 38–41.

[5] H. Cox, *A History of the Reform Bills of 1866 and 1867* (1868), p. 201.

[6] Parl. Debates, 3rd series, clxxxvii (17 May 1867), 717.

conservative policy to endeavour to settle the question, or, if I may use the expression, to let the pot go on boiling till it over-flows and brings us to a much worse state of things?'[1] In the laconic words of Trevelyan: 'During April little had been done to improve the Bill in Committee. But in May the tide turned."[2]

If the sixth May has been forgotten while the tenth April is remembered, that reveals more about the values of historians than it does about the magnitude of the events themselves.[3] The humiliation of the Governing classes in Hyde Park can provide quite as good an insight into the laws of motion of the British political system as does the humbling of the Chartists at Kennington Common. To suggest, as one able historian has done, that the issue on 6 May was the right of public meeting rather than the question of Reform,[4] is to indulge in finer distinctions than either political theory or historical experience warrant. At least from Peterloo onwards—and Peterloo was recalled on more than one occasion in May 1867[5]—there had been the closest of associations between the two. It would be the height of naivety to suppose that what was involved at the Common in 1848 and the Park in 1867 was simply the right to hold meetings or stage processions. Two powers confronted each other—'The Secretary of State's proclamation is confronted by President Beales' proclamation'[6]—one party had settled upon a trial of strength, in the knowledge that whichever side prevailed must gain enormously in self-confidence while the other would, to a degree, be broken and demoralised. An explanation of why the Government surrendered in the Park cannot but be relevant to an understanding of why it yielded on Reform. The historians, however distinguished and luminous their writings, who have

[1] Parl. Debates, 3rd series, clxxxvii (20 May 1867), 800–1.

[2] Trevelyan, op. cit., p. 375.

[3] Neither of the standard histories, Woodward, *The Age of Reform* (Oxford 1937) nor Briggs, *The Age of Improvement* (1959), mention 6 May. H. Paul, *A History of Modern England*, iii, 1905, p. 83, misses the significance of the event by writing as if Walpole had merely warned the public against attending the meeting and as if the Prime Minister had said *in advance* that nothing would be done to prevent it.

[4] J. H. Park, *The English Reform Bill of 1867* (New York, 1920), p. 128.

[5] By John Bright, who asserted that Peterloo had left an animosity that still endured; Parl. Debates, 3rd series, clxxxvi (3 May 1867), 1957. Also by C. Bradlaugh in his speech in the Park, *National Reformer*, 12 May 1867.

[6] *Standard*, 6 May 1867, citing the *Saturday Review*.

omitted all mention of 6 May have inevitably understated and misunderstood the part played by mass agitation in carrying the Second Reform Act.

II

Why did the Government, having declared that the meeting was 'prohibited' and having assembled an army for the apparent purpose of suppressing it, make no attempt to arrest the speakers or disperse the crowd? A section of the conservative press suggested that there had been a last minute discovery that the Government had no legal authority to act in this manner. However, as early as 28 July 1866 the Government had received an opinion from the Law Officers of the Crown as to its right to disperse by force a meeting held by persons who had already entered the Park, presuming that a general notice prohibiting such a meeting had already been given. The Law Officers had replied that persons who attended prohibited meetings could be treated as trespassers and removed.

But [they added] we are bound to state that, though the legal right of removal is such as we have described, we do not consider that in the case of any large assembly the right could practically be exercised with safety, or that such an assembly could be 'dispersed by force' in the sense in which that term is ordinarily understood. The right of removal is a right to remove each separate individual as a trespasser, by putting him out of the Park, using just so much force (and no more) as is necessary for that purpose. It is a separate right against each individual. The assembly (assuming it to be orderly) are not united in doing an illegal act, and there is no right to disperse them, or coerce them as a body of rioters or disorderly persons. It appears to us that it would not be practicable to remove each individual, or any considerable number of persons, and to prevent them returning; and it is also highly probable that the effort to remove any particular person or persons with the degree of force that would be justifiable would or might soon become confused by a resistance from bystanders, which would introduce into the operation elements of great difficulty and embarrassment. On the whole, we should answer the question proposed to us by saying that, in our opinion, there is not for any practical purpose a legal authority to disperse by force a meeting of the kind supposed, consisting of a large number of persons, and that whether notice has or has not been given beforehand.[1]

It will be observed that in this opinion the Law Officers did not confine themselves to legal technicalities, but offered their views on political expediencies. The Government would have been within the law had it chosen to remove Beales and his colleagues, but in fact it would have been a perilous proceeding. In the House of Lords, the Prime Minister insisted that they had never really intended to take the risk, but hoped to conceal this from the League.

> I did not think it expedient to say to these persons: 'You may hold your meeting in defiance of the Government with perfect impunity.' I preferred that the course of the Government should be left to their discretion, instead of giving public notice that although the holding of the meeting was prohibited it was not our intention to take any steps whatever.[2]

Beales, however, had grasped the meaning of the studied ambiguity with which Government spokesmen talked about how they would deal with the meeting. He read the signs of weakness in the announcement that there was to be a Park's Bill ostensibly designed to make the existing rights of the Crown more easily enforcible. The arguments which Mill had employed successfully nine months before had lost their persuasive power. Conscious of the challenge which he would have to face from the more militant members of his own Council if he shrank from the issue, he resolved to act and Lord Derby found that his bluff had been called.

The Prime Minister left it to his more vulgar supporters to pretend that it was the 'pendulous' character of Mr. Walpole which was responsible for the disaster. It might plausibly have been suggested that had General Peel or Lords Cranborne or Caernarvon been at the Home Office matters would have

---

[1] Parl. Debates, 3rd series, clxxxvii (9 May 1867), 221–2.

[2] Parl. Debates, 3rd series, clxxxvii (9 May 1867), 226. While there was no 'public notice', private assurances were made. Beesly heard on 4 May that the Government had promised Bright that they would not interfere with the meeting, 'but they did not like to say so last night. They will let it go on; so they have just left doubt enough in the public mind to ensure a walk (?) to the Park! Donkeys! How cock-a-hoop Bradlaugh will be.' (Beesly to Harrison, 4 May 1867. B.Coll. U.C.L.)

turned out differently. But then these 'strong men' had already despaired of the Government and resigned their seats in the Cabinet. Robert had done his sums and knew that 'fifteen minus three equalled nothing'.[1] If Walpole was vacillating and weak, he possessed the qualities appropriate to the character and situation of the Government in which he served. He made a convenient scapegoat, but it was his Cabinet colleagues who were alleged to have pressed him to issue his proclamation of 1 May; a step which he took against his own better judgement.[2] The advice which was offered to him both before and after the meeting had been held was singularly unhelpful and obscure. Thus, on the eve of 6 May, *The Times* expressed its uneasiness about Walpole: 'He may desire, as the mood takes him, to show his conciliation or his firmness, to fraternise with Mr. BEALES or to rout his followers. He will go surest,' it added, 'in the middle path.'[3] The unfortunate Home Secretary might be forgiven for failing to discover where that path lay. A similar objection applied to Lord Russell's dramatic recommendation of 'the course taken in 1848'. What did this mean? O'Connor had not called the Government's bluff, since there was little reason to suppose that the Government was bluffing. Russell's advice ignored the weakness of authority.

There was one contemporary observer who furnished a shrewd and penetrating analysis of this weakness. Frederic Harrison, rightly relating the Park's issue to the wider question of Reform, saw in 'the great Surrender' of 1867 the character of panic. Various forms of authority were growing feeble, lacked prestige, and were practically denuded of real power.

A centralised bureaucratic system [he wrote] gives a great resisting force to the hand that commands the Executive. Our Executive has nothing to fall back upon. There are practically no reserves. The few bayonets and sabres here and there are perfectly powerless before the masses, if the people really took it into their heads to move; beside which it is an instrument which they dare not in practice rely on. A few redcoats may be called upon to suppress a vulgar riot; but the first blood of the people shed by troops in a really popular cause would, as we all know, make the

---

[1] A Briggs, *Victorian People* (1954), p. 285.
[2] S. Walpole, *The History of Twenty Five Years*, Vol. 2 (1904), p. 197.
[3] *The Times*, 3 May 1867.

Briton boil in a very ugly manner. There are only the police, hardly a match for the 'roughs' as we know to our cost. The Government would be mad which seriously attempted to face an angry people on the strength of seven thousand police staves. It was very easy to abuse an unlucky set of ministers about Hyde Park. But what were they to do? To have used the army would have been the end of the British Constitution. There were seven thousand policemen, but what were they among so many? The Executive in this country has absolutely nothing to fall back upon but the special constable, the moral support of the cheesemonger and the pork-butcher. Real and powerful so long as the pork-butcher is in good humour. But wait till the windows of the pork-shop are being smashed, and all about a quarrel to keep you in office and you will see the ungrateful pork-butcher turn and rend you like one of his own herd . . .

Property has, no doubt, an enormous social and moral *vis inertiae*. But Government as such, has singularly small material forces. Our greatest soldier in this age saw it perfectly and so did Lord Derby last year [1867]. The fact is that our political organism of the constitutional type was based on a totally different theory from that of force at all. The governing classes never pretended to rely on force. They trusted to maintain their supremacy by their social power, and their skill in working the machine. Local self-government, representation of the people, civil liberty, was all the cry, until at last the tone of English public life became saturated with ideas of rule by consent, and not by force. Very excellent theories of a certain kind—but you must abide by them, and never dream of force, for you have cut yourself off from the right to appeal to it. The least suggestions of force puts the governing classes in an outrageously false position, and arrays against them all the noble sentiments of liberty on which they based their own title to rule. Club blusterers jeering at Trades Unionists in Pall Mall may talk about grapeshot and dragoons, but men with heads on their shoulders know that an appeal to force would be the end of English society; and what is even more to the purpose, that there is no force to appeal to . . . for years the governing classes had kept Democracy at bay behind some imposing ramparts. But one day the Reform League discovered that they were mounted with canvas and logs.[1]

Used as a rejoinder to Lord Russell, Harrison's analysis is marred by an over-emphasis on the Government's lack of

[1] F. Harrison, 'Order and Progress' (1875), pp. 182–5. (Reprinted from the *Fortnightly Review* for April 1868.)

material forces. For the purposes of 6 May they would, no doubt, have proved sufficient. Lord Cranborne had a very good, if young, head on his shoulders and he would not have hesitated to prosecute Beales and his colleagues for conspiracy or to have removed them from the Park. Armed with his 'natural history of Revolutions', the future Prime Minister was not to be intimidated by the prospect of an insurrection in London. London, as John Bright also pointed out, but to a very different purpose, was not Paris. 'One night's neglect may place a mob in the Tuileries and terminate a dynasty.' But in England the authority of the capital was not so decisive. If a mob took control of London it would be 'a frightful thing', but it would not 'shake the allegiance of a single English county'. From this it followed that 'the British Constitution has nothing to fear from revolution unless the owners of property are beguiled into helping to undermine the institutions which protect them'.[1] To invite an attempt at proletarian revolution was, in Cranborne's eyes, clearly preferable to yielding to Democracy.

> Discontent, insurrection, civil war itself, will, in the long run, produce no worse dangers than absolute or unrestrained democracy. Such commotions can only end in a military government; and the despotism of a successful soldier is a lighter burden than the despotism of the multitude. Resistance, therefore, even to the uttermost, to such claims as these (manhood suffrage and the ballot) may be contemplated without misgiving as to the result; for it may, and probably will, succeed, and at worst; its failure will be no worse than yielding.[2]

Cranborne's hopes about the probable outcome of a collision would appear to have been entirely justified in any short run view. If the balance of material forces had been the decisive consideration on 6 May, then the warnings of Collet and Connolly would have been well advised. If the police force was small it was expanding rapidly. Indeed, in London the absolute and relative increase in the number of full-time police officers was greater in the 1860s than in almost any other decade in police history.[3] Had the Government adopted the policy of

---

[1] 'Parliamentary Reform', *Quarterly Review*, April 1865, pp. 562-3.
[2] Ibid., pp. 570-1.
[3] J. M. Hart, *The British Police* (1951), p. 34. Much of the expansion may have been concentrated in the last years of the decade.

Cranborne or Peel, the police and soldiers would have broken up the meeting and given the London workmen a sound thrashing. The day would have ended, not in a humiliating surrender for the Government, but in the rout of the League which, despite its slight essays in organising its own constabulary, would have proved no match for a disciplined force.

It was not, in Cranborne's view, want of material power, but want of nerve, which explained the 'Conservative Surrender'.

> When the troops run away at the first charge, it is of course difficult to decide whether they have lost because they could not win, or because they dared not try to win . . . the world generally assumes that when an army does not discover its hopeless inferiority of strength until the powder begins to burn, its nerves are more to blame for the result than its numbers. A school, however, has arisen in recent days that formally denies that the bloodless conflicts of the political world have any analogy, either in the feelings of honour which should animate them, or the rules by which they should be judged, with the conflicts of the field. According to their teaching, nothing ought ever to be fought out . . . The desperate resistance which our fathers made to the last Reform Bill is blamed, not so much because their views were mistaken, as because it was madness to defend those views against so formidable an assault. It is said,—and men seem to think that condemnation can go no further than such a censure—that they brought us within twenty-four hours of revolution. Their successors boast that their prudence will never go so near to the heels of danger. No one will suspect them of it. But is it in truth so great an evil, when the dearest interests and the most sincere convictions are at stake, to go within twenty-four hours of revolution?[1]

Was the Government's surrender on Reform, to which, it is insisted, its surrender of 6 May served as harbinger and analogue, to be explained by an unjustifiable timidity and cowardice? If Derby is to be believed, then, in relation to the Park, he had been bluffing all along. He had been driven to this course because he did not wish it to appear that the Government was acting under duress on the Reform Question. He needed a moral victory over the League so as to remove the impression that he was not a free agent. But being a more mature statesman than Lord Robert, he recognised that it had

---

[1] *Quarterly Review*, October 1867, pp. 542-3.

to be a moral and bloodless victory or none at all. He might look confidently to the immediate issue of an engagement between the Reformers and the military, but the triumph would have been bought at too high a price. At best, it would have meant the exclusion of the Tories from office for the rest of the century (for if the Whigs had given their approval in private, they would certainly have protested in public); at worst, it would have struck at the very foundations of the political system and have caused the ruling classes to be confronted, not by a Reform agitation, but by a Revolutionary Movement. Marx was not the only one to appreciate that 'these thick-headed John Bulls, whose brainpans seem to have been specially manufactured for the constables' bludgeons, will never get anywhere without a really bloody encounter with the ruling powers'.[1] That encounter had to be avoided, even if it meant that instead of preserving its dignity the Government exposed its weakness.

It was, of course, most inconvenient that the London working men refused to be overawed by the impressive proclamations of the Government. In consequence, poor Walpole had to be offered up as a sacrifice to the outraged dignity of the upper and middle classes and the Prime Minister had to face the bitter reproach of having fought just long enough to 'betray the weakness of the garrison and the poverty of the defences'. This was precisely the charge which Cranborne brought against the Government's management of the entire Reform question.

> It may [he wrote] be a bed of roses upon which we are now swiftly descending; but even if that be the issue, the surrender will scarcely be less disastrous. If the upper and middle classes had made up their mind to this tender trust in the people with which they have become suddenly inspired seven years ago, or even one year ago, no harm would have been done beyond that which might result from the particular measure they were passing . . . But they have fought just long enough to betray the weakness of the garrison and the poverty of the defences. The dullest of their antagonists perfectly understands that they have not yielded to argument or sentiment; that the apostles of reform who have the real credit of their conversion are the mobs who beat down the

[1] K. Marx to F. Engels, 27 July 1866. (*Marx and Engels on Britain*, 1954, p. 495.)

palings of Hyde Park, or went out marching with bands and banners in the towns of the North.[1]

Ultimately, what separated Lord Robert from the great majority of men of influence and power was that, while he wished to suppress revolution, they desired to break up the formation of forces which were potentially revolutionary. To this majority the disintegration of such forces was the overriding priority, but how and by whom this should be accomplished was a matter which was necessarily decided, not 'objectively', but in relation to sectional and party interests, and in the light of differing estimates of the degree of menace from without. Within a regime which allowed full play to these interests, strategic withdrawals were bound to be associated with dissension and delay, exposing those in command of the operation to just those charges which Cranborne brought against his Party leaders. But what Lord Robert missed was the capacity of the system to withstand the shock of such surrenders. And the source of his error here was that he mistakenly supposed that there was no hope of protecting the 'garrison' with part of the 'besieging force'.

Cranborne's aristocratic instincts unfitted him for government. He had to learn to operate the system by practice and experience. He was so far unreconciled to a bourgeois society that he wanted to treat it as if it was the *ancien régime*.

In the end, all the most influential men of property and power were persuaded that they must make a substantial concession in order to break up the agitation and remove the danger that prolonged intransigence, accompanied by police violence, would cause the popular forces to assume a truly menacing character. With the exception of the small group close to Cranborne, no one quarrelled with the principle of Gladstone's advice that they must 'be wise in time'.[2] They differed only as to the lateness of the hour and to the exact form and extent of the concession to be made. It was also true that to the extent that Reform could be made to appear as a 'boon granted' rather than as a 'fortress stormed', it would be an object of Party ambition to have the credit of the measure.

[1] 'The Conservative Surrender', *Quarterly Review*, October 1867, p. 556.
[2] Parl. Debates, 3rd series, clxxxii (12 April 1866), 1149.

In the spring of 1866 John Bright did his best to rouse the House to the danger that prolonged resistance would provoke. He recalled how in 1848 a Noble Lord had sought him out and anxiously impressed upon him that he (the Lord) had always favoured an extension of the suffrage. The nobleman had believed that there was going to be revolution and thought that Bright would be in the provisional government. 'Of all the follies and crimes which Governments commit,' concluded the great Radical, 'that of a constant distrust of their subjects, of their citizens, of their country, is about the wildest and most foolish.'[1]

This argument was developed with exceptional clarity and force by 'educated Liberals' outside Parliament.

When the rich declare their own interests to be incompatible with those of the rest of the nation [wrote James Bryce] and resolve upon this ground to keep the government, or the chief share in it, to themselves they give a formal challenge to the poorer part of the community, and oblige it—unless it be wholly helpless—to assert its rights by agitation. Abnegating their own functions of leadership for the common good—a function which the poor, when fairly treated, have always been found willing to concede to them—they throw the humbler class into the hands of men who come forward as its advocates and their assailants. Such men may do their work better or worse. They may ally themselves with the more liberal members of the ruling class, and seek to improve or widen the Constitution without destroying its ancient features. Or they may—as happened in Greece and Rome, and might happen even in England were agitation to be long protracted—they may appeal to the lower passions of our nature, and proclaim a war of the poor against the rich. But in either case it is primarily upon the mistaken policy of those who rule the state that such agitation must be charged, for experience shows that the working class, unless under the pressure of the severest physical misery, is in a large country comparatively indifferent to political power, and does not clamour for it until irritated by a long course of scornful refusal.[2]

The point was made with more brutal directness by another contributor to the same volume.

[1] Parl Debates, 3rd series, clxxxii (12 April 1866), 221–2.
[2] J. Bryce, 'The Historical Aspect of Democracy', *Essays on Reform* (1867), p. 272.

. . . the introduction of a larger popular element into our ancient constitution is, after all, not a matter of free choice, but an alternative. If we refuse this Reform, we accept the responsibility of governing an unwilling and reluctant people: if we reject what may be, in some instances, a representation of defective knowledge and short-sighted speculation we must be prepared to encounter an organised ignorance from without and the boundless Utopia of revolutionary expectations: if we will not admit the Working-men into the great school of Public Life, we leave them to the free exercise of their instincts and their passions: if we will not teach them political wisdom, they will teach us political disaster.[1]

But even when the issue was only Gladstone's relatively small Bill and when it was proposed to enfranchise 'only those who are already powerful' so as to enlist their help against the ignorance and turbulence of the lowest stratum, Lowe failed to see the force of the argument.

If driven to it we must, of course, submit, and it may perhaps be better to do so than to give rise to a great internal commotion or civil war; but it will take a very severe compulsion to induce me to counsel suicide. The advice to yield at once lest a worse thing befall us, reminds me of the lines—

He thought with a smile upon England the while,
And the trick that her statesmen had taught her,
Of saving herself from the storm above
By putting her head under water.[2]

As for the Tories, they showed an understandable distaste for any change and strongly suspected that Gladstone's proposals exactly expressed the small tradesman class from whom they felt they had, as a party, most to fear.[3] So long as they were out of office they supposed that they could treat the warnings of Bright and Gladstone with contempt. But from the second half of 1866 onwards the agitation rapidly undermined their confidence. The Queen sounded the first note of alarm and warned

[1] J. Bryce, 'The Historical Aspect of Democracy', *Essays on Reform* (1867), p. 66. (Lord Houghton, on the admission of the working classes as part of our social system and on their recognition for all purposes as part of the nation.)

[2] A. P. Martin, *Life and Letters of the Rt. Hon. Robert Lowe, Viscount Sherbrooke*, vol. ii (1893), p. 255.

[3] Caernarvon's Memorandum on Reform, 8 November 1866, Cabinet Notes 1866–7, 99–108 (Caernarvon Papers, P.R.O.).

her Prime Minister that unless he and his colleagues took up Reform in earnest 'very serious consequences may ensue'.[1] Derby was the first to understand; Disraeli followed, and soon all the ablest among the Tory gentry were afraid, 'with that wise old English fear of their fellow countrymen which has done as much to save England as many more heroic virtues'.[2]

Blackwood's mirrored the progress of Tory thinking. The valour of January gave place to the discretion of March. In January bloodshed was contemplated with a good imitation of comparative equanimity. In March it was discovered that the Irish were ripe for armed uprising and that there was a danger of a coalition being formed with the League.

> Who can doubt, had the attack on Chester Castle succeeded, but that in St. Giles, perhaps at Islington, not less than in Kerry, disturbances would have broken out? And, blood once drawn, especially in the metropolis, it would be hard to say what consequences might not follow. In like manner, the Trades Unions, departing from the purposes for which they came at first into existence, are ranging themselves on the side of democracy . . . A weak Government confronted in the legislature by a numerous yet divided Opposition, while both are libelled and threatened by well organised bodies of men out of doors,—this is a state of things which no thoughtful person can contemplate without alarm. It is precisely such a disposition of moral forces as has in all times past preceded and worked up to revolution; and there is too much reason to apprehend that, unless counteracted and restrained in the Legislature by a principle loftier than mere impulse of party, it will, in our case, precede and work up to revolution again.[3]

From this followed the conclusion that to postpone legislation on Reform

> would be tantamount to challenging the masses to do their worst, and though we entertain no doubt respecting the issues of a collision, if collision with roughs be forced upon the Government, there is nothing which we would more deprecate, save only the surrender of the Constitution itself.[4]

[1] Monypenny and Buckle, op. cit., p. 191.
[2] G. M. Trevelyan, *Life of John Bright* (1913), p. 363.
[3] 'The Ministerial Resolutions', *Blackwood's Edinburgh Magazine*, March 1867, pp. 381-2.
[4] Ibid., p. 387.

Had there been any reason to suppose that there was a ceiling to the agitation, some limit beyond which it could not go, Disraeli would never have been able to boast that he had 'educated' his party. If he had introduced a measure more advanced than Russell's he would have split his own party while a smaller one, not having been worth carrying, would have been laughed out of the House. But as month by month the agitation grew more menacing, the realisation came home to more and more Members that fifteen years of 'busy idleness' on Reform could no longer be continued. For the House to reject a Liberal measure one year, and a Tory one the next, would be taken as evidence of 'a permanent Parliamentary incapacity to deal with the subject';[1] a thing of the utmost danger. Hence the discovery in May 1867 on the Tory backbenches that:

> If events had become too strong for them, and they were being hurried beyond what most of them desired, it behoved them to come to some agreement on the question with all speed, for no one could watch what was passing in the country, or read the newspapers, without coming to the conclusion that, if the question of Reform were kept open much longer, the hon. Member for Birmingham (John Bright) would be in the position of a Girondin.[2]

Mr. Lowe's demolitions of historicist fallacies were no longer received with rapturous applause, the Tories had discovered 'destiny and fate'. 'Surely there were social tendencies and movements of events so strong as almost to amount to destiny. M. Guizot once declared "Destiny stands before you and is greater than you are." '[3] Thus, under the expert direction of Mr. Disraeli, the House learned to convert each fresh humiliation into a triumph. To 'settle the question', to 'extinguish the agitation', became its ruling idea. The leader of the House might pretend that he was uninfluenced by danger signals from without, but he admitted in private that his object in accepting Hodgkinson's amendment was to 'destroy the present agitation and extinguish Gladstone and Co.'.[4] The possibility of reaching the second of these objectives rested entirely upon the necessity of accomplishing the first.

[1] G. Cecil, *Life of Robert, Marquis of Salisbury*, Vol. 1 (1921).
[2] Parl. Debates, 3rd series, clxxxvii (13 May 1867), 417 (Grant Duff).
[3] Ibid., (20 May 1867), 810 (Bailie Cochrane).
[4] Monypenny and Buckle, op. cit., p. 274.

The argument for yielding so as to prevent the formation of revolutionary forces had a power to convince members of the upper and middle class only to the extent that they were already persuaded that the working class was still 'loyal'; that their heads were not full with 'the boundless utopia of revolutionary expectations'; that they would answer to 'good will' shown by their 'betters'; and that the new political opportunities which were going to be opened to them were in fact of a very limited sort. Were the 'occult and unacknowledged forces which are not dependent upon any legislative machinery'[1] strong enough to allow the upper classes to make even a far-reaching measure into a 'good Reform Bill'? A good Reform Bill being one which would silence the agitator and satisfy the criterion laid down by Lord Cranborne: 'The test by which a good Reform Bill may be distinguished from a bad one is that under it the working classes shall not now, or at any proximate period, command a majority in this House.'[2]

One of the contradictions in the history of the second Reform Bill was that assurances of the required sort were likely to become scarcer the longer Parliament delayed. But such assurances there had to be if Lowe's objection, from analogy of sheltering from storms by putting one's head under the water, was to be removed.

Perhaps the consideration which weighed most heavily with the upper and middle classes and which helped to prepare them for far-reaching concessions to the urban working class was what might be termed the 'Rochdale' argument. Gladstone argued that that place 'has probably done more than any other town in making good to practical minds a case for some enfranchisement of the working classes'.[3] Rochdale was used as a symbol for all the advances made by Labour since 1832.

> It is not denied on any hand—whether we take education in schools; whether we take social conduct; whether we take obedience to the law; whether we take self-command and power of endurance, shown under difficulty and privation; whether we

[1] Leslie Stephen, 'On the Choice of Representatives by Popular Constituencies', *Essays on Reform* (1867), p. 107.

[2] Parl. Debates, 3rd series, clxxxiii (27 April 1866), 16.

[3] Parl. Debates, 3rd series, clxxxii (12 March 1866), 37.

take avidity for knowledge and self-improvement—if we take any one of these tests, or any other test that can be named, there can be no doubt at all that if the working man was in some degree fit to share in political privileges in 1832 he has, at any rate, attained some degree of additional fitness now.[1]

Within Parliament, Baines, Hughes and many other Members enlarged on this, while out of doors Beales pointed out that

> the working classes themselves are deeply interested in the pre-
> servation of law and order, of the rights of capital and property;
> of the honour and power and wealth of our country. They are as
> members of co-operatives, building and other societies, daily be-
> coming themselves capitalists and land-owners; there are among
> them men of large intellectual capacity, and earnest unaffected
> christian principle . . .[2]

Bright was able to point out that neither the President nor the Secretary of the Rochdale Equitable Pioneers Society had the vote and that there were many men charged with the manage-ment of co-operative enterprises, in which tens of thousands of pounds had been invested, who were non-electors.[3]

Observing that many a wild elephant had been tamed ere now by being coupled with tame ones, W. Graham, M.P., asked what confiscatory measures had they to fear?

> Look at the savings banks and the trade unions. Are not the
> working classes learning the value of capital? Look at the co-
> operative building and manufacturing societies. Are they ignorant
> of the value of property? Are they dishonest more than ourselves
> that they should wish to seize what they know is not theirs?[4]

W. E. Forster scorned the familiar bogy that the Trade Unions would become engines of political power. 'We who are em-ployers know how difficult it is to maintain these trade organ-isations and we are not afraid of them.' But he added that they might have some cause to fear them if Parliamentary obstinacy organised them into a class. He explained that the real object of the Russell–Gladstone Bill was to 'fight against a class much

---

[1] Parl. Debates, 3rd series, clxxxii (12 March 1866), 38.
[2] Speech of Edmond Beales, Esq., M.A., President of the Reform League, At the Meeting in St. Martin's Hall, In Support of the League (1865), pp. 11–12.
[3] Parl. Debates 3rd series, clxxxii (23 April 1866), 1891–7.
[4] Ibid. (19 April 1866), 1657–8.

more to be dreaded than the holders of the £7 franchise—I mean the dangerous classes in our large towns. If we can get into Parliament those who are more immediately above them, we shall be able to legislate more effectively for them.'[1]

These arguments, as presented in 1866, failed to convince the Adullamites and Tories for two reasons. First, they suspected that while the élite of the working class might be safe as far as the Constitution and property in general were concerned, they would provide a decidedly dangerous contingent of supporters for Bright and Mill. It was considered most ingenuous of 'advanced liberals' to ask why, if large employers of labour were unperturbed, the holders of broad acres should be alarmed.[2]

Second, the exact extent and distribution of this élite was unknown. It was extremely difficult to tell precisely what sort of electoral qualifications would let them in, while excluding the 'residuum'. And there was uncertainty as to the size and characteristics of that stratum which was thought to lie between the 'labour aristocracy' and the residuum. Gladstone offered no satisfactory definition of the 'working class'. His figure of the existing working-class electorate, which he estimated at about a quarter of the whole, included small employers, keepers of beer shops and the like.[3] An examination of the papers of Tory Cabinet ministers reveals that Gladstone's opponents were in dire need of information and were really uncertain about the make-up of the class with which they had to deal. Dean Mansel begged Caernarvon not to let the Cabinet act without a preliminary enquiry. Everything was dark and obscure. 'Would the representatives of many of our towns be at the mercy, not of the working men as a body, but of Mr. George Potter and his brother terrorists?' Would the religious consequences of a serious measure of Reform not be the 'preponderating influence of secularism and infidelity'? 'Is Bright's portrait of the lower classes or Lowe's the better likeness?'[4]

---

[1] Parl. Debates 3rd series, clxxxii (16 April 1866), 1392–4.

[2] Ibid. (16 April 1866). 1464–76. (These remarks by Sir Hugh Cairns clearly express the fear that workmen would follow Bright in seeking abolition of the law of primogeniture.)

[3] 'I am bound to say that our definition (of the working man) is a large definition.' Parl. Debates, ibid., 36.

[4] H. L. Mansel to Caernarvon, 26 October 1866. Caernarvon Papers, op. cit., 71–5.

'I wish,' noted Caernarvon, 'we could get information on the component parts and proportion of the "working class".'[1] Bagehot told him that if the Tories had to act they could only do so by going down very low in the suffrage. Then rank and position and wealth, combined, might give them control o fthe big towns.[2] But the editor of the *Economist* plainly thought that they would have to stop, well before they reached the residuum. For the residuum had no known system of internal stratification. It might be cowed, but it did not know the meaning of deference. If it was found to answer without conscience to the temptations of corruption, it might equally, without pangs of conscience, rouse itself to violence and pillage. 'Is that,' Mr. Punch asked the carpenter pointing to a drunken 'rough', 'is that the sort of "Manhood" you wish to be mixed up with?'[3]

It was not. There was almost complete agreement, even if it was only tacit, about the exclusion of the residuum. The differences arose over the problem of just how extensive this group might be. Its supposed boundaries were being continually redrawn in accordance with political expediency. Its size depended on the degree of the speaker's pre-occupation with it. Thus, it came to loom larger in Bright's thinking in 1867 than it had done in the previous year, while for most Tories, it grew 'wonderfully less' as the agitation progressed. But no matter who the speaker happened to be, the term was generally employed to cover more than the lumpen proletariat or lazzaroni, even if it was the inclusion of this element which gave the residuum its cutting edge. For the bourgeois, thinking in the tradition of the New Poor Law, extreme misfortune and destitution shaded into crime: 'the labouring classes merged into the dangerous classes'.[4] It was unthinkable that the sort of

[1] Cabinet 21 November 1866, Caernarvon's Memo, Caernarvon Papers, op. cit., 110.

[2] Memo of conversation with Bagehot on Reform, 2 November 1866, Caernarvon Papers, 89–90.

[3] *Punch*, 15 December 1866.

[4] See J. C. Symons, *Tactics for the Times as Regards the Condition and Treatment of the Dangerous Classes*, London, 1849, p. 1. 'Every country has its dangerous class. It consists not only of criminals, paupers and persons whose conduct is obnoxious to the interests of society, but of that *proximate body of the people who are within reach of its* contagion, and continually swell its number.' (My emphasis.)

people who were known to respectable society only through the police, the courts and the guardians, should become electors. They were not to be enfranchised, because, having no organisation there was no need to enfranchise them [1] and, had they been able to attain to organisation, they still would not have been enfranchised since they would have been far too terrible to have been assimilated by the political system.

It was a fact of very great importance that the Reform League hedged its demand for Manhood Suffrage with the qualifications 'Registered and Residential'. Its leaders insisted upon these qualifications in a way which suggested that they were not to be dismissed as a mere form. They would not and could not relinquish a slogan which had all the traditions and the attractive simplicity of 'Manhood Suffrage', but they could show that they were realists and sensible men. In emphasising that they were demanding 'Registered and Residential Manhood Suffrage' they implied that they were being 'business-like' and 'practical'. These clauses released the League leaders from the old, uncompromising rigidity and opened the way to several attempts at trimming. Thus, after the fall of the Liberal Government, Beales wanted to collaborate with the National Reform Union. He told his followers that 'household suffrage in combination especially with the lodger franchise, is, practically and substantially, all but equivalent to what the advocates of residential and registered manhood suffrage require'.[2] No more than the 'advanced Liberals' in Parliament were they seriously concerned to press the claims of 'the class of persons they saw at the corners of the streets of the Seven Dials . . . the stalwart navvies with red handkerchiefs who made our railways . . . the hordes of Irish labourers . . . that class which, in common Parliamentary language, was designated as the dangerous class.'[3]

Karl Marx apparently sensed that there was something behind the League's insistence on 'Registered and Residential'. Ernest Jones did his best to reassure him: 'Registered manhood suffrage means that the elector shall have been *registered* as having *lived* in a boro' for a certain time (say six months) before he can give his vote at an election. It was embodied in the

[1] J. Bryce, op. cit., p. 273.   [2] Bell, thesis, p. 320.
[3] G. Leeman, M.P., Parl. Debates, 3rd series, clxxxii (26 April), 2127.

"Universal Suffrage" of the Charter, and is nothing new.'[1] Had
the lawyer not momentarily eclipsed the politician in Jones, he
would have had to admit that the emphasis was quite new.
Behind this difference lay the fact that the Leaguers, unlike the
Chartists, lived lives which were remote from the experience of
the lower depths. They had quite lost the old sense of the identity of the poor, of the wage earners. When they talked about
the 'working class' in a laudatory way it was a comparatively
narrow stratum of it which they had in mind. They never
looked like calling the entire working class into united political
action.[2]

The political leaders of the upper and middle classes might
resist Reform, they might be uncertain about the implication
for Parties of going down to different social levels, but here they
could find their ultimate security. The prospect of all the
heterogeneous elements within the working classes, being
drawn into a disciplined force behind leaders inspired with the
'boundless Utopia of revolutionary expectations' seemed highly
remote. Derby, who had learned to overcome his terror of the
working class as a result of his experience in Lancashire during
the cotton famine,[3] could freely speculate on the possible success
of his party among the factory populations of the North. The
Gladstonians could look with some optimism towards the skilled
craftsmen and Trade Unionists. Disraeli, in turn, could look 'to
household suffrage giving birth to a class of electors who would
be independent of the influence of the Trade Unions and their
leaders, and *pro tanto* less revolutionary in their views and a less

[1] E. Jones to K. Marx, 25 February 1865. (Micro-film from Marx–Engels–
Lenin Institute Moscow. Courtesy of Mrs. D. Thompson.)

[2] Dr. A. D. Bell, in his unpublished thesis, The Reform League from its
origins to the Reform Act of 1867 (D.Phil., Oxford 1961), has shown (p. 157)
that of the 114 branches of the League in London only 27 were in the East
End. There were 23 south of the Thames. Hobsbawm, op. cit. p. 204, points
out that in 1871 the Engineers, Bricklayers, Carpenters and Masons Unions
had 10 branches in the East End, but 31 south of the Thames. Since
membership of these Unions was confined entirely to members of the labour
aristocracy, the relatively higher number of East End branches of the League
provides a rough guide to the extent of its infusion with 'plebeian' elements.
However, the main conclusion to be drawn from a study of the geographical
distribution of the London branches of the League is that it relied heavily
upon the same stratum as that which belonged to the 'new model' Unions.

[3] W. D. Jones, *Lord Derby and Victorian Conservatism* (Oxford 1956), p. 323.

danger to the state.'[1] He might have to retreat, but it was 'to a new position to carry on his defence of the British Constitution'.[2] If Reform had become imperative that was, in part, because it had also become safe.

III

'Rochdale' certainly helped to convince the upper and middle classes that if it was dangerous to resist it might be safe to yield. By 1867 the ideals of self-help had found solid institutional expression among the highest stratum of the working class. Benefit Clubs, Co-operative Societies and New Model Unions had given the workmen a stake in the country. Such developments were mainly due to the operation of the impersonal forces of economic and social change. But Gladstone and others saw that the benign influence of such forces might be effectual if re-enforced by what he termed 'good will'.

As early as 1847, Sir Robert Peel (from whom Gladstone learned so much) had said: 'I do feel that the point at which we all ought to strive is to improve the conditions and elevate the feelings of the great labouring class. I tell you it is not safe unless you do it.'[3] When Gladstone was taken to task by an aristocratic relative for encouraging the demand for Reform in 1865, he replied:

> After all, you are a peer, and Peel used to say, speaking of his peer colleagues, that they were beings of a different order. Please to recollect that we have got to govern millions of hard hands; that it must be done by force, fraud or good will; that the latter has been tried and is answering; that none have profited more by this change of system since the Corn Law and the Six Acts, than those who complain of it.[4]

Sir William Hutt, the Member for Gateshead, gave a clear, if crude, illustration of this complex idea. During one of the Reform debates he recalled how, in 1843, Gladstone had

[1] Earl of Wemyss and March, *Memories 1818–1912*, Vol. 1 (1912). Printed for private circulation. (Courtesy of the present Earl of Wemyss.)

[2] C. J. Lewis, 'Theory and Expediency in the Policy of Disraeli', *Victorian Studies*, March 1961, p. 252.

[3] Jephson, op. cit., p. 418.

[4] J. Morley, *Life of Gladstone*, Vol. 2 (1903), p. 133.

brought in a Bill to release the coalwhippers of London from the bondage in which they were held by the owners of beer shops and gin shops. In 1848 these men had thanked Gladstone for his kind interest and announced their intention of being sworn in as special constables. Their spokesman had called on Sir William himself and had assured him 'that wherever else there might be disturbance, he might depend upon it that peace and order should be preserved at Wapping'![1]

The argument was supported by less parochial examples. Reactionaries who expressed their fear of a House of Commons filled with Feargus O'Connors[2] betrayed their ignorance of the altered state of things. Where was the Charter? Where was the *Northern Star*? Where the prosecutions for sedition? 'All these things have passed away.' By objecting 'altogether to the use of the word "class" '; by recognising that there were 'as many divisions and subdivisions' among workmen as in any other section of the community; by putting 'trust' in the people; the employment of the 'demagogues' who had flourished thirty years ago had been greatly reduced.[3] In place of the dreadful utterances of Bronterre O'Brien or George Julian Harney, opponents of Reform had nothing better to frighten themselves with than a few odd remarks by George Odger or Professor Beesly.[4] They might try to make John Bright serve the purpose,

[1] Parl. Debates, 3rd series, clxxxii (19 April 1866), 1683.

[2] 'He was not afraid of the working classes, but he should not like to see the House of Commons filled with Feargus O'Connors; yet that Gentleman was looked up to as a great oracle in Yorkshire', J. Hardy (Dartmouth), Parl. Debates, 3rd series (13 March 1866), clxxxii, 237.

[3] Ibid. (16 April 1866), 1438–50 (A. H. Layard).

[4] Odger was attacked for a speech in which he argued that one of the objects of Reform must be to help agricultural labourers who were trying to live on 8s. a week. See Lowe (13 March 1866) 152 and Cranborne on the same evening 233. Beesly had expressed the belief that recasting our institutions would before long supersede the question of reforming them. For this he was attacked by Lowther (16 April 1866) 1403 and by Cairns on the same evening (1490). Layard (1457–8) (16 April 1866) and Goschen (23 April 1866) 1970 ridiculed the idea of making the working men responsible for the opinions of a Professor who had been educated at Oxford. However, on 26 April 1866, Lowe returned to the attack on 'inspired apostles of a new Religion of Humanity' (2078). All in Parl. Debates 3rd series, clxxxii. Beesly defended himself in the *Spectator*, 21 April 1866. For his attitude to Reform and Parliamentary Government see my 'E. S. Beesly and Karl Marx', *International Review of Social History*, Vol. 4, pts. 1 and 2, 1959.

but he was not really a lion—only Snug the Joiner.[1] 'Good will' had been tried and was answering.

Of course, it had to be clearly recognised that 'good will' was to be understood, not in the Kantian, but in the Gladstonian, sense of the term. It belonged not so much to the realm of ends, as of means. If it was conceived as the 'better way' than force or fraud, it was also the substitute for them. Its moral excellence was matched by its political convenience. It was the condition whereby 'we' were to continue to govern 'millions of hard hands'. It was the policy with which to eke out what Beesly, criticising Bagehot, called 'all the most contemptible tricks and hypocrisies of the British Constitution'.[2] To carry it to the length of enfranchising a large part of the urban working class would, in the absence of pressure from without, have required considerable daring. But to have used cutlasses on 6 May, or to have shown prolonged resistance to the League, would have been to squander an immense fund of valuable social and political capital. Beesly might sneer at a policy of cheating the masses being regarded as the crowning proof of political sagacity, but long before 1867 there was evidence that 'good will' was viable. It was left to a few immature or seemingly incorrigible reactionaries like Cranborne to complain of it. After the passing of the Act, he reported, with feelings in which incredulity was mixed with indignation, that the upper and middle classes flattered the new electors to their faces while in private they discussed their boundless pliability.[3]

Upper class confidence in 'good will' was under-pinned by their faith in the efficacy of the 'occult forces'. These were evidently at work already for, if the working classes wished to plunder the rich, they had no need to wait to be enfranchised before they set about it. They already had the physical power to do so.[4] 'Where,' as Sir Francis Goldsmid asked, 'would the

---

[1] Parl. Debates, 3rd series, clxxxii (16 April 1866), 1453 (A. H. Layard).

[2] 'A clever writer in the *Fortnightly Review* has lately been picking out for special eulogy all the most contemptible tricks and hypocrisies of the British Constitution. To cheat the masses . . . is in this gentleman's eyes the crowning proof of political sagacity. Some kinds of education seem to be worse than none at all.' E. S. Beesly, *Spectator*, 14 April 1866.

[3] 'The Conservative Surrender', *Quarterly Review*, October 1867, pp. 533–4.

[4] Goldwin Smith, 'The Experience of the American Commonwealth', *Essays on Reform* (1867), p. 220.

landowners and great employers of labour now be if their influence in elections were merely proportionate to their numbers in the constituencies?'[1] Those who knew the workmen did not share Bagehot's doubts as to whether the saving quality of deference was as prevalent among them as it was with the petit bourgeoisie.

> Take the English, as a nation, at home. They are devoured with the idea of 'bettering themselves', and that idea with them means 'rising in the social scale'. 'Respectability' is consequently their idol ... They look up to the higher classes as a sort of divine Olympus, beautiful, sacred, above all things *intelligible*, just near enough to be perhaps not quite unattainable by their children, just far enough to lend enchantment to the view. So far from these men being levellers or potential levellers, if you could dive into their hearts (for what they exactly say with their lips is not the test) you would find what every unconscious indication reveals —that to deprive them of their Olympus would be to deprive them of their earthly heaven and ultimate aspiration. To offer to pull it down for them would fill them with horror, grief and concern, by offering to deprive them of their only earthly ideal. And those are the men whom you are afraid of admitting to the Constitution, to tell you in your own House, in their own words, where the shoe pinches them, and what they want.[2]

Lowe's fears that Reform would destroy the character of the House of Commons were, according to this writer, quite unjustified. It was imperishable. 'In this country if you had manhood suffrage, with womanhood suffrage thrown in to the bargain, you would not and could not have democracy, for democracy in this country, in Mr. Lowe's sense of democracy, is impossible.'[3] The wage-earners, as Forster told the House, admired 'gentlemen'. And if, after Reform, England were to become 'a little less of a rich man's country and gentlemen were to fall in the market, they would still have excellent cards in their hands'.[4]

Reform did not mean any substantial transfer of power. It

[1] Parl. Debates, 3rd series, clxxxii (13 April 1866), 1278.

[2] B. Cracroft, 'The Analysis of the House of Commons, Or Indirect Representation', *Essays on Reform* (1867), p. 187.

[3] Ibid., p. 181

[4] *Pall Mall Gazette*, cited in Blackwood's *The Progress of the Question*, July 1867, p. 120.

was said that a substantial measure of Reform would make the workmen 'masters of the situation'. 'They may be able to decide whether a Whig or a Tory shall be elected,' replied J. S. Mill, 'they may be masters of so small a situation as that.'[1] It was obvious to informed and intelligent men that there was little immediate prospect of workmen being elected. The vast 'cousin-hood' of the Parliamentary families had largely survived 1832 and it would survive 1867.[2] And even if workmen were elected they would soon catch the tone of the House.

> To a careful observer there is nothing more interesting than the growth of moderation and justice which unconsciously takes place in the minds of violent or narrow men, after they have taken a parliamentary position. Nothing short of fanaticism can withstand it; and fanaticism soon becomes silent and slinks away.[3]

Why, with all these assurances, did the House resist Reform for so long? Why did men of outstanding intelligence, such as Cranborne and Lowe, resist to the end and, even after the Bill was passed, spend their curses on those who feared to go 'within twenty four hours of Revolution'?

The approximate answer is that the House as a whole was too comfortable to move until it became an evident necessity. As

---

[1] Parl. Debates, 3rd series, clxxxii (13 April 1866), 1257.

[2] B. Cracroft, op. cit., p. 173, refers to an ex-governor of the Bank of England who declared that he was related to thirty other Members of the House all of whom were sitting with him at that time. One imagines that Cracroft would be suitably gratified to learn of the impressive kinship ties of contemporary governors of the Bank of England: see C. S. Wilson and T. Lupton, 'The Social Background and Connections of "Top Decision Makers"', *The Manchester School of Economic and Social Studies*, Vol. xxvii (1959), pp. 30–51. Cracroft p. 162 et seq. tried to demonstrate the socially exclusive character of the House of Commons by reference to its educational background and argued that Reform would make little difference to this. He gives the following figures for the House of Commons elected in 1865. The figures in brackets relate to the House elected in 1951 and are taken from J. F. S. Ross, *Elections and Electors*, 1955, p. 415 et seq. Public School Boys, 429 (321); Eton, 105 (81); Harrow 52 (24); Oxford 136 (141); Cambridge 110 (89). In interpreting these figures it has to be remembered that in 1865 the House was larger than it is now and numbered 652 Members. Although the social composition of the undergraduate population has been greatly altered, it is believed that 80% of the boys at Eton today are the sons of fathers who also went to Eton. (See *Sunday Times*, 13 August 1961.)

[3] Lord Houghton, op. cit., p. 59.

for the incorrigible resisters, their intelligence was not matched by the quality of their information. No one who reads the speeches of Lord Robert could suppose that he was a reliable authority on the political disposition of the mid-Victorian workman. When he went on his sleep-walking expeditions at Hatfield House the phantoms whom he prepared to repulse came in the guise of Federal soldiers or of *sansculottes* at the head of a revolutionary mob.[1] When awake, he still saw his adversaries in much the same insurgent shapes. There were occasions when Robert Lowe, a very different personality, showed himself to be scarcely better informed. He was apparently ready to believe every story about the indolence, extravagance and violence of the working man which any down-at-heel commercial traveller or failed professional man chose to tell him.[2] The forebodings of these most capable men often appeared far-fetched, trivial or over-dependent upon foreign experience which was of doubtful relevance. Thus, it was assumed that Reform would require the Commons to turn itself into an academy for the refutation of the fallacies of Fourier or Saint Simon,[3] and that much time would have to be spent in resisting proposals for the establishment of *ateliers nationaux*.[4]

There were occasions when the eloquence of the extreme reactionaries struck a false and faintly comic note. Thus, Beresford Hope talked of the 1867 Reform Bill as if it was the equivalent of 4 August 1789. Primogeniture and freedom of bequest would be dashed down. 'Then farewell to the old halls rising over the tall trees, and the spacious deer parks, for the peasantry in their ignorance and cupidity would soon be set fancying that these broad acres would best serve their purpose if cut up into freehold allotments.'[5]

While Beresford Hope saw the Jacquerie in the countryside, Lowe and Cranborne imagined levellers and socialists in the towns. They were unaware that virtually the only clear-headed revolutionaries in the country were German refugees. It was true that these revolutionaries had a high opinion of their own influence. Marx claimed that the Reform League was the work

---

[1] G. Cecil, op. cit., p. 170.   [2] A. P. Martin, op. cit., pp. 313–14.
[3] Parl. Debates, 3rd series clxxxii (26 April 1866), 2099 (Lowe).
[4] Ibid. (13 March 1866), 233 (Cranborne).
[5] Parl. Debates, 3rd series clxxxvii (20 May 1867), 802–3.

of the International[1] and that he himself had played a great part until he saw that the agitation was 'set going',[2] but this was probably tall talk. Marx had a penchant for taking the credit whenever a success was scored by anyone who happened to belong to the I.W.M.A.[3]

Of course there were also the Positivists. Cranborne and Lowe made the most of them and plainly saw in them that 'auxiliary contingent from among the educated classes'[4] which is necessary for the success of the multitude. 'The inspired apostles of a New Religion of Humanity', as Lowe called them,[5] had influence over Trade Unionists and might be able to direct their energies into dangerous courses. The Positivists were certainly bent on social reconstruction, and they were pleased to state that it was the political function of the working class to bring the revolutionary element into the British political system.[6] Such language concealed the fact that they had no desire to destroy existing property relations, but sought only to 'moralise' them. During the Reform agitation Frederic Harrison explained: 'I would never say anything which could have an incendiary effect.' He thought it 'impossible to produce any strong feeling, much less action'. Besides, in the most 'sacred

[1] K. Marx to F. Engels, 1 May 1865, op. cit., p. 494.

[2] K. Marx to L. Kugelmann, 9 October 1866, Marx/Engels, Sel.Corr. (1956), p. 223.

[3] Marx kept up a close correspondence with Ernest Jones during the early stages of the agitation, but there is no evidence that he was aware that political forces of a fighting kind came on the scene in July 1866. Indeed, he expressed doubt as to whether they had. (See his reply to George Howell in the *Secular Chronicle*, 4 August 1878.) He never attempted a sustained analysis of the Reform Question nor did he refer to the debate on the nature of Revolution which went on during it. Yet this debate provided a valuable test of the perspicacity of the 'class enemy'. Marx, had he bothered with it, would have been forced to allow that Cranborne had some correct insights. There was much discussion on the relation between 'base' and 'superstructure'. Thus, progressives like Leslie Stephen complained that it was 'too common to argue as though constitutional arrangements created, instead of giving effect to, the existing social forces . . .' Lowe tried to rebut this type of reasoning, but was not at his most lucid. (Parl. Debates, clxxxvii [20 May 1867], 788–90.)

[4] 'Parliamentary Reform', *Quarterly Review*, April 1865, p. 574.

[5] Parl. Debates, 3rd series, clxxxii (26 April 1866), 2078.

[6] F. Harrison, *Order and Progress* (1875, p. 221. Being a lecture of March 1868).

circles' of the ruling families, like the Russells, they quite liked a little 'playful Radicalism'.[1] His tone is well represented by an enigmatic remark he made on 6 May 1867: 'I think I have put a stopper on one of the dirtiest tricks that d——ed Jew ever tried on about Hyde Park. What fun it is. I am off to it.'[2]

When Beesley failed to attend the meeting because of a dinner engagement, Harrison scolded him: 'Fancy Cataline not being able to attend the *comitia* in the Forum because he had to sup with a certain knight.'[3] When a lady of Beesly's acquaintance was described as an extreme reactionary, Harrison asked whether she was enough of a Charlotte Corday to stab Beales.[4]

When the Positivists talked about the Reform Agitation in relation to the revolutionary tradition it was always with a factitious intent, except when they were thinking in terms of the longer run. Beesly—who saw Robespierre as a 'Calvin', a 'narrow fanatic'—remarked: 'I see among my operative friends more than one capable of playing Robespierre, but alas, not one Danton.'[5] He and Congreve may, at times, have thought in terms of organising physical force, but not of a revolutionary seizure of power.[6] The Positivists were out of sympathy with the democratic mania of the masses. Indeed, they had a high regard for Lowe so far as intellectual method went. They thoroughly endorsed his view that Reform ought to be judged by the probable consequences which would follow from it, rather than in terms of abstract rights or other metaphysical principles.[7]

The opinions of the English Positivists coincided with those of Marx over a range of issues, and Beesly and Marx had an affectionate regard for each other, but the Positivists were neither revolutionaries nor socialists. It was absurd to regard them as being actually or potentially leaders of a revolutionary

---

[1] F. Harrison to Mrs. Hadwen, 3 March 1866. F. H. Papers, L.S.E. Box 1.

[2] F. Harrison to E. S. Beesly, (6?) May 1867, F. H. Papers, L.S.E. Box 1.

[3] F. Harrison to E. S. Beesly, Wed 1867 (May.)

[4] F. Harrison to E. S. Beesly, Easter 1867.

[5] E. S. Beesly to H. Crompton, 26 October 1865 (B.C.U.C.)

[6] E. S. Beesly, 'Reform Constables', *Bee-Hive*, 25 November 1866. [Congreve 'is, indeed, for strong measures, processions and physical force'. F. Harrison to E. S. Beesly (n.d. 1866?)]

[7] F. Harrison to E. S. Beesly, 22 Feb. 1867. [Lowe 'is the only one of them with the true key. And how perfectly his case is stated.']

proletariat.[1] However, to understand Cranborne and Lowe, one must recognise the correctness of their insights as well as the absurdity of their mistakes. They were to be proved right over an impressive range of issues. They saw clearly that the Bill must be the first step towards complete political democracy. Mill might talk of the workmen being masters, only in relation to the small matter of whether they would be represented by Whig or Tory. Cranborne and Lowe recognised that with a working-class electorate Whig and Tory must become much altered. They were right in observing that land, which was a sedative in the New World, must be an irritant in England and that Reform would be followed by attacks on the landed interest. However mistaken their opinions about the then existing characteristics of Trade Unions, they were right in believing that they could and would become engines of political power. They were right in believing that this surrender could not be the last, but must form a precedent for many more in the future. In the longer run they were right about the advent of subsidised housing and the progressive income tax and the coming of Socialism.

Lowe, when he knew that all was lost, asked if any Member of the House would favour him with a précis on the political opinions of unskilled labourers earnings 8s. a week. He fancied that some of his new constituents would fall into this class.

> The fact is [he said] that the great mass of those you are going to enfranchise are people who have no politics at all ... But they will not be always without politics; and what will they be? What must be the politics of people who are struggling hard to keep themselves off the parish? ... their politics must take one form—Socialism. What other aspect can politics bear in their eyes ... What man will speak acceptably to them except the man who promises somehow or other to re-distribute the good things of this world more equally, so that the poor will get more and the rich and powerful will get less? ... History affords no instance where political power has been given to the lower classes and taken back from them without civil war or violent convulsion. What you do now is absolutely irreversible; and your repentence—bitter as I know it will be—will come too late.[2]

[1] See my 'Professor Beesly and the Working Class Movement', *Essays in Labour History*, ed. A. Briggs and J. Saville (1960), pp. 205-44.

[2] Parl. Debates, 3rd series, clxxxvii (20 May 1867), 788-99.

It has been said that the division on Reform crossed party lines and really lay between the optimists and the pessimists.[1] But if Lowe and Cranborne were pessimists that was because they were reasoners before they were observers, and philosophers before they were politicians. They were more concerned with what the logic of the situation would cause the working class to become than they were with its present characteristics. They were ready to run close to 'the heels of danger' for the sake of a hypothesis. If Lowe denounced the *a priori* method in politics at one level, he applied it himself at another. He tended to argue from certain supposed laws of history and human nature to what the political character of the working class must be. Similarly Cranborne granted that the working class were, in essence, like everybody else. However, their circumstances were different, exposing them to special temptations which necessarily made them dangerous. Assuming that everybody was alike 'in essence', these philosophic reactionaries concluded that the proletariat must exhibit the same degree of class consciousness as they possessed themselves. This assumption was, perhaps, the greatest hindrance to the discovery of the conservative possibilities of democracy.

The preoccupation of men like Cranborne and Lowe with the more remote consequences of Reform lent to their utterances a deceptive air of statesmanship. They were unsparing in their criticisms of the 'short sightedness', timidity and the absence of principle by which they supposed their colleagues to be characterised. When someone remarked that the Tory country gentlemen displayed greater zeal in the matter of the cattle plague than in opposing the Reform Bill, Lowe remarked: 'That is quite intelligible for the cattle Bill ruins ourselves, the Reform Bill only our children.'[2] Cranborne preferred to run a risk of a collision with the Reform League rather than submit to what he termed a 'revolution by inches'.[3]

Speaking in the House of Commons, Sir E. Bulmer-Lytton distinguished between Revolution and Reform. The former consisted of the transfer of power from one class to another; the latter, of the modification of the conditions under which power

[1] A. Briggs, *Age of Improvement* (1959), p. 515.
[2] M. E. Grant Duff, *Notes from a Diary 1851–1872*, Vol. II (1897), p. 119.
[3] 'Parliamentary Reform', *Quarterly Review*, April 1865, p. 564.

was exercised by the existing ruling class, by the correction of 'abuses'.[1] At any particular moment this distinction might appear to be clear and satisfactory, but it did not distinctly preclude the possibility of a long Revolution, a Revolution by a thousand 'modifications'. For a time the House was ready to be terrified by this prospect of a 'Revolution by inches'. It lost its fear only when the progress of the agitation obliged it to choose between removing an immediate peril or coping with distant dangers. The common-sense conception of Revolution is essentially 'holistic'. In theory, the same results might be accomplished over a long period and in a piecemeal manner. There is, however, a deep-seated belief that the results which are produced by the one process will not, in fact, be the same as those produced by the other. A 'Revolution' which works itself out within the existing political tradition is not a Revolution at all.

To this consideration was added another of still more compelling force. The English empiricist tradition taught that the politician who took account of the second order consequences of his actions was a statesman; and that to try and do more than this was evidence of metaphysics or megalomania. Cranborne and Lowe were ignoring this lesson and inviting immediate disaster on the pretext of avoiding ultimate catastrophe. It was all very well to complain that Derby adopted an attitude of 'après moi le déluge', but there were circumstances in which that discredited maxim became the last word in sagacity.

IV

It is widely acknowledged that the history of the Second Reform Act raises problems of exceptional complexity. Some historians have been content to proceed eclectically,[2] while one or

---

[1] Parl. Debates, 3rd series (13 April 1866), 1238.

[2] J. H. Park, *The English Reform Bill of 1867* (New York, 1920) is the best example of eclecticism. It is also one of the best and fullest accounts. Park inclined to the view that the Bill was the result of public opinion as stirred up partly by economic and social conditions, partly by the Reform League, partly by John Bright, partly by Trade Unions. It was also partly the result of party competition and, in particular, the calculations of Disraeli (p. 232 et seq.). F. E. Gillespie's useful *Labor and Politics in England*,

two dispense with the labour of enumerating the various factors involved and simply refer the reader to 'the Spirit of the Times'.[1] However, the great majority of historians of the Second Reform Act fall into one or other of two camps according to whether their interpretation is couched in terms of class struggle or of party conflict.

The first camp is by far the smallest, and the best of its contributions is so cursory and dogmatic that its opponents can be excused for neglecting it altogether.[2] In a more or less *a priori* fashion, historians of this persuasion argue that the ruling class was forced to concede Reform as a result of pressure by the masses. They do not explain why it was that a revolutionary proletariat confronting a relatively weak state apparatus in the 'thirties and 'forties was unable to force this concession which was secured by a reformist labour movement against a far more powerful executive two or three decades later. They make light work of the immense significance of the concession itself. They neglect the fact that this was the first occasion upon which a substantial portion of the working class secured the vote in a country in which the Executive was accountable to the popularly elected branch of the legislature. They ignore, rather than rebut, the argument that Reform was the result of the party system and party manoeuvring. They make the cardinal error of treating party rivalries as *mere* simulacra behind which one discovers the *arcana imperii*: the realities of class rule. In doing so they cut themselves off from an understanding of how party conflict may cross, as well as express, class antagonisms; how, in intriguing for office, the ruling oligarchies find their rivalry becoming informed by external interests and purposes; how the habit of peaceful political change, and the appeals to the principle of consent, debilitates the propertied classes, undermines

---

[1] W. D. Jones, *Lord Derby and Victorian Conservatism* (Oxford 1956), p. 326.

[2] T. Rothstein, *From Chartism to Labourism* (1929), p. 187. A. L. Morton and G. Tate, *The British Labour Movement* (1956), pp. 118–21.

1850–1867, (Durham, North Caroline, L1927) is in the same tradition, but attaches less importance to Tory statesmanship. The most recent historian of the Reform League, [H. Katz, *Liga Reformy* (Lodz) 1962] also appears to belong in this tradition. He explains that he has 'resisted the temptation of theoretical speculating and therefore has been rather frugal in his conclusions . . .'.

their powers of resistance, leaving them, to a degree, imprisoned by their own hypocrisies.[1]

However, if it is grotesque to write a history of Reform without reference to Party, it is scarcely better to attempt it without regard to the problem of Revolution. This would be freely acknowledged in relation to 1832, but it is taken to be possible in the case of 1867. Thus, at the end of the Victorian years, G. Lowes Dickinson thought it clear that 'the disturbance of the settlement of 1832 and the series of measures which culminated in the Reform Act of 1867, are to be attributed not to popular pressure from without, but to the free and spontaneous choice of the governing class'. He suggested that 'the phenomenon, curious though it be, might no doubt be explained by the manoeuvring of parties . . . reform of Parliament was treated merely as a weapon in the political game'.[2]

Lowes Dickinson's contention that 'the Bill of 1867 was introduced not so much in deference to public opinion, as in pursuance of a series of measures which had originated in the House itself, and in redemption of voluntary pledges of a succession of governments',[3] has been taken up and elaborated by Professor Herrick.[4] He asserts that 'the idea of revolution present in the agitation preceding the act of 1832 and close to the roots of

---

[1] In practice, Marx himself did not entirely neglect the importance of 'party'. As early as 1855 he foresaw that 'a real change might come about only under a Tory Government' (*Marx and Engels on Britain* [1954], p. 406). But most of his followers prefer to recall only his grander over-simplifications. See, for example, R. Fox, *The Class Struggle in Britain*, n.d. (1932?), p. 27.

[2] G. Lowes Dickinson, *The Development of Parliament During the Nineteenth Century* (1895), p. 54.

[3] G. Lowes Dickinson, *The Development of Parliament during the Nineteenth Century* (1895), p. 84.

[4] It is not only historians who have followed Lowes Dickinson. One of the best and most influential textbooks in political philosophy contains the following passage: 'The extensions of the franchise in nineteenth-century Britain were carried out by parties outdoing one another in the search for votes, rather than pursuing the interests of the propertied classes which financed them. Those classes have unquestionably lost many of their former advantages as a direct result of this competition.' This highly simplified and misleading account occupies a crucially important position in a chapter devoted to 'Democracy'. (S. I. Benn and R. S. Peters, *Social Principles and the Democratic State* [1959], p. 339.) Is it wise of our educational reformers to assume that a knowledge of the second law of thermodynamics is more important than a knowledge of the second Reform Act?

Chartism was conspicuously absent'.[1] In an earlier article, he declared that

> there is absolutely no evidence that Bright or Beales or Odger, the popular leaders, ever considered the use of violence, as was most certainly done by Reformers in 1832.[2] If their followers could not vote and did not make trouble, why should Conservatives give in to their demands? Real disturbances had not moved them during the Chartist agitation.[3]

He tries to interpret the Act of 1867 in terms of the maturing of certain ideas, and in terms of the earliest proposals for Reform— the abortive Bills brought forward in 1852, 1854, 1859 and in 1860 and 1866. In his first contribution to this discussion, Herrick places special emphasis on 'the necessities of political parties'.[4] The point being, presumably, that both the Radicals and the Tories had an interest in ending twenty years of Whig supremacy, while the Whigs themselves had to feign an interest in the question.

Professor Herrick has completely missed the problem of Revolution in relation to Reform. Many of his propositions about Party calculations are undoubtedly correct but they hardly add up to satisfactory interpretation of events. The Herrick–Lowes Dickinson analysis is open to a whole series of challenges. For example, if Reform was a gamble taken in the interests of Party expediency, what was it that transformed the harmless flutters of the 'fifties and early 'sixties into the relentless game of brag which began in February and ended in August 1867? The Act went far beyond anything which had been desired before 1866. It was surely the presence of the Reform League which stopped the players crying off as they had done so often in the past. If the pressure exerted by the League is held to be negligible, then innumerable public and private

---

[1] F. H. Herrick, 'The Second Reform Movement in Britain,' *Journal of the History of Ideas*, Vol. 9, 1949, p. 178.

[2] It has been shown that Bright and Beales did 'consider' violence, although they did not encourage it. J. B. Leno, *The Aftermath* (1892), p. 71 alleges that at the meeting with Cleusart in July 1866 at which he (Leno) was present, Odger spoke in favour of violence.

[3] F. H. Herrick, 'The Reform Bill of 1867 and the British Party System', *Pacific Historical Review*, Vol. 3, pp. 223–4.

[4] F. H. Herrick, 'The Reform Bill of 1867 and the British Party System', *Pacific Historical Review*, Vol. 3, pp. 229–30.

admissions about the influence of its agitation have to be discounted; the widespread preoccupation with preventing the formation of revolutionary forces has to be ignored; and the proximity to revolutionary situations in 1866 and 1867 has to be neglected.

Of course, Party rivalries and calculations were important, but such rivalries and calculations all depended upon the stage of development attained by the Labour Movement. Unless a synthesis is made between the 'party conflict' and 'class struggle' interpretations, the history of 1866–67 is unintelligible. Unlike the Chartist years, the agitation of 1866–67 had a character which allowed the leaders of the traditional parties to think of Reform in terms of what might be 'in it' for them. Unlike the years of the abortive Reform Bills, there was an agitation which could only be ignored at the cost of reviving and sharpening the class-consciousness of the workmen and helping on the formation of revolutionary forces.

In the 1860s the British working class exhibited certain 'contradictory' characteristics. If it was increasingly 'respectable', it was increasingly well organised. If it had abandoned its revolutionary ambitions, it had not wholly lost its revolutionary potentialities. It left no doubt that these potentialities might be speedily developed if it was too long thwarted in its desire to secure political equality. In short, it had attained precisely that level of development at which it was safe to concede its enfranchisement and dangerous to withhold it. It was this circumstance, rather than the death of Palmerston, which determined the timing of Reform.[1]

Professor Briggs has attempted the kind of synthesis which is required. He makes a distinction between the *timing* of events and their *pattern*.[2] Unlike Lowes Dickinson and Herrick he finds room for the Reform League. He contends that the agitation

[1] Trygve R. Tholfsen, 'The Transition to Democracy in Victorian England', *International Review of Social History*, Vol. vi, 1961, pt. 2, pp. 226–48, provides a useful corrective to the narrowly 'political' interpretations of Reform. However, the tensions, conflicts and inconsistencies which characterised the mid-Victorian Labour Movement tend to be obscured by his emphasis upon the way in which workmen acted out roles prescribed for them by middle-class radicalism.

[2] A. Briggs, *Victorian People* (1954), p. 281.

determined the timing of events. 'Pressure from without' was necessary in order to break through the barrier presented by the complex of petty, Parliamentary interests and to open the way for the already mature aim and strategy of the Tory Statesmen. However, for Briggs this is a 'subsidiary factor . . . More important than external pressure was the desire of the Conservative leaders to secure a comprehensive settlement.'[1] He sees in this desire the main determinant of the 'pattern' of events.

It is not clear whether Briggs' distinction between 'timing' and 'pattern' would allow him to accept the statement made on p. 112 above. There it was suggested that when Disraeli asserted that he aimed 'to destroy the present agitation and extinguish Gladstone and Co.', the possibility of reaching the second objective depended entirely upon the necessity of accomplishing the first.[2] If this contention is accepted then the attempt to assign relative weights to 'parliamentary manoeuvre' and 'pressure from without' would have to be revised or discarded as unrewarding.

Perhaps the difference between Professor Briggs' position and the one taken up here reduces itself to a matter of emphasis. There can be no question about the fact that the mysterious nature of Disraeli's genius made its contribution to the passing of the Reform Act. The problem is how far he should be regarded as the master, rather than as the not unwilling prisoner, of circumstance. It is certain that for a number of years Disraeli had sensed that there might be a possibility of using a section of the non-electors to help restore the fortunes of his Party. As the prospect of restoring the old Toryism faded, the preoccupation with ending a prolonged period of Whig supremacy grew. He had never had scruples against using the Radicals to further his own ends. But Disraeli's skill at self-advertisement has encouraged his vague premonitions to be treated as if they were cold calculations. Ideas which were half-formed or slowly maturing were taken for developed aims and a clear cut strategy.

Those who try to make the history of Reform intelligible in

---

[1] A. Briggs, *Victorian People* (1954), p. 295.
[2] In discussing Disraeli's response to Hodgkinson's amendment, Briggs only cites that part of Disraeli's phrase which refers to Gladstone. (See A. Briggs, *The Age of Improvement*, 1959, p. 511.)

terms of Disraeli's skill and cunning are inclined to forget that, in the first months of the Tory Ministry, he was not at all anxious to deal with the question and had to be convinced by the Queen and Lord Derby that it was imperative.[1] There is a tendency to overlook the fact that he was forced to make up his mind about important amendments on the spur of the moment.[2] He and Derby frequently talked with a flippancy which is only possible for men who have surrendered to events. Thus, while the Prime Minister could refer to Household Suffrage as a wonderful hare to start,[3] the Chancellor of the Exchequer could request Stanley to come and speak on the Lodger clause, explaining that it made no difference whether he spoke for it or against it, so long as he spoke.[4] The Tory Statesmen were bowing to a process which it was beyond their power to control. To employ the equestrian imagery which was so popular at the time: Disraeli gave the horse its head without care for how far it might carry him so long as he managed to stay on its back. If a minority Government was to carry a measure, it could not be too particular about what sort of measure it was. Walpole's successor in the Home Office understood it perfectly. He shared the conviction of his colleagues that 'our security is going lower than the combining classes'.[5] This conviction helped to reconcile him to developments which he neither whole-heartedly welcomed nor pretended to control. He found in the experience of 1867 'a new proof that a great measure ought not to be in the hands of a minority but those who can mould and resist the moulding of others'.[6]

The strength of the Government lay, not so much in the weakness and division of the Opposition, as in the fact that a Reform Act had become essential. A great majority in the House was brought to the conclusion that the whole institution of Parliamentary government would be discredited and imperilled by yet another false start. Had it not been for this consideration

---

[1] W. E. Monypenny and G. E. Buckle, *The Life of Benjamin Disraeli* (1929 New Edition), Vol. 2, p. 187 and p. 191.
[2] Ibid., p. 274.   [3] Ibid., p. 218.   [4] Ibid., p. 269.
[5] A. E. Gathorne-Hardy, *Gathorne-Hardy, First Earl of Cranbrook* (1910), Vol. 1, p. 211.
[6] Ibid., p. 210.

then Disraeli could never have carried so many members of his own party with him. Peel, Carnarvon and Cranborne would have become the leaders of a Tory 'cave'. All the Adullamites would have followed Lowe in offering a continued resistance. The Radicals, many of whom were uneasy about the extent of the measure as well as its supposed paternity, would have made it their first interest to defeat the Government.

The largely forgotten events of 6 May throw light on the character of the challenge with which the Government had to deal. When it allowed a reformist movement to score a revolutionary triumph, it showed that it understood the choice before it. A humiliation had been suffered; a humiliation which gave notice that henceforth 'good will' rather than 'force' or 'fraud' was to be the main instrument. It was in accordance with the curious dialectic of the British Political System that it was able to make a strength of its weakness. It exchanged the associations of Peterloo for those of Hyde Park. After 6 May Hyde Park gradually became an established tradition. It stood for freedom in relation to the pretensions of aristocratic privilege, but it also stood for the powerlessness of democratic enthusiasts in the face of those 'occult and unacknowledged forces which are not dependent upon any legislative machinery'.

IV

THE REFORM LEAGUE AND THE GENERAL ELECTION OF 1868

I N 1867 social philosophers might point to the presence of 'occult and unacknowledged forces' which would help to preserve the *status quo*, but party managers could take little comfort from such reflections. The Reform Act had opened up a new world where they made their way with halting steps and much foreboding. Thus, G. G. Glyn, one of the partners in the great banking house of Glyn, Mills and Co., had recently become Liberal Chief Whip and he felt obliged to warn Gladstone that the Reform Act of 1867 had made a general election an incalculable business: 'All is new & changed & large & I fear I must say in some respects *dark*.'[1] The size of the electorate had been just about doubled and none of the established party leaders could be sure that ways would be found of organising and controlling the new voters. Indeed, there was some reason for supposing that the newly enfranchised workmen might bring forward their own candidates or, short of that, exert independent pressure on both parties in the interests of a distinctive programme of their own.

The materials required to produce such effects appeared to be present. The legal status of the Trades Unions was in question. The security of their funds had been imperilled by the decision of the Court of the Queen's Bench in the case of Hornby *v.* Close, and their freedom to engage in strikes was

---

[1] A. F. Thompson, 'Gladstone's Whips and the General Election of 1868', *English Historical Review*, April 1948, p. 189.

endangered by the application of the law of conspiracy to a dispute in the London tailoring trade. To make matters worse, the terrorist activities of a few workers in Sheffield had been exploited to bring the whole Trade Union movement into bad odour. A Royal Commission had been set up to enquire into the workings of the Unions and it was feared that its recommendations might lead to further restraints being imposed upon them.[1]

Under these circumstances it was not altogether surprising that one of the Unionists' most influential advisers, Professor Beesly, was hard at work trying to persuade Unionists and working-class reformers to break through the closed ring of established party politics. Even before the Reform Bill had become law, he had drawn up a six point programme in which the main emphasis was placed on securing a satisfactory legal settlement for the Unions. He urged that this issue, together with demands for an extension of the Factory Acts, a reduction in indirect taxation, and a system of national, secular and compulsory primary education, should be given priority over all other questions. He expressly warned against the danger of subordinating this programme to that of the middle-class Radicals. He regarded it as 'quite certain' that 'many candidates who swallow the Ballot, or even warmly support it, would go dead against workmen's interests on intellectual and social questions'.[2]

Beesly had been asked to draw up this programme by the Bradford Trade Unionists and Reformers, and in 1867 he felt that there were workers all over the country who were ready and willing to take his advice.[3] However, he had only limited success with the 'Junta'. The Conference of Amalgamated Trades was prepared to take up and develop his ideas on labour law reform, but it showed a characteristic reluctance to merge the special interests of Trade Unionism in a general class programme.[4]

Yet, despite the almost total absence of socialist ideas, there were indications that workmen might feel their way towards

[1] S. and B. Webb, *History of Trade Unionism*, (London, 1920), pp. 259–73.

[2] E. S. Beesly, 'The General Election of 1869: Programme for Trade Unions', Coll. E. Section B. vol. cxx, item 41, WTUC.

[3] E. S. Beesly to R. Congreve, 28 August 1867. PABM. Add. MSS. 45227–64.

[4] Minutes of the Conference of Amalgamated Trades, 30 September 1867. WTUC.

independent political activity. The small, but exceedingly energetic, London Working Men's Association held discussions on labour representation and the possibility of building up an electoral fund. Its platform contained most of the planks in Beesly's programme, but they were tagged on to the end of the usual democratic demands.[1]

In the autumn of 1867 it would have been excusable for a political observer to predict that Labour would appear as a distinct force in the next election. It had numbers, grievances, its own programmes and projects to discuss and, in the Reform League, it had by far the largest and most perfect political organisation in the country.

By July 1867 there were approximately 600 branches of the Reform League including ward and auxiliary organisations. There were one hundred branches in London alone. In May of this year the League's Secretary had supplied 65,000 membership cards. The branches were grouped in 'Departments' in Scotland, Ireland, the Midlands, the North, the North East, the West Riding and in Oxford. In terms of size it quite overshadowed its middle-class rival, the Reform Union which was centred in Manchester. At the beginning of 1867 the Union could claim less than one third of the League's membership organised in only one quarter of the number of branches. However, its financial resources were considerable and it advanced a long way towards its target of £50,000 for its guarantee fund. The League could never think in these terms.[2]

All members in England paid a minimum subscription of 1s. per year—a third of which went to the centre. George Howell, a bricklayer who had been prominent in many trade and political movements, was employed as full-time secretary with a salary which reached £2 10s. per week.[3] In addition to Howell,

---

[1] G. D. H. Cole, *British Working Class Politics 1832–1914*, London 1941, pp. 39–44.

[2] For the Reform Union see *Bee-Hive*, 23 February 1867. For the League see 'A List of Departments and Branches of the National Reform League', 1867, in Volume of *Election Reports* (H.C.). The Reform League's organisation has been subjected to detailed examination by A. D. Bell, 'The Reform League from its origins to the Reform Act of 1867' (D.Phil Oxford, 1961).

[3] Cash Book of the Reform League, entry for November 1867. HC. (All other references to manuscript material in this chapter relate to the Howell Collection unless otherwise stated.)

the carpenter, W. R. Cremer, served as a full-time organiser and fund-raiser.[1] At various times James Finlen,[2] a French-polisher and an associate of Ernest Jones; George Odger,[3] shoemaker and Secretary of the London Trades Council; and George Mantle,[4] an old Chartist who had served several prison sentences, were employed as lecturers and agents. William Parsons, the Rev. W. H. Bonner and the Rev. Goalen were also employed for considerable periods.[5] The President was Edmond Beales, who was one of the Revising Barristers for Middlesex until he was deprived of his appointment. He enjoyed an unequalled prestige among all sections of working-class Reformers. It was correctly said that 'he lost his practice, his office, his voice, his health in the people's cause'.[6] These officers worked under the formal control of an Executive Committee which was in its turn accountable to a General Council consisting of representatives from the branches.

It would be a mistake to imagine that the rivalry between the League and the London Working Men's Association represented a crippling division in the ranks of working-class Reformers. The strength of the L.W.M.A. lay almost entirely in London and largely depended upon its control of the *Bee-Hive* newspaper. In 1867 the League had almost as many branches as the L.W.M.A. had members.[7] Potter and Hartwell had shown that they were capable of bringing large numbers of workers into the streets of the metropolis, and that their followers might manage to infiltrate into the Reform League's General Council, but they could neither dislodge their opponents from office nor seriously undermine their authority as national leaders. The League was unquestionably the most

[1] H. Evans, *Sir R. Cremer: His Life and Work*, London 1909. For Cremer's remuneration as a League agent, see G. Howell to W. R. Cremer, 29 November 1867.

[2] J. Finlen, *Mr. J. Finlen's Defence of Himself Against the Attacks Made Upon Him By the Parliament and Press of England* (London, 1868?), p. 16.

[3] D. R. Moberg, 'George Odger and the English Working-Class Movement' (Ph.D. Thesis, London School of Economics, 1953).

[4] G. Howell, Draft Autobiography. Note on 'G. H. Mantle, 1865–1870'.

[5] A. D. Bell, 'The Reform League from its origins to the Reform Act of 1867' (D.Phil. Oxford, 1961).

[6] Ibid. (6) ('Edmond Beales').

[7] 'Report of Saint Martin's Hall Conference', *Bee-Hive*, 9 March 1867.

important organisation of working-class Reformers. At the end of 1867 it had ceased to be sure of itself, but this had little to do with George Potter and his friends.

I

If the organised working class was going to make itself felt in the approaching General Election then it could only be through the powerful machinery of the Reform League. Yet no sooner was the Reform Act passed than it found itself beset with financial and political problems which threatened to deprive it of any further influence.

Within the General Council there were violent debates on the question of Fenianism. Benjamin Lucraft,[1] George Odger and other well-known leaders announced their sympathies with the Irish. Odger went so far as to declare that had he been an Irishman he would have been a Fenian.[2] Important sections of the press fastened on these statements and interpreted them as evidence that the League favoured terrorism and approved of physical force policies. George Howell soon found that he had to write reassuring letters to professional and middle-class friends who were alarmed by these reports.[3] He was unable to prevent a number of resignations and he could see no way of putting a stop to the League's decline unless these divisions on the Irish question were healed. 'Now is the time when unity is required,' Howell observed, 'for some people are easily defeated after a victory.'[4]

However, unity required some agreement about the future work of the League. In December 1867 the General Council called for joint action with the Unions to secure the return of Labour representatives to the next Parliament in numbers 'proportionate to the other interests and classes at present represented in Parliament', but no practical steps were taken to help

[1] G. H. Dyer, *Benjamin Lucraft*, 1879.

[2] Minutes of the General Council of the Reform League, 23 October 1867. (Hereafter referred to as G.C.R.L.)

[3] Howell to Prof. Thorold Rogers, 23 November 1867, and to W. E. Forster, M.P., 17 December 1867.

[4] Howell to C. Hills, 26 November 1867. (Howell kept carbon copies of letters, which are bound in date order in a series of letter books.)

carry this out.[1] Howell had great misgivings about such resolutions and he explained in private that he did not see his way clear in this matter.[2] 'As to working-men representatives as a rule, our time is not yet come. We want *good men* no matter whence they come or what they are.'[3] Talk of Labour representatives was likely to give further distress to middle-class patrons of the League who were disturbed enough by the debates on Fenianism.

From its inception the League had received some financial support from wealthy Liberal manufacturers. Of the total national receipts, amounting to £3,101 in the financial year ending in April 1867, half was accounted for by 'donations'. Some of the contributions under this heading came from workmen. 'A few engineers, £1'; 'Three of the venal and the ignorant, 2/6'—there are many such entries in the League's cash books. But the greater part of this money came in much larger sums and from other quarters. Thus, between 10 November 1866 and 17 April 1867 ten Liberal politicians and manufacturers, headed by Samuel Morley and Titus Salt, made contributions totalling £1,150. There were many other middle-class men who subscribed sums of under £50.[4] Samuel Morley was said to have 'erected benevolence into a business'[5] and Howell knew all such men, if they gave generously, brought to their giving the same shrewdness and calculation which they displayed in their investments. They needed to know their man before they parted with money and they expected a proper account of how it was spent. Not one of them could be counted as an uncritical admirer of the League's programme. Not one of them would give a penny so long as there was any doubt or uncertainty about where the League would stand in the coming election.

Throughout the winter of 1867–68, Howell recorded a steady worsening of the financial position, which he explained in terms of the separation of the League from its middle-class friends. It was a deplorable situation whether regarded from the stand-

---

[1] Minutes G.C.R.L., 4 December 1867.
[2] Howell to Elk, 27 October 1867.
[3] Howell to Clayton, 28 February 1868.
[4] Reform League cash book, 1866–67.
[5] Samuel Morley, *Dictionary of National Biography*.

point of his political ideals or equally in relation to his personal interests. Although one of Howell's earliest recollections was of George Snell calling at his father's house before going off to die in the Newport Rising of 1839,[1] Chartism and Owenism were objects for him of sentimental curiosity rather than of serious commitment. When he came to London in the 1850s he saw Robert Owen and gave some support to Ernest Jones, but his object was to equip himself for public life and to fulfil his three ambitions: to speak in the Exeter Hall, to publish a book, and to enter the House of Commons.[2] He came into the Labour Movement during that period of half-light in which Chartism had not yet passed finally away nor the new institutions firmly established themselves. But by the time he was Secretary of the Reform League he had long ceased to drink at the old Chartist water-holes and he recommended his working-class correspondents, 'as to works on politics and political economy, get Mill on Liberty and Political Economy. There are many other works, but go to the fountain head at once. Mill, Gladstone and Bright are great authorities on politics, taxation and government.'[3]

At first sight, Mill, Gladstone and Bright make a strange trio. Yet despite profound differences of mind and character, these three men had achieved a substantial measure of political agreement during 1867–68. They certainly shared a quite remarkable prestige among working-class reformers as a whole. Even Professor Beesly admitted that 'no workman would cast his vote against such men as Mr Bright, Mr Mill or Mr Gladstone, let the opposing candidate promise what he would'.[4] But if Beesly faced what he took to be the facts, Howell rejoiced in them. If Beesly thought of Mill, Bright and Gladstone as exceptional individuals whom workmen could not be induced to oppose, Howell saw them as representatives of social and political forces with which the working class must be aligned. For Howell was firmly convinced that workmen would never accomplish anything in politics without the help and advice of professional

---

[1] Howell, Draft Autobiography.   [2] Ibid.

[3] Howell to W. Thomas, 4 May 1868.

[4] Beesly, E. S., 'The General Election of 1869: Programme for Trade Unions'. (Undated, but 1867.) WTUC, Coll. E. Section B. Vol. cxx, item 41.)

teachers such as Goldwin Smith, Thorold Rodgers, Frederic Harrison and Mill. He believed that, if they were to exercise any serious influence, they had to work closely with progressive parliamentarians like James Stansfeld and Walter Morrison. While Beesly looked forward to the supremacy of working-class interests, Howell declared:

> I have never been, and never shall be, an advocate for merely changing our masters. I neither want aristocratic rule, nor the rule of the middle classes, nor the rule of the working classes. I want a government of the entire people—where wealth and intellect will have its fair share of power—no more.[1]

Howell's most immediate fear in the winter of 1867–68 was that a separation from the middle-class Liberals would result in the League's falling into the hands of ultra Radicals. If this happened the only consequence would be that the manufacturers would be driven back into the arms of the Whigs. As he explained to one of Francis Place's old friends: 'The greater the element of our middle classes in these movements, the less violent and more progressive will be the results. For then there will be no fear of counter-plotting and reaction.'[2]

The political considerations that led Howell to deplore the withdrawal of middle-class support were powerfully reinforced by personal financial problems. Several times in his life he had seemed within measurable distance of escaping from the insecurity and drudgery of a working-class existence. His father had been a stone-mason in the West Country. He had managed to become quite a substantial subcontractor, but had lost out heavily in a legal dispute. When Howell came to London as a young man he managed to earn a skilled worker's wage and, with only a wife and one child to support, his responsibilities were relatively light. But, as a result of his activities in the great strike and lock-out in the London building trades, he was victimised by the masters and forced to find employment elsewhere.[3] In 1867 he enjoyed what he described as his 'very first year of real comfort'. In the course of the year he was able 'to buy a few things and not really pinch for it'. He added, 'Yet I

---

[1] Howell to Morrison, M.P., 30 November 1868.
[2] Howell to Dr. Black, 22 February 1868.
[3] Draft Autobiography.

have not lived extravagant [*sic*], but very moderately and carefully. Never felt that I should live fast or spend in gaiety.'[1] Indeed, he had managed to save £6 and was thinking of buying a house. He told his brother, 'If I can get over this year (1868) I shall feel quite safe and at my ease. It will be a great struggle, but then the victory will also be great.'[2]

Howell's prospects were jeopardised by the weakness of the League and, in particular, by the reluctance of the middle-class sympathisers to continue their subsidies. While his wife and son visited friends or went to the Comic Opera, he employed the winter evenings studying French, reading Machiavelli, and drawing up plans for a personal canvass of rich supporters in the north of England.[3]

In February 1868 Howell visited Bradford, a town where the class conflicts within English Radicalism appeared with exceptional sharpness and clarity. Here there were many workmen who were ready to follow Professor Beesly and Dr. Bridges, and to argue that the Tory Radicalism of Oastler and the democratic Radicalism of Bright and Cobden were equally perishing species which ought to yield to a new social philosophy in which the control of capital would appear as the paramount issue. Arrayed against them were the men whom Howell had come to see, the influential textile manufacturers, Robert and S. C. Kell, vigorous supporters of further political reform, who resented any attempt to introduce disruptive questions about the legal status of Trade Unions.[4]

Howell was immediately made aware of the intense class-consciousness which prevailed in the town. He recorded that he

went to Kells; saw Mr. S. C. Kell; had a long chat. But he was very shy about cash ... Went in the evening to hear Mundella's lecture on Arbitration versus Strikes. I found the Committee room full of employers, Chamber of Commerce men, and they evinced their partiality for the employers' view of the question in the way they applauded every hit at the workmen. But the men met the

[1] Howell's Diary, 1868. (Personal Financial Review for the past year.)

[2] Howell to 'Dear Brother', 14 April 1868.

[3] Howell's Diary, 3 January 1868.

[4] For this controversy, see *Bradford Review*, 31 August to 28 December 1867. This was a continuation of an earlier struggle: see *The Commonwealth*, 12 May to 16 June 1866.

charge well. Never was I more convinced of the necessity of the Unions than this night.

But he immediately added: 'I was asked to speak, but refused as I saw I must say some things which would be disagreeable to those I came to see and I knew it would be unadvisable. Workmen, defend your Unions! say I.' [1]

Howell's diplomacy was not rewarded.

Met Arthur Illingworth; had a long talk. They were all close-fisted ... saw Titus Salt ... no cash whatever, not even a direct promise. Illingworth strongly insisted on a union of Manchester with London, Kell the same. My private impression is that the manufacturing class are rather afraid of the power the People now have. They are beginning to be shy. [2]

On returning to London Howell wrote to thank Kell for his hospitality:

I sincerely hope that Mr Titus Salt will give us some help for we are sorely pressed for cash and quite unable to move. It does seem strange that after doing such good service for two years, and being capable of much more service for some time to come, we should be in such crippled circumstances for a few hundred pounds. [3]

The same day, Howell had to explain to Illingworth that there was no immediate prospect of combined action between the League and the middle-class Reform Union, the condition to which the Bradford manufacturers attached so much importance. [4] In fact, Edmond Beales was thoroughly roused by the attempted interference and, at the Executive Committee meeting of 12 February, he strongly condemned middle-class dictation. [5]

Fortunately there was in London a Liberal politician who was far more polished and experienced than the blunt men of Bradford. James Stansfeld, who was closely associated with Glyn, had worked with Labour leaders over a number of years. [6]

[1] Howell's Diary, 5 February 1868.   [2] Ibid., 6 February 1868.
[3] Howell to R. Kell, 11 February 1868.
[4] Howell to A. Illingworth, 11 February 1867.
[5] Minutes of the Executive Committee of the Reform League, 12 February 1868. (Hereafter referred to as E.C.R.L.)
[6] Sir James Stansfeld, 1820–93. D.N.B. Also J. L. Hammond and Barbara Hammond, *James Stansfeld: A Victorian Champion of Sex Equality*, London 1932.

He saw that it was a mistake to complicate the task of building a class alliance by insisting that an end should be put to the organisational rivalries between the Reform Union and the League. Howell went to see him and he promised to help him to raise £500. Howell was delighted: 'Nothing could be kinder than his reception. He is indeed, one of the *best* of our public men.'[1]

Stansfeld did not want to impose conditions upon the Labour leaders, but to cultivate closer relations between them and men of his own social and political position. To this end, he had tried to induce Howell, Applegarth and others to join the Century Club, where there would be an opportunity for them to meet Liberal intellectuals and Parliamentarians.[2] The workmen found the subscription prohibitive, so he devised a scheme for a new club. The initial capital was to be supplied by Liberal manufacturers, but it was to be run by a Committee on which workmen were to be represented. It was eventually established in the premises of the Reform League at Adelphi Terrace and its object was declared to be—'doing something to bridge over the gulph which now exists between different classes and thereby developing a more kindly feeling than has hitherto existed'.[3] A large number of professional men, including Mill, joined the Club and sent books for its library. Titus Salt, Samuel Morley and others supplied the funds. Professor Beesly was the only middle-class friend of Labour who refused to have anything to do with it.[4]

A few weeks after Howell's interview with Stansfeld, the financial position of the League began to improve. Funds were now available for an important series of lectures which Howell planned to organise in London. The series had already been opened by Ernest Jones, who had created a very bad impression among middle-class friends. Samuel Morley complained about Jones' lecture and described him, rather oddly, as 'a wild Irishman'.[5] The remaining lectures in the series were given by such

[1] Howell's Diary, 8 February 1868.

[2] Howell to J. Stansfeld, M.P., 18 November 1868.

[3] Draft Appeal for the Adelphi Club, 9 April 1869. (Howell's letter book for 1868.)

[4] E. S. Beesly to Geo. Howell, 26 April 1868. (Letters to Howell are kept in packages for each year and arranged in alphabetical order.)

[5] Howell's Diary, 11 December 1867.

reliable men as W. E. Forster, M.P., A. J. Mundella and Stansfeld himself. Little difficulty was experienced in persuading M. T. Bass, Edmund Potter, M.P., H. C. E. Childers, M.P., and others to help supply the money.[1]

Within the League, Howell counselled members to adopt moderate and 'realistic' policies. In March he told the Pimlico branch that there were four issues which ought to be put before the country: further democratic reform of the electoral system; justice to Ireland; national education; and Trades Unionism. This was virtually the last occasion upon which he placed any emphasis at all upon the problem of securing a sound legal status for the Unions. At Pimlico he explained: 'While I adhere to my Radical creed with all the tenacity of a partisan, I still think that we in England can only permanently succeed by compromise.'[2]

He discussed the question of candidates with the Secretary of the Scottish Department of the League.

> We must go in for the best we can get to come forward, but better have *new* Liberals than old Whigs. I *hate the Whigs*. They have ever been our enemies and are now . . . We must fight the next election tooth and nail and *if the Whig is doubtful* I personally should prefer a Tory. But of course this is a delicate matter and one which requires care in the working out . . . but we must tell the professing Liberals that their programme must be a good and bold one and their pledges must be kept or they will not do for us.[3]

Howell had already made clear that in his view, the selection of working-class candidates was not a serious proposition.

While he was elaborating these general principles, Howell was already engaged in trying to place 'good men' in constituencies. Mr. B. Samuelson, the Liberal Member for Banbury, who was no great friend to Trades Unionism, wished his son to join him in the House of Commons. Howell wrote about the matter to one of his correspondents in Cheltenham.

> I am desired by a well known and good Liberal member of the House of Commons to enquire of you as to the chances of success for a good young Oxford Liberal. His father is a good man and

[1] Howell's letters of thanks to Potter and to Childers, 24 March 1868.

[2] Howell's draft of Lecture to Pimlico Branch, 24 March 1868. (In letter book for 1868.)

[3] Howell to Geo. Jackson, 11 May 1868.

one of great ability and standing in the House. But he is desirous of his son being elected without resort to any corrupt or dubious means, or in any way compromising his own feelings of integrity. The family is wealthy and very liberal in all good works. Please treat this letter as *private* and tell me the chances for such an one, and also whether you are free to support him if he should come out for Cheltenham.[1]

The matter was managed successfully and H. B. Samuelson was adopted. Howell thanked his father for a donation of £10, adding, 'I think our League will do good service.'[2] He told Titus Salt, 'We feel that to disband (the Reform League) before the next General Election would be a national misfortune for the Liberal Party.'[3] Salt's earlier doubts on this subject were by now subdued and he contributed £100.[4]

By offering general assurances and performing small services, Howell prepared the way for the more formal and comprehensive agreement which was concluded with the Liberal Whips in the middle of 1868.

Glyn and Stanhope now joined Stansfeld in the negotiations. They regarded a deal with the Reform League as a very delicate matter which had to be kept as secret as possible. It would not be desirable to have the proceedings discussed in the General Council. In so far as it was practicable they wanted to confide only in Howell and Cremer. The election of a new Executive Committee in May made it much easier to satisfy these conditions. Lucraft, who had been associated with the left wing of the old Executive, was not re-elected.[5]

The first act of the new body was to establish a Parliamentary Sub-Committee for 'registration and electoral purposes'. It consisted of a professional election agent, James Acland; a wealthy merchant, Joseph Guedalla; Beales' friend, Col. Dickson; W. R. Cremer, George Odger and Thomas Mottershead.[6] The delegation by the Executive of its powers to this Committee; to a small finance committee and, on occasion, to Howell and Cremer directly, allowed negotiations to proceed confidentially and discreetly. It was not until the election was over that Howell and Cremer were charged with exceeding their authority.

[1] Howell to C. Hiscot (?), 2 April 1868.
[2] Howell to B. Samuelson, M.P., 30 April 1868.
[3] Howell to T. Salt, 3 April 1868.   [4] Ibid., 25 April 1868.
[5] Minutes E.C.R.L., 6 May 1868.   [6] Ibid., 9 May 1868.

The Parliamentary Sub-Committee lost no time in displaying its usefulness. In June it sent six men down to the Bristol by-election to organise support for Samuel Morley.[1] Morley had been a candidate for Parliament before, but had been unseated on a petition. This time he was elected. Shortly after this, Cremer reported to the Executive that he had had an interview with one of Gladstone's Whips, H. S. Stanhope, 'in reference to the pending General Election and as to funds being made up for the use of the League'. At the same meeting Howell referred to interviews which he had had with the Liberal Whips.[2] It was decided that a deputation consisting of Howell, Cremer and Worley, should 'wait upon Mr Stanhope, Mr Adams or others in reference to the elections and with regard to funds'.[3] By the end of July, Howell was able to tell the Executive that he had seen Samuel Morley and that Morley had donated £250 to the League. Cremer spoke of 'the negotiations now pending for raising a fund of £1,000' for preliminary election expenses.[4]

The Minutes of the Executive—which it must be remembered were kept by Howell himself—suggest that there was scarcely any sustained questioning about the precise conditions under which the money was received. In the General Council, Whitfield and a few others complained that the Executive was arrogating too much power to itself, and wanted to know whether sums of money were distributed among its members without the Council's sanction,[5] but members of the Executive simply expressed their dissatisfaction with these questions, condemned them, and then went into a month's adjournment.[6] It was only when the election was over that some sort of general explanation was offered to the membership as a whole. They were then informed that in order to carry out the declared policy of the League—the return of as many 'Advanced Radical Reformers' to the next Parliament as possible—it was necessary to make a large outlay,

> much larger than the funds of the League permitted. In this emergency, Mr Samuel Morley, who has ever been the foremost of our supporters, consented to act as Treasurer of a 'Special Fund', to be

[1] Minutes E.C.R.L., 17 June 1868 on the Sub-Committee's report.
[2] Ibid., 15 July 1868.   [3] Ibid.   [4] Ibid., 31 July 1868.
[5] Minutes of E.C.R.L., 24 June and 13 July 1868.
[6] Ibid., 31 July and 6 August 1868.

raised for the above purpose. The first sum raised was £1,000, to be specially devoted to a preliminary investigation into the condition of such Borough constituencies as had heretofore returned *one or more Conservative Members*.[1]

To this the three members of the Finance Committee, Mottershead, Weston and Worley (all members of the International), added their own ingenuously qualified remarks.

The League, having been called upon from outside its ranks, to aid in returning as good a Liberal Parliament as possible under the circumstances; an extra special fund, was established with that object, and in part placed at our disposal. Under some restrictions it was made available, so far as possible, after meeting other expenses, to assist in defraying expenses of members of the League as candidates for election to the House of Commons.[2]

In fact, Morley was not merely Treasurer of the 'Special Fund'. Between 8 August and 20 November he supplied £1,900. The money was not paid over in a lump sum, but in a series of instalments, which had the effect of keeping the League leaders on a tight leash.[3] The first £1,000 was, indeed, used for the 'preliminary investigation'. It was because many members of the Executive were fully employed on this work that that body adjourned in August, but the reports were sent to Glyn and Stanhope.[4] Far from being used to help League candidates at the election, the money was given on the express understanding that 'not a shilling' would be used to empower anybody to fight against Liberals. This term was interpreted as covering Whigs like Sir Henry Hoare in Chelsea and Lord Henley in Northampton.[5] The whole operation was under the general supervision of Glyn and the other Whips, and they had assigned to

[1] Reform League Report and Balance Sheet for 1 May–30 November 1868.

[2] Ibid.

[3] Reform League Cash Ledger, 'Special Fund', Folios 127–33. (Samuel Morley sent £100 on 8 August and the same amount on 15 and 24 August. The same amount again on 5 and 15 September. He sent £200 on 19 September and the same sum on 1 and 23 October. He sent £300 on 7 November and the final instalment of £500 on 20 November.)

[4] Howell's copy of letter to Stansfeld, 26 August 1868 in small black diary for 1868.

[5] Howell to S. Morley, M.P., 1 December 1868.

Howell and Cremer direct responsibility for work in particularly tricky constituencies which Glyn had designated as 'special'.[1]

The first interest of Gladstone's Whips was simply in the provision of information. The organisation of the new electorate required the development of a new Party apparatus, but this could not be accomplished overnight. Political power still lay, very largely, in the constituencies. It was exercised by local magnates, landlords or great capitalists; cliques of socially influential persons; or, rather exceptionally, by middle-class wire-pullers who had built up a caucus within which some shop-keepers and workmen were organised. It was exceedingly difficult for Glyn to move without offending these local interests, which were bent on protecting their autonomy. To add to his difficulties, the Whigs were suspicious of Gladstone and were not making their customary contributions to the coffers of the Party. Glyn complained endlessly to his chief about their miserly and obstructive conduct.[2] Brand, who had come back to help Glyn in the management of the election, clearly indicated the source of the trouble when he told Gladstone, 'in many quarters there is apprehension that the Church and the rights of property are not safe in your hands!!!'[3] Deprived of the support of the Whigs, Glyn was fearful of upsetting the balance within the Party which Gladstone was interested in maintaining. He saw a danger of putting himself 'too much in the hands of those to whom I do not think I should be under an obligation'.[4] Short of money and faced with the old local party managers who refused to recognise the altered state of affairs, the Liberal Whips lacked the basic data without which they could not help in ensuring the fullest registration of Liberal voters, discreetly push forward, or pull back, prospective candidates, or properly perform several other tasks which were in the interests of the Party.

As a result of his negotiations with Howell and Cremer in July, Glyn was able to arrange for fifteen experienced working-

[1] Howell to J. Stansfeld, M.P., 6 January 1869.

[2] A. F. Thompson, 'Gladstone's Whips and the General Election of 1868', *English Historical Review*, April 1948, p. 193. (Glyn to Gladstone on 31 August and 14 September 1868.)

[3] Ibid., Brand to Gladstone, 4 August 1868, p. 33.

[4] Ibid., Glyn to Gladstone, 12 September 1868, p. 195.

class organisers to visit more than seventy boroughs which had hitherto returned one or more Conservative members and to furnish him with reports on the political situation in each one of them. By this arrangement he got some of the essential work of his office done efficiently and cheaply. Such lines of communication as he already had with the constituencies were not likely to supply him with information about the state of opinion and organisation among the new electorate. In addition to these great advantages, Glyn had removed, at one stroke, a potential source of mischief. He certainly regarded his agreement with Howell as an asset of the highest value to the Liberal Party. He congratulated himself on his achievement and he had every reason for doing so.[1]

II

Throughout August 1868 Howell, Cremer and their agents were visiting the constituencies and drawing up their reports, which were then compiled by Howell and sent on to Glyn and Stanhope.[2] In addition to Howell and Cremer, there were fifteen other men involved, most of them having had considerable industrial or political experience. George Odger and the working-class poet and publicist, J. B. Leno,[3] were extremely well known and had, like Cremer and Howell themselves, been members of the Central Provisional Council of the International Working Men's Association. So had W. C. Worley.[4] The other ten agents were not so prominent, but their reports show that many of them were shrewd and intelligent. They were Charles Bartlett, a bricklayer who had befriended Howell when the latter had first come to London,[5] A. J. Bannister, S. Brighty, J. Coffey, G. Davis, T. Saunders, C. J. Walsher and William Osborne (who is not to be confused with the John Osborne who was a foundation member of the I.W.M.A.), C. Wade, and Thomas

---

[1] Glyn to Gladstone, 10 September 1868. (B.M. Add. MSS, 44, 348 F 157.)

[2] 'Election Reports'—a volume in the Howell collection, hereafter referred to as ER. The volume contains reports on boroughs arranged in alphabetical order and gives the names of the reporters. All future references will take the form 'ER: Andover: Leno and Worley'.

[3] J. B. Leno, *Autobiography*, London 1892.

[4] L. E. Mins (editor), *Founding of the First International*, New York 1937, pp. 43–4.

[5] Howell's Draft Autobiography.

Connolly, a stonemason and a distinguished working-class orator, who became 'dissatisfied with the *arrangements* and *terms*' and, since he swore that he would not abide by them, was not sent out. Connolly chattered about what was going on to Robert Hartwell, the old Chartist and sometime editor of the *Bee-Hive*, and this caused both Stansfeld and Howell some anxiety.[1]

Connolly had no objection in principle to being paid for electioneering. Frederic Harrison told Beesly, 'Connolly—the "Irish Mason"—has been here. He gives rather a dark picture of these people. Potter, whom he sticks to is "honest enough for the purpose". Cremer is a "most false scoundrel" etc. etc. He and Potter have been electioneering at Birkenhead at £10 a head and their expenses!'[2]

Howell instructed his agents 'to get all the information you can as to *who are the candidates*, what their politics, how they stand, either locally or otherwise. What Associations there are in the town, where they meet, and on what nights, the names and addresses of their secretaries etc. etc. In fact, let our reports be full of information.'[3]

These directions were faithfully carried out with the result that Howell's volume of election reports provides a major source of information about British political conditions on the eve of the 1868 election. The reports cover the 65 boroughs which the agents visited[4] and the picture which emerges must be taken

[1] Howell to J. Stansfeld, M.P., 26 August 1868. (Copy in Howell's small black leather diary for 1868.) The minutes of the Executive Committee of the League for 6 August 1868 mentions fifteen men being selected to work under 'Special Fund' arrangements. They include Connolly and William Dell, sometime Treasurer of the I.W.M.A. He did not go out. Bartlett and Wade appear to have taken the places of Connolly and Dell.

[2] F. Harrison to E. S. Beesly, 21 November (1865?) FHC.

[3] Howell to Hales and Brighty, 13 August 1868.

[4] Andover, Bath, Beverley, Birkenhead, Bolton, Boston, Brecon, Bridport, Buckingham, Cambridge, Chichester, Chippenham, Christchurch, Cockermouth, Colchester, Coventry, Cricklade, Devizes, Derby, Dorchester, Durham, Exeter, Grantham, Guildford, Harwich, Haverford West, Helston, Hereford, Huntingdon, Ipswich, Knaresborough, Kidderminster, Leeds, Lichfield, Liverpool, Newcastle-under-Lyme, Ludlow, Macclesfield, Maldon, Marlborough, Monmouthshire, Newark, Newport, Northallerton, Preston, Plymouth, Pontefract, East Retford, Stamford, Southampton, Sunderland, Tewkesbury, Thirsk, Tiverton, Truro, Warwick, Warrington, Weymouth, Westbury, Whitehaven, Whitby, Wigan, Wilton, Winchester, and Woodstock.

into account in any estimate of the problems and possibilities of working-class politics at this time. (Some of the agents visited, but did not send written reports on conditions in other places such as Middlesborough, Hartlepools and Stockton. There were no written reports on the 'special' constituencies which Howell and Cremer handled directly. These constituencies were Blackburn, Rye, Stafford, Stoke, Brighton, Shoreham and Northallerton.)

The reports usually began with an estimate of how far the electorate had been increased as a result of the Reform Act and then went on to describe the progress which was being made by both Parties in getting new voters on to the register. The reporters (they usually travelled in twos or threes) then attempted to identify the centres of power and influence in the Borough; the issues which loomed largest; the political position of such candidates as were already in the field and the main problems confronting the Liberal Party.

From many constituencies it was reported that power was still in the hands of a great landlord or landed family; direct pressure being brought to bear on tenants and trades people. Such was the position, for example, in Andover, Buckingham, Chichester, Dorchester, Huntingdon and Marlborough. Hales and Brighty declared that in Knaresborough nearly all the land in the vicinity

> belongs to two rampant Tories, Sir Charles Sligsby and Mr. J. Collins; and most of the working men hold small allotments under them, and they are getting the screw on as tight as they possibly can. Mr. Collins has already dismissed a boy who was in the Charity School because his father promised to vote for Illingworth.

From Chippenham, Geo. Davis and W. Osborne described the activities of Squire Ash 'who has large estates and a great deal of cottage property in the Borough . . .' From Huntingdon it was reported that the local nobleman had taken revenge for a Liberal victory at the last municipal election. 'Every tenant of the Earl of Sandwich who voted for Liberals was at once turned out, and every voter in the employ of a Tory was immediately discharged.'[1] Mottershead and Bannister described how feeling

---

[1] ER: Huntingdon: Hales and Brighty.

in Whitehaven was running high against the 'Lonsdale' or 'castle influence'. 'This power,' they said, 'sits like an incubus upon the town, controlling its local affairs, returning its M.P., and in the belief of the people, generally paralysing the industry of the port.'

Occasionally the agents sent in accounts of attempted resistance by tenants and workmen to aristocratic control. For instance, in Woodstock efforts were being made to form an agricultural workers' Association capable of defying the Duke of Marlborough whose power in the town was already under challenge. Many a tough quarryman was incensed by the Duke's savage sentences for offences against the game laws, and the spirit of independence seemed to be growing, even among labourers who paid 4*d*. or 5*d*. a week rent for their 'wretched cottages'.[1]

Elsewhere the place of the powerful landlord or landed family was taken by a capitalist or a great company. In Beverley, the Tory Member exercised control through a substantial interest which he held in the local iron works.[2] At Harwich, the Tory was Vice-President of the Great Eastern Railway Company, and was able to exercise a large amount of patronage.[3] From Macclesfield it was reported that 'the Brocklehursts, who have furnished one member since 1832, are the greatest employers of labour in the Town, and are in possession of the Whig influence'. The Tories were capable of making a fight of it, because their candidate had bought a mill and put it to work and there were three other manufacturing Tories who expected their employees to vote that way.[4] A better instance of a single, overriding capitalist interest was supplied by Birkenhead—'an utterly hopeless case'.

> The political feeling of this Borough is Liberal, but such a pressure is put on all those employed on Laird's works and shipyard, and other works of a similar nature, that the Liberal feeling is stultified and the Tories have it all their own way. It is the general opinion of the working and middle-class leaders that there is no

[1] ER: Woodstock: Walsher and Bartlett.
[2] ER: Beverley: Sanders and Wade.
[3] ER: Harwich: Davis.
[4] ER: Macclesfield: Mottershead and Bannister.

hope for Liberalism in this Borough, until the death of Mr. Laird or the introduction of the *Ballot*.[1]

The shipping interest was alleged to exert a comparable influence in Southampton. The local secretary of the Reform League told Howell's agents that the P. & O. Steamship Company would 'put the screw' on all its hands in favour of the Conservatives.[2] In Liverpool the shipping interest re-enforced the power which the Earl of Derby held over persons whose leases were about to expire. 'The Secretaries of the principal trades are Liberal—even Radical—but dare not act in consequence of the complex character of their respective trades.'[3]

In some constituencies the controlling interest still lay, in whole or in part, with traditional corporate interests, the Cathedral and the University. In Cambridge, the University aided the Tory party through its hold on college servants and its large custom with the shop keepers.[4] But it was in such constituencies as these that the old patterns of power and influence were most likely to be disturbed by the Reform Act; the University could not save the Tory at Cambridge. Similarly, the Reform Act created the conditions for an assault on the traditions of what might be described as 'compact Boroughs'— Boroughs in which there was a traditional arrangement between the Whigs and the Tories. Truro[5] and Weymouth[6] were compact boroughs, while in Ipswich 'there seemed to be an understanding that, though they always like a contest, perhaps for the pleasure of bleeding the candidates, yet, still, one and one are to be returned'.[7] Akin to the 'compact boroughs' were nomination boroughs such as Brecon, which was 'alternatively provided for by Lord Camden, Liberal, and Lord Tredegar, Tory'.[8] In some small boroughs of this kind the traditional pattern was not upset by the Reform Act. In Stamford, where there was little manufacture and where the tradespeople were in

[1] ER: Birkenhead: Sanders, Wade and Bartlett.
[2] ER: Southampton: Worley and Leno.
[3] ER: Liverpool: Sanders, Wade and Bartlett.
[4] ER: Cambridge: Osborne and Davis.
[5] ER: Truro: Odger and Coffey.
[6] ER: Weymouth: Bartlett and Walsher.
[7] ER: Ipswich: Davis and Osborne.
[8] ER: Brecon: Leno and Worley.

consequence dependent upon the local gentry, it was still as impossible to get a contest as it had been when the constituency was in the pocket of the Marquis of Exeter. All the lawyers in the place received £10 10s. a year as a retaining fee from the nominee M.P.[1]

As against those boroughs in which the Reform Act without the ballot had made little difference, there were many others in which its impact was considerable. If there were still constituencies in which the Castle and the Cathedral, the great landowner and the large employer, concentrated power in their own hands, there were others in which power was more diversified and in which the pattern of conflicting interests and influences was far more complex and subtle. Places like Bridport, where the Liberal was supported by the Gundry family; merchants, manufacturers and lawyers who all exercised considerable influence from the number of hands they employed, but who also enjoyed 'outside' support conferred by a dissenting minister; a coal merchant; the principal banker; a flax and twine merchant and the officials of the Working Men's Institute. The Tories in Bridport relied upon the support of an opposing team of merchants and manufacturers.[2] In Guildford, Howell's agents declared that the principal wire-pullers on the Tory side were a brewer, a banker and a gentleman farmer. The Liberals were led by solicitors, a chemist, an ironmonger and an upholsterer.[3] In Cockermouth, the Tory power based on traditional social and economic influence was confronted by a newly-created Liberal organisation. On the one side, 'the Wyndham family holding lands and Cockermouth Castle in the centre of the Town—often keeping great revel in it. Giving tradesmen large orders for goods and half-yearly invitations to dine at the Castle.' On the other, a Committee composed of manufacturers, traders and workmen which was divided into eleven district sub-committees within each of which a hundred electors were organised.[4]

At this level it may well have been the case that the reports merely confirmed information which was already in the hands

[1] ER: Stamford: Hales and Brighty.
[2] ER: Bridport: Unsigned (Bartlett?).
[3] ER: Guildford: Leno and Worley.
[4] ER: Cockermouth: Mottershead and Bannister.

of the Whips. Stanhope told Howell that he tested several of the reports and that they 'harmonised' with his own knowledge of the political condition of several constituencies.[1] No doubt they helped to bring the Whips up to date. It may have been of real practical value to know that in Andover 'the old solicitor is dead',[2] while in Cricklade they should have nothing to do with Mr. F. Rowland Young, once a Chartist, 'now a Unitarian, who used all his influence at the last election on behalf of the Tory'.[3] However, news of individual wire-pullers was probably of less interest and importance than the light which was thrown on the state of working-class morale, opinion and organisation. This was the kind of information which Howell's agents were particularly well qualified to supply.

The over-all picture was not encouraging. In addition to those constituencies in which the new electors were subject to control through intimidation or patronage, there were one or two others in which they were said to be completely demoralised politically and ready to sell their votes to the highest bidder. Guildford provided an extreme example:

> The political morality of this town is, to say the least, extremely discouraging; not one but nearly all with whom we came in contact, estimate the value of the vote by what it will fetch in the market, and openly proclaim (with the approval of all present saving myself) that their votes would go to the highest bidder— that candidates for election were guided by no principle, and hence no discredit attached itself to those who traded on their desire for personal advancement.[4]

The Tories were alleged to be debauching the electorate in their Public Houses; the Liberals had only three Public Houses in the entire Borough.

In Guildford, Trade Unionism was effectively confined to the bricklayers and the tailors. This was fairly representative of the smaller boroughs. Either there were no Trade Unions at all, as was the case in Thirsk or Christchurch; or Unionism was confined to the carpenters, engineers and tailors, which was the

[1] Howell to J. Stansfeld, M.P., 26 August 1868. (Copy in Howell's small black leather diary for 1868.)
[2] ER: Andover: Leno and Worley.
[3] ER: Cricklade: Davis and Osborne.
[4] ER: Guildford: Leno and Worley.

position in such places as Bath, Beverley and Hereford. There were, however, a number of significant constituencies in which unions were well established and looked capable of wielding considerable influence. There were powerful Union branches in Leeds,[1] and in Preston a large Trades Council was in the habit of transforming itself into 'The Working Men's Political Association' whenever it wanted to engage in politics.[2] From Derby, Hales and Brighty reported that there were twenty-two Trades Societies and that eight of them came together in the Trades Council. Hales' own Union, the elastic web weavers, organised three hundred members, the A.S.E. had two hundred and seventy-five engineers and the Steam Engine Makers a further forty-five. In Derby, even some of the labourers were organised.[3]

In Sunderland, there were said to be as many as a thousand men in a General Labourers' Union, while two thousand more were enrolled among the iron ship builders, boiler makers and smiths. The movement was headed by the Shipwrights Society which had one thousand six hundred members.[4] The position in Wigan confirmed the impression that Unionism was rather stronger among the labourers than has been generally supposed, for in that Borough there were, in addition to the powerful miners' lodges, three hundred labourers organised in their own Union.[5]

Yet even where a borough did happen to be a stronghold of working-class organisation, there is little indication that workmen were making themselves felt, or that they were determined to push their own distinctive demands forward as issues in the approaching election. Howell and Cremer, who visited Carlisle, found that the workers there were mainly preoccupied with the Labour Laws.[6] But, in general, Marx was quite right in saying that 'the Irish question dominates'.[7] The indignation of the parsons over Gladstone's threat to the Irish Church loomed far

---

[1] ER: Leeds: Hales and Brighty.
[2] ER: Preston: Sanders, Wade and Bartlett.
[3] ER: Derby: Hales and Brighty.
[4] ER: Sunderland: Mottershead and Bannister.
[5] ER: Wigan: Sanders and Wade.
[6] Howell's notes of his trips to the factory districts. (Small black leather diary for 1868.)
[7] Marx to Kugelmann, 6 April 1868. (*Letters to Kugelmann*, London 1936, p. 67.)

larger than the anger of the Trade Unionists over the treatment which they received in the courts. When any reference was made to working-class opinion, in the reports which Howell's agents submitted, it was more likely to turn on feeling about the Permissive Bill[1] than on the prospects for new Labour legislation.

However, the reports did not give Glyn grounds for indulging in unrestrained rejoicing. If workmen showed little sign of exerting independent pressure, they were by no means as wholeheartedly behind Mr. Gladstone as the leaders of the Reform League or, for that matter, the printing workers of Cambridge where, in one establishment, 77 men out of 80 declared themselves to be Liberals.[2] From the factory districts and the larger Boroughs came distressing reports of Tory sympathies among workmen. In Coventry, where the Reform League had 700 members, the depressed state of the silk trade was explained by reference to the French Commercial Treaty, and the Conservative Workingmen's Association made five hundred recruits.[3] The French Treaty was also an issue with the weavers in Macclesfield, men who 'never had any strong love for the Manchester School'. Here the weavers' Secretary was a Liberal, but was uncertain about the membership as a whole. Howell's agents reported that these weavers were very independent and could not be intimidated by the employers.[4]

In Kidderminster, the power loom for carpet weaving had reduced the population by 25% over the past thirty years. These looms were now being brought back to the Borough and the emigrants were returning home after being through the 'political school of the North'. This did not preclude the Tory working man. 'The form in which the Conservative working man is developed in Kidderminster is that of Benefit Societies, organised, patronised and liberally assisted by the swell Conservatives.'[5] This device commended itself to Howell's agents: '*We* can found a great politico-provident society, self-supporting, with head-quarters in London, and ramifications all over

[1] The Permissive Bill was designed to permit a majority of ratepayers to impose prohibition on a district.
[2] ER: Cambridge: Osborne and Davis.
[3] ER: Coventry: Hales and Brighty.
[4] ER: Macclesfield: Mottershead and Bannister.
[5] ER: Kidderminster: Davis and Osborne.

the provinces.'[1] The unsuspected political associations of Friendly and Benefit Societies appeared elsewhere. In one Borough all the Oddfellows were said to be Tories, while the Foresters were all Liberals.[2]

From Preston there was a call for Odger or Cremer to come down and strengthen the trades. There were indications that some of them 'might go Tory'.[3] In Sunderland, the 'advanced' Liberal's advocacy of arbitration made the shipwrights 'fretful and fearful'. They had already had some experience of employers who went to arbitration and abided by its rules only when it suited them.[4]

Although the main business in August was to gather information, Howell's agents frequently addressed meetings and helped to establish local Liberal Electoral Committees. In Bolton, Sanders and Wade held a general meeting of trades delegates and formed a 'Liberal Trades Political Association'. They also founded a working men's committee in Warrington. Mottershead and Bannister established a branch of the Reform League in Cockermouth, but in other Boroughs branches of the League were transformed into Liberal Registration or Electoral Associations.[5] In Newcastle-under-Lyme, Hales and Brighty set up a new Liberal Committee with the object of taking matters out of the hands of a few lawyers—it was still customary to find solicitors playing an important part in the management of elections. However, the new committee was dominated by tradesmen and the workers had little influence. In many places workmen were already organised, while in others, such as Beverley, it was thought to be impossible to do anything with them, 'so few of them having Political Honesty'.[6]

Apart from setting up new organisations, Howell's agents did their best to develop understanding and active collaboration between the Whig cliques and the old electors on the one hand, and the new men of the lower middle and working classes on the other. Glyn explained to Gladstone that this was one of his

[1] ER: Kidderminster: Davis and Osborne.
[2] ER: Colchester: Davis.
[3] ER: Preston: Sanders, Wade and Bartlett.
[4] ER: Sunderland: Mottershead and Bannister.
[5] ER: Warwick: Hales and Brighty. Also ER: Whitby: Mottershead and Bannister.
[6] ER: Beverley: Sanders and Wade.

biggest problems. 'The great difficulty,' he said, 'is that the old local party managers do not realise the altered state of matters & if they do they are extremely slow in coalescing with the new men.' [1] After the reports had been submitted to the Whips, Howell laid particular stress on this question:

> In *most* cases our opinion is that the only thing to be done is to lay the foundation for a thorough organisation of the Liberal Party in which organisation the working men shall be consulted and called into active political life.
>
> One great cause of failure in the past has been ignoring the working-class voter. This must not now be. They are a power and must be consulted and subjected to discipline. We find no difficulty with them when treated fairly. [2]

In public, one of the most distinguished leaders of the League had said:

> We must look to our organisation at the approaching general election. I sincerely trust that the American caucus system will be shortly introduced into this country; it is, beyond doubt, the most equitable and most efficient system yet devised. It would give the working classes a commanding influence they can never otherwise possess . . . No constituency ought to be divided in the Liberal interest. [3]

In practice, Howell's agents found that, even if the several elements within the Party were united behind a candidate, they often met separately. In Whitby, Mottershead and Bannister found that this was the case. Although the middle-class men were well intentioned, they were 'scarcely ought but a fossilised lot of old Whigs . . . seeming to think that they can carry the election by the same machinery they could use in contesting for the Parish Beadle'. They visited both sides and tried to impress upon them the need for closer unity. [4]

Again in Bath and in Derby the Liberal electors were agreed on their candidates, but were organised separately in their own Associations. In the former place closer collaboration was

---

[1] Glyn to Gladstone, 8 October 1868. B.M. Add. MSS: 44347 f. 190.

[2] Howell to J. Stansfeld, M.P., 26 August 1868. (Copy in small black leather diary for 1868.)

[3] J. Guedalla, *The Political Situation*, London, 1868, p. 32.

[4] ER: Whitby: Mottershead and Bannister.

ensured by an arrangement whereby representatives of the two Associations came together in a special electoral committee.[1]

If the question of unity within the 'Liberal camp' was important in constituencies in which there was a straight fight with a Tory, it took on an added significance in double member constituencies, in which there might be a compact either to return one Liberal and one Whig, or even one Whig and one Tory. Glyn made it a general rule not to interfere in fights between Liberals unless a Tory appeared.[2] If he interfered at this stage, it was with the greatest caution. There was a deep and widespread prejudice against taking the control of elections out of local hands and establishing a centre for 'Liberal Candidate Manufacturing'.[3] Whenever he did interfere, Glyn had to avoid exposing himself to the charge that he was pushing Gladstonians against the Whig interest. A. J. Mundella who was contesting Sheffield against the Whig, Roebuck, explained to Howell: 'I have written to Parliament Street. The fact is that they (the Whips) are frightened out of their wits lest R. should get in; and they dare not appear to do anything to help me.' Under these circumstances Mundella wanted Howell to send his agents up to Sheffield and prevent the workmen falling for the 'debauching influences'.[4] This was at the end of August and Howell, after he had managed to negotiate the second major instalment of the 'Special Fund', duly obliged. But even while the agents were out on their 'preliminary investigation' they were actively concerned about the claims of rival candidates, since this was the issue around which the most serious divisions in the 'Liberal' ranks generally centred. They sometimes suggested that a particular Liberal should be induced to withdraw. For example, in Maldon they reported that the Whigs had called a meeting of the old Liberal electors and chosen a candidate. This arrogant procedure was also followed in other places, but in Maldon it produced an immediate reaction. A self-made man, a manufacturer of agricultural machinery, named Bethall, resented this dictation and decided to stand himself. He employed hundreds of men and he set to work organising them on

[1] ER: Bath: Davis and Osborne.
[2] Glyn to Gladstone, 28 October 1868, B.M. Add. MSS. 44347 f. 220.
[3] The *Halifax Guardian*, 24 October 1868.
[4] A. J. Mundella to George Howell, 29 August 1868. (H.C.B.I.)

his own behalf. Howell's agents suggested that Glyn should be asked to get Bethall a straight fight with the Tory and this appears to have been done.[1]

Things worked out differently in Kidderminster where the division was between 'the excellent Bristow', who had been nominated by the local branch of the League, and Mr. Lea, 'a *promising* Liberal, but with nebulous ideas ... He is the nominee of the manufacturers and the old Whig party, and seems only to have been brought forward out of jealousy of the working class.'[2] Mr. Lea was duly elected. At Kidderminster, explained Howell: 'I was most careful as reports in the papers will show.'[3] And a few days later to Samuel Morley he modestly stated: 'We have done something to secure the withdrawal of Mr. Bristowe from Kidderminster. The Liberal is now safe.'[4] However, this is to anticipate work which was done after August.

From Hereford and Sunderland there were reports of probable Tory victories as a consequence of a split vote among the Liberals. In Sunderland the workers were divided in their allegiance between Gouxley, a ship-owner and merchant, who aspired to 'getting Mrs. G. presented at Court', and the Whig, Thompson, who was a barrister and coal proprietor.[5] The absence of a Tory allowed the matter to be fought out without interference. A similar situation was found in Newark where the Whigs supported Dennison, an opponent of the Ballot, and the Radicals followed Handley, a strict Gladstonian Liberal. Hales and Brighty remarked that 'it would be dangerous to interfere'.[6]

In a number of instances Howell's agents drew attention to openings which existed for a 'good Liberal Candidate'. Only Mottershead and Bannister suggested that the Reform League as such should supply a vacancy, and their choice fell upon the unlikely Borough of Whitehaven. From Cricklade it was reported that the new men wanted a candidate and would

---

[1] ER: Maldon: Davis and Osborne.
[2] ER: Kidderminster: Davis and Osborne.
[3] Howell to H. S. Stanhope, M.P., 29 October 1868.
[4] Howell to S. Morley, 4 November 1868.
[5] ER: Sunderland: Mottershead and Bannister.
[6] ER: Newark: Hales and Brighty.

'prefer a moderate one, and if possible a local man'.[1] A good, moderate, Liberal candidate was required in Dorchester; while in Warwick there was room for 'an advanced Liberal of good position'.[2]

From his side, Howell was trying to place candidates. During August he helped to get one of Goldwin Smith's friends, Dr. Sandwith, adopted for Marylebone.[3] He sent a private and confidential letter to the land reformer and journalist, A. A. Walton, enquiring: 'Is there an opening for a good candidate in Brecon? If so, will Mr. Passmore Edwards have a chance?'[4] He also sounded out the position at Nottingham.[5]

It is not surprising that the Liberal Whips were delighted with the 'election reports', not only for the information which they provided, but for the evidence of work done. The general spirit of these working-class organisers was obviously excellent. Glyn told Gladstone: 'I should like to show you some of the reports made by the working men. They are so sound and so sensible & in most places their great object is to unite the two sections of the party *for you* & not to put up their own or any extreme men.'

This was a fair judgement on the quality of the reports as a whole. One can imagine the sort of passages which Glyn had in mind. For example, when Odger and Coffey were touring the West Country they reported that

we had several interviews with that thorough-going old Radical, Mr. Rowcliffe. He regrets that a member of the League did not come forward upon the principles of the League. [This was in Tiverton where the Liberal candidates were Geo. Denman and Heathcote Amory.] But after some conversation he accepted our opinion, that as there are two Liberals before the constituency having the confidence of the majority of the voters, it would be extremely undesirable for the Radicals to entertain any doubts which would be calculated to weaken Liberal interest in the Borough; more especially as the State Church in Ireland would form the question upon which the strength of the two parties is to be tested.[6]

[1] ER: Whitehaven: Mottershead and Bannister.
[2] ER: Warwick: Hales and Brighty.
[3] Howell to Dr. Sandwith, 6 August and 8 August 1868.
[4] Howell to Walton, 7 August 1868.
[5] Howell to W. Smith, 7 August 1868.
[6] Glyn to Gladstone, 9 September 1868. B.M. Add. MSS: 44347 f. 154.

Odger and Coffey spoke to the same effect in Exeter, where the local branch of the Reform League resented its exclusion from the selection of the Liberal candidates.[1]

However, there were much more striking instances than these of the uncritical and unwavering loyalty which some of Howell's agents showed towards Mr. Gladstone and his supporters. A good example is provided by the report on Wigan:

> The Liberal Candidates for this Borough are Messrs. Wood and Lancaster. The first-named gentleman being the sitting member. His election is sure, but as the election of the second gentleman depends largely on the miners, and they having a serious trade dispute with him, his success is not so certain.
>
> Mr. Lancaster is chairman, and a large shareholder, in the Wigan Coal and Iron Company. The dispute arises out of the difference between weighing and measuring coal; the men demanding weight as more just than measure. He is also disliked for tyrannical strictness to the hands, and for calling upon the police to assist him in a recent trade difficulty. He is nevertheless a Liberal in politics, will go for the ballot, security to Trades Union Funds, and will give his support to Mr. Gladstone. If the miners could be persuaded to support him, it is thought that he would use his influence with the company to give or compromise [*sic*] the demands of the men. The miners have 3,000 votes, but some of these are commanded by the Conservatives who have coal and iron works, but their influence is not great.[2]

Subsequently, Howell wrote a letter headed '*Private*' to Mr. Leigh Ellis, Esq., Liberal Committee Rooms, Wigan. It ran:

> We are taking very important action in reference to Trades Societies, but we must deal with each Boro' separately and differently.
>
> We are managing the unions in Blackburn, Bristol, Preston and a great many of the large towns at this moment and will, if you desire it, send down a man at once to do something in Wigan. At Sheffield our delegates have done what the local agents could not do viz., unite the numerous trades into one committee for electoral purposes.
>
> The enclosed card will indicate the way in which we do our work. But in all instances we take independent action, so as not to

---

[1] ER: Tiverton: Odger and Coffey.
[2] ER: Wigan: Sanders and Wade.

commit the candidates in any way. They pay us by giving a donation to our special Fund, Mr. Morley Treasurer.[1]

A day or so later Howell was making enquiries as to 'who is the general sec. of the Miners Union?'[2]

There was a similar case involving some railway workers in Swindon. Howell invited Glyn to bring some pressure to bear on the company directors while he was 'setting things all right with the railway men'.[3]

Thus, the leaders of the Reform League and their agents paid no heed to Professor Beesly when he warned them to be content with nothing but the clearest of pledges on Trade Union questions and added:

> Employers who look to nothing but money-making, or who have made themselves conspicuous by attempts to crush Unions, ought to be opposed with the greatest determination. They are the most dangerous enemies of Labour. No profession of Radicalism, not even to the extent of manhood suffrage and the ballot, ought to gain them a moments hearing.[4]

III

In the middle of September Howell wrote to James Stansfeld: 'I understand that Mr. Glyn is much pleased with our reports; Mr. Stanhope has also spoken highly of them. We shall be glad if Mr. Glyn and yourself will write to Mr. Morley on this subject if you feel satisfied with our preliminary work.'[5]

Most of the first £1,000 in the 'Special Fund' had been spent. Howell was eager to go on; to enlarge the number of his agents in the field and to use his contacts with national Trade Union secretaries to gain access to local lodges.[6] As he told Stansfeld: 'We are preparing for the next part of our contract—work.'[7] But 'work' required a steady flow of cash. The agents were paid

---

[1] Howell to Ellis, 12 October 1868.

[2] Howell to John Holmes, 14 October 1868.

[3] Howell to G. G. Glyn, M.P., 30 September 1868.

[4] Beesly, E. S. 'The General Election of 1869'.

[5] Howell to James Stansfeld, M.P., 18 September 1868.

[6] Howell to D. Guile, 23 September 1868, and on 24 September letters to Allan, Applegarth, Coulson and the secretary of the cordwainers.

[7] Howell to J. Stansfeld, M.P., 22 September 1868.

10s. per day for their time; a further 10s. per day for their expenses; and on top of this they were given their railway fares.[1] Morley, who had paid £630[2] towards the first £1,000, thought that the time had come for others to take a greater share of the burden. He drafted an appeal which was submitted to Stanhope. It was intended to be 'strictly private' and to be sent only to 'safe' friends, 'about 25 or 30 in number'. It was not to be printed or lithographed.[3] Despite these precautions, Stansfeld did not favour this proposal.[4] It was not consistent with the whole transaction being as secret as possible. Morley would just have to make the best of it and Howell would have to keep him happy with a stream of flattering notes.

Throughout September and October, Howell kept reminding Morley that 'the entire Liberal Party will owe you a debt of gratitude for the great aid you have rendered them in this election'.[5] At the same time he stressed the amount of useful work that still might be done. Stansfeld

> told Cremer and myself when we came together to see you that we *must go on* and some arrangement would have to be made with you.
>
> I have applications *today* for men to go to Sheffield, Whitehaven, Cockermouth, Droitwich, Worcester and many other places. We have men out now involving a large outlay and I feel therefore rather anxious. We told Mr. Stansfeld that it would require £2,000 and I think it will, but it will not exceed that. I will write to a few men to send you cash towards the amount.[6]

This was written four days after Morley had sent Howell a cheque for £200[7] and only a week elapsed until Howell was begging for more. 'We have gone on increasing expenses up to date and have already exceeded the amount received by nearly £200. This morning I have received a letter from H. Scudmore Stanhope . . . wanting us to deal with no less than 14

[1] E.C.R.L. Minutes of 'Special Meeting', 10 August 1868.
[2] Howell to James Stansfeld, 6 January 1869.
[3] Howell to J. Stansfeld, 26 September 1868.
[4] Howell's letters to S. Morley and J. Stansfeld, 2 October 1868.
[5] Howell to S. Morley, 30 September 1868.
[6] Howell to S. Morley, 26 October 1868.
[7] Howell to Morley, 22 October 1868.

Boroughs.'[1] This brought £300 from Morley and a hefty contribution came in from the Kells at Bradford.[2] Nevertheless, right up until the end of the election Morley got a stream of requests for money.

> I am requested to write to you for a further advance. We now think, as the election will take place earlier than some of us thought, that about another five hundred pounds will complete the entire scheme. Mr. Stansfeld, at our last meeting, considered the repayment to you quite safe.
>
> It was at first thought that £5,000 would be required, but the entire amount up to now will be but £1,400.[3]

Morley paid up once more. His cheque for £500 made up the total, already mentioned, of £1,900 on account of the 'Special Fund'.

Armed with these fresh supplies, Howell increased his staff of workers who were hurrying from one part of the country to another establishing committees, addressing meetings, giving advice to the local unions and generally employing themselves as the Liberal Candidates in the boroughs thought best. Howard Evans, Blackburn, Hinton, Young, Mead and Nicolson joined the original fifteen agents.[4] The accounts of the special fund show that veterans such as Lloyd Jones, Ernest Jones and Holyoake, 'the thin-voiced, intrusive, consequential Holyoake' as Marx called him,[5] also received small amounts for expenses.

If these men were not fully employed in boroughs to which they were directed as a result of instructions from Glyn or Stanhope, Howell would write to a Liberal candidate and offer his assistance. This sometimes gave rise to misunderstandings. William Rathbone at Liverpool, for example, suspected that there must be political conditions attached to offers of working-class support. In a revealing letter Howell sought to reassure him. 'You are quite mistaken as to the import of my letter. You are not supposed to *endorse anything*, only *tell me how to serve you* . . . in no case would you be mixed up with our movement either

---

[1] Howell to S. Morley, 31 October 1868.
[2] Howell to Kell and Co., Bradford, 4 November 1868.
[3] Howell to S. Morley, 9 November 1868.
[4] Cash Ledger, Special Fund Folios 127–33, Ref. 4058.
[5] Marx to Engels, 27 July 1866.

in Liverpool or here.'[1] While Lloyd Jones, who would only work for candidates who were sound on the Labour Question, went to Blackburn;[2] while such men as Hales and Mottershead were helping Dronfield and the Sheffield workers to defeat Roebuck[3] (there cannot have been a politically conscious worker in the country who would not have preferred Mundella, for all his brass-voiced cunning, to Roebuck); Howell and Cremer were devoting more and more of their own time to dealing with Glyn's 'special' constituencies. Wherever there was a really 'delicate' situation they were on hand to deal with it directly.

When Samuelson, whose son Howell had helped to place in Cheltenham, started arousing dissatisfaction among Radicals and Trade Unionists in his own constituency of Banbury, the Reform League's Secretary did his best to silence the critics.

Mr. Samuelson is not quite up to our mark [he confessed] but he is considered as a sound Liberal, even more so than the one you name. He is sound on Education, and advanced on the subject of capital and labour and generally votes right in the *House*. He has aided us in the agitation for reform, although not going in for our programme. If we advised any contest, the Liberal Party would say that we were dividing the Liberal interest and [he added] we should lose friends.[4]

Howell got Robert Applegarth, Secretary of the Amalgamated Society of Carpenters and Joiners, to go down to Banbury and try to ease matters. But he had to explain to Samuelson that he had the reputation of being opposed to Trades Unions.[5] Although he sent £5, the Honourable Member for Banbury resented being censured. Howell thanked him for the money and tried to smooth the path with a remark which was characteristically at once 'Liberal' and Olympian: 'Trades Unionists, like Employers, are not over wise, they want everything their own way. But some of us must step between them

[1] Howell to W. Rathbone, M.P., 27 October 1868.
[2] Lloyd Junes to Howell, 26 October 1868 and Howell to Mottershead, 27 October 1868.
[3] Howell to A. J. Mundella, 26 October 1868 and to Hales and Brighty on 2 and 7 October, and on 10 November 1868.
[4] Howell to J. Butcher, Esq., of Banbury, 22 September 1868. (Headed 'private'.)
[5] Howell to B. Samuelson, M.P., 1 October 1868.

and folly and try and test all questions by reason and common sense.'[1]

The possibilities of a serious split in Banbury were probably not very great. Howell devoted his best efforts to more serious cases. He told Stanhope: 'We are trying all in our power to close up the Liberal ranks in several places and I think we shall have some success.'[2] Five days earlier Glyn had cancelled a visit to Gladstone, explaining:

> I had a private intimation late last night, that I must see Beales *today* upon some matters of very pressing and immediate importance which admit of no delay & which I dare not depute to my Secretary. I have done it, & though it has cost me my little holiday I feel that good will come of it. Nothing can be more striking than the moderation of these men & their loyalty in *your* cause *but* direct communication with them is a very delicate matter—2 or 3 places will I hope be put right now and I have the comfort of feeling that I have not lost my pleasant visit to you for nothing.

To this he added a note:

> Please let no one know of my visit to Beales.[3]

Despite the heavy air of mystery surrounding all Glyn's references to his work with the League, it is not difficult to conjecture where the 'two or three places' were, or the methods which were employed to—in Howell's phrase—'close up the Liberal ranks'. From other letters in the Gladstone and Howell collections it seems likely that the three constituencies involved at this stage were Kidderminster, Brighton and Stoke.

Reference has already been made to the position in Kidderminster. Howell might tell provincial officers of the League: 'Your men are our men. We shall never be disloyal to our branches';[4] but within a week he was able to tell Morley that he had helped to dispose of 'the excellent Bristowe', the choice of the Kidderminster Reform League.[5]

Brighton was one of Glyn's 'special' constituencies. It was a double-member one and Henry Fawcett sat as the junior representative. Despite his devotion to many of the teachings of the

---

[1] Howell to B. Samuelson, M.P., 7 October 1868.
[2] Howell to H. S. Stanhope, M.P., 29 October 1868.
[3] Glyn to Gladstone, 24 October 1868. B.M. Add. MSS. 44347 f. 212.
[4] Howell to R. White of York, 24 September 1868.
[5] See p. 34.

Manchester School, Fawcett had some qualities that might well commend him to working-class electors. Professor Beesly had gone out of his way to recommend him when he first came forward for Brighton in 1864.[1] Odger declared that no man had done more than he had to help amend the Master and Servant Acts.[2] John Stuart Mill pointed out that he was a friend of co-operation, an advocate of the claims of the agricultural labourer, and was in favour of compulsory education and the payment of election expenses out of the rates.[3]

The complication at Brighton arose from the fact that William Conningham, who had once been one of the two representatives, decided to come forward as a candidate. Unlike Fawcett, Conningham had been closely identified with the Reform League and was one of its Vice-Presidents. Howell tried, without success, to find him a seat elsewhere. There was a real danger that the working-class vote would be split, for Fawcett was already running in harness with the senior member, James White. Because he was well known in the town and in the League, Conningham had considerable working-class support. He even managed, and it was a brilliant stroke, to get Col. Dickson to turn up at one of his opponent's meetings and declare it a duty to 'support those who supported the Reform League'. Dickson said he was for Fawcett and Conningham. 'Mr. White looked so comfortable that he was sure that he could take care of himself.'[4] Meanwhile, a Tory who saw an opportunity of profiting from these divisions had arrived on the scene.

Doubtless Howell himself preferred Fawcett to Conningham and would not follow Dickson in regarding the choice before the Brighton electors in any other light. The Whips always were likely to favour the incumbents except in such unusual circumstances as those at Sheffield. Consequently, Howell wrote to the Secretary of the Brighton branch of the Reform League in favour of Fawcett: 'The working men of England cannot afford to lose the services of one of their best and most uncompromising champions . . .'[5] The branch subsequently organised a large

[1] E. S. Beesly, 'The Brighton Elections', *Bee-Hive*, 13 February 1864.
[2] *Brighton Guardian*, 18 November 1868.
[3] Ibid., 11 November 1868.
[4] *Brighton Guardian*, 11 November 1868.
[5] Howell to J. Thompson, 28 October 1868.

meeting in favour of Fawcett at which Odger was the principal speaker.[1] Odger was one of the favourite targets of the more vulgar middle-class newspapers. 'He has not derived any benefit from the repeal of the duty on soap,' said the *Brecon County Times* (31 October 1868). The *Pall Mall Gazette* commented that 'his father was a miner and his mother was mad'. It is interesting to note that Fawcett went out of his way to pay a tribute to Odger and to protest that 'a bitter personal attack may possibly frustrate all hope of obtaining that united action that all true Liberals ought to desire'.[2] Conningham finished at the bottom of the poll and resigned from the Reform League.[3]

Like Brighton, Stoke was on Glyn's list of 'special' constituencies, and it probably figured in his conversation with Beales. If the affair at Brighton caused unpleasantness, the arrival of Robert Hartwell at Stoke in mid-October was much more serious politically. Hartwell said that he 'came there to ask them to support an interest which he regarded as being superior to either Liberal, Conservative or any Party interest; he came to ask them to support the interests of Labour'.[4] His programme included distinctively working-class demands, and he placed a considerable emphasis upon them. He could present himself, as Conningham could not, as an authentic working-class leader. There was no Tory in the field, and one of the adopted Liberals, Rodin, was an ironmaster who had been reproached with trying to crush Unionism. Thus, Stoke raised issues of principle which were absent in Brighton. Glyn told Gladstone: 'I am doing all I can to get Hartwell away from Stoke.'[5] However, an account of his efforts and of the attitude of Howell towards Hartwell's candidature is best reserved for discussion in the last part of this chapter.

Wherever a Trade Unionist, or a Reformer, or someone with a recognisable claim to the confidence of working-class electors came forward, he found he had to enter the lists against the Whig cliques; that these cliques had frequently come to an arrangement with the middle-class Radicals to divide the repre-

[1] *Brighton Guardian*, 18 November 1868.
[2] Ibid., 30 October 1868, reprinting a letter from the *Daily News*.
[3] Howell to W. Conningham, 21 November 1868.
[4] The *Staffordshire Sentinel*, 17 October 1868.
[5] Glyn to Gladstone, 3 November 1868. B.M. Add. MSS. 44347 f. 226.

sentation of the Borough between them, and that he was faced with the choice of withdrawing or 'dividing the Liberal interest'. There was never any money forthcoming from the Reform League to support such men. There was not even any encouragement, but rather the reverse. There were public letters from Beales and private letters from Howell which had the effect of disowning and undermining them. There were private visits to constituencies by Howell and Cremer which gave rise to rumours of intrigue and charges of betrayal.

When Alexander Macdonald, the miners' leader, came out as a candidate for Kilmarnock, he was supported by Professor Beesly. Beesly observed that the sitting member, the Whig, Bouverie, belonged to a class 'who only want to keep things as they are—workmen, if they know their own interests, want to make almost everything different from what it is ...' He told Macdonald, 'You are one of the few representatives of Unionism I know who would be able to fight the battle with effect in such an Assembly as the House of Commons.' He concluded with the remark, 'Those who begin do a great thing and deserve to be remembered.'[1]

Howell took no interest in the Scottish elections—except in Kilmarnock. A few days before Macdonald's candidature was announced he wrote to a correspondent there informing him that Edwin Chadwick intended to stand for that constituency. 'If he does, do aid him all you can; at any rate do not give your pledges too early for any one else.'[2] One can only conjecture as to whether Howell knew at the time of writing that the foremost leader of the British miners was about to enter the field. At any rate, Macdonald found himself embarrassed by discussions about the attitude of the Reform League towards the election[3] and this—combined with a shortage of money—forced his retirement. Chadwick had declared himself delighted with the very advanced programme of the workmen of Edinburgh and Leith, and Macdonald, in retiring, spoke in his favour.[4] However, the electors apparently preferred the persecutor of Ernest

[1] E. S. Beesly to A. Macdonald, 7 September 1868. *Kilmarnock Standard*, 12 September 1868.
[2] Howell to McEwen, 24 August 1868.
[3] *Kilmarnock Advertiser*, 31 October 1868.
[4] Ibid., 14 November 1868.

Jones to the author of the new Poor Law. He was soundly defeated.

In Nottingham, there were, at one time, four Liberal candidates in the field for the two seats. One of them was J. J. Merriman, a barrister, a member of the International and a prominent figure in the Reform League. A. J. Mundella had helped to establish an elaborate Liberal Electoral Association in this Borough, ostensibly with the object 'that the working men should have the honest choice of one representative, and the moderate party another, and he hoped that the two would work together . . . it must not be said that a large constituency like that was in the hands of a clique Number 30 or anything else . . .'[1]

Merriman, anticipating the criticisms of Ostrogorski, argued that this machine gave the appearance of popular participation while leaving power in the hands of an oligarchy. He was not surprised when another 'Working Man's Candidate' appeared on the scene in the shape of P. W. Clayton. Clayton does not appear to have been any more of a working man than Merriman himself, and his views on the mutual responsibilities of labour and capital were fairly described in the local press as such as 'the wealthiest millionaire might have listened to with complacency'.[2]

Merriman made it plain that he was not going to abide by the decision of a 'primary', in which Ward Committees whose officers were nominated from on top were accorded an important role.[3] But he found the Reform League unsympathetic. In September he participated in a stormy meeting of the General Council and

> complained of the conduct of the 'two persons' who had visited Nottingham. He thought himself badly treated. The Secretary replied to the attacks on himself and Mr. Cremer, and assured the Council that the statements upon which the complaints were founded were inaccurate in every particular. The Council generally accepted the explanations given.[4]

When Clayton was officially adopted, the Executive expressed its satisfaction at the manner in which the Liberal Party in

---

[1] Speech by A. J. Mundella, *Nottingham Review*, 4 September 1868.
[2] *Nottingham Review*, 25 September 1868.   [3] Ibid., 6 November 1868.
[4] G.C.R.L. Minutes, 4 September 1868.

Nottingham had chosen its nominees and urged that they be supported 'to the exclusion of all personal considerations'. It added: 'The surest and quickest mode of ensuring the triumph of our principles is to be found in the most complete organisation of the Party.'[1] Merriman retired from the fight with a general denunciation of everyone connected with the proceedings, including Samuel Morley,[2] who had refused to arbitrate.

A still more dramatic problem was presented by Halifax. In this borough the electorate had been raised, as a result of the Reform Act, from 1,900 to 9,442. The workmen wanted to choose at least one of the representatives for themselves and they sent a deputation to the Whig-controlled Liberal Registration Association to negotiate about this. The Whigs refused to even discuss the matter and they hurriedly formed an alliance between their man, Edward Akroyd, and the other member, who was none other than James Stansfeld.

The local branch of the Reform League adopted the well-known co-operator E. O. Greening as their candidate and despite the fact that Greening was not prepared to make a financial contribution to his own expenses, they swore that they would return him.[3] The working class was exceedingly well organised in Halifax and the threat had to be taken seriously. Ernest Jones and John Stuart Mill both publicly supported Greening. Jones had earlier told Marx that Greening was: 'A very good, clever and honest young man, a good speaker, a good writer and a good democrat.'[4] However, Stansfeld refused to accept the suggestion that he should break with the Whig.[5] Akroyd was a large employer and his committee had met the whole expense of registration.[6]

Howell did not shy away from this embarrassing situation. He told Stansfeld that Stanhope had spoken of 'the complication at Halifax. Shall we run down to see you or will you be in

[1] E.C.R.L. Minutes, 4 November 1868.

[2] *Nottingham Review*, 6 November 1868.

[3] T. Crimes, 'Edward Owen Greening, Manchester, 1923; E. O. Greening to T. Hughes, 4 September 1868', *Halifax Guardian*, 24 October 1868.

[4] E. Jones to K. Marx, 25 February 1865. Bulletin of the Labour History Society, No. 4 (Sheffield), spring 1962.

[5] *Halifax Guardian*, 7 November 1868.

[6] E. Akroyd to T. Hughes, 9 September 1868, *Halifax Guardian*, 24 October 1868.

London this week?'[1] A few days later he wrote, 'We shall be very glad to see you and consult as to Halifax.'[2] A day or so later he was expressing the hope that 'things are all right at Halifax'.[3] Beales intervened by making it plain that the Reform League at national level was not going to follow the local branch. He acknowledged Greening's respectability, his integrity, his sound principles, but he declined to do anything which might run a risk of getting Stansfeld defeated.[4] Tom Hughes, who served with Stansfeld and P. A. Taylor as an arbitrator in Chelsea, where he found against Odger, refused an invitation from Greening to arbitrate in Halifax.

As the campaign went on, Greening found that the wind was going out of his sails. Stansfeld used great skill in focusing more attention on his disagreement with Greening on the Permissive Bill than on their common agreement against Akroyd on the ballot. Greening's personal honour was the object of determined Whig attacks and he referred with some justification to the way in which they 'dipped their hands in the gutter and hurled a social Finlen at him'.[5] He managed to win on the show of hands, but was well beaten at the poll. He himself summed up the lessons of the election:

> In this democratic borough they had found that local influence, wealth and position, and the respect men paid to good employers could hold their own against the political enthusiasm and manifest class interest of working men . . . Those influences to which he had referred were as able now to hold their own and were as omnipotent as in times gone by.[6]

To which he might have added that if the Secretary of the Reform League hated Whigs, he loved middle-class Radicals more. 'I am,' said Howell to Stansfeld, 'truly glad to find you in office and in a position to be close to Mr. Gladstone.'[7]

---

[1] Howell to Stansfeld, 15 September 1868.
[2] Ibid., 18 September 1868.   [3] Ibid., 22 September 1868.
[4] *Halifax Guardian*, 3 October 1868.
[5] Ibid., 31 October 1868—the reference is to James Finlen being hounded out of public life by Parliament and the press for his defence of the Fenians. Finlen was accused of driving his wife mad and leaving his children to starve.
[6] *Halifax Guardian*, 12 December 1868.
[7] Howell to Stansfeld, 11 December 1868.

Hackney was another problem borough. It was here that Col. Dickson, a long-standing and active member of the League, came forward as one of the five Liberal candidates who contested for the two seats against a single Tory. Dickson had been a most loyal supporter of both Beales and the Secretary. Howell recalled the 'military pride' with which the Colonel used to say: 'We must support those in authority.'[1]

In October 1868, Dickson's supporters in Hackney tried to get a grant of money from the Reform League to aid his candidature. This was turned down on the grounds that there was no cash available.[2] The Hackney leaders, if not Dickson himself, were most indignant about this and since there was obviously a lot of money available for other purposes they threatened to 'publish the proceedings'. 'I don't know what you mean,' replied Howell, 'come to the Council and all information can be given.'[3] Regret was officially expressed when Dickson ended up at the bottom of the poll, but it is quite certain that if his friends had come to the Council all information would not have been given.

A few months after the election was over, Howell wrote a letter addressed to one of the other Liberal candidates who had stood at Hackney asking him for money. He stated: 'We had nothing whatever to do with the Hackney election—we tried hard to keep one of our men away, but he would stand in spite of us. I think it is good to tell you this, now that it is all over, or perhaps you might think that some of us played a double game.'[4]

Dickson was a genial person, but not all those who had held high office in the League behaved with his decorum when they found that they were denied support or intrigued against. Charles Bradlaugh, who offered himself as a candidate for the double member constituency of Northampton, had already acquired a great reputation for truculence and aggression. Like Greening in Halifax, Bradlaugh was unable to persuade the sitting Liberal, Gilpin, to break his alliance with the Whig, Lord Henley; Glyn told Gladstone that 'Bradlaugh will do harm, but

---

[1] Howell's Draft Autobiography.
[2] Minutes E.C.R.L., 14 October 1868.
[3] Howell to C. Royal, 16 October 1868.
[4] Howell to C. S. Butler, 5 April 1869.

Henley (if either) is in danger. B. is not amenable to the League or I think I'd manage him.'[1]

Howell had to be exceedingly careful. In July he explained to a correspondent in Northampton that he had

> never had any official communication to make to Mr. Bradlaugh whatever. He came to this office on June 24th when our Election Committee was sitting and stated that he *was* a candidate and meant to fight it out to the last. He then wished for our aid. The Committee gave no pledge at all, but Mr. Odger was appointed at the next meeting to visit you and ascertain whether he *was accepted by you* and then to report to us.[2]

Bradlaugh had already announced that his candidature had the 'sanction and knowledge' of the Reform League,[3] and the Northampton branch was being congratulated on its choice by branches in other parts of the country.[4]

Howell was in touch with Gilpin. He promised to draw the attention of his colleagues to one of Gilpin's letters, and went on to remind the Honourable Member for Northampton that 'you were kind enough to partially promise me some little towards our new Club'.[5] The League defined its attitude towards Northampton in two resolutions: one expressed the earnest hope that Gilpin would be returned; the other commended Bradlaugh's plan to submit to the choice of the Liberal electorate as expressed in some kind of primary.[6] However, the Whigs would have nothing to do with Bradlaugh's proposal. It might have been expected that the League would there and then endorse their own man, but instead, Howell and Cremer arranged to get together with the Northampton Branch Committee 'to talk over matters quietly and confidentially'.[7] Howell wrote to the local President, 'I trust the tenor of the resolutions will not cause any breach with our Northampton Branch.'[8]

[1] Glyn to Gladstone, 10 September 1868. B.M. Add. MSS. 44347 f. 157.
[2] Howell to S. Clarke, 11 July 1868. (Clarke was corresponding Secretary of the Northampton Branch. He was charged with withholding correspondence favourable to Bradlaugh. *National Reformer*, 23 August 1868.)
[3] *National Reformer*, 5 July 1868.   [4] Ibid., 12 July 1868.
[5] Howell to C. Gilpin, M.P., 29 July 1868.
[6] Minutes of G.C.R.L., 22 July 1868 and Howell to the editor of the *Daily Telegraph*, 6 August 1868.
[7] Howell to Yorke, Secretary of Northampton Branch, 14 August 1868.
[8] Howell to F. Wells, 10 August 1868.

In fact, the local branch split and Bradlaugh plainly thought that Cremer, who warned against the electoral consequences of adopting an atheist, made matters worse.[1] The seceders joined forces with the teetotallers to support a rival candidate, Dr. F. R. Lees, an eccentric Hegelian. Bradlaugh declared, very plausibly, that had Dr. Lees been a paid agent of Lord Henley he could hardly have acted differently.[2] He was extremely suspicious about the exact part played by Howell and Cremer, and he kept the General Council, and then the Executive, occupied with his grumbling and searching questions.[3] But he did not dare to complain too loudly in public, for open hostility with the League leaders might have been more damaging to his cause than was their ambiguous neutrality. Howell was able to boast to both Goschen and Glyn: 'Bradlaugh has felt aggrieved with us. He thought that we could give him money for his election, but we kept to our arrangement and would not swerve even for one of our own Council.'[4]

By this time Odger was also feeling 'aggrieved'. A brilliant orator and probably the most popular working-class leader of the day, he was optimistic and easy-going to a fault. Unlike Howell he had no taste for administration and was most unreliable. He was always promising to go to Northampton or Stafford or somewhere else and then failing to turn up. During his visit to the West Country in August he got separated from Coffey and could not be found for several days. Unlike most of his contemporaries in the Labour leadership, Odger could unbend. He enjoyed visiting pubs where, standing upon a table, he would give a recitation from Shakespeare. Both before and after the election, Howell found cause to complain of Odger whom he accused of talking bosh;[5] behaving badly[6] and speaking 'in very bad taste';[7] being dilatory;[8] getting in the sulks;[9] and even of getting 'nearly drunk' and suggesting 'to settle some difference with a fight. His conduct was disgusting.'[10]

The shoemaker seems to have assumed that as a result of his

[1] *National Reformer*, 23 August 1868.   [2] Ibid., 22 November 1868.
[3] Minutes G.C.R.L., 4 and 16 September 1868. Also Minutes of E.C.R.L., 13 January 1869.
[4] Howell to Glyn, 30 November 1868.
[5] Howell's diary, 16 January 1868.   [6] Ibid.
[7] Ibid., 17 January 1868.   [8] Ibid., 25 March 1868.
[9] Ibid., 6 January 1869.   [10] Ibid., 3 August 1868.

services in August he would be found a seat, if not in Stafford then in Chelsea, where the 'Chelsea Association of Reasoners' were looking for a working-class candidate.[1] In the London constituency he confidently agreed to the issue between himself and Whig, Sir Henry Hoare, being decided by a panel of three advanced Liberals: P. A. Taylor, Tom Hughes and James Stansfeld. It was a great shock to him and to his supporters when the verdict went against him.[2] Howell described Odger's reaction to Glyn: 'Mr. Stansfeld, Mr. Hughes, and Mr. Taylor are supposed to be tools for getting rid of the Working Man's Candidate for that miserable Tory, Sir H. Hoare.'[3] However, on the eve of the election Glyn was becoming frightened. He told Gladstone: 'The ultra party, so loyal throughout are beginning to give me anxiety . . .'[4] From the beginning Glyn had been astonished by the moderation of the Reform League leaders and their unconditional loyalty to Gladstone, and he was not surprised that they were showing some signs of restiveness. He admitted to his Chief that he would have liked to have seen one or two workmen in the House. Howell and Cremer were the obvious choice, but they had never said that they wanted to be candidates until the last moment, when they came forward for the hopeless constituencies of Aylesbury and Warwick.[5] Howell's agents had reported that Warwick needed 'an advanced Liberal of good position'.[6] Howell had asked, 'What do you think of the Hon. Lyulph Stanley, son of Lord Stanley of Alderley? He is a fine Liberal, good speaker, and of good family.'[7] Cremer hardly fulfilled this last condition and he was unable to make any headway against a Whig–Tory compact.

There was a similar compact in Aylesbury where Howell tried to induce the Whig, Rothschild, to enter into an alliance with him. Glyn observed:

Howell has no chance at Aylesbury, *but* I am very much disappointed at the line Rothschild has taken. He has refused today

[1] *National Reformer*, 23 August 1869.

[2] *Chelsea News*, 31 October and 7 November 1868.

[3] Howell to Glyn, 3 December 1868 (headed 'Private').

[4] Glyn to Gladstone, 12 November 1868, B.M. Add. MSS. 44347 f. 241.

[5] Ibid., 13 November 1868, B.M. Add. MSS. 44347 f. 107 (catalogued as if written in March).

[6] ER: Warwick: Hales and Brighty.

[7] Howell to R. S. Gold of Warwick, 4 September 1868.

to combine or act & in strong terms—I have done all I can—
Howell is a true man & has been of great use to me. He has unfortunately chosen the wrong place & went to A. against my
advice—a stranger cannot win there & Rothschild's treatment
has done harm & will create bad feeling. The upper part of our
party are so jealous & (. . .) just now—I have written to Howell,
Morley, Goschen, Forster, & others have all written to me in his
favour—The League are very angry, but they have waited too
long.[1]

Rothschild explained that his principal supporters would
have left him if he had made an alliance with Howell. These
people had added that 'in consequence of the warm contest in
the Borough an ill-feeling had sprung up between the labourers
and their employers'.[2] Apparently the mere appearance of a
working man, even one whose election address contained no
reference to the Trades Union Bill and who favoured every
effort to 'economise on national expenditure',[3] was the signal
for a furious class struggle. In fact the root of the matter would
appear to have been simple Whig resentment that any kind of
working man should presume to enter the best club in Europe.
There was nothing left for Howell to do but recall his own
adage: 'Well, caste is not confined to any class, it rankles in all
of us.'[4]

IV

'Everywhere the proletariat is the rag, tag and bobtail of the
official parties, and if any party has gained strength from the
new voters, it is the Tories.'[5] It was in these terms that Engels
summed up his first impressions of the results of the election of
1868. The Conservative press consoled itself with the same
thought: in the factory districts, in the large boroughs, Disraeli
had more support than Gladstone. J. S. Mill had referred to
Gladstone as 'the one English Minister of past or present times
who has best deserved, and obtained in largest measure, the

[1] Glyn to Gladstone, 13 November 1868. B.M. Add. MSS. 44347 f. 107.
[2] N. M. de Rothschild to Howell, 23 November 1868.
[3] G. Howell: Address to the Electors of the Borough and Hundreds of
Aylesbury, 22 October 1868.
[4] Howell's Diary, 20 January 1868.
[5] Engels to Marx, 18 November 1868.

confidence of the working classes'. But the Tory *Standard* pointed out that Gladstone owed his good fortune to 'sectarian ascendancy' and to a 'despotic priest-hood', not to the workmen. The Conservatives were victorious in Lancashire and the big Towns; Gladstone in 'bigotry-ridden' small boroughs.[1] This was a gross over-simplification, but it had an undeniable element of truth in it.

'Not a single working-class candidate had a ghost of a chance, but my Lord Tomnoddy or any parvenu snob could have the workers' votes with pleasure.'[2] This was a matter about which virtually the entire press, whether Liberal or Tory, expressed its thankfulness and relief.

> The notorious BEALES, the blasphemous BRADLAUGH, HARTWELL, ERNEST JONES, and every man of the same kind has been rejected, unless we are to place Mr. CARTER of Leeds in the same category, and that we cannot properly do, as he came out not as a nominee of one class, but of the party as a whole . . . The working men of our land are not wishful for separate representation or for class legislation.

This dispelled the last fears of 'abuse of the electoral power'.[3] 'Next to the triumph of the Liberal Party, the most original feature in the elections is the utter collapse and downfall of the League and its adherents: No single member of the Hyde Park connection, from Mr. Beales down to Mr. Howell, has obtained a seat.'[4]

A week or so before the election the Reform League and its leaders were being mocked and taunted in the Tory press.

> BEALES and ODGER and BRADLAUGH gather the sweets, and HOARE, and DILKE and VERNON HARCOURT consume them. We trust that working men are satisfied with this division of labour. They may be tempted to grumble, possibly, at a dispensation which gives them all the work, and their aristocratic friends of the Whig connection all the wages, but they should be careful, lest by their murmurs they 'divide the Liberal Party'.[5]

---

[1] Standard, 18 December 1868.
[2] Engels to Marx, 18 November 1868.
[3] *Huddersfield Observer*, 21 November 1868.
[4] *Northampton Mercury*, 21 November 1868.
[5] *Standard*, 2 November 1868.

The satirical journal, *Judy*, printed a cartoon entitled 'No Third Class'. Various middle-class Liberals were shown on board 'the underground railway to Westminster'. A notice announced: 'Work-men's train will not run.' Tom Hughes appeared as a porter informing a crowd of carpenters, builders and shoemakers:

> No Third Class can travel! Why must I repeat?
> Some Lord or some swell has bespoke every seat.
> So 'step it' my hearties! Pack off with your tools
> Directors have power to alter their rules.[1]

Within the League Howell tried to put the best face he could on matters. Beales' defeat was explained by the absence of the Ballot; Col. Dickson was too late in the field; Odger's withdrawal was 'a matter to be deeply regretted by us all'. The defeat of Cremer and himself was chiefly due to the action taken by the Whigs. He suggested that they could derive some satisfaction from the return of a number of friends: Samuel Morley for Bristol; Sir Wilfrid Lawson for Carlisle; Samuel Plimsoll for Derby; Dr. Brewer for Colchester; Mr. James Howard for Bedford and Mr. R. M. Carter for Leeds. All these men were Vice-Presidents, but Howell could not carry his colleagues with him when he went on to suggest that they could also congratulate themselves on having Mundella, Illingworth; Holmes and Reid (the members for Hackney!); Dilke *and* Hoare (the members for Chelsea!) and MacArthur for Lambeth in the new Parliament. This was drastically amended in the final report, and one new passage was added stating that

> the League will not feel restrained, at its discretion, from presenting and supporting candidates at future Elections, merely because there may happen previously to be other candidates in the field, provided there appears to be in any such case, a fair portion of the constituency in favour of the League candidate.[2]

In public Howell expressed his disappointment and associated himself, albeit reluctantly, with the resolve to pursue a

[1] *Judy*, 11 November 1868.
[2] Howell's draft of the Report and Balance Sheet of the Reform League, 1 May–30 November 1868. (In letter book for 1868, folios 829–833. The Report was adopted in the E.C.R.L. Minutes after the entries for 25 July 1868.)

more independent policy in future; in private, he spoke proudly of what had been achieved. He described to Samuel Morley the difficulties with which Cremer and himself were confronted, and made an estimate of the contribution which had been made to the Liberal victory.

> Mr Bradlaugh thought that we should have given him pecuniary and other help. This we absolutely refused, because the money was given to us for a *special object* viz. to try and win a number of seats from the *Tories*. We had a list given to us containing the names of 92 Boroughs returning no less than 109 Conservative members, all of which were open to attack. Not one shilling of the money was given to us to empower any man to fight against Liberals, unless indeed we include Mr. Roebuck under this term.

(The fact that this express condition was attached to the 'Special Fund' nowhere appears in the League Minute books. However, members of the Executive knew that negotiations about cash were being carried on with Gladstone's Whips; they were certainly ingenuous if they imagined that all Mr Morley's cheques would be blank ones.)

Howell's letter to Morley continued:

> Now I felt, as the man having more control over the fund than anyone else, as the Executive Officer, that I should not be doing my duty if I allowed the money so subscribed to be used in Northampton against Lord Healey. In addition to this Col. Dickson thought that we could find him money for the contest in Hackney and deputations were sent asking for large sums. This Mr. Cremer and myself refused. Even Mr. Odger seemed aggrieved that we did not turn our attention to Chelsea. We felt obliged to refuse except sending a speaker to aid now and again when they had returned to town for a day or two. This has placed us rather in antagonism. But as to the expenditure of the funds, our finance committee went over the whole of the accounts up to the Saturday before the Council meeting and everything was examined and certified as correct. So that there was no complaint as to the keeping of the accounts, or indeed spending of the money, but they wanted the names for the *public papers* of those who had been the means of raising *this* fund. You are aware, Sir, that Mr. Stansfeld and Mr. Glyn strongly object to their being known in connection with the matter. I think yours had better not appear either except you allow it to be used simply as the Treasurer for the Fund. That the money has been honestly and fairly used I

186

pledge my honour and will allow any fair inspection of the accounts, but I will never dishonour myself by giving names except first being authorised to do so.

Mr. Cremer and myself will call tomorrow (Wednesday) at one o'clock to consult you on this subject. [Throughout all the discussions which took place on the Special Fund, Howell attempted to treat criticisms of his *political* honour as if they were criticisms of his *personal* honour in money matters.]

As for the work done—this will tell its own tale.

We sent out deputations of two each to 85 Boroughs covering the whole of England and Wales. We employed 27 men, good speakers and adapted for electioneering work. These men were employed from August 1st up to the end of the Election, a period of seventeen weeks.

We held about 240 public meetings, sent out circulars and other printed matter, and embodied our first labours in the reports which you have read and which Mr. Glyn so much praised and valued. This money has paid time, travelling and all other expenses, except that I find a printer's bill in London for about £16, so that the work done with the money spent, is not a matter to be ashamed of.

I think that we helped to dislodge about thirty conservatives from old strongholds and where they beat us was where our friends were over-sanguine of success and consequently not earnest enough in their work.

These will tell pretty well the work done without all the minute details. We will give more when we call if you require it.[1]

In the nature of the case it is exceedingly difficult to verify Howell's claim respecting the number of seats won. He told Glyn: 'We secured 49 of the seats which we attacked as you will find on investigation.'[2] A month later he sent Stansfeld a list of the 85 Boroughs, the amount spent in each, and indicated 'those constituencies where we consider that we did some service towards securing the success of the Liberal candidate'.[3]

There were forty-seven such constituencies.[4] This estimate

[1] Howell to S. Morley, 1 December 1868 (headed 'Private').
[2] Howell to Glyn, 12 December 1868.
[3] Howell to Stansfeld, 6 January 1869.
[4] Of the 47 seats listed as 'won' the following were mentioned in the 'Election Reports': Bath; Buckingham; Cambridge (2 seats); Cheltenham; Derby; Durham; Exeter; Grantham (2 seats); Guildford; Helston; Ipswich; Kidderminster; Knaresborough; Leeds; Liverpool; Maldon; Marlborough; Newport; Sunderland; Tewkesbury; Tiverton; Warrington; Whitby;

can be made to coincide with the one given to Glyn, because Howell explained in an accompanying letter that he could have added Bristol, 'where we prepared the way beforehand', and Brighton, where 'we prevented Mr. Conningham doing serious mischief'. In the eight Boroughs returning fourteen members which Glyn had classed as 'special', the results were definitely disappointing. Mundella was returned at Sheffield, and Brighton and Stoke were secured, but elsewhere the Tories were victorious; although in Rye and Northallerton it was by the narrowest of margins.

In fact, the figure of 49 represents the total number of Liberal gains from the 109 Tory seats which were attacked, while the earlier reference to 30 gains is apparently an estimate of the number of cases in which Howell, Cremer and their agents worked to decisive effect either by agitation and organisation among workmen as in Sheffield; by helping to secure the withdrawal of a candidate, as at Kidderminster; or by depriving the 'rogue elephant' of support, as at Brighton. There is no evidence that this estimate was questioned by Morley, Glyn or Stansfeld, all of whom showed by word and deed that they were highly satisfied with the services rendered. Thirty seats might seem neither here nor there in a majority of 112, but had the League pursued an independent policy of applying pressure from without, an embarrassingly high price might have had to be paid for a much smaller majority.

Two matters required special emphasis. The immense value to Glyn of getting a great deal of information and routine electoral work done cheaply, work which had to be done even if it

---

Wigan; Christchurch; Cockermouth; Colchester; Cricklade; Monmouth and Newark. (30 places, 32 seats.) The reader will note Guildford is included—it was won by 20 votes. The inclusion of Liverpool suggests that Howell's claims to have helped ought not to be taken too seriously. The city returned 3 members, and before Joseph Chamberlain showed the way in Birmingham, the minority party could count on securing one seat.

The other 15 seats listed as won were: Burnley; Bodmin; Canterbury; Carlisle; Devonport; Dover; Gravesend; Kendal; Salisbury; Wenlock; Windsor; Bedford; Montgomery; Sheffield and Stoke. ('Secured' was written against the last named.)

Canterbury had been represented by Butler-Johnstone. Sympathetic to the claims of Labour, he was a Tory. In Grantham, Kendal, Marlborough, Tiverton [sic], Wenlock and Montgomery, there were no contests.

is impossible to make any exact measure of its importance in terms of seats gained. The expenditure of the 'Special Fund' was made up as follows:[1]

	£	s.	d.
Payment for time, etc., of deputies .	701	16	0
Expenses, etc., of deputies . . .	593	9	6
Railway and other fares . . .	313	0	0
Meetings, halls, etc.	141	17	8
Printing and Stationery . . .	172	15	6
Postage, parcels, telegrams . . .	18	1	5
Bill posting and miscellaneous . .	31	7	6
	£1972	7	9

It will be seen that this represents an outlay of about £17 10s. per seat attacked and—if the figure of 49 is taken as the number of seats gained—then the cost of each gain was only £40. The money was, in fact, expended fairly evenly over the boroughs visited; Blackburn, in which £103 2s. 8d. was expended, was easily the most expensive of the 85 boroughs.[2]

The second feature of the way in which the agreement worked, which must have given Glyn special satisfaction, was the manner in which secrecy about it was preserved. 'We believe,' said Howell and Cremer, 'that you are satisfied that we preserved our connection with you as secret as *possible* considering the peculiar organisation and body of men with which we had to deal.'[3]

No doubt secrecy was important to Glyn for a variety of reasons. The Whigs could not be expected to share his confidence in the men of the 'Hyde Park connection' and would have suspected, no matter how unjustly, that he was everywhere using the League, as he was in Sheffield, to support the Liberal and Radical wing of the party against them. They might have construed the whole agreement as a conspiracy to undermine local autonomy and establish a powerful central office staffed with the most unsavoury representatives of the mob. And how

[1] Report of the Finance Committee (Mottershead, Weston, Worley), 9 December 1868.

[2] 'Copy of Expenditure on Account of the "Special Fund" at the late General Election, 17th November, 1868', accompanying Howell's letter to Stansfeld, 6 January 1869.

[3] Howell and Cremer to an unnamed correspondent, 13 February 1869 (headed 'Private').

could Glyn reassure them without discrediting Howell and Cremer among working-class electors? It was hardly likely that the working-class leaders whom he used would have enjoyed the same influence if it was generally known that they were all being paid three or four times the skilled workers' wage out of subsidies supplied by Samuel Morley, and that their labours were being directed by Stanhope, Stansfeld and himself.

In the event, very little appeared in the press at the time, beyond a paragraph or two in the *Standard* which referred to 'the mysterious funds' of the Reform League.[1] This could easily be ignored or dismissed as an insinuation calculated to aid the Tory Party. It was not until some years later that charges began to be made in public, and there was talk of the corruption and destruction of the League by political mercenaries working in the interests of 'that ghastliness, that knavery called Liberalism'.[2] In 1871, Beesly explained the passage of the Criminal Law Amendment Act by the fact that workmen had been sold at the election of 1868. He said that some Trade Union officers had got money or 'money's worth' by working for wealthy politicians instead of for their members.[3] Howell was not mentioned by name, but he unwisely rushed forward to repudiate these 'dastardly' and 'unmanly' attacks.[4]

This was followed by Marx' more general reference at the Hague Congress to 'almost all' the recognised English Labour leaders being sold to 'Gladstone, Morley and Dilke'. It was not until 1874 when a German paper, *Der Volksstaat*, published an unsigned article by Engels that some precise and detailed disclosures were made.

Engels used the elections of 1874 as an excuse for a review of the condition of working-class politics in England. He pointed to the absence of an independent workers' Party and argued that this was

> understandable in a country in which the working class has shared more than anywhere else in the advantages of the immense expan-

---

[1] *Standard*, 16 December 1868.

[2] The *Republican*, 1 September and 1 October 1870.

[3] E. S. Beesly, 'The Division on the Trades Union Bill', *Bee-Hive*, 29 July 1871.

[4] G. Howell, 'Professor Beesly and the Pall Mall Gazette', *Bee-Hive*, 4 November 1871.

sion of its large-scale industry. Nor could it have been otherwise in an England that ruled the world market; and certainly not in a country where the ruling classes have set themselves the task of carrying out, parallel with other concessions, one point of the Chartists' programme, the People's Charter, after another.

However, he saw the Reform Act of 1867 as a 'turning point'. 'Whereas under the old franchise the workers had been to a certain extent compelled to figure as the tail of the Radical bourgeoisie, it was inexcusable to make them go on playing that part after the Reform Bill had opened the door of Parliament to at least sixty working-class candidates.' Nevertheless this is what they did.

In order to get into Parliament the 'Labour leaders' had recourse, in the first place, to the votes and money of the bourgeoisie and only in the second place to the votes of the workers themselves. But by doing so they ceased to be workers' candidates and turned themselves into bourgeois candidates.[1] They did not appeal to a working-class party that still had to be formed but to the bourgeois 'great Liberal Party' . . . The Radical bourgeoisie has sense enough to realise that the election of workers to Parliament is becoming more and more inevitable; it is therefore in their interest to keep the prospective working-class candidates under their control and thus postpone their actual election as long as possible. For that purpose they have their Mr. *Samuel Morley*, a London millionaire, who does not mind spending a couple of thousand pounds [*sic*] in order, on the one hand, to be able to act as the commanding general of this sham labour general staff and, on the other, with its assistance, to let himself be hailed by the masses as a friend of labour, out of gratitude for his duping the workers.

Engels then referred to

the Potters, Howells, Odgers, Haleses, Mottersheads, Cremers, Eccariuses and the rest of them—a conclave of people everyone of

---

[1] This point had been made at the time by Beesly: 'It is said that all candidates who offered themselves expressly as representatives of workmen were rejected. I ask, in what sense did they represent workmen? What did they offer to Labour? Why, the very workmen who stood laid but faint stress on the industrial question . . . Perhaps they feared to alienate middle-class supporters and expected the workmen to divine their benevolent intentions. This was a fatal mistake.' *Bee-Hive*, 12 December 1868.

whom had served, or at least had offered to serve, during the previous Parliamentary elections (1868), in the pay of the bourgeoisie, as an agitator for the 'great Liberal Party'.[1]

There is no evidence that anybody in England paid the least attention to this article nor is there any reason to believe that Glyn, who by this time had succeeded to his father's title as Lord Wolverton, would have lost a moment's sleep over it. Engels' charges were not supported, nor have they been up until now, by detailed documentary material.

What really requires some explanation is how it was that the working-class press, and more particularly the *Bee-Hive*, never made any disclosures about the 'Special Fund'. Up until 1868 there had been the most deadly enmity between George Potter, the manager of that paper, and the Junta with which Howell and Cremer were associated. Howell and Cremer claimed credit, and quite rightly, for the skill with which they silenced noisy and troublesome critics within the League, but on the face of it, it was a still greater achievement to have persuaded Potter to forego the pleasure of exposing the intrigues of the 'filthy pack'. Here, surely, was a theme ready made for Hartwell. One can imagine him assuming his nom de plume of SCOURGE and laying about the conspirators who, hiding behind a veil of secrecy, made a deal with Gladstone; sacrificed their own colleagues and lined their own pockets. Nothing of this sort appeared, but there is no evidence that Potter was employed or rewarded with any of the money in the 'Special Fund'.

The solution to this problem appears to be that the ubiquitous Samuel Morley, along with the usual collection of wealthy employers and Liberal politicians, had made a quite separate arrangement with Potter. During the election of 1868, Potter supported the candidature of Daniel Pratt at Lymington. J. M. Hare, in introducing Potter to a meeting, said: 'Ask Samuel Morley, and other great men, his character, and they will tell you they depend in a great measure on George Potter for keeping the working men of England right.'[2]

[1] F. Engels, 'The English Elections', *Der Volksstaat*, 4 March 1874. (Reprinted in English in *Karl Marx and Frederick Engels on Britain*, Moscow, 1953, London, 1954, pp. 464–70.)

[2] S. Coltham, 'George Potter and the Bee-Hive Newspaper', D.Phil. Thesis, Oxford, 1956, p. 200.

This dependence of Morley upon Potter, and still more of Potter upon Morley, is confirmed by the discovery of a circular, headed 'Confidential': 'The General Election and Working Men'. It reads in part:

> Several influential members of Parliament and other Gentlemen, friends of the working classes, seeing that the general election is close at hand, when the newly enfranchised working men will be called on to exercise their rights as citizens in the election of representatives to serve in the new Parliament; and believing that the *importance* of the support of the working classes to the Liberal Party cannot be over-estimated, have readily subscribed towards a fund for the purpose of helping the conductors of the *Bee-Hive* to extend the circulation of that paper among the industrial classes.
>
> They intend also to publish *a series of special articles* upon political subjects of the deepest interest, and circulate them widely among working-class voters, to guide them at this important crisis in sustaining the LIBERAL PARTY . . .

The circular gave the names of seventeen person who had already subscribed £440. Morley and Daniel Pratt had supplied £100 each; while A. S. Ayrton, C. S. Butler and Sir Henry Hoare—opponents of Beales, Dickson and Odger respectively—were numbered among the other subscribers.[1]

This document would appear to provide a sufficient explanation of the silence of the *Bee-Hive* on the Glyn–Howell agreement. Further, it helps to explain the *rapprochement* between Potter and the Junta. It was difficult to continue a quarrel in which both parties were receiving blessings from the same source. Together with some letters in the Henry Solly collection[2] it helps to substantiate Marx' charge that the *Bee-Hive* 'is really the organ of the renegades, sold to Sam Morley and Co.'.[3]

If Howell and Cremer could take no credit for keeping Potter quiet, they were entitled to congratulate themselves on how they handled some of their colleagues on the Executive Committee of the Reform League. Gladstone had declared after the election that his mission was to pacify Ireland; Howell had a

---

[1] Dr. Coltham discovered this circular in the cover of one of the duplicate volumes of the *Bee-Hive* kept in the John Burns Collection.

[2] S. Morley to H. Solly, 17 October and 2 December 1870, and 3 January 1871. (Solly Collection, British Library of Political and Economic Science.)

[3] Marx to Beesly, 12 June 1871.

similar task within the Reform League and, for a time, it looked as if it was going to be just as exacting. He told Glyn: 'I have never had so much badgering over anything in my life as over this piece of work. Still I feel that we did our work fairly honestly, and well.'[1]

George Odger began the attack by insisting that 'The E.C. instruct the Secretary to respectfully write to Mr. Glyn to know the grounds upon which Mr. Samuda was supported in his candidature by the Liberal Party at the expense of dividing the Liberal interest and after a truer Liberal—Mr. Beales—was in the field . . .'[2]

Odger followed this up by demanding a committee of enquiry into the Tower Hamlets election and also 'into the particulars of the visit of Messrs Howell and Cremer to Northampton in reference to Mr. Bradlaugh's candidature and to enquire into and report upon the manner in which the Electoral Committee, or Committees, have conducted their affairs'.[3]

This was carried. But in the middle of December a resolution moved by Holyoake and seconded by Davis, 'That the report of the Financial Committee do pass' was defeated by one vote.[4]

Howell and Cremer were by now wishing that the League was dead and buried, but it was not so easily despatched. Howell declared that the conduct of Odger and his allies was 'inexplicable' and 'calculated to injure the Reform League in the estimation of its patrons and also to do me personally immense injury'.[5] Cremer resorted to the familiar tactics of bringing counter charges against Odger. After recalling the shoemakers' failure to keep appointments and carry out instructions, he asked:

> Is there any truth in the report that you received any money or promise of money, either directly or indirectly, from Mr. M. T.

[1] Howell to Glynn, 12 December 1868.

[2] E.C.R.L. Minutes, 2 December 1868. (Moved by Odger, seconded by Dell.)—J. A. Samuda was a notorious foe of Trade Unionism. After he was returned in 1868 he is alleged to have implored Gladstone to make no concessions to the unionists. (Henry Crompton, 'The Defeat of the Workmen', *Bee-Hive*, 2 September 1868.) He beat Beales, but this may well have been due to the intervention, not of Glyn, but of Newton of the Engineers, who also stood for Tower Hamlets.

[3] E.C.R.L. Minutes, 2 December 1868.

[4] Ibid., 16 December 1868.   [5] Howell to Beales, 10 December 1868.

Bass, Mr. A. Bass or any other person speaking for them either directly or indirectly? . . . Did you receive any promise direct or indirect, from Messrs M. T. or A. Bass, or from any other person speaking or acting for them, directly or indirectly, that either of the Basses or any other person would allow you £100 or any other sum per year towards your maintenance provided you would not come to Stafford and could get a seat elsewhere.[1]

The basis of this impressive questioning was a rumour that Odger, Connolly and Cremer himself had received £500 'as an inducement to withdraw Mr. Odger from contesting Stafford'.[2] There seems no doubt that M. T. Bass did offer to contribute £100 per year to a fund for the support of working men who were elected to Parliament.[3] Mottershead was instructed to go to Stafford to investigate the whole matter, but the League was dead before his report was received.[4]

Apart from trying to show that their critics were as much implicated in private financial transactions with brewers and manufacturers as they were themselves, Howell and Cremer called upon Morley, Glyn and Beales to help exonerate them.

After many desperate appeals from Howell, Glyn was induced to address a letter to the League about his attitude to the Tower Hamlets election. It began with the haughty observation:

I can scarcely admit that I should be called upon to respond to the 'minute' of which you send me a copy. [But he added] You are at liberty to tell your friends that I am not aware that any action was taken by myself or others which can justify the supposition that Mr. Samuda was supported by the Party at the expense of dividing the Liberal interest . . . I never attempted any interference and I am quite at a loss to understand the data upon which the allegation in the minute is based.[5]

Although this answer was hardly satisfactory from Odger's point of view it closed the discussion. The whole affair at Tower

---

[1] Minutes of E.C.R.L., 2 December 1868. The Basses were the famous brewers. M. T. Bass was the Member for Derby. He played an important part in the early history of Trade Unionism on the railways. (See G. W. Alcock, *Fifty Years of Railway Trade Unionism*, London, 1922.) Arthur Bass had been a candidate for Stafford (one of Glyn's 'specials') but withdrew.
[2] Minutes of E.C.R.L., 9 December 1868.
[3] Ibid. (Remarks by Connolly, Mottershead and Odger himself.)
[4] Ibid.
[5] Copy of Glyn's letter in E.C.R.L. Minutes, 16 December 1868.

Hamlets was complicated by Newton's candidature. Cremer wanted an enquiry as to whether Allan, Applegarth and 'other leading Trade Unionists' had taken voters to the Poll to plump for Newton.[1] Beales was the *one* 'League' candidate who had received help from the Special Fund and he was satisfied with Glyn's explanation.[2]

Howell's great difficulty was the rejection of the report of the Finance Committee. Bradlaugh and others were determined to conduct a close enquiry into the expenditure of the Special Fund. Special meetings of the E.C. had to be held at which Odger, Cooper, Bradlaugh and others examined accounts and vouchers.[3] Howell knew that the source of their discontent was the absence of any financial support for their own candidatures. In private, he spoke like Guizot, *'enrichez vous'*. 'If Mr. Bradlaugh or Col. Dickson wants money to fight with, let them get it . . .'[4] At the Executive he 'misunderstood' all this probing and investigating. He behaved as if it was based on a suspicion that he had abused his official position for personal gain. This allowed him to whip himself up into a state of righteous indignation, for at the time of these debates neither Cremer nor himself had received special preferential rates for their work. (They received their reward privately and only *after* the debate in the League had ended; nothing was allowed to appear in the accounts.)

Howell complained to Beales:

> I had *every item ready* for the Executive last night. Why then, I ask, did not Mr. Odger allow the balance sheet to be read and discussed in proper form and time instead of leading off into quite a different subject? Perhaps vile insinuations will serve their purpose better than the facts of the Balance Sheet.[5]

Beales eventually got the Balance Sheet adopted.[6] Mr. Cooper said he never called the accounts in question,

---

[1] Minutes E.C.R.L., 5 December 1868.

[2] Howell to Glyn, 17 December 1868. (Beales was seeking favours from the Ministry, Howell to Beales, 12 December 1868.)

[3] Minutes of Specially Summoned E.C.R.L., 8 January 1869.

[4] Howell to Beales, 2 December 1868 (headed 'Private').

[5] Howell to Beales, 10 December 1868.

[6] Minutes E.C.R.L., 23 December 1868. Adoption moved by J. B. Langley, seconded by Wm. Osborne.

what he deprecated was the policy involved in the matter; we had been used as Whig tools etc. The President replied that that was a very different matter and did not in any way interfere with the Report of the Finance Committee and the Balance Sheet. It was then put to the meeting and adopted.[1]

Howell explained to Samuel Morley:

I feel truly thankful that I have been able to give satisfaction to those who have chiefly sustained our great movement during the four years of its existence. As to the Special Fund, all have felt satisfied. Of course, there were a very few who have always more or less felt the same antipathy to the 'Whigs' as William Cobbett— but things are now greatly altered. All classes are drawn nearer to each other, and I hope it will not be long before the present jealousy will be considerably modified.[2]

The adoption of the balance sheet did not formally close the matter, because a rider was added 'that the E.C. reserve its right to discuss the propriety and authority of a certain part of the expenditure',[3] but most of the critics had never been well placed to sustain their attack. They had tied their own hands in advance by their concessions and compromises. Those of them who stood as 'League' or 'Working Men's' candidates produced programmes which were little more advanced than those of such middle-class Radicals as Mundella or Stansfeld. They all announced that, if elected, they would give general—or at most, 'independent'—support to Mr. Gladstone. Bradlaugh, for example, always did his best to win the confidence of the Liberal chief. He sent him a copy of his election address and, when he was planning a popular campaign against the obstruction of the House of Lords, he told Gladstone that he did not want to do anything that might be detrimental to his plans. 'The feeling of the people is so strong on the matter that controlled it may be useful, uncontrolled it will be dangerous.'[4]

Given the fact that men like Bradlaugh laid less stress on what distinguished them from other Liberals than they did on what they had in common with Gladstone, they were not well placed to criticise their officers for putting first the overriding interests of the Party, as interpreted by Gladstone's Whips.

[1] Howell to S. Morley, 24 December 1868.
[2] Ibid., 21 January 1869.   [3] Minutes E.C.R.L., 23 December 1868.
[4] Bradlaugh to Gladstone, 9 June 1869. (Date in pencil by another hand.)

Some of those who were employed by Howell with money from the 'Special Fund' may have known little about how the money was raised. This was true of Lloyd Jones, who stipulated that he would only work for candidates who were sound on the Labour Question and who refused to take any payment even for expenses, for work done in London.[1] But Odger and most of the others certainly knew a good deal of what was going on. Howell alleged that Odger was well aware that the Liberal Whips did not want any discussion about the 'Special Fund' in the General Council, and that they were only satisfied when Cremer and himself conducted all negotiations. Odger had received £58 for his work and had made no complaints until he was forced out of Chelsea.[2] Having allowed Howell and Cremer to assume more and more power it was a bit late in the day to start complaining about the results.

All this mutual recrimination was finally ended early in 1869. With only Osborne and West offering serious resistance, it was agreed to wind up the Reform League.[3] A month or so before, members had been asked to console themselves for failures in the election by remembering that the League had 'secured a hold on the constituencies never before attained by the Democratic Party';[4] now it was discovered that this impressive machine had outlived its usefulness. Howell explained that the League had accomplished its main purpose; that he had every confidence in Mr. Gladstone and that continual political agitation was bad for the country.[5]

Instead of reproaching each other about money matters everyone now agreed that everyone else's expenses ought to be met. It was agreed, in principle, that Cremer should receive a commission of £90 on the last £900 raised in the Special Fund;[6] that Howell's debt of £136 at Aylesbury should be treated as a collective responsibility;[7] finally, it was unanimously agreed that Odger should be voted £75 for his election and other expenses.[8]

[1] Lloyd Jones to Howell, 26 October 1868.
[2] Howell to Beales, 10 December 1868.
[3] Minutes E.C.R.L., 12 March 1869.
[4] Report of the Finance Committee of the Reform League, 9 December 1868.
[5] Howell to Beales, 10 March 1869.
[6] Minutes E.C.R.L., 13 January 1869.
[7] Ibid., 20 January 1869.   [8] Ibid., 12 March 1869.

On 13 February 1869 George Howell wrote two letters which, when placed side by side, provide a final, most revealing comment, on workmen, money and the General Election.

The first of these letters was to a correspondent in Stoke. It will be remembered that Stoke had been the scene of Hartwell's candidature and a source of great anxiety to Glyn.[1] In the end the old Chartist retired from the contest on the grounds that he had insufficient supplies. It was arranged that he should be paid £280 to enable him to meet the expenses which he had already incurred, but he was swindled out of the money.[2] He tried to take action through the courts to restrain those who had defrauded him and, in consequence, the episode became public knowledge.

Rumours were current in the Potteries that Howell was trying to discredit Hartwell, and that he was actively involved in the intrigue against him.

> I cannot but regret that my name has been mentioned in connection with your election [wrote Howell]. I do not think that I was treated fairly in the matter. However, I frankly state that I did not (?) know that Mr. Hartwell was to be bought off or 'induced to retire' as the expression was used. I sincerely respected my informant and I begged him not to dirty his fingers with the transaction. I own to an impression at the time that I was to be selected to do something in the matter. But so strongly was I opposed to it that I was told that it would be smashed up. I imagine that it was—so far as the first attempt was concerned. I felt that if working men's candidates were to be open to influences of this nature the cause of Labour was low indeed. Working men's candidates when once selected and in the field, must fight the battle out *fairly*, *honestly* and persistently to the end.
>
> I would not retire from Aylesbury on any account. I felt that the honour of our class was in my hands, and I left the constituency with my name cherished not only by the 1,000 who voted for me, but by all who had any pretension to the name of Liberal.[3]

The second letter was sent to an unnamed correspondent. Its terms had been carefully discussed and it was signed by Cremer as well as by Howell. It read:

[1] See p. 174.   [2] *Standard*, 20 November 1868.
[3] Howell to A. Smith of Stoke, 13 February 1869.

Private: Dear Sir, In the various interviews we had with you during the late electoral campaign, you were pleased to acknowledge that the work which we had undertaken to perform had been done in a satisfactory manner and that we had rendered an essential service to the Liberal Party. We believe that you are satisfied that we preserved our connection with you as a secret as *possible* considering the peculiar organisation and body of men with whom we had to deal. The difficulties of our task are only known to ourselves, especially, with regard to some circumstances which arose out of the Northampton, Hackney and Chelsea elections.

An endeavour was made to connect you with the movement, but completely failed inasmuch as we never would mention your name under any circumstances. Hence the public has never been any the wiser, although we got a little more abuse.

So far as we are concerned we were the least paid of all who went out, as our expenses were much heavier, whilst our pay was just the same in amount as any one of our co-workers, however humble his abilities or inadequate his work. Circumstances therefore compel us to ask you to consider our claims . . .[1]

Cremer annoyed Glyn by the strong terms of his demands[2] and irritated Stansfeld by wanting to claim money as a fee in the same way as a professional agents such as Acland.[3] In the end Stansfeld advised that they should be paid £200.[4]

Howell had already received substantial help with his election expenses from Samuel Morley. 'My gratitude,' he said, 'shall be shown by my future devotion to the same good work . . .'[5]

In March and April 1869, Howell proposed that the 'same good work' could best be carried on through a private Registration and Election Agency.[6] He had already told Glyn that: 'In any work for the future I would see to it that I dealt only with

---

[1] Howell and Cremer to an unnamed correspondent, 13 February 1869 (headed 'Private'). The correspondent was almost certainly Glyn. Howell's diary for 13 February 1869 reads: 'sent letter to Glyn about fee [*sic*] for work done . . .'

[2] Howell's Diary, 3 February 1869.

[3] Ibid., 20 February 1869.

[4] Ibid.

[5] Howell to Morley, 21 January 1869.

[6] Howell to Stansfeld, 24 April 1869.

those who found the money, and let all accounts, vouchers, etc. etc. be rendered to them.'[1]

Morley, Glyn and Stansfeld supplied Howell with £500 to establish this agency,[2] but with the formation of the Labour Representation League at the end of the year Howell found himself in some danger of being isolated. He proposed that the balance of the £500 should be made over to him personally so that he could be independent. 'I own that I do not like trusting entirely to politics for one's bread. It lessens a man's moral influence and independence. I want to preserve both.' He hastened to explain that he wanted to be independent, not of Morley or of Glyn, but of his own class. 'I cannot always lend myself to all the foolish movements of working men.'[3]

Howell's proposal was accepted on the understanding that he would, in his words, continue to 'as truely and fairly carry out the intention of the subscribers as though he went on as he was now doing'.[4]

At the end of 1867 Howell was delighted to have £6 in the bank; two years later his assets amounted to more than £850.[5] Both he and Cremer invested their money in old houses which they renovated.[6] Howell tried to make his property the starting point for a bigger venture—a philanthropic building society which was to pay 6%.

In view of all this, it was quite an achievement for Howell to be able to assume a high moral tone about the misfortunes of Hartwell, and to be able to declare that he would only be comforted when he knew that none of the 'base money' reached him.[7]

However, Howell did not feel that he himself had been treated over-generously and he complained at frequent intervals about the 'stinginess' of the Gladstonians. Even in 1871,

[1] Howell to Glyn, 12 December 1868.
[2] Howell's rough notes on Balance sheet of Registration and Election Agency.
[3] Howell to Stansfeld, 2 November 1869.
[4] Ibid.
[5] Howell's Diary, 1868, 'Personal Financial Review for the past year' and the cash account at the end of the diary for 1869.
[6] H. Evans, *Sir R. Cremer: His Life and Work*, 1909, p. 48, and Howell to S. Morley, 20 July 1871.
[7] Howell to E. Hind, 3 December 1868.

when he was Secretary to the Parliamentary Committee of the T.U.C., Howell was looking for favours from the Ministry and asking Beales to approach Glyn on his behalf. Glyn would do no more than 'bear the matter in mind'.

> I sincerely thank you [wrote Howell to Beales] for your kindness, and hope that Mr. Glyn will bear the matter in mind, for there are plenty of chances wherein he may, if he so pleases.
>
> Mr. Glyn should remember not merely good offices rendered, but the abstention from adverse criticism upon many points of the Government promise and performance. I, of course, could not do anything which would run the risk of a Liberal defeat, but upon some questions they have really invited it, and if we had been hasty in taking up the cudgels I think considerable dissatisfaction would have been the result.
>
> I wonder if Mr. Stansfeld ever remembers how some of us worked for him, now that he is reconstructing his office. Surely there would be a chance of some good appointment where my qualifications would be a fair test.[1]

Beales had already received his judgeship. Howell and Cremer both had to wait until the 1880s before becoming Lib–Lab Members of Parliament.

V

As far as mere matters of fact are concerned it is no longer possible to dismiss Marx' judgement about 'almost all' the recognised English Labour leaders' being sold to Gladstone and Morley. There is no real release from this conclusion in pointing out that there were other 'recognised leaders' apart from Howell, Cremer, Potter, Odger, Hales, Mottershead and the rest of them. In the first place, Marx qualified his charge. In the second, such men as Applegarth had, by the time Marx spoke, started to engage privately in work for 'Glyn and the Government'.[2]

It is, however, possible to argue that Howell and Cremer ought not to be judged by the political moralities of either

---

[1] Howell to Beales, 23 August 1871.

[2] A. J. Mundella to R. Leader, 13 October 1871. Sheffield University Library. (A postscript to the letter headed 'Private' runs: 'Applegarth works for Glyn whenever needed, and is always ready to help the Government.')

Chartism or of Socialism. It is not self-evident that Howell was betraying his own social and political values when he made his agreement with Glyn. It might be suggested, and very plausibly, that Cremer and he were empiricists; practical men who believed that any programme that looked beyond limited improvements was delusory and nonsensical. They believed, with equal sincerity, in Mr. Gladstone; in 'new model' unionism; and in the adage about the half loaf. They could see little incompatibility between the interests of their industrial organisations and their political loyalties.

Once this is granted, their secrecy, their shiftiness, the readiness with which they sacrificed their friends take on the aspect of unpleasant, but indispensable, expedients.

It must not be forgotten that most contemporary Labour leaders shared Howell and Cremer's attachment to Liberalism. For example, John C. Proudfoot, a leading Trade Unionist in Scotland, was even more attached to the principles expressed in the essay 'On Liberty' than they were themselves. Proudfoot told Lord Elcho: 'I agree with your Lordship in believing that this class (the working class) is in great need of being taught that the true liberty is individual or personal liberty, and that communal or mob liberty, or happiness, or progress, at which most of their would-be leaders aim, is . . . tyranny over body and mind.'[1] Proudfoot favoured 'labour representation', provided that there was no suggestion of independent class policies and that 'the right men' were chosen. 'I do believe in the propriety of a few working men getting into Parliament as I deem it a *sine qua non* that all classes should be represented, but Potter and Co. are not the men.' (He was discussing Hartwell's candidature at Stoke.) 'I believe them as destitute of the necessary intellect as of honesty and that is saying something considerable I deem. Potter himself is about as honest as any of them, though certainly not the ablest, although his vanity would lift him over all heads.'[2]

An apologist for Howell and Cremer could argue that the workmen and reformers who came forward as candidates in Hackney or Nottingham, Halifax or Northampton, were not

[1] J. C. Proudfoot to Lord Elcho, n.d. (Gosford House archives. Courtesy of Earl of Wemyss and March).
[2] Ibid., 8 August 1868.

advancing programmes which were conspicuously different from those of many middle-class Gladstonians. The challenge which they made to local Whig interests or to middle-class wire-pullers was therefore dangerous where it stood any chance of letting in the Tory, and merely trivial where it did not. If mere labour representation was all that was wanted, it was more likely to be secured by services rendered to the Whips than by making a nuisance of yourself in the constituencies.

If Howell and Cremer were rewarded with a 'small independence' for themselves, there was nothing particularly reprehensible about it. Applegarth and Coulson had occupied the official positions which they might otherwise have expected to have secured for themselves and they had made a notable contribution to supplying Mr. Gladstone with the majority upon which his first, great administration depended.

It could be maintained that when the reforms of that first administration are remembered: the disestablishment of the Irish Church; the improvement in the Irish land laws; the beginnings of army reform; the Education Act of 1870; and the introduction of the ballot; faith in Gladstone does not appear to have been misplaced.

Even if Howell knew (as he did) that the middle-class Radicals of Bradford and elsewhere were doubtful friends to Trade Unionism, what else could he do? Even if he saw (as he did) support for 'advanced radical reformers' degenerating into general support for all candidates approved by the Whips, what could he do? Given the state of political opinion in England and the structure of politics at that time, it may be questioned whether there was any alternative course open to the leaders of the League except collaboration with Gladstone.

The plausibility of this defence largely depends on showing that Howell and Cremer had no choice, or that if they had a choice, they were not aware of it; or that if they were aware of it they conscientiously rejected it.

There was an alternative policy, although it must be recognised that it was neither well articulated nor strongly supported. Engels was being wildly unrealistic when he said that the Reform Act opened the door of the House of Commons to sixty labour M.P.s—this showed no appreciation of the importance of the ballot or the tremendous cost of elections. Taking account only of legitimate election expenditure, it appears to have cost the majority of candidates who contested English boroughs in 1868 a sum between £500 and £2,000.[1] But it might have opened the door to some, had workmen been more conscious of their strength and encouraged by their leaders to use it. Glyn was obviously astonished by the modest ambitions of the Reform League leadership and amazed by their unconditional support of Gladstone. Had they demanded concessions on matters of policy and a share of representation he might well have tried to help them to get it.

The alternative to Howell's policy of complete identification with middle-class Radicalism was most clearly set forth in Professor Beesly's programme.[2] It will be recalled that Beesly attached no importance to mere labour representation as such. A few workmen in the Parliamentary Liberal Party would simply have come up 'night after night to the crack of Mr. Glyn's whip; compromising their convictions, soiling the purity of their own consciences and ruining their chances of future usefulness'.[3] A few working-class candidates would be useful provided their appearance was part of a larger strategy of mass pressure behind a distinctive programme.

There are a number of reasons why it would be quite wrong to dismiss Beesly's ideas as a sheer flight of fancy. The first, and most impressive of them, is that the essentials of his strategy were taken up and applied at a number of by-elections in the early 'seventies and at the General Election of 1874. This made an important contribution to securing the satisfactory legal settlement for the Unions in 1875.[4] Howell's policy, on the other hand, broke down in 1872 when his industrial and political loyalties came into open conflict with each other. As secretary of the Parliamentary Committee of the T.U.C. he could not carry out Congress' instructions to bring mass pressure to bear on the Liberal Government and to settle for nothing but the total repeal of the Criminal Law Amendment Act.[5] His

[1] W. B. Gwyn, *Democracy and the Cost of Politics in Britain*, 1962, p. 34.
[2] See p. 138.
[3] E. S. Beesly, 'The Election', *Bee-Hive*, 12 December 1868.
[4] R. J. Harrison, 'The English Positivists and Labour Movements', D.Phil. Thesis, Oxford, 1955 and Chapter VI.
[5] See the controversy between Beesly and Harrison on the one hand and Howell on the other in the *Bee-Hive* between 13 January and 14 June 1872.

earlier commitment to Glyn and Gladstone made it impossible for him to do this. Congress would have better understood the strange reticence of its secretary had it known that he had made an impressive contribution to the Government's majority, and that he had been set up in business by the Whips on the understanding that he would continue to work for the Party.

But even in 1868, Beesly was not alone in pointing to an alternative. There were workmen who were feeling their way towards independent political action along the lines which he suggested. For example, there was the Scottish workers' programme, developed by the men of Edinburgh and Leith. It consisted of fifteen test questions for candidates on questions of social legislation of interest to the working class. The first question was: 'Are you in favour of extending the full protection of the law to the funds of Trades Unions . . .?' Other questions covered: widening the penalties for employers' negligence; the extension of the factory acts; further amendment of the Master and Servant Acts; more legislation and inspection for mines and sea-going vessels; state ownership of railways; a national compulsory, unsectarian, system of education; and compulsory provision of full house accommodation for workmen evicted from their homes as a consequence of civic improvements or other causes.[1]

The acceptance of the Gladstonian principles of public finance and total rejection of state intervention in economic and social life was by no means as widespread in the 1860s as has sometimes been supposed. The London working-class leaders knew the *Fortnightly Review* in which the Editor talked of jargon about 'retrenchment' being essentially hollow and hypocritical; a favourite phrase of the 'unidea'd rich'. And went on to speak of the ragged flag of economy being paraded as if it were a holy lance.[2]

All the way from Lloyd Jones and Hartwell at one extreme to Applegarth and Odger at the other, workmen retained the sense of their own identity and distinct interests. This awareness might be dulled but it could not be wholly eradicated. It was there behind the halting and uncertain gestures of some of the

[1] The *Kilmarnock Advertiser*, 31 October 1868.
[2] J. Morley, 'Old Parties and New Policy', *Fortnightly Review*, September 1868.

working-class candidates in 1868. It helps to explain the rise of British republicanism in the 'seventies, and it was at the source of the continual tension that characterised the inner history of both the Reform and Labour Laws agitations. The policies of empiricism and compromise were always under a challenge; usually muted and feeble; occasionally stern and formidable. Howell knew about this. It was at the root of most of his problems in managing the League. It was always threatening to assume the shape of an alternative policy. As he told Stansfeld: 'Some of us have to stand in the character of obstructives because we will not consent to the revival of the old Chartist practice, that of opposing all parties except those pledged to labour questions.'[1]

One can understand neither the movements nor the men of the mid-Victorian Labour Movement if the ambivalent attitudes of workmen are not understood. Liberalism at the front of the mind, and old working-class sentiments and traditions at the back of it, produced the characteristic vacillations and inconsistencies. Applegarth secretly working for Glyn and the Government, and at the same time valuing his membership of the International; Odger in 1868, at once party to an agreement with the Liberal Whips and yet in rebellion against it.

The point is illustrated by the superb irony of Odger's peroration at Fawcett's eve of poll meeting in Brighton. The shoemaker took as his theme that most cherished and ambiguous of Victorian virtues, self-help.

> Rely upon yourselves! Self-reliance,—that rising, animating, soul-stirring, heart-inspiring quality which whispers to a man;—no matter whether he be a shoemaker in his kitchen or a tailor in his garret, an engineer at his lathe, a bricklayer or a mason on his scaffolding,—whoever he may be, be strong in the spirit of self-reliance, the faithful monitor which whispers into the deepest recesses of his soul, and says in gladdening tones—'Look up! There's a brighter and happier future before you'.[2]

The general working-class sympathy with Liberalism and Radicalism would not have been enough in itself to have prevented some advance along the lines of Beesly's programme. The intellectual dependence of the Labour leaders upon the

[1] Howell to J. Stansfeld, 8 November 1869.
[2] *Brighton Gazette*, 18 November 1868.

Gladstonians was never so great as to make their financial dependence upon them unimportant or merely incidental. It was this 'iron power', as Howell himself termed it,[1] which enabled Glyn to re-enforce and consolidate the exceedingly skilful social and educational efforts of Stansfeld and Mundella. If the Amalgamated Engineers could have been induced to give £3,000 to a working-class electoral fund, as they were induced to give the same sum to the London builders, the history of the 1868 Election might have been very different.

The secret agreement of 1903 may have had beneficial consequences for both parties; it is an arguable matter.[2] The agreement of 1868 was essentially what Howell called it—'a contract'. From this contract, the Liberal Party derived immense benefits at very little cost; the Labour Movement derived no obvious benefit at all. As a result of the negotiations with the Whips, support for 'advanced Radical Reformers' became synonymous with support for Whigs like Akroyd and Lord Henley. And if there was any advantage in returning Mundella for Sheffield it was balanced by helping to defeat Butler-Johnstone at Canterbury. By their unconditional support for Gladstone, Howell and Cremer helped to create a Government with so vast a majority that it became insensitive to the claims of Labour.

Howell and Cremer derived undeniable advantages for themselves by their deal with the Whips. Yet it is apparent from Glyn's remarks to Gladstone that they began by putting too low a price upon their services, and that had they played their cards properly they might have been rewarded with more promising constituencies than Warwick and Aylesbury. Perhaps they under-priced themselves because they did not appreciate that Glyn was full of doubts and anxieties about the outcome of the election. At the beginning of 1868 they could hardly have guessed that the Liberal Whips would come to attach so much importance to the machinery of the Reform League. It seems probable that Howell always believed that the Liberals would

[1] Howell to J. D. Nieas, 22 August 1868.
[2] For the secret electoral pact concluded between Macdonald and Hardie on the one side and the Liberal Whips on the other see F. Bealey and H. Pelling, *Labour and Politics 1900–1906*, 1958. Also P. P. Poirer, *The Advent of the Labour Party*, 1958.

win the Election. He may well have interpreted the close-fisted behaviour of the Northern manufacturers during the winter of 1867–68 as a sign that they shared his confidence. If victory was certain, then the Reform League could only be of marginal importance.

It was only as the election campaign developed that Howell gradually recognised how much Glyn needed the League. If he lamented his missed opportunities and came to complain about the stinginess of Glyn and Stansfeld, he could console himself with the thought that he had made enough to make him, in his own words, 'independent'. However, he lived under the constant strain of the invidious position in which he had placed himself. His relations with his associates became charged with bitterness and mutual contempt. He came to talk of his old friend Dickson as 'simply a man about town, he never was a politician'. Mottershead, he accused of writing 'scurrilous rhymes, without power or reason, or common sense, to lampoon or libel all with whom he comes in contact. Shunned by all . . .' 'As to the cantankerous little dog Cremer, he is doing all the mischief in his power as usual.' Odger 'has done us much harm during the last two years by his foolhardiness and by his ill-governed temper. But it pays him somehow, for he is well up for cash . . .'[1] 'Whoever found Cremer working for long with any party except pay kept him quiet for a while?'[2] Howell's correspondence abounds with this sort of thing. He acquired, in turn, an unenviable reputation as a man who had 'never worked for or been identified with any reform movement where the money was scarce and hard work the only reward'.[3]

The historical significance of the 1868 agreement is that it marked the real beginning of the Lib–Lab era in working-class politics; an era which was to last well beyond the formation of the Labour Representation Committee in 1900. Surrounding that meeting in the Memorial Hall there was an unnoticed irony—the money for the building had been largely supplied by Mr. Samuel Morley.[4]

---

[1] Howell to C. Bartlett, 27 June 1871.   [2] Ibid., 9 January 1871.
[3] F. W. Soutter, *Recollections of a Labour Pioneer*, 1923, p. 120.
[4] The *Englishman*, 10 June 1876. ('This is MORLEY's Shop, he having been the largest contributor to the erection of the building, and it is the home of very (every?) milk-and-water kind of gospel . . .')

V

THE REPUBLICANS: A STUDY
OF THE PROLETARIAN LEFT,
1869–73

ENGLISH Republicanism in the nineteenth century was heavily dependent for its inspiration on foreign examples. Sir Charles Dilke made an effective defence of its Englishness, but the names that he recalled numbered many whose enthusiasm for the Republic had been kindled by events abroad.[1] During the decline of Chartism, Republican sentiments were most commonly expressed by those who gave particular attention to international affairs. In the 'sixties, the American Civil War did something to revive this spirit, Beesly referred scathingly to the 'passionate loyalty' which the press wished to believe characterised the feelings of working men towards Victoria and he insisted on underlining the Federal victory as a Republican triumph.[2] His fellow Positivist, Dr. J. H. Bridges, commended the *Commonwealth* newspaper to its readers by remarking that the word 'commonwealth' was a good English equivalent for what the French understood by the Republic.[3] Politically-conscious workmen may have had some general sympathy with these opinions and they demonstrated this by occasionally refusing to sing 'God Save the Queen' or by some such gesture.[4] This sort

[1] S. Gwyn and G. M. Tuckwell, *Life of Sir Charles Dilke* (1917), p. 145.

[2] E. S. Beesly, 'Passionate Loyalty', *Bee-Hive*, 7 March 1863 and 'The Republican Triumph', *Bee-Hive*, 29 April 1865. See also his 'Court Dress', *Commonwealth*, 17 February 1866.

[3] J. H. Bridges, 'The Commonwealth', *Commonwealth*, 24 February 1866.

[4] *Bee-Hive*, 16 January 1864.

of thing was quite enough to cause excited reactionaries to declare that it would be better to see the Thames flowing with blood than to witness the Republic in England. But it was not until the proclamation of the Republic in France in September 1870 that Republicanism captured the imagination of large numbers of working-class people and became a serious political force.

It would, however, be a mistake to interpret the Republican movement as merely a response to events on the Continent. Alarm about a war which was held to have had its origin in 'dynastic rivalries', and enthusiasm for the Republic which arose from it, were brought into relation with purely English concerns. The Royal Family was costly, and lazy. The heir to the throne was known to be debauched and some suspected that his mother was little better.[1] The marriage of Princess Louise was not well received. Distress in London was exceptionally severe. Pauperism was higher in 1869–70 than it had been in any year since 1848.[2] Workmen felt that this was no time to go round jangling the 'Royal begging box'. The disillusionment which invariably follows constitutional reform began to make itself felt. Little had changed. Far from getting better, large sections of the London working class found times worse than they could remember. Evidently the Reform Act had not cut deeply enough. In varying degrees their leaders concurred in this opinion. They not only failed to get themselves elected to Parliament: they found it almost impossible to get a seat on the London School Board. When George Howell had resigned his secretaryship of the Reform League in March 1869 he had explained that one of his reasons for doing so was that 'his

---

[1] From the standpoint of the history of Republicanism it is more important to notice that these rumours—they even got into print—were widespread than it is to determine their accuracy. Yet it is odd that such outspoken critics as Lytton Strachey and Kingsley Martin dismiss them so lightly. Had the image of Victoria as the model of domestic purity so great a hold that even the boldest thinkers drew back appalled at the prospect of shattering it? The more circumstantial stories respecting the Queen's relations with John Brown deserve to be the subject of serious historical criticism. It is unfortunate that Mr. E. E. P. Tisdall's, *Private Life of Queen Victoria*, 1961, falls short of such a standard.

[2] The London ship-wrights were injured by the rise of iron ship building. See S. Pollard, *Econ. Hist. Rev.*, second series, Vol. 3, 1950–51.

profound faith in our great Liberal leader—Mr. Gladstone—makes me feel all the more secure as to the future'.[1] This confidence was not shared by all his colleagues, some of whom wished to replace the League with a Republican organisation. 'Cooper, Odger and the Clerkenwellians seem determined,' he noted, 'to convert the (Reform) League to ultra-Republicanism.'[2] Within a few months Howell was isolated and Republicanism had become a serious issue.

The Republicanism of the early 'seventies was not all of a piece. This is not merely a matter of the vulgar, 'Civil List' republicanism of the masses on the one hand and the gentlemanly, philosophic sort of republicanism on the other. There were two tendencies in the Republican Movement, just as there were in the land agitations and the movements for the organisation of the unskilled which were associated with it. Republicanism, in whatever shape it came, was joined to these other movements through its personnel and by its own essential nature. It was never merely an attack on Monarchy.

In terms of the first of these two tendencies, the Republic was conceived of as a meritocracy: a regime resting upon equality of opportunity. Englishmen were thought to be separated from it by obstacles of a purely constitutional and legal sort. The Monarchy was objectionable because it enshrined the principle of aristocratic privilege at the heart of our national life. Republicanism in this form was directed exclusively against the landed interest. To an attack upon an aristocratic privilege in political institutions it joined an attack upon the law of primogeniture and entail which prevented free trade in land. The leaders of this tendency looked with a special solicitude upon the sufferings of the agricultural labourer and often associated themselves with his attempts at Trade Union organisation. Sir Charles Dilke was the most prominent representative of this kind of Republicanism and was credited by the Queen and the national press with leadership of the entire movement. Charles Bradlaugh was its most energetic and effective propagandist and organiser. John Stuart Mill, although not directly identified with Republican propaganda, was its teacher and as far as the land question was concerned, the author of its

---

[1] G. Howell to E. Beales, 10 March 1869 (H.C.).
[2] G. Howell, diary entry for 29 January 1869.

programme and the head of its most influential organisation: the Land Tenure Reform Association.

The second tendency saw the Republic socially as well as politically: in terms of organisation as well as of liberty: to *la République démocratique* it opposed *la République démocratique et sociale*. It was frequently more authoritarian and sometimes contrasted Republican statesmanship with democratic inefficiency. If the Republic maintained itself by public opinion rather than by force, this did not mean that it was inseparable from ballot boxes and still less from parliamentarianism. Some characterised the head of state in the Republic as one who would govern but not reign. Cromwell, Danton, Lincoln, all the great Republican chiefs were far more kings of men than most monarchs.[1] What would make the Republic legitimate would be the quality of its purpose rather than any perfecting of democratic legality. The Republic stood for the provision of social welfare as well as for widening opportunities for personal advancement. The Monarchy was objectionable, not merely because it exalted aristocratic privilege, but because it consecrated the principle of the unworthiness of labour (they characterised the ruling class as the *commercial* aristocracy). Some of the most sophisticated exponents of this kind of Republicanism declared that it was historically necessary that the political revolution should find its complement and reach its climax in a social revolution. The political republic had endorsed the five great principles of emancipation: of the mind, the man, the land, the nation and the minority. But the Republic could only fully realise its own ideals by becoming social. Thus, if the political revolution's first principle was the emancipation of the mind, the social revolution's must be universal education. If the land had been 'emancipated' in France and was in the course of emancipation in England, then this must soon be followed by the emancipation of labour through the abolition of 'wages

---

[1] In particular, the Positivists emphasised the distinction between democracy and republicanism. J. H. Bridges, 'Republicanism', *Commonwealth*, 24 March and 6 May 1866. The fullest exposition of their views will be found in F. Harrison, *Order and Progress*, 1875, pp. 116–24 and 300–47. Harrison is acknowledged by Kingsley Martin (*The Magic of Monarchy*, 1937, p. 40) to have been the most serious theoretician of the republican movement, but he fails to draw attention to Harrison's differences with Dilke, Herbert, Fawcett and others.

slavery'.[1] Whereas the bourgeois Republicans concentrated their fire on the landed interest and demanded land tenure reform, the proletarian republicans insisted on tagging on to attacks on the landlords, attacks on the 'money-lords' as well. They made their first demand, not reform of the land laws, but nationalisation of the land. Land nationalisation was linked to plans for 'Home Colonisation' and was intended to bring relief to the urban as well as to the agricultural workers. With this difference of emphasis, there went a corresponding difference in the approach to the problem of organisation among the unskilled. For the bourgeois Republicans this was seen to relate exclusively to the agricultural labourers: for the proletarian Republicans it involved active assistance to the unskilled workers in the towns. If the first trend in Republicanism was associated with Mill and the Land Tenure Reform Association, the second owed much to Marx and the Land and Labour League.

The boundaries between these two tendencies were fluid. Sometimes when the workers did insist upon their independence, they seemed to be unable to supply any rational or wholly convincing reasons for doing so. It took the Commune to expose the indeterminate nature of the demand for the Republic. It could be plausibly suggested that there was no incompatibility between going in for Land Tenure Reform and asking for nationalisation. Similarly, there seemed to be no contradiction between organising labourers in the countryside and helping them to do the same thing in the towns. The demarcation line was blurred because, with a few exceptions, the proletarian Republicans were not socialists and the bourgeois Republicans were exceedingly flexible. Thus, while the former made little or no attempt to push the demand for nationalisation beyond the land and certain aspects of banking,[2] the latter were ready to accommodate themselves to the increasingly leftward trend

---

[1] T. Smith, *The Law of the Revolution*, Nottingham, 1872, p. 20. This was the most distinguished working-class contribution to Republican thought and was praised by Marx and Beesly and treated with respect by J. S. Mill.

[2] An exception was the platform of the *International Herald* which added to these demands a call for the nationalisation of railways, mines, canals, docks and harbours (*International Herald*, 18 May 1872). However when Dupont attempted to get the British section of the International to endorse nationalisation as a general principle to be applied to industry as well as land he was defeated (*Eastern Post*, 27 July 1872).

that ran through the Labour Movement in these years. With the exception of George Potter, who was unambiguously associated with the bourgeois grouping, the 'recognised' leaders of British Labour moved uncertainly between the two tendencies. They were caught between the need to respond to a great upsurge of militancy from below and the desire to maintain friendly relations with those who were better off and socially more distinguished.

I

The story of proletarian Republicanism begins in the Autumn of 1869 with the foundation of the Land and Labour League. This body was not at first an avowedly Republican one, but it soon became the principal forum and clearing-house for that trend in the movement. Its history has never been adequately written, for Cole was confused about its leadership[1] and Mac-Coby could not get beyond 'tantalising indications surviving of a forgotten Land and Labour agitation conducted on what was, perhaps, a more radical and less careerist basis than the Labour Representation Movement proper'.[2]

The League was established at a working men's conference which was held at the Bell Inn, Old Bailey on 13, 20, and 27 October 1869. With the burial of the Reform League earlier in the year, the question was raised as to what organisation could take its place. In September the formation of the Labour Representation League provided an organisation with a platform that corresponded to the deepest concerns of the 'recognised' Labour leaders, but it hardly satisfied the rank and file. In the democratic clubs of the metropolis various schemes were canvassed for a more radical organisation which would push Land Nationalisation or Republicanism. At a meeting of the Holborn branch of the old, O'Brienite National Reform League, William Osborne and John Johnson proposed the summoning of the conference at the Bell Inn.[3]

---

[1] G. D. H. Cole and R. W. Postgate, *The Common People*, p. 393.

[2] S. MacCoby, *English Radicalism 1853–1886* (1938), p. 164.

[3] For the preliminary moves and for the inaugural meetings see the *National Reformer* from 19 September 1869.

As soon as the Land and Labour League was born, Karl Marx staked his claim to paternity. He told Engels that it was 'directly inspired' by the International and that it signified that 'the workers' party disassociates itself completely from the bourgeoisie'.[1] In a confidential circular issued by the General Council of the International, Marx stated: 'We can initiate measures (such, for example, as the foundation of the Land and Labour League), which later, in the public execution of their tasks, appear as spontaneous movements of the English working class.'[2] There were many tendencies within the League, but at its inception Marx was justified in believing that his was the dominant one.

This is evident from a study of the character of the League's Programme and from the form and content of its Inaugural Address. It is equally apparent in the character of its founders and leading personnel, and in the usefulness of its early work in relation to the specific line taken by Marx in the International.

Marx attached particular importance to the first plank in the Programme, the nationalisation of the land. This had been the first of the ten 'despotic inroads on the rights of property, and on the conditions of bourgeois production' which had been proposed in the *Communist Manifesto*. At the Basle Congress of the International, held only one month before the founding of the Land and Labour League, it had been declared that 'Society is entitled to abolish individual ownership of the soil and to make the land communal property.'[3] In advance of the Congress, Marx had won the English delegates for this proposition. He attached special importance to it in the English context because of its bearings on the Irish question which he saw as decisive for the future development of the British Labour Movement.[4]

For the rest, the Programme of the League was presented in a disjointed and unsystematic way, but it contained some of the measures which were bound to separate workmen from the middle-class Radicals and which would, if adopted, be bound

[1] K. Marx to F. Engels, 30 October 1869 (*Gesamtausgabe*).
[2] K. Marx, *Letters to Kugelmann*, 1936, p. 107.
[3] G. M. Stekloff, *History of the First International*, 1928, p. 141.
[4] K. Marx to L. Kugelmann, 29 November 1869.

to 'outstrip themselves (and) necessitate further inroads upon the old social order'.[1] These measures were:

2. Home Colonisation.

3. National, Secular, Gratuitous and Compulsory Education.

4. Suppression of Private Banks of Issue. The State only to issue paper money.

5. A direct and progressive property tax in lieu of all other taxes.

6. Liquidation of the National Debt.

7. Abolition of the standing army.

8. Reduction of the numbers of the hours of labour.

9. Equal electoral rights, with payment of Members.

The hand of old Chartists, Owenites and currency reformers can be seen in some of these demands. Land nationalisation itself was supported on a wide variety of grounds. Even in its early stages some members of the League were found reviving old arguments based on the 'Norman Yoke'; arguments that had been employed by Winstanley and Lilburne two hundred years before.[2] Thus, M. J. Boon, in one of the first publications of the League, referred to the workers as 'nothing but white wage-slaves to the same classes who have always been licensed by the Land Robbers to rob and plunder their forefathers from the time of the Norman Conquest . . .'.[3] Others, such as Frederick Riddle who was subsequently to become Secretary of the League, turned to scriptural authority.[4]

Indeed, the programme showed the vitality of the popular radical tradition which taught that the private control of land and credit was qualitatively different from the private control of the means of production in general. 'True theories of Money' which could be traced back to Yarranton or Bishop Berkeley had a long historical association with demands that the land should be recovered from the descendants of those who had stolen it. Land and credit were regarded as being more subject

[1] K. Marx and F. Engels, *The Communist Manifesto.*

[2] C. Hill, 'The Norman Yoke', in J. Saville (editor) *Democracy and the Labour Movement*, 1954, pp. 11–66.

[3] M. J. Boon, *A Protest Against the Present Emigrationists*, 1869.

[4] F. Riddle, 'Deus Rex', reprinted in C. M. Davies, *Heterodox London* (11), 1874.

to monopoly and inherently more important than anything else—although there was little reason for supposing this to be so, except in terms of the experience of small farmers and petit bourgeois.[1] If many members of the Land and Labour League continued to associate land and credit in this way it was because they saw land nationalisation, not as an inroad on bourgeois production, but as a measure to be taken along with Home Colonies in order to reduce unemployment. The Home Colonists, once established, would require cheap credit.

Paradoxically, the Basle Congress itself may have given some impetus to this type of 'deviation'. The delegate from the American National Labour Union, A. G. Cameron, was a currency reformer who had had his fare paid by the leader of that school in the United States, Horace Day. As early as 1870, F. A. Sorge was obliged to tell Marx that 'the National Labour Union which had such brilliant prospects in the beginning of its career, was poisoned by Greenbackism and is slowly but surely dying'.[2]

An early tract of the Land and Labour League was entitled, 'The Bank of England and the Greenback Banks of Issue'. But in its first months of existence the League did not give excessive attention to these theories and a leading currency reformer, James Harvey, asked reproachfully, 'why land and not money?'[3] Marx might well feel that he could ignore the ecleticism of the League's programme and the retrograde and unscientific character of some of the interpretations which were placed upon it. He was all the more entitled to do so because the Programme was over-shadowed by the Address which accompanied it. This was clearly modelled on his own Inaugural Address written for the International five years before. Like that famous indictment of capitalism, the Address of the Land and Labour League to the Working Men and Women of Great Britain and Ireland, attempted, with a single impressive sweep, to lay before the reader the condition of the working class as a *whole*. It directed attention to the same crucial issue; the supposed tendency to an inverse ratio between the expan-

[1] However, for the high concentration of land ownership see J. H. Clapham, *Economic History of Modern Britain*, Vol. 2, 1932, p. 253.

[2] P. S. Foner, *History of the Labour Movement in the United States* (New York, 1947), p. 429.

[3] *National Reformer*, 9 April 1871.

sion of productive power and the growth of national income on the one hand, and the share of that income going to the working class on the other. Even the style owed something to Marx, although here dialectics hardly rose above paradox.

> They promised retrenchment; they have enormously increased the public expenditure instead. They promised to lift the burden of taxation from your shoulders; the rich pay but a fractional part of the increased expenses . . . They promised to minimise pauperism, they have made indigence and destitution your average condition—the big loaf has dwindled into no loaf. Every remedy they have applied has but aggravated the evil, and they have no other to suggest—their rule is doomed!

In so far as this 'Address' took the whole of capitalist economy under review, it dwarfed the League's own limited and disjointed programme; in so far as it indicted existing society in the name of the working class as a whole, it set itself far in advance of the Labour Representation League which shrank from any developed statement of principle,[1] and concerned itself with little more than sending the leaders of the skilled workmen into the House of Commons.

The Address appeared over the names of John Weston as Treasurer and of Martin J. Boon and J. George Eccarius as Secretaries.[2] All three were members of the International and Eccarius was still one of Marx' most devoted disciples. It was expected that Eccarius would become the paid Secretary of the League,[3] but his hopes, so often disappointed in the past, were to be dashed again. The League's constitution provided that 'as soon as the funds are sufficient, a paid Secretary shall be appointed by the Council', but with an annual subscription of 1s., they never proved sufficient. Indeed the low subscription and the ultra-democratic character of the League's constitution— with its emphasis upon the autonomy of its branches—ought to have given Marx pause before he assumed that it would be a convenient instrument. For the time being he was doubtless content that members of the International such as Osborne, Lucraft, Hales, Johnson, Mottershead and Jung should figure

[1] So much so that Bradlaugh refused to join it on these grounds, and Odger was soon disowning his membership of it.

[2] See the appendix to this chapter.

[3] K. Marx to F. Engels, 30 October 1869, op. cit.

prominently among the thirty-seven members of its Council.[1] The office of President had been abolished in the International. The League followed suit when a conflict between Odger and Bradlaugh looked as if it might split the organisation. When it was finally decided that there must be a President, the choice fell upon the tailor, Patrick Hennessey. As an Irish Trade Unionist, he provided just the sort of figure-head that Marx would have welcomed.

The formation of the Land and Labour League was doubly welcome to Marx. First, because it appeared to put a stop to all the badgering of Hales and others for an English National Council within the International. Second, because of the good which it appeared to be capable of doing in its own right. Hales had been pressing for an English section of the I.W.M.A. since 1866.[2] Marx—distrusting the theoretical capacity and revolutionary spirit of the English—wished to keep the management of British affairs in his own hands.[3] Hales tried at the outset to get the Land and Labour League constituted as the English department of the International.[4] Two years later, when the English Federal Council was established, it was frequently confused with the Land and Labour League.[5]

The League began its career by taking up precisely the issues which Marx would have wished it to tackle. The Irish question loomed large. Before the League was formed Hennessey appeared in Trafalgar Square with Bradlaugh, Weston, Charles Murray and others on behalf of the Fenian prisoners.[6] This spirit was carried over into the League's inaugural meetings. The members listened sympathetically to Mr. Dicker of Londonderry, who represented 2,500 Irish tenants who were being evicted by two London companies. While in the Cabinet they were considering the Irish Land Bill, and 'both Argyll and Lowe were very much afraid of admitting arguments that, as Gladstone put it, might one day cross the water';[7] Patrick

---

[1] *National Reformer*, 7 November 1869.

[2] H. Collins, 'The English Branches of the First International' in A. Briggs and J. Saville (editors), *Essays in Labour History*, 1960, p. 248.

[3] K. Marx, *Letters to Kugelmann*, op. cit.

[4] *National Reformer*, 17 October 1869.

[5] *Eastern Post*, 9 December 1871.

[6] *Bradford Review*, 25 September 1869.

[7] J. L. Hammond, *Gladstone and the Irish Nation*, 1938, p. 93.

Hennessey was explaining to the League the propriety of occasionally shooting an Irish Landlord. When Benjamin Lucraft tried to reprove Hennessey, he was over-ruled by the meeting.[1] Marx saw fraternal relations between the British proletarian and the Irish nationalists as the *sine qua non* of the defeat of the aristocracy and the arrival of a class-conscious Labour Movement in Britain.

The League also broke with the traditional attitude of the Labour aristocracy towards the unskilled and the unemployed. In 1869 there were 1,032,000 in receipt of relief, a higher number than in any year since 1849 if one ignores the figures for the cotton famine year of 1862. The position in the East End of London was exceptionally bad and unemployment persisted in the South-East after recovery had become general elsewhere.[2] This was largely due to the decline of ship-building on the Thames. Between 1865 and 1871 it is estimated that the numbers employed in ship-building and marine engineering fell from 27,000 to 9,000.[3] The League sought to place itself at the head of the unemployed and the great demonstration which it organised in Trafalgar Square on Good Friday 1870 aroused much interest. *The Times* made the activities of the League the subject of repeated editorial comment. The League's speakers were denounced for displaying 'the grossest ignorance ever exhibited by popular pretenders to knowledge'. It was monstrous, in the eyes of *The Times*, to suggest that the price of bread could be reduced by reclaiming waste lands or to contend that it was being kept artificially high by landlords.[4] Howell found that 'the abuse of Gladstone was simply intolerable'.[5]

Emigration was the simplest and the most familiar response of many Victorians to the problem of unemployment and faith in its efficacy was expressed by Trade Union leaders even if it never figured as a very important element in their actual policies. With unemployment reaching serious levels in London, George Potter was pushing emigration in the *Bee-Hive*. This

[1] *Reynolds' News*, 17 October 1869.

[2] 'Debate on Unemployed Labour', 17 June 1870, *Hansard*, 3rd Series, Vol. 27.

[3] S. Pollard, 'The Decline of Ship-building on the Thames', *Econ. Hist. Rev.*, Second Series, Vol. 3, 1950–51, p. 88.

[4] *The Times*, 12 and 16 April 1870.

[5] G. Howell, Diary, 15 April 1870.

panacea now came under violent attack by the spokesmen of the League. When Potter closed the pages of the paper to them, they published their letters to him in the form of tracts.

> The emigrationists [wrote Martin J. Boon] are treacherous Tories, cunning Judas-like Whigs, and Half-hearted reformers ... They seek to deprive our country of that bone, sinew and brain, that would enable us to bring about those reforms that would save us from the Land and money sharks within, and the disturbing enemies without.

He continued in a tone that must certainly have won Marx' approval:

> We are told by the advocates of emigration, that our wants arise from too great a number of people. This is a monstrous untruth. Our wants do not—they cannot arise from too great a number of people for many years to come. They arise from the fact of one-third part of the people living in idleness, luxury and splendour, while the mass of the people are compelled to live upon less than one-fourth part of the produce of their own labour. Therefore, let the useful classes say emphatically, 'No! We will not emigrate!' If emigration is needed, let those who have never done anything to add to the happiness of the human race, go and begin in a fresh land ... Some tell us that it is a law of nature that causes the present distress: that population tends to increase faster than the means of subsistence. No! no! the cause is—and the only cause is—the law—and not, as Mr. Malthus and his mistaken disciples say, the Law of Nature.

Boon appended to his tract a draft of a Bill which Gladstone was called upon to introduce. It specified that 'on and after the first day of March 1870, all forests and untilled lands throughout the United Kingdom be used for National Purpose, the same to be held as National Property, and under no circumstances to be sold to private individuals: the future rents of such lands to be used to defray the legitimate expenses of the Country'. The whole object was to bring relief to the unemployed. They were to be started on small co-operative farms which were to be financed by borrowing 'a sum of National Notes free from all interest, such notes to be legal tender for all taxes and purposes of trade ...'.[1] This proposal reflected the influence of

[1] M. J. Boon, op. cit.

O'Brien and also of the celebrated Guernsey Market experiment which was frequently referred to by members of the Land and Labour League.[1]

There was yet another aspect of the League's work which might have been a source of satisfaction to Marx. It was at its formation a direct triumph for his line in the Labour Movement at the expense of John Stuart Mill and Mill's admirers and followers. On 22nd July 1869, Mill, together with a group of radical M.P.s, issued invitations to a private conference at which it was intended to establish the Land Tenure Reform Association. The invitations were headed with the words of Cobden: 'I would have a League for free trade in Land, just as we had a League for free trade in corn.' The first object of the Association was to be the promotion of the free transfer of land and 'to restrict within the narrowest limits the powers of tying up land'. Positive measures by the State were to be limited to providing 'facilities' by which—'without unjust interference with private rights'—the tillers of the soil might acquire an interest in the land.[2] While this new organisation was still in a provisional state, Mill learnt that among the workers there was a party of 'Nationalisers' of which Odger, Cremer and Lucraft were members. While he agreed with them 'in principle', he held that the Association would not gain support from any but a portion of the working classes if it openly endorsed their views. 'It is possible,' he wrote, 'that the active spirits of the working classes may think nothing worth trying for, short of this, and may consequently withhold their support from the Association. I think this would be a great mistake, but we must be prepared for the possibility of it . . .' He went on to demonstrate the extent of his intransigence by opposing a change in the Articles of the Association which would have allowed that the working classes generally, as distinct from those who worked on the land, had a peculiar interest in the land question.[3] When he heard of the establishment of the Land and Labour League he

[1] J. T. Harris, with preface by S. Webb, *An Example of Communal Currency*, 1911. (The best account of the Guernsey Market House.)

[2] Records of Land Tenure Reform Association (H.C.).

[3] J. S. Mill to A. Reid, 5 October, 1869, H. S. R. Elliot (editor) *Letters of John Stuart Mill*, 1910, II, pp. 214–15. The end of the letter, not published by Elliot, shows Mill's opposition to changing the articles of the Association. I am indebted to Mr. Peter Jackson for showing me a copy of this.

did not know whether to be glad or sorry. 'The furious and declamatory violence of their resolutions and some of their speeches seems to show that they would have been a very intractable element in the other association, and that it is well rid of them.' [1]

Mill's correspondent, Andrew Reid, went to the inaugural conference of the Land and Labour League as a kind of emissary. He found that his statesmanlike proposals for the abolition of primogeniture were 'laughed down'. Marx had all too recently been reading lessons to the English members of the International on the 'incorrect formulations' of Bakunin, which also placed a special emphasis upon the laws of inheritance. It had been impressed upon them that such proposals started at the wrong end and merely created obstacles to the final settlement of the land question through nationalisation. As for Mill in particular, Marx had already—through the medium of Eccarius—dealt with his notions of political economy in the pages of the *Commonwealth*. He allowed that

> Mr. Mill has a faint anticipation of a state of things in which the satisfying of wants, and that alone, might be the incentive to production, but he cannot elevate his conception above a state of society in which the materials of and instruments of production are the private property of individuals.[2]

George Potter, who was also associated with the Land Tenure Reform group, came along with Reid to the inaugural meetings of the League. He did his best to prevent attacks on 'the monied aristocracy' being tagged on to resolutions against the landlords. He told workmen that they now had a Government 'which would respectfully listen to the representatives of working men', but his interventions were greeted with cries of derision.[3] Heedless of such warnings, Potter allowed himself to be nominated to the Council of the League. To the intense satisfaction of Marx, he was soundly defeated.[4]

For a time the most 'respectable' Labour leaders—and perhaps Mill himself—imagined that they could adopt a con-

---

[1] J. S. Mill to H. Fawcett, 24 October 1869 in *H. S. R. Elliot*, p. 223.
[2] J. G. Eccarius, *Commonwealth*, 17 February 1867.
[3] *Reynolds' News*, 17 October 1869.
[4] K. Marx to F. Engels, 18 November 1869.

descending attitude towards the League. When George Howell's employer, Samuel Morley, told him that he ought to join all the popular movements of the day, Howell replied:

> There are some movements in which I cannot take part, such as the Land and Labour League—a body which goes in for the most wild theories as to the Land and Social and Political questions generally. But these theories will yield to the influence of more practical suggestions as they become the topics of general discussion.

In the event, the yielding was on the other side. By April 1870 Mill was negotiating with Robert Applegarth, W. R. Cremer and others in the hope of finding a new programme 'on which the land reformers of the working classes can co-operate with those who do not go to the length of the nationalisation of all the land of the country'. Cremer stated publicly that he could not have joined with Mill on the basis of the original programme. Thus it was that the celebrated 'unearned increment clause' came to be written into the policy of the Land Tenure Reformers. Some middle-class supporters withdrew from the Association as a consequence of these changes. Mill told them:

> It is not without deliberate consideration that I have concurred in a course of policy for the Association which we knew would prevent many persons whose support would have been valuable from joining it. We had to choose, however, between possessing their adhesion, and depriving ourselves of all support whatever from the working classes . . . as an Association we should have no power or usefulness whatever unless we could enlist in our support the most intelligent part of the working classes; who are very generally adopting as their creed the entire resumption of the land from private hands into those of the State. We thought it the wisest course, therefore, instead of limiting our demands so as to obtain the greatest attainable amount of adhesion among the higher and middle classes, to go as far towards the demands of the working classes as we conscientiously could, provided that by this means we could induce them to support us and act with us . . .[1]

As will be shown, this gambit met with some success, but it exposed Mill to the charge that he had compromised his reputation as a philosopher and concealed his real opinions,

[1] J. S. Mill to J. Boyd Kinnear, 22 July 1870, *H. S. R. Elliot*, op. cit., pp. 263–4.

'which are not so revolutionary as he tries to make out'.[1] It was not until May 1871 that the Land Tenure Reform Association managed to hold its first public meeting and to begin 'ousting' the Land and Labour League. There was some truth in the Tory allegation that if the League was ousted, it was yet, paradoxically, 'really in possession of this land agitation'.[2] But even at this level, Mill's Association was never wholly in possession of the field or able to entirely wean away such eminent leaders as Odger from the Land and Labour League.

II

While Mill was trying to find a formula which allowed Cremer and his friends to support his Association, discussions were beginning in the branches of the Land and Labour League on the possibilities of establishing a new journal. By this time the *Bee-Hive* had altogether ceased to pretend to militancy, and 'improving' articles were taking the place of news spiced with salacious titbits. The absence of any distinctively working-class principles among the top level Labour leaders was reflected in the banality of its columns. Matters were made still worse at the beginning of 1870 when the Rev. Henry Solly was appointed joint conductor of the paper. Engels sized the situation up very astutely:

> It is really lucky that the *Bee-Hive* shows its bourgeois colours so impudently and so stupidly. Such a lousy number I have never seen yet. This crawling before Gladstone, and the whole bourgeois-condescending-philanthropic tone must break the neck of the paper and make a real worker's newspaper a necessity. It is very good that just at this moment, when the workers are awakening from this Liberal trance, their only newspaper becomes more and more bourgeois.[3]

In September 1870 the new journal appeared. It was not officially the organ of the Land and Labour League, although the League was virtually the only organisation which received its consistent support. It gave extensive coverage to the League's activities. The proprietor of the copyright was Daniel Chatter-

[1] *Standard*, 20 March 1873. Also *Pall Mall Gazette*, 18 April 1871.
[2] *Standard*, ibid.
[3] F. Engels to K. Marx, 1 November 1869 (*Gesamtausgabe*).

ton, one of the League's most active propagandists and a member of its General Council.[1] The name of the paper was the *Republican*.

The choice of title was not merely a salute to the new regime in France. Beneath the surface of events, Republican sentiments had been growing for some time past. Just as the International—no doubt to the amused contempt of Marx—adopted the Republican mode of address before the rise of the Republican movement, so the Land and Labour League adopted the symbols of the Republic before they were being displayed by anyone else. At the demonstration on behalf of the Unemployed on Good Friday 1870, members of the League wore 'broad scarlet sashes, not over the shoulder, but around the waist, in the exact pattern current among the *sans culotes* of the first French Revolution, and, in a further imitation of that class, poles were born aloft with the emblematical caps of liberty'.[2]

In 1870, the *Republican* expressed, far better than the *Bee-Hive*, the dominant mood of the London workmen. Solly set before his readers the ideal of workmen as 'working bees rejoicing in cheerful labour . . . true to their brother bees of every class, and to the Queen Bee on her honoured throne'.[3] This at a time when the workers were sickened by the 'stimulated ecstasy, slavish tone and meaningless, unmanly, drivelling' about the Royal Family.[4] They were heartily behind the Land and Labour League which led the protest against the dowry to Princess Louise. Well-informed observers knew that in the workshops curses both loud and deep were heaped upon Royalty as the callous despoilers of the poor. 'Men—decent, steady artisans . . . speaking amid applauding circles of shop-mates, wished that the whole tribe of Royalty were under the sod; while women, mothers themselves, prayed that its women might be made unfruitful, so that the race of royal paupers might not be increased.'[5]

[1] In the 'eighties Chatterton produced a scarcely legible sheet called *Chatterton's Commune*. It had no programme beyond the physical extermination of the bourgeoisie to the last man, woman and child.

[2] *Times*, 16 April 1870.

[3] *Bee-Hive*, 19 February 1870.

[4] 'A Working Man', 'English Republicanism', *Frasers' Magazine*, N.S., Vol. 3, January–June 1871, p. 754.

[5] Ibid., pp. 755–6.

When the French Republic was proclaimed in September 1870, the British working class became as enthusiastically pro-French as it had been pro-North after the Emancipation proclamation. However, the witless Solly was staunchly for the Prussians. The French, he explained, had been 'desperately demoralised' by Voltaire and Auguste Comte. Thus, the *Republican*, born at this time of disappointed hope at home and crisis abroad, was able to point with some effect to the 'political pauperism by which the working class is surrounded' and which is becoming 'more transparent and obvious every day'.[1] If its voice was shrill and its questions rhetorical, the new paper was in close accord with the spirit of the time. It directed its fire at the Howells and Cremers with deadly effect. Where was the Reform League? It had been destroyed by hired political mercenaries in the interests of 'that ghastliness, that knavery called Liberalism'.

> Christ, a Social and Political Reformer of his day, we are told was sold for thirty pieces of silver; we fear that there are many traitors who would sell the workers for less than that amount, if by so doing it enabled them to present themselves at Court, or drive with the professed friends of the people . . .[2]

What was the Labour Representation League doing? 'The wires of this Society are pulled from Downing Street.'[3] 'To us,' declared the Republican, 'there is nothing so hateful, so detestable, as a patronising, mendacious magnanimity.'[4]

The Labour leaders whom the *Repulican* (somewhat prematurely) characterised as 'the abandoned tools of commercial philanthropy',[5] soon found that they could not afford to ignore the new forces which the paper represented. The Land and Labour League now advanced by leaps and bounds. Between September 1870 and the end of the year three new branches were established in London.[6] Soon support was coming in from the provinces. Working Men's Clubs and other associations in

[1] *Republican*, September 1870.

[2] *Republican*, October 1870.

[3] Ibid. (This had some foundation in fact. See G. Howell's diary, 30 May 1870 (H.C.).)

[4] *Republican*, May 1871.   [5] Ibid.

[6] Report of the Land and Labour League, *Republican*, January 1871.

Cardiff, Bristol, Oxford, Southampton and elsewhere applied for membership.[1] In relation to the protest against the failure of Gladstone to recognise the French Republic, the established leaders of Labour found themselves being pulled along in the wake of a vast movement which they could not pretend to control. Charles Bradlaugh now appeared as the leading spokesman. The main agency for organisational purposes was the Anglo-French Intervention Committee, presided over by Richard Congreve, which was set up by the Land and Labour League in conjunction with the International Democratic Association.[2] The Positivists, who were francophils on a religious scale, largely inspired these developments. They no longer turned to the *Bee-Hive* or the well-known Labour leaders, but in the first instance, to the branches of the Land and Labour League. All these branches took a vigorous part in the pro-French agitation.

By the beginning of 1871, the Rev. Henry Solly no longer controlled the *Bee-Hive* and the Labour Representation League had been forced to identify itself with the great pro-French and Republican upsurge. Its leaders were kept up to the mark by the militancy of the rank and file. When George Howell was bold enough to ask, at a great meeting organised by the Positivists in conjunction with the Land and Labour League: 'Would Englishmen have surrendered at Metz?' a strong voice from the Hall replied, 'Yus, if they had been led by the Duke o' Cambridge.'[3]

In the spring of 1871 the League was at the height of its power. No other organisation conducted such intensive activities. The *Republican* from being issued monthly was turned into a fortnightly and then into a weekly. It was not until May that the Land Tenure Reform Association held its first public meeting and when P. A. Taylor introduced a petition to the House of Commons opposing further enclosures it was from the Land and Labour League. The militant policies with which the League was identified seemed everywhere in the ascendant. Yet it soon ceased to make any further real headway. Just as it had anticipated the rise of the general Republican movement, so

[1] Third Half-Yearly Report, *Republican*, September 1871.
[2] *Republican*, November 1870.
[3] *Eastern Post*, 14 January 1871.

it declined somewhat ahead of it, and this despite the fact that it managed to maintain some kind of existence until the close of the 'seventies.

III

The fortunes of the Land and Labour League in particular, and the Republican movement in general, have to be understood in terms of both political and economic developments. Events in France accelerated the growth of English Republicanism, but they also contributed to its confusion and disintegration. Unemployment in London provided a valuable agitational field and helped to create a favourable climate within which the League could work. When this problem diminished during the rapid expansion of the early 'seventies, the League (or some of its members) still found valuable work to do among workmen who were untouched by established forms of Trade Unionism. What they could not cope with was the vastly more profound problem which was posed by the onset of the Great Depression.

When the Franco-Prussian War broke out, Patrick Hennessey invited John Stuart Mill to assist a public meeting to be organised by the Land and Labour League. The objects of the meeting were to resist any attempt to involve England in the war: to call for the abolition of standing armies: to demand that all able-bodied men in the country should have a thorough military training as the best safeguard of peace and the best defence in war.[1] Mill replied:

> I so far agree with the promoters of the meeting to which you do me the honour of inviting me, as to be very desirous to see a movement commenced for the thorough military training of the general population. I wish the mass of soldiers to be identical with the mass of citizens, standing armies to be eventually dispensed with, except the scientific corps, and probably a permanent staff of carefully trained officers, and not taken as at present from one class of the community, but from all.
>
> But I do not agree with what seems to be implied in a 'Protest against this country being brought into the War'. To declare beforehand that no amount of iniquity perpetrated before our

[1] P. Hennessey to J. S. Mill, 25 August 1870. (Mill–Taylor Collection, folio 361–2, L.S.E.)

eyes shall induce us to go to war would be the best way of ensuring wars abroad and would infallibly, like all other selfishness and cowardice, finally redound to our own cost. If war between nations is ever to be put an end to it can only be as war between individuals has been checked in civilised societies—by the creation of a police and an impartial umpire to settle quarrels. To create such a system it is necessary that all courageous and right-thinking men should be as ready to suffer in protecting the weak in politics as they ought to be in civil life.[1]

Within a few days Hennessey's stand of strict neutrality had changed into one of passionate sympathy with the French. Working-class London seemed to be riding as one man to demand the recognition of the Republic. The Positivists, encouraged by Marx, joined with the Bradlaugh and the leaders of the Land and Labour League in bringing the entire movement's weight to bear on the Government. But little time elapsed before Beesly and his friends had transformed the demand for recognition into a demand for armed intervention by Britain on behalf of France. The Land and Labour League and many other workmen went forward with them. It was easy to present the pacifists of yesterday as the war-mongers of today:

> Yes, Mr. Merriman, sound your alarms,
> Odger and Applegarth, shout ye: 'To arms!'
> At the war's outbreak you peace were all for,
> Now have your windpipes grown trumpets of war.[2]

Mill was quite out of sympathy with the demand for war and he blamed the Positivists for uniting the workers behind them in raising it.[3] Marx and Engels, who had a more correct appreciation of the state of working-class opinion, reproached them with splitting the workers up.[4] Police reports to the Gladstone Cabinet support Marx' interpretation of what was happening. After making some suitable observations to the effect that the 'quasi-respectability' of such men as Beesly ought to have separated them from those who referred to the Premier as 'Coercion

---

[1] J. S. Mill to P. Hennessey (Draft answer), n.d. 26 August 1870? (Mill–Taylor Collection, folio 363–4, L.S.E.)

[2] *Punch*, 28 January 1871.

[3] J. S. Mill to J. Morley, 6 January 1871, *H. S. R. Elliot*, II, p. 292.

[4] For Engels' Criticisms, Minutes of General Council of the I.W.M.A., 31 January 1871 (IISH).

Bill' and to the Queen ('Mrs. Brown') in 'terms that would be-
fit a brothel', these reports state that the call for war with
Prussia led to secessions from the movement.[1] Beesly explained
to Marx, 'I do not anticipate that England will act even in the
mildest way. But all this excitement is leavening the mass for
us.'[2] Two years later, Beesly's chief, Richard Congreve, summed
up: the London workmen were

> practically unanimous in proclaiming the French Republic, and
> always insisted that the Government should recognise it without
> delay. But when it came to the question of war, the division was
> very pronounced: they drew back before this prospect, and this
> division was fatal to the exercise of any serious influence upon the
> general politics of the country.[3]

The Revolution of the Commune healed the breach between
Positivists and Marxists, but it had the most divisive effects on
the Land and Labour League and the Republican movement
generally. With one stroke it exposed the hopelessly indeterminate nature of the demand for 'the Republic' and broke English Republicanism up, not only along the lines of the two tendencies which had always been latent in it, but into a host of
quarrelsome, competing sects.

As far as the respectable Labour leaders were concerned,
Beesly and Marx in defending the Commune, might as well
have been addressing the inhabitants of another world. The
chasm which separated working-class thinking in London and
Paris was vividly demonstrated by the experience of a committee set up early in 1871 on which George Potter and other
workmen sat alongside Baron Rothschild. The object was to set
up a fund so that the Parisian workmen might get their tools out
of pawn.[4] Across the Channel this philanthropic gesture was being rendered superfluous by the Parisians themselves who were
abolishing the pawn-shops! Most of the English Trade Union
leaders seem to have supposed that the Commune could have

[1] Summary of Police Reports registered in the Home Office, with reference to political meetings held in the Metropolis during the years 1867–70
inclusive, Gladstone Papers. (Brit. Mus.) 44617, f. 95.

[2] E. S. Beesly to K. Marx, 20 September 1870 (MELI).

[3] R. Congreve, 'L'Union des proletariats anglais et français', Essays:
Political, Social and Religious, 1874, I, p. 464.

[4] Bee-Hive, 8 April 1871.

been averted by a timely translation of *Cassell's Encyclopaedia of Useful Knowledge*. The Bookbinders' Secretary, T. J. Dunning, was speaking with the authoritative voice of the Trade Union oligarchy when he announced that economic categories were immutable and that the Communards must be mad since they dared to contemplate the abolition of rent.[1]

The rank and file were probably not so much hostile to the Commune as bewildered by it. Engels could not find a good word to say for them,[2] but they were at least free from the hysteria which infected other classes of society.[3] Some observers found that while the British workers were opposed to Communism—'it would make the skilful and thrifty workmen suffer for those who are neither'—they sympathised with the Communards. They respected them as patriots, republicans and courageous men, and were passionately indignant when their prisoners were butchered.[4] Their most popular tribunes, Bradlaugh and Odger, refused to endorse the principles of the Commune and began the break-up of the Land and Labour League by pushing their own sectarian movements. Thus, by the middle of 1871, Bradlaugh was emerging as 'the coming Cromwell', the President of the London Republican Club which was reputed to have some 30,000 supporters loosely organised under his personal leadership.[5] Odger gave to the idea of the Republic rather

[1] T. J. Dunning, 'The Commune in Paris', *Bee-Hive*, 8 April 1871.

[2] Minutes of the General Council of the I.W.M.A., 8 August 1871 (I.I.S.H.).

[3] Hysteria was not, of course, universal in any class. Harrison told John Morley: 'Half the people I meet here secretly (but very secretly) sympathise with the Commune' (9 June 1871). He reported that Mill 'was against Versailles' (21 June 1871), and referred to rumours that Carlyle agreed with his line on events in Paris (9 June 1871). Harrison's work for the communard refugees throws interesting light on English attitudes: 'Every day brings me letters in which the British public is displayed in all its colours—its eccentricity, its good nature, its profound generosity, its Yankee quickness to do a job, its impertinence, its selfishness, its hypocrisy. Pinching housewives write on scented notepaper for a "distressed" maid-of-all-work at £1 per year . . . Procuresses want "an inexperienced girl of 17". Oxford men want a Communist by the next train to live with them. Well-to-do people offer a home and their friendship. An M.P. sends £100, an "old housekeeper" sends £5 . . .' (F. Harrison to J. Morley, 13 February 1872 H.C., L.S.E.).

[4] 'The Journeyman Engineer, The English Working Classes and the Paris Commune', *Frazer's Magazine*, July 1871, pp. 62–8.

[5] *Eastern Post*, 21 October 1871, citing a report in the *New York World*.

more of a social content than did Bradlaugh, but he too turned to the development of his own personal following, which he organised around the publication *Odger's Monthly*. He rejected the moderation of the Labour Representation League ('I found it serving the Whigs') and also the intransigence of the International ('the most unfit persons I have ever come in contact with to represent the working classes').[1] The *Republican*, and a section within the Land and Labour League, complained about his attitude towards the International and made him the subject of violent criticism. In consequence, Odger began to give increasing support to Mill without formally breaking with the League.[2]

What of the pro-communard element? The Positivists saw the Commune as 'perhaps the most striking event (as yet), of the nineteenth century';[3] the 'first act of the most momentous historical drama of modern times'.[4] Beesly in the *Bee-Hive* and Harrison in the *Fortnightly* both wrote superbly in its defence.[5] The social character of 'left' Republicanism was momentarily given an extremely sharp expression.

> As I have always insisted, *civil war* in France has long been inevitable. There stands there the people of Paris and other large cities, for the purest, most honest, direct, and intelligent part of France, its real intellectual head and its true vital heart, who will have a Republic, and a real Republic, a government that is for the sake of the whole and not of the rich. Opposite stand the professional and trading class—mere adventurers who want to keep society as it is, and who alternately make use of armies, police, priests and peasants as their instruments. There stood the workmen resolved that society should not go on as it has done, armed and ready to fight. On the other side the rich resolved to keep society as it is, and ready to use any weapon, especially lying, fraud, legal and parliamentary chicanery and the rest of their dodges to keep society as it is . . . Society as it is now constituted is not worth keeping together. The right to grind out of the work-

---

[1] *Republican*, August 1871.
[2] G. Odger, 'The Land Question', *Contemporary Review*, August 1871.
[3] F. Harrison to J. Morley, 22 March 1871. FHC.
[4] E. S. Beesly: 'The Fall of Paris', *Bee-Hive*, 27 May 1871.
[5] See the *Bee-Hive* between 25 March and 17 June 1871 for a dozen articles by Beesly on the Commune. Harrison in the *Fortnightly* for May and August 1871.

man, his wife and child the uttermost farthing; to leave him naked, half-starved, ignorant, filthy, whilst you choke yourself with luxuries and cover the earth with your whims i.e. political economy, is a right he will not admit. Your right to property, that is selfishly to consume, or wantonly to waste, what the combined toil of many has made, is no right at all. *La propriété (comme vous la possédez) c'est la vol.* That is quite true. *Your* goods, *your* shops, *your* coffers! are being robbed! Yours? What made them yours? Society put you in charge of them, but from the ill-use you made of them Society takes them away from you.

Nothing that the rich can suffer, no death or torment, is worse than they deserve—lying, cheating, selfish, callous, calumnious brutes. There is only one word—*ces bougres du bourgeois* . . .

Dimly and under many cries these workmen say—we want Society organised so that all its plums shall not fall on [*sic*] the rich, and all its weight on us—and that means the Republic—a government which is not the prize of a class—but the protection of the weak, and the helper of the suffering . . .

Legitimacy of the National Representatives: I deny it all. I refuse to be bound by suffrages. The whole thing is a protest against the lying sham called universal suffrage. The whole theory of the suffrage is only one of the tricks of the *bougres*. It is not the national will, it is not even the majority. The best men have *a right* to serve the nation in a crisis. It is as Carlyle said—take away the bauble of the ballot box. The 2,000,000 workmen in Paris and other great towns are the 'best men'. There are not 2,000,000 *bougres*, not 500,000, but having hocused a lot of peasants they call themselves the majority. Majority or not we won't have them. Legitimate government be damned!

In an epoch of revolutions every government is but the issue of a fresh *coup d'état* . . . But election or not I deny that suffrage is a test, I deny parliamentary government, I deny the suffrage is the source of right altogether. I fall back on force. And here we are. What do the *bougres* fall back on? Why, force . . .

I beg your pardon for the use of the word '*bougre*'. It comes from Marat and Père Duchesne. Nothing else can express the feeling of loathing and contempt we feel for the order. It is made up of idle bourgeois, money-makers, lawyers, priests and so forth and the official military, legal and literary creatures they employ.[1]

In the shelter of a private correspondence Harrison felt free to express the boundless passion which events in Paris aroused

---

[1] F. Harrison to J. Morley, 22 March 1871. FHC.

in him. In public he showed rather more discretion, rather more light and rather less heat. Yet even before the onset of civil war, he told Morley: 'I think there is only one thing left to preach—the Abolition of the Bourgeoisie. Its ignorance, super-stition, cowardice and selfishness ruins all in France and else-where. Love is its prophet—*The Times* its teacher and W.R.G. its toady. Damn its sordid soul—damn everybody who has money in the funds.'[1] He complained about

> the inherently metaphysical and impotent nature of modern Radicalism. I am struck with it most in its concentrated form in J. S. Mill. You know my admiration for the personal character and philosophic power of the wise old man . . . Yet politically Mill is utterly wrong-headed . . . He reasons, argues and syllogizes about politics . . . Now you ought not to reason about politics . . . Politics is a matter of feeling. Right feeling, trained, intelligently trained feeling, I grant—but not of syllogisms. Mill teaches you all to chop logic in politics—very good logic no doubt, but you ought to feel with a mysterious force of nature. Politics are like virtue in Aristotle, the same thing in fact.[2]

Social Republicanism, in a high passion, hit upon 'abolition of the bourgeoisie', but it did not pursue this idea in its calmer moments nor had it any adequate conception of how it might be accomplished. What Harrison said in private was echoed in the public pronouncements of some working-class Republicans. J. Johnson, the 'Marat of Walworth Common', was ready to raise an International Brigade to go to Paris and declared him-self ready to destroy existing society in England root and branch. Osborne of the London Patriotic Society and some of the contributors to the *Republican* valued the Commune as 'a sort of transcendental poetry' which would, somehow, quicken and transform political existence.[3] But these proletarian Republi-cans got no encouragement from the Positivists despite the in-stinctive affinities that appeared to be present. Beesly deprecated the attempt of John Hales and others to impress 'a sectarian character upon the Communard movement'.[4] He told the Left Republicans that if they wanted to make a Revolution they had

[1] F. Harrison to J. Morley, 8 February 1871. FHC.
[2] F. Harrison to J. Morley, 10 (?) February 1871. FHC.
[3] *Republican*, 9 May 1871.
[4] E. S. Beesly to F. Harrison, 13 March 1872. BUC.

better do some thinking and organising instead of parading about with bands and banners. He regarded them as vulgar, shallow and essentially unserious when compared with their opposite numbers in Paris.[1] The Positivists did consider bringing out a paper to be called the *Republican* which would 'give the working class element a distinct point', but they never managed it.[2] No doubt Marx and Engels shared this view, but lest anyone should look to the Positivists for leadership they took care to point out that ' the Comtists are not properly a working-class party. They advocate a compromise to make wages–labour tolerable, to perpetuate it; they belong to a political sect who believe that France ought to rule the world.'[3] Despite the friendship and co-operation which characterised the relations of Beesly and Marx, both men were anxious that there should be no confusion between Positivism and Communism.[4]

Thus, the pro-Communard forces were divided among themselves even as they were separated from those Republicans who drew back from the dictatorship of the proletariat. Just as Odger and Bradlaugh hived off to devote most of their time to their own enterprises, so the supporters of the Commune within the Land and Labour League tended to do likewise. Thus in April 1871, some Social Republicans, including Boon, Weston and Le Lubez formed the Universal Republican League. It was modelled organisationally on the I.W.M.A. and most of its followers were disgruntled members of it. It had corresponding secretaries for Scotland, Ireland, Germany and other countries, and included a long list of 'welfare' demands in its immense programme.[5] The subsequent formation of two rival National Councils of the I.W.M.A. added to the confusion of competing organisations.

The *Republican*, highly cantankerous at the best of times, fell increasingly under the influence of currency reformers. They attacked the Unionists as 'the worst of monopolists' and

---

[1] E. S. Beesly, 'London Republicans', *Bee-Hive*, 24 June 1871.

[2] F. Harrison to E. S. Beesly, 27 October 1870 (?). FHC.

[3] F. Engels, Minutes of the General Council, I.W.M.A., 31 January 1871. IISH.

[4] R. Harrison, 'E. S. Beesly and Karl Marx', op. cit.

[5] *National Reformer*, April 1871.

declared that their Unions were 'deadlier than any capitalist's possible weapon.'[1] Odger was singled out for special abuse and this brought protests from John Weston and some branches of the Land and Labour League.[2] The editor claimed to have enjoyed the friendship of George Julian Harney and Bronterre O'Brien, and he enlivened his columns with attacks on Feargus O'Connor as well as Odger. In the end the paper buried itself under the weight of its own vituperation. Bradlaugh's opinions on religious matters were drawn into discussion of Republicanism. Its last issue compared atheists unfavourably with the Sultan of Turkey, the Czar of Russia and the Pope.[3] It perished in February 1872, its place quickly being taken by the *International Herald* which tried to be rather more generous towards its contemporaries.

Had the Land and Labour League enjoyed formal control over the paper and had it possessed substantial funds, it might have been able to have restrained some of this sectarianism and prevented quite so great a proliferation of competing organisations. As it was, it was badly placed to deal with the blandishments which Mill now addressed to working-class land reformers. He appealed 'to the active and influential portion of the working classes' who opposed all private property in land, to recognise that his proposals would, by increasing the number of landlords, reduce the price of land and therefore the cost of compensation if it was later nationalised.[4] This was a gambit which effectively split the League. Some of its members were for an uncompromising class struggle on the land and other questions, the rest based their actions on a Liberal interpretation of the League's constitution. This expressly commended 'co-operating with, or accepting the co-operation of other associations or individuals, who, while they may not be pre-

[1] E. L. Garbett, 'The Coming Holy War', *Republican*, 1 August 1871. In the issue for 1 June 1871 Wm. Maccall wrote, 'Between the governing classes and a revolution, stand a million of paupers and the dense mass of trades' unionists . . . And what is trade unionism but selfishness and despotism?'

[2] *Republican*, 15 April 1871.

[3] 'Republicanism versus Bradlaugh and Atheism', *Republican*, 1 February 1872.

[4] 'Explanation' added by J. S. Mill to Programme of the Land Tenure Reform Association, 1871.

pared to cast in their lot with us, are honestly desirous of promoting the same ends'.[1]

Boon and Johnson went along to Mill's inaugural meeting and put an amendment stating that the Land Tenure Reform Association was unworthy of the support of the working classes because it advocated 'an extension of private ownership in land for the advantage of the middle classes'. Not only was this amendment lost, but John Weston, the first Treasurer of the Land and Labour League, moved a vote of thanks to Mill in which he reprimanded his comrades for their opposition.[2] George Howell, comfortably ensconced as financial agent of Mill's Association, must have enjoyed this situation.[3]

If the League was fast becoming a forum and clearing house for the proletarian left rather than a centre of power, not all those members who branched out into independent activities wasted their time in sectarian wrangling. Patrick Hennessey not only helped P. O'Leary to form the Metropolitan Home Rule Association,[4] he joined with other members of the League in pioneering work among the unorganised workers in the East End.

In July 1871 the employers of the East and West India Docks resolved to abolish the contract system. But they combined this decision with another which involved the reductions of wages from 3s. to 2s. 6d. per day. The Rector of Bethnal Green, the Rev. S. Hansard, sided with the men, but advised them not to strike since they had no Union. He told them: 'At present they were without a champion and . . . they were not of the aristocratic class of working men. Feeling that they required others' services, he had asked Mr. Patrick Hennessey to attend.'[5]

By the end of November, Hennessey had helped the dockers to organise a Labour Protection League. The entrance fee was fixed at 6d. with a weekly subscription of 2d. Hennessey presided at the inaugural meeting and became a trustee. A docker

---

[1] 'Constitution of the Land and Labour League', *Republican*, September 1870.

[2] *Land Tenure Reform Association*: Report of the Public Meeting in the Freemason's Hall, 15 May 1871.

[3] G. Howell to C. Bartlett, 26 September 1869. (In this letter Howell gives a long list of his offices in various organisations.)

[4] *Irish Vindication*, 30 September 1871.

[5] *Eastern Post*, 4 November 1871.

named Caulfield was elected secretary at a salary of 24s. a week.[1]

By the spring of the following year, Hennessey was working for the new League in close collaboration with Charles Keen. Keen had succeeded Hales as secretary of the British Federal Council of the I.W.M.A.[2] and frequently addressed meetings of the Land and Labour League. He was widely experienced in this type of work and had helped to establish the Kent Agricultural Labourers Union.[3] Hennessey had not spared the Rev. S. Hansard's feelings from the moment he had joined the Dockers' Union. He spoke bluntly about the class war and cursed the 50,000 Christian ministers, when but two only could be found to support the workers.[4] Keen followed suit, and when Hansard presumed to give an address to the Prince of Wales, ostensibly on behalf of 10,000 labourers, Keen denounced him for 'Toadyism and Twaddle'.[5]

By July 1872 the League was growing fast and Keen replaced Caulfield as Secretary. He and Hennessey addressed numerous meetings around the demand for a 6d. an hour minimum and a reduction of hours, explaining that these demands could only be attained through strengthening the Labour Protection League. They adopted a policy of selective strike action, leaving the large docks over the water alone, and concentrating on the smaller wharfs and warehouses at the season when these were most vulnerable to pressure. Short, sharp strikes met with success and as much as 33% was secured in increases for some men. 'Six weeks ago,' declared T. Venner, the President of the League, 'as little as 3d. an hour was paid by Col. Beresford's wharf—(hisses)—the Gun Shot wharf 3½d. and others 4d. None of them now paid less than 5d.'[6] They were resolved to go on until they had won 6d. an hour with extra for overtime and had abolished the contract system.

The Labour Protection League grew at a prodigious rate. In May it had 1,200 members, but by October it claimed 30,000 organised in 54 branches.[7] In June it had begun extending beyond the docks and had started to organise engineers'

---

[1] *Eastern Post*, 16 December 1871. [2] H. Collins, op. cit., p. 252.
[3] *Eastern Post*, 4 May 1872. [4] Ibid., 4 November 1871.
[5] Ibid., 7 July 1872. [6] Ibid., 7 July 1872.
[7] Ibid., 4 May and 19 October 1871.

labourers in Millwall. In September it began to found branches among the dustmen, slopmen and scavengers. According to the representative of these men the average weekly wage in East London was 7*s*. per week. On the other hand, in Whitechapel, men worked for between 9*s*. and 10*s*. per week, in Limehouse 12*s*. and in St. Luke's 18*s*.[1]

At the end of the year Keen convened a conference attended by representatives of the Labour Protection League, the Railway Servants Association, the Carmens Society and the Amalgamated Lightermen and Watermen's Association. The carmen and lightermen had recently failed in strike action and it was proposed to establish one joint executive so as to centralise their power and bring it to bear on any one branch of the 'transit trade'. Although it was to be called 'The Amalgamated Labour Union', it was to be a federation in which each of the constituent bodies preserved its own autonomy, but elected six representatives to a Council. The Council was to decide on strikes and on parliamentary action. Keen, pointing to the Master and Servant Acts, stressed the importance of the Union having political purposes.

> Mr. C. Keen believed that they were on the right road to redress their grievances in the future. Strikes had failed in consequence of the aristocracy of mechanics and artisans ignoring the underpaid labourer. It was from the lowest remunerated class that the employer recouped himself. It should be their effort, and the effort of the skilled mechanic, to elevate the lowest strata of society. The Labour League was doing it, but the amalgamation of the four associations would more effectively accomplish it.[2]

It is not clear what became of the intended amalgamation, but the London and Counties Labour League which the Webbs describe as having been established in 1872,[3] and which shared in the glory of 1889, was no doubt a descendant of the body led by Keen, Venner and Hennessey.[4] Other members of the Land and Labour League interested themselves in promoting Trade

---

[1] *Eastern Post*, September 1872. [2] Ibid., 22 December 1872.
[3] S. and B. Webb, *History of Trade Unionism* (1920), p. 403.
[4] According to R. Groves, *Sharpen the Sickle*, 1949, p. 85, this was the descendant of the Kent and Sussex Labourers Union. If this is so it still leaves Keen with the credit of a founding father since he appears to have played a significant part in organising the labourers in Kent.

Unionism among the police and the case of the alleged victimisation of P. C. Goodchild for engaging in this activity.[1] These men or others like them may also have had a share in the organisation of agricultural labourers. This was evidently so in Kent and may have been so in other districts. But most of the agricultural workers' Leagues and Unions placed great stress on the value of emigration and this ran counter to one of the earliest and most distinctive doctrines of the Land and Labour League. Besides, this work was smiled upon by Mill, and supported by Samuel Morley and the Trade Union oligarchy, so there was correspondingly less scope for organisers from 'the Left'.[2]

In 1873 the League still served as a meeting place for land-nationalising Republicans, even if the main commitments of the more prominent ones lay with other organisations. In March of that year Weston became President; Boon, Vice-President and Le Lubez, Treasurer. The Secretaries were nonentities, but Odger, Bradlaugh, Shaw and Shipton were among the members of the Council.[3] Just before Mill held his last public meeting, the League reiterated its objections to his position. Peasant proprietors were not a 'universal good', even if they were preferable to aristocratic ones. Such proprietorships would not result merely from the abolition of primogeniture and entail. Mill's proposals were calculated to reform landlordism in the interests of perpetuating it. Why did he propose to appropriate only the *future* unearned increment of the landlord's rent?[4] Odger and Shipton put amendments in the sense of these

---

[1] Anon. (but printed and published by D. Chatterton) *The Revolution in the Police and the Coming Revolution in the Army and Navy* (n.d. 1872?).

[2] Arch claimed that between 1871 and 1881 the Unions helped 200,000 persons, agricultural labourers with their families, to emigrate. Certainly in 1874–75 Arch's Union spent £3,367 on emigration as well as £2,630 on migration. (Groves, op. cit., p. 67.) W. Hasbach, *A History of the English Agricultural Labourer*, 1908, declares that Mill greeted the agricultural labourers Unions as important allies (p. 279) and relates this to the powerful tendency within them which looked to a solution in terms of 'peasant proprietorship' (p. 281). Dilke and Bradlaugh joined the many non-conforming Christians who gave outside support and advice. The A.S.E. contributed £1,000 to the agricultural labourers' lock-out in 1874 (Groves, op. cit., pp. 69 and 77).

[3] *Eastern Post*, 1 March 1873.

[4] *National Reformer*, 23 March 1873.

objections at Mill's meeting, but they were rejected. The Land
Tenure Reformers had, as the Tory *Standard* put it, 'ousted the
Land and Labour League'.[1]

After Mill's death the programme of his Association was reconstructed under the direction of Admiral Maxse whose
article on 'Our Uncultivated Waste Lands' had done much to
carry the land question into the forefront of English, as distinct
from Irish, politics.[2] From October 1874 the famous 'unearned
increment' clause was replaced by a proposal that local authorities should acquire land in and around expanding towns and
cities. Two months later the *Bee-Hive* reported a speech by
Maxse in which he complained that members of the Land and
Labour League were wrecking the work of sincere reformers.
Warning his audience of the fate that befell what he termed 'the
Spencian Land and Labour League Societies of 1816', Maxse
went on to say that,

> all movements on behalf of Land Tenure Reform are being ren-
> dered abortive by wild amendments in favour of raw schemes
> which are scouted by the community. Not even the reputation of
> J. S. Mill—not even his unswerving devotion to the cause of the
> proletariate—was sufficient to save him from this treatment at the
> Freemasons Hall on the part of a couple of raw politicians, one of
> whom was not able even to express himself in decent English. I
> say that if there be any dignity or wisdom in the London Demo-
> cracy, it will give no encouragement to such insane behaviour in
> future . . .

It was difficult for the League to reply to the charge that its
role was an obstructive one, for while it found out the bourgeois
limitations of its rival, it could work out no systematic alternative of its own.

IV

Republicanism was an attempt to break out of the closed ring
of party politics, but it was inadequate to the task. It could
neither be used to unite the workers behind a radicalised
Liberal party, nor could it supply the basis for an independent

---

[1] *Standard*, 20 March 1873.
[2] Captain Maxse, 'Our Uncultivated Waste Lands', *Fortnightly Review*,
August 1870.

Labour party. Its most obvious consequence for the party system was apparent in the help which it gave to the Tories, who rejoiced in assuming the role of the Beefeater Party. The formula of 'the Republic' masked and inhibited the two tendencies and prevented them from working themselves out. As with the Reform League, so with the Land and Labour League; Marx congratulated himself on the appearance of independent, class organisations and concealed from himself the precarious basis of that independence. His high hopes ended in disappointment because neither the material nor the intellectual pre-conditions were sufficiently developed. During the late 'sixties and early 'seventies, the years of sharp economic fluctuations; of the Trade Union 'explosion'; of the Labour Laws agitation; disillusionment with the results of Reform and the rise of Republican protest; these conditions did appear to be ripening. But all advances were nipped in the bud by the onset of the Great Depression. This brought both the frost which caused present blooms to perish and a change in the climate which was eventually to allow hardier plants to arise.

The Land and Labour League shared in the pathos which marked the decline of the English Republican Movement. Just as the secularists' Hall of Science eventually passed into the hands of the Salvation Army, so the Hole-in-the-Wall (headquarters of the London Republicans) had its name changed under pressure from the Holborn magistrates to the Crown and Anchor.[1] Martin J. Boon, first secretary of the Land and Labour League, and resolute opponent of the emigrationists in 1869, was obliged to emigrate himself five years later.[2] The League lingered on to the late 'seventies, but like its contemporaries it was little more than a shell from which all life had been scooped out.[3] Its practical achievements had been small, although it may have done something to check the enclosure movement. On the other hand, its anticipation of future lines of development had been remarkable. Among some of its leaders Republicanism had been meant to be more than the last

---

[1] *Bee-Hive*, 16 March 1872.

[2] M. J. Boon, *How to Construct Free-State Railways*, 1884.

[3] Some time after 1877, probably in the following year, the League issued a leaflet, calling for a 'recommencement' of activities. It is undated, but refers to the late George Odger. Odger died in 1877.

word in Radicalism; it had occasionally been a recognisable anticipation of the Socialism of the next decade. 'We must,' said J. Johnson, who was generally more distinguished by his passion than his intelligence, 'prepare the way, not simply for a change of government, but for the coming social revolution and the redemption of labour.'[1] The League's land agitation prepared the ground for Henry George's triumphs in the 'eighties. The hand of fellowship to the unskilled was equally an anticipation of what the S.D.F.'s Trade Unionists were to attempt again some fifteen years later. If The New Unionism failed to establish an enduring organisational basis before the late 'eighties that was because it required higher real wages, wider educational experience, a jolt to the complacency of the labour aristocracy and the repeal of the Criminal Law Amendment Act.

It would be difficult to over-stress the analogy between the early 'seventies and the late 'eighties. It extended even to the language of protests. The term 'the unemployed' is held not to have become part of our vocabulary until the 'eighties when the Socialists popularised it through the demonstrations which they organised on behalf of the jobless. In fact, the expression was repeatedly used by the Land and Labour League from 1869 onwards. By going out to organise them it gave them a new identity.[2]

But the proletarian Left in the 'seventies did more than merely anticipate future developments; to an extent it prepared opinion for them. Some of those who took part in the earlier movement went on to join in the later ones. Indeed, the 'pioneering' achievement of some of the men of the 'eighties—notably Henry George—needs to be reassessed in the light of the process shown to have been already made by working-class opinion in the 'seventies.[3] The Labour Emancipation League,

---

[1] *Republican*, 5 August 1871.

[2] The O.E.D. (1926) credits the *Pall Mall Gazette* with introducing the term for the first time in 1882. The Land and Labour League used it in its 'Address'. See p. 246 and in its call to the demonstration of 1870. I can discover only one earlier use of the term: on 2 January 1863 the General Commanding the Northern District sent a confidential report to the Home Secretary in which he observed, 'the unemployed remain very quiet' (H.O. 45 7523 A/4).

[3] J. Saville, 'Henry George and British Labour', *Science and Society* (New York), Vol. xxiv, No. 4, pp. 321–33.

which bridged the gap between the advanced Republican and Socialist traditions, drew part of its programme from that of the Land and Labour League.[1] Although Patrick Hennessey failed to get the League re-established in 1881,[2] its title was kept alive by the Scottish section of the S.D.F. in the 'eighties,[3] and by a Hertfordshire Labourers Union centred on Hitchin in the 'nineties.[4] Hennessey himself went on to become a leader of the English Land Restoration League.[5] There were many other such names linking the Republicanism of the 'seventies to the Socialism of the 'eighties.[6]

APPENDIX

ADDRESS OF THE LAND AND LABOUR LEAGUE TO THE WORKING MEN AND WOMEN OF GREAT BRITAIN AND IRELAND

Fellow Workers,—The fond hopes held out to the toiling and suffering millions of this country thirty years ago have not been realised. They were told that the removal of fiscal restrictions would make the lot of the labouring poor easy; if it could not render them happy and contented it would at least banish starvation for ever from their midst. They raised a terrible commotion for the big loaf, the landlords became rampant, the money lords were confounded, the factory lords rejoiced—their will was done—Protection received the *coup de grâce*. A period of the most marvellous prosperity followed. At first the Tories threatened to reverse the policy, but on mounting the ministerial benches, in 1852, instead of carrying out their threat, they joined the chorus in praise of unlimited competition. Prepared for a

[1] E. P. Thompson, *William Morris*, 1955, p. 331.

[2] *Radical*, 8 January 1881.

[3] Manifesto of the Scottish Land and Labour League—Being the Scottish Section of the Social Democratic Federation, Edinburgh, October 1884.

[4] R. Groves, op. cit., p. 87.

[5] Information from Mr. Alfred Peacock.

[6] J. Morrison Davidson provides a leading example: see his *The Annals of Toil* (1899) particularly p. 386.

pecuniary loss, they discovered to their utter astonishment that the rent-roll was falling at the rate of more than 2,000,000*l*. a year. Never in the history of the human race was there so much wealth—means to satisfy the wants of man—produced by so few hands, and in so short a time, as since the abolition of the Corn Laws. During the lapse of twenty years the declared value of the annual exports of British and Irish produce and manufactures—the fruits of your own labour—rose from 60,000,000*l*. to 188,900,000*l*. In twenty years the taxable income of the lords and ladies of the British soil increased, upon their own confession, from 98,000,000*l*. to 140,000,000*l*. a year; that of the chiefs of trades and professions from 60,000,000*l*. to 110,000,000*l*. a year. Could human efforts accomplish more?

Alas! there are stepchildren in Britannia's family. No Chancellor of the Exchequer has yet divulged the secret how the 140,000,000*l*. are distributed amongst the territorial magnates, but we know all about the trades-folk. The special favourites increased from sixteen, in 1846, to one hundred and thirty-three, in 1866. Their average annual income rose from 74,300*l*. to 100,600*l*. each. They appropriated one-fourth of the twenty years' increase. The next of kin increased from three hundred and nineteen to nine hundred and fifty-nine individuals: their average annual income rose from 17,700*l*. to 19,300*l*. each: they appropriated another fourth. The remaining half was distributed amongst three hundred and forty-six thousand and forty-eight respectables, whose annual income ranged between 100*l*. and 10,000*l*. sterling. The toiling millions, the producers of that wealth—Britannia's Cinderellas—got cuffs and kicks instead of halfpence.

In the year 1864 the taxable income under Schedule D. increased by 9,200,000*l*. Of that increase the metropolis, with less than an eighth of the population, absorbed 4,266,000*l*., or nearly a half. 3,123,000*l*. of that, more than a third of the increase of Great Britain, was absorbed by the City of London, by the favourites of the one hundred and seventy-ninth part of the British population: Mile End and the Tower, with a working population four times as numerous, got 175,000*l*. The citizens of London are smothered with gold; the householders of the Tower Hamlets are overwhelmed by poor-rates. The citizens, of course, object to centralization of poor-rates purely on the principle of local self-government.

During the ten years ending 1861 the operatives employed in the cotton trade increased 12 per cent; their produce 103 per cent. The iron miners increased 6 per cent; the produce of the mines 87 per cent. Twenty thousand iron miners worked for ten mine owners. During the same ten years the agricultural labourers of England and Wales diminished by eighty-eight thousand one hundred and forty-seven, and yet, during that period, several hundred thousand acres of common land were enclosed and transformed into private property to enlarge the estates of the nobility, and the same process is still going on.

In twelve years the rental liable to be rated to the poor in England and Wales rose from 86,700,000*l*. to 118,300,000*l*.: the number of adult able-bodied paupers increased from one hundred and forty-four thousand five hundred to one hundred and eighty-five thousand six hundred.

These are no fancy pictures, originating in the wild speculations of hot-brained incorrigibles; they are the confessions of landlords and money lords, recorded in their own blue books. One of their experts told the House of Lords the other day that the propertied classes, after faring sumptuously, laid by 150,000,000*l*. a year out of the produce of your labour. A few weeks later the President of the Royal College of Surgeons related to a jury, assembled to inquire into the causes of eight untimely deaths, what he saw in the foul ward of St. Pancras.

Hibernia's favourites too have multiplied, and their income has risen, while a sixth of her toiling sons and daughters perished by famine, and its consequent diseases, and a third of the remainder were evicted, ejected and expatriated by tormenting felonious usurpers.

This period of unparalleled industrial prosperity has landed thousands of our fellow toilers—honest, unsophisticated, hard-working men and women—in the stone yard and the oakum room; the roast beef of their dreams has turned into skilly. Hundreds of thousands, men, women and children, are wandering about—homeless, degraded outcasts—in the land that gave them birth, crowding the cities and towns, and swarming the highroads in the country, in search of work to obtain food and shelter, without being able to find any. Other thousands, more spirited than honest, are walking the treadmill to expiate little thefts, preferring prison discipline to workhouse fare, while the wholesale swindlers are at large, and felonious landlords preside at quarter sessions to administer the laws. Thousands of the young and strong cross the seas, flying from their native firesides, as from an exterminating plague; the old and feeble perish on the roadside of hunger and cold. The hospitals and infirmaries are overcrowded with fever and famine-stricken: death from starvation has become an ordinary everyday occurrence.

All parties are agreed that the sufferings of the labouring poor were never more intense, and misery so widespread, nor the means of satisfying the wants of man ever so abundant as at present. This proves above all that the moral foundation of all civil government,

'THAT THE WELFARE OF THE ENTIRE COMMUNITY IS THE HIGHEST LAW, AND OUGHT TO BE THE AIM AND END OF ALL CIVIL LEGISLATION' has been utterly disregarded. Those who preside over the destinies of the nation have either wantonly neglected their primary duty while attending to special interests of the rich to make them richer; or their social position, their education, their class prejudices have incapacitated them from doing their duty to the community at large by applying the proper remedies: in either case they have betrayed their trust.

Class government is only possible on the condition that those who are held in subjection are secured against positive want. The ruling classes have failed to secure the industrious labourer in the prime of his life against hunger and death from starvation. Their remedies have signally failed; their promises have not been fulfilled. They promised retrenchment; they have enormously increased the public expenditure instead. They promised to lift the burden of taxation from your shoulders; the rich pay but a fractional part of the increased expenses; the rest is levied upon your necessities—even your pawn tickets are taxed—to keep up a standing army, drawn from your own ranks, to shoot you down if you show signs of disaffection. They promised to minimise pauperism: they have made indigence and destitution your average condition—the big loaf has dwindled into no loaf. Every remedy they have applied has but aggravated the evil, and they have no other to suggest—their rule is doomed. To continue is to involve all in a common ruin. There is one, and only one, remedy. Help yourselves. Determine that you will not endure this abominable state of things any longer; act up to your determination, and it will vanish.

A few weeks ago a score of London working men talked the matter over. They came to the conclusion that the present economical basis of society was the foundation of all the existing evils—that nothing short of a transformation of the existing social and political arrangements could avail, and that such a transformation could only be effected by the toiling millions themselves. They embodied their conclusions in a series of resolutions, and called a conference of representative working men, to whom they were submitted for consideration. In three consecutive meetings those resolutions were discussed and unanimously adopted. To carry them out a new working-men's organisation, under the title of the 'LAND AND LABOUR LEAGUE' was established. An executive council of upwards of forty well-known representative working men was appointed to draw up a platform of principles arising out of the preliminary resolutions adopted by the Conference, to serve as the programme of agitation by means of which a radical change can be effected.

After mature consideration the Council agreed to the following: Insist upon the State reclaiming the unoccupied lands as a beginning of its nationalisation, and placing the unemployed upon it. Let not another acre of common land be enclosed for the private purposes of non-producers. Compel the Government to employ the army, until its final dissolution, as a pioneer force to weed, drain, and level the wastes for cultivation, instead of forming encampments to prepare for the destruction of life. If green fields and kitchen gardens are incompatible with the noble sport of hunting, let the hunters emigrate.

Make the nine points of the League the Labour programme, the touch-stone by which you test the quality of candidates for parliamentary honours, and if you find them spurious reject them like a counterfeit coin, for he who is not for them is against you.

The success of our efforts will depend upon the pressure that can be brought to bear upon the powers that be, and this requires numbers, union, organisation and combination. We therefore call upon you to unite, organise and combine and raise the cry throughout Ireland, Scotland, Wales and England 'THE LAND FOR THE PEOPLE'—the rightful inheritors of nature's gifts. No rational state of society can leave the land, which is the source of life, under the control of, and subject to the whims and caprices of, a few private individuals. A government elected by, and as trustee for, the whole people is the only power that can manage it for the benefit of the entire community.

You are swindled out of the fruits of your toil by land laws, money laws, and all sorts of laws. Out of the paltry pittance that is left you, you have to pay the interest of a debt that was incurred to keep your predecessors in subjection; you have to maintain a standing army that serves no other purpose in your generation, and you are systematically overworked when employed and underfed at all times. Nothing but a series of such radical reforms as indicated on our programme will ever lift you out of the slough of despond in which you are at present sunk. The difficulty can be overcome by unity of purpose and action. We are many; our opponents are few. Then working men and women of all creeds and occupations claim your rights as with one voice, and rally round, and unite your forces under the banner of the 'LAND AND LABOUR LEAGUE' to conquer your own emancipation!

JOHN WESTON,   Treasurer

MARTIN J. BOON   ⎫
                        ⎬Secretaries
J. GEORGE ECCARIUS ⎭

VI

THE POSITIVISTS: A STUDY
OF LABOUR'S INTELLECTUALS

━━━✦✦✦✦━━━

THERE were many intellectuals who enjoyed some standing or influence in the Labour Movement in the 'sixties and 'seventies. T. H. Huxley and Herbert Spencer had importance as educators. Carlyle and Ruskin exercised an influence which grew with time. J. S. Mill and J. M. Ludlow were among the friends of Labour whose counsel received respectful attention. But it was the English Positivists who established the closest ties with the Trade Union leaders and working-class politicians and who exercised the most decisive influence upon men and events. The Christian Socialists still counted for something, but the Positivists far surpassed them in the numbers which they brought to the work and the energy which they displayed. E. S. Beesly, Frederic Harrison, Henry Crompton, the brothers Vernon and Godfrey Lushington and (to a lesser extent) J. H. Bridges and Richard Congreve, filled the columns of Labour newspapers; came in as advisors to key committees and appeared on the platform at the most significant Trade Union and political gatherings.

Positivism (with a small 'p') was the most distinctive intellectual tendency in England between 1860 and 1880. 'Advanced thinkers' accepted Comte's view of the scientific method as the only source of knowledge, properly so-called. Sometimes, as with Mill and John Morley, they owed a direct debt to Comte. In other cases, as with Huxley or Tyndall, they shared many of the conclusions of the Positivist Philosophy without having come to them by Comte's road. The more literary side

251

of the intellectual movement owed less to Comte, but it is a
measure of the pervasive character of Positivism that Ruskin
and Matthew Arnold felt obliged to define their positions in
relation to it. The Positivists, Frederic Harrison and Patrick
Geddes, had little difficulty in showing that Ruskin had more in
common with Comte than he realised.[1]

The defenders of established institutions saw their antagon-
ists as Positivists and took little heed of 'denominational' distinctions.

> Wise are their leaders beyond all comparison—
> Comte, Huxley, Tyndall, Mill, Morley and Harrison.
> Who will adventure to enter the lists,
> With such a squadron of Positivists?
>
> There was an APE in the days that were earlier,
> Centuries passed and his hair became curlier,
> Centuries more gave a thumb to his wrist,—
> Then he was MAN,—and a Positivist.[2]

The work of the English Positivists has to be understood in
terms of two traditions. First, as the disciples of Auguste Comte,
they were secular religionists. They sought to exchange the
consolations of theology for those of history. By the Religion
of Humanity they expected to resolve the conflicts of capital
and labour; order and progress; religion and science. Through
Saint Simon and Robert Owen, John Francis Bray, Colin and
Comte; the tradition of secular religiosity is joined to the formative stages of Labour and Socialist evolution.[3] Admittedly, not

---

[1] P. Geddes, *John Ruskin, Economist*, 1884. F. Harrison, *John Ruskin*, 1902.

[2] M. Collins, *Poetical Works*, 1886, pp. 87–8.

[3] In general, see G. D. H. Cole, *History of Socialist Thought*, Vol. I. *The
Forerunners*, 1953. For Colin see Cole's second volume, *Marxism and
Anarchism*, 1954. The reader who wishes to spare himself the immense
labour of reading Comte's major work will find all the essentials in
the following: *The Fundamental Principles of the Positive Philosophy* (translated and edited 'for workmen' by E. S. Beesly), 1905: *A Discourse on the
Positive Spirit* (translated and edited 'for workmen' by E. S. Beesly), 1903:
this work provides the best evidence of what Comte took to be the fundamental unity of his life and doctrine. But also see *A General View of Positivism*
(translated by J. H. Bridges), 1865. The standard interpretation is *La
Jeunevie d'Auguste Comte et la Formation du Positivisme* (Paris), H. Gouthier,
1933–41, 3 vols.

The most convenient introduction to Comte's opinions on the Labour

all these men were equally preoccupied with—or equally successful in—religion building. But even in Owen's case it would be unwise to dismiss it as the mere borrowing of certain religious forms to cover purely secular activities. There would be still less justification for treating it as simply a latter-day aberration or eccentricity.

The hall-mark of a secular religion is that it replaces God with some other agency which is supposed to be subject to empirical investigation. Just as righteousness had consisted in acting in accordance with the Will of God, so now it is identified with actions which are in conformity with the laws of this newly discovered agency. The conflict between religion and science disappears and moral rules at last become scientifically demonstrable. While Christian fundamentalism was being tormented by scientific progress, and Christian enquiry was turning away from explorations into the nature of God in favour of a heightened interest in relations between Him and the individual soul, the secular religionists proclaimed the reconciliation of science and religion and restored the apocalyptic vision which the theologians could no longer sustain. Robert Owen had little or no historical sense and his religious projects are consequently rather emaciated when set beside those of Saint Simon or Comte. Owen's 'rational religion' is less impressive because—while it embodies the 'scientism' essential to all secular religion—this is not re-enforced by 'historicism'. Nevertheless it was no accident that, when Richard Congreve tried to inaugurate the Religion of Humanity in England, he found that old Owenites provided the most receptive audience.[1]

It is largely through secular religion that the intimate alliance of philosopher and proletarian is sealed and the intellectual becomes progressively identified with the Labour Movement.

[1] R. Congreve to H. Edgar, 11 May 1860 (Wadham, C.).

Movement in its relation to his secular religion is *Le Proletariat dans la société Moderne*, Textes Choisis, avec une introduction de R. Paula Lopes (Paris), 1946. See also Delegation Executive de l'Eglise Positivists du Brasil, *Appreciation du Communisme* par Auguste Comte (Rio de Janeiro), 1948.

The best short accounts of Comte in English are H. B. Acton, 'Comte's Positivism and the Science of Society', *Philosophy*, xxvi, 1951, pp. 291–310, and the chapter on Comte and Scientism in D. G. Charlton, *Positivist Thought in France During the Second Empire* (Oxford), 1959, pp. 24–50.

Marx and Marxism stand in a complex relationship to these developments, but the association of Positivists and Marxists are not to be understood out of this context.

The English Positivists aspired to establish a Church, but in their effective influence they never became more than a ginger group. Valuing no vocation as highly as that of priest or teacher, they became men of affairs. Believing that redemption could come only through a vast change in hearts and minds, they worked a modest change in law and opinion. It was almost despite themselves that they came to occupy a kind of 'middle' between the Utilitarians and the Fabians. While they never lost their character as secular religionists, they assumed significance in the line of politico-philosophic societies that have done so much to determine the shape of social thought and legislation in England in the nineteenth century. It is primarily in this second capacity that they will be treated here, although their religiosity must not be lost sight of since it helped to determine the scope and limits of their effectiveness as an intellectual pressure group.

I

The success of any intellectual school in politics depends upon the presence of certain characteristics. First, the leading spirits must be bound together by close ties of personal friendship extending over many years. From this relationship arises a common commitment to ideas that are the products of several minds. As a Fabian wrote of the Utilitarians:

> The history of any definite 'school' of philosophic or political opinion will generally show that its foundation was made possible by personal friendship. So few men can devote themselves to continuous thought that, if several think on the same lines for many years, it is almost always because they have encouraged each other to proceed. And varieties of opinion and temperament are so infinite, that those who accept a new party name, and thereby make themselves responsible for each other's utterances, are generally bound by personal loyalty as well as by intellectual agreement.[1]

Second, the school must arrive at principles which have such fecundity that they can supply and replenish legislative programmes.

[1] G. Wallas, *Life of Francis Place*, p. 65.

Third, they must be able to create at least that minimum of organisation without which they cannot popularise their principles. They must have some command over journals and platforms.

Fourth, they must be able to win the confidence of powerful and dissatisfied groups interested in change. At the same time they need to combine their special relations with the leaders of such groups with some access, however limited, to the highest circles of established power.

Fifth, they must be able to promote direct political action either through the 'permeation' of existing parties or by means of their 'own' candidates or both. Yet the leading spirits are usually most effective when they are free from personal political ambition. For the moment they enter parliament they tend to compromise their intellectual independence and reduce the volume and effectiveness of their research and propaganda.

The Utilitarians and Fabians met most of these conditions. The Positivists, partly because they were never fully reconciled to this sort of role, met them more unevenly and imperfectly. It was almost (but not quite) as if the Fabians had tried to do the work for which they became famous without breaking with the Fellowship of the New Life.

English Positivism grew out of personal friendship. Beesly, Harrison and Bridges were all at Wadham College, Oxford, together as undergraduates, Godfrey Lushington was at Balliol during the same period—the years immediately following on the Revolutions of 1848.[1] Beesly and Bridges were both the sons

---

[1] F. Harrison, *Auto-Biographic Memoirs*, I and II, 1911. A. Harrison, *Frederic Harrison, Thoughts and Memories*, 1926. S. Liveing, *A Nineteenth Century Teacher:—J. H. Bridges*, 1926. M. A. Bridges, *Recollections of J. H. Bridges* (privately published), 1908. F. H. Torlesse, *Some Account of J. H. Bridges and his Family* (privately published), 1912. Beesly is not in the D.N.B. but there is a note in the 11th edition of the *Encyclopaedia Brittanica*. A slight but spirited sketch of him by a contemporary appears in J. M. Davidson, *Eminent Radicals in and out of Parliament*, 1880. See also my 'Professor Beesly and the Working Class Movement' in A. Briggs and J. Saville (editors), *Essays in Labour History*, 1960.

Lushington—later Sir Godfrey Lushington—was Bridges' contemporary at Rugby as well as at Oxford. See obituary by E. S. Beesly, *Positivist Review*, March 1907, pp. 70-1. There is a history of organised Positivism in England by J. E. McGee, *A Crusade for Humanity*, 1931. It contains a valuable bibliography but was written without access to the papers of Congreve, Beesly,

of evangelical ministers and their tutor, Richard Congreve, was regarded as the rising hope of the Evangelicals within the University. In fact he was already profoundly dissatisfied with the state of the world in general and Oxford in particular. He was passing under the influence of Comte and within a few years he was to resign his fellowship at Wadham and come to London to study medicine and qualify himself for the Positivist priesthood.[1]

Congreve's discontent and his developing sympathy with Positivism were soon detected by Beesly and his friends. They had formed themselves into a society known as Mumbo Jumbo in which they tried to find their way out of the religious and political chaos by which they felt themselves to be surrounded. They left Oxford united in their respect for Congreve, their affection for each other and their resolve to make themselves felt in the world.

In the 'fifties they were not yet Positivists, nor were they all of one mind. They were looking for a religion which would allow them to retain the moral earnestness of their evangelical forefathers without committing them to a shallow and untenable theology. They were in search of a Cause, but they could recognise no political or social forces with which they felt able to identify themselves. In relations with Congreve it was difficult to escape from *statu pupillari* and Harrison had reservations about accepting his leadership. 'His moral power of command, his independent thirst for rule, and broad sweep of aspiration is more than what his intellect can sustain or justify, and in his strength of will he claims more extensive work than his powers of understanding can master . . .'[2] As he saw Bridges drawing

[1] D.N.B. also F. Harrison, op. cit.

[2] F. Harrison to E. S. Beesly, 1852. FHC. (Many of the early letters in this collection are undated, or dated by the author thirty of forty years after they were written. Harrison presumably tried to date them when he was preparing his Memoirs. He made errors. All letters by Harrison are in this collection unless otherwise stated.)

Harrison and others used in this study. McGee adds nothing to what the Webbs had to say about the Positivists in their *History of Trade Unionism*, as far as their association with labour is concerned. The present work went to press before I had an opportunity of reading W. M. Simon's *European Positivism in the Nineteenth Century* (Cornell), 1963.

closer to Positivism he feared for him. 'Be the system true or false—it seems to me to paralyse the minds of its best followers.'[1] As for Beesly, Harrison always chided him with being cast in a severe mould and declared him to be the most truculent of mortals. But differences were not allowed to get out of proportion.

> Mumbo might quarrel and disagree seriously, but he must always exist. We each differ wholly, widely in much and perhaps must always—but in the main bond must always agree . . . Just consider how much we three, Bridges, you and I, hope for in common: an entire reconstruction religious, social and intellectual in which no institution, class or practice is to go unexamined or 'be saved but by its own merits'.[2]

On another occasion he told Beesly, 'I cann't say that I seriously imagined any permanent difference between us. It is quite impossible. I should shut up altogether before it came to that.'[3]

In the 'fifties, with the distintegration of parties at home and the Crimean War and Indian Mutiny abroad, Harrison and Beesly were possessed by a furious sense of outrage and helplessness. They tried vainly to form a small syndicate of like-minded young men who would work the press on political, particularly foreign political, issues.

> What a vile system it is where you and I can't get a morning paper to print our remarks on politics, and a puppy like that (the Hon. F. Lyzon) is actually in the government—30 millions of whites and about 100 millions of blacks governed by a doll whose face I should like to smack—let us pull it all down together.[4]

The only public figure for whom they felt any admiration was John Bright.

> I thoroughly like and trust the old fellow [remarked Harrison], but I more and more grow out of the position of English radicalism. A more harmonious system is gradually growing rooted in me. I once was as far gone as anyone in the subversive revolutionary spirit . . . I think even you might modify or rather develop your views were you to give the other side a fair chance. Read the *Politique*—Take the third vol.[5]

[1] F. Harrison to E. S. Beesly, 1856.   [2] Ibid., 1858.   [3] Ibid., 1859.
[4] Ibid., 1859—a different letter from the one cited above.
[5] Ibid., 1857. (Beesly eventually translated it.)

Bright alone among public men appeared to them to be associated with healthy social forces.

> It appears to me clear that the upper classes can no longer furnish
> even working statesmen. They will not even fight as a class. They
> are scrambling on the very battlefield. The middle class, com-
> mercial as opposed to manufacturing—shop keepers, money
> dealers, traders—appear to me sunk in selfish apathy. They care
> for nothing, they do nothing and they hope nothing—The
> Northern manufacturers alone have the pluck to direct—the
> horny handed millions alone the heart to trust.
>
> I am sick of those among whom we live. Their stale sneers—
> their ignorant commonplace—their mean fears disgust me. They
> stifle me. I will go and make friends with the hard hands and
> rough tongues—in whom content has not overgrown human
> nature nor success made selfish nor convention hypocrites—who
> can trust and love and hope.[1]

Harrison told Beesly that he must abandon his teaching post
at Marlborough College, come to London and make the acquaintance of Bright. 'You and he are made for one another.'[2]

> At least let us show the public that men of education and reflec-
> tion join heart and soul in John Bright's attack on the aristocrats—
> and that there are other people besides cotton-spinners who know
> them for the cowards and fools they are. Well, let us write to John
> Bright and say some young fellows disgusted with the howl raised
> around them, wish to ask him how best they can serve his cause.[3]

While seeking an alliance with Bright, the young Positivists
had a shrewd appreciation of the limits of Bright's social philosophy and the weakness of his political situation.

> I quite agree with you about Bright—I regret to see him sheer off
> from the people and yet alarm the bourgeoisie. I fear he has not
> enough of the demagogue—although his popular sympathies ap-
> pear to me to grow stronger every year. Bright however knows
> this. The mass of the people are not yet suffering enough to rouse
> them—His *point d'appui* must be the ambitious section of the middle
> class and the highest orders of the artisans, especially in the North
> of England. We are not sufficiently of the people to do much with
> our puerile education to agitate—but we could do a little to alarm

[1] F. Harrison to E. S. Beesly, 185– ?.   [2] Ibid., 1859, not cited before.
[3] Ibid., 1858, not cited.

EDWARD SPENCER BEESLY

GEORGE HOWELL

the upper classes and render them ridiculous—Now then, if after careful consideration, you are willing to move, write a letter to that effect to Bright.[1]

When Beesly and the other Oxford friends came to London at the end of the 'fifties they were better placed to work up this association with Bright and they did so to important effect. Yet from the beginning some at least of them felt that their attempt to rehabilitate the old notion of *les industriels*, with Bright at the head of an alliance of northern manufacturers and labour aristocrats, could only meet with limited success. For a time Beesly appears to have identified himself with Bright on all essentials, but Harrison observed:

> I fear your position as to the Ten Hours Bill is Bright's—one which I repudiate—I do reject political economy. I used to think Comte very unfair—but further reflection and a wider comprehension of his system convinces me that a study of the laws of wealth apart from political science as a whole is a pernicious fallacy.
>
> You see, turn which way I will, the ground is cut from under me as a supporter of Bright viz. my belief in a system really opposed to his and yours.[2]

He noticed that Ernest Jones was hostile to Bright and wondered whether Jones represented London workmen.

In the event, it was as much through the development of their differences with Bright on social questions as through their concurrence with him on political ones, that the young Positivists came to be in a position to render him the services which they had an ambition to perform. Their first concerted action in public affairs was taken on behalf of the London Builders and this immediately gave them a standing in the Trade Union world at a most formative period. They immediately employed the good will they had won to draw the Unions into political action and to associate them with Bright on the American question. 'We are going to have a great emancipation demonstration by the Trade Unions which Beesly has in some measure organised—Bright in the chair—to be a sort of reconciliation between him and them.'[3]

[1] F. Harrison to E. S. Beesly, n.d. (1859?), not cited.
[2] Ibid., n.d. (1858?).
[3] F. Harrison to Mrs. Hadwen, 24 March 1863.

Positivism helped to lead Harrison and his friends into association with both Bright and Trade Unionists and their experience of these associations came to re-enforce the lessons of Comte's teachings upon them. It was a creed which exactly hit off the aspirations of the more ambitious and adventurous section of the rising young intelligentsia. Positivism was modern, emancipated, scientific and systematic. As a syllabus—and Comte was an incorrigible pedagogue—it compared very favourably with the archaic and discredited conceptions still current at Oxford. In its programme for social reconstruction it conferred an exalted role upon the intellectual—provided he was a Positivist, he was to have power without office and this was to be conferred upon him by the proletariat which was unspoilt, open to large ideas, interested in fundamental change and increasingly able to secure it.

Comte was among the first to recognise the existence of the intellectuals as a distinct social stratum and to discuss their position *vis à vis* the proletariat. He wrote:

It is among the working classes that the new philosophers will find their most energetic allies. They are the two extremes in the social series as finally constituted; and it is only through their combined action that social regeneration can become a practical possibility. Notwithstanding their difference of position, a difference which indeed is more apparent than real, there are strong affinities between them, both morally and intellectually. Both have the same sense of the real, the same preference for the useful, and the same tendency to subordinate special points to general principles. Morally they resemble each other in generosity of feeling, in wise unconcern for material prospects, and in indifference to worldly grandeur. This at least will be the case as soon as philosophers in the true sense of that word have mixed sufficiently with the nobler members of the working classes to raise their own character to its proper level. When the sympathies which unite them upon these points have had time to show themselves, it will be felt that the philosopher is, under certain aspects, a member of the working class fully trained; while the working man is in many respects a philosopher without the training. Both too will look with similar feelings upon the intermediate or capitalist class. As that class is necessarily the possessor of material power, the pecuniary existence of both will as a rule be dependent upon it.[1]

[1] A. Comte, *A General View of Positivism* (trans. J. H. Bridges), 1865, p. 136.

This corresponded fairly precisely with the instinctive re-action of men like Beesly and Harrison to the unidea'd rich and with their readiness to take a positive, indeed rather romantic, view of the proletariat.

It is this stony impenetrability to ideas, of which the British middle class have made a sort of gospel, and in which the aristocratic class (who ought to know better) please to encourage them, that so revolts a man of any cultivation and a grain of imagination. Where is such a one to be found, not absolutely absorbed in politics or business, who is not visibly mocking at the whole apparatus (Parliament, Bible and Free Trade) in his heart? A lively writer of this class has opportunely transplanted the German name of Philistine. This happily describes that insurrection of the brain against the official and mercantile thrall which has driven those who believe in the force of ideas into closer sympathy with the people.[1]

If on closer acquaintance Beesly and Harrison found that working men were not so free from personal ambition or con-ventional hypocrisy as they had dared to hope, they were by no means totally disillusioned with them.[2] They admired their organisational capacity and in the presence of the hardships of the worker's life, the sufferings of strikers, the miseries of the Communard refugees they felt a genuine humility. They had indeed the intellectual's characteristic sense of guilt about the contrast between the comfort of their own circumstances and the insecurity which their working class friends experienced. When Frederic Harrison's father pressed a house upon him he remarked: 'Here am I just 40—who preach about Aristotle and St. Paul on Sundays, slowly being drawn down by the gentle pressure of truly loving hands into the final slough of Respect-ability. I assure you it makes me writhe with discontent.'[3] 'I

[1] F. Harrison, *Order and Progress*, 1875, p. 186.

[2] One of the first English Positivists, James Winstanley, was involved in the building strike and helped to prepare the ground for the formation of the First International by putting English workers in touch with their opposite numbers in Paris. He found in George Howell 'a kind of intellectual, moral and even physical beauty' (J. Winstanley to P. Lafitte, 30 August 1861), Le Musee d'Auguste Comte. Twelve years later when Howell 'lost' the paper which Harrison read to the T.U.C. at Leeds, the Positivist remarked: 'In dealing with workmen one has a constant struggle with a set of lying, thieving, jealous, vain, ignorant, irritable, lot of self-styled leaders to treat with' (F. Harrison to J. Morley, 21 January 1873).

[3] F. Harrison to J. Morley, 24 April 1871.

have got a house into which I am ashamed to bring one of these starving devils (the Communards) whom I call citizen and address with fraternity and whose shoes in the Kingdom of Heaven I am not worthy to black.'[1]

Comte had warned about the backwardness of the English workmen and feared that they were marked down for Communism, but the young Positivists found them in profound sympathy with much that was fundamental to the Positive Polity. Most of the leaders of the London workmen were emancipated from theological prejudices. They did not need to be persuaded that, as Comte held, it was to industrial and social, rather than to political action, that they must look for the solution of their problems. Yet they were ready to join hands with the Positivists and Bright on the great issue of British neutrality during the American War. Thus, they convincingly demonstrated that they had a wider and more generous vision than other classes. If they showed a distressing tendency to approach the question of Reform in a merely democratic or 'metaphysical' spirit instead of pressing for it in positive terms as a means to those measures which would be of substantial benefit, they were open to persuasion on this point. Above all, they were eager to have the friendship and collaboration of the young Oxford men. They treated their advice with respect; they welcomed their contributions to the Labour press and their defence of Unionism in the middle-class one; they visited them to seek their advice about the education of their children.[2]

This was just the style of relationship which Beesly and his friends wished for. One of the attractions of Positivism was that it offered the intellectuals a prospect of power without office; of ideological leadership without administrative responsibility. Comte warned his philosophers to avoid parliamentarianism and the sort of journalistic activity that involves an exclusive preoccupation with day to day events and the management of periodicals. If the young Positivists felt the temptations of parliamentary candidatures and editorships, they resisted them. Beesly presided at the inaugural meeting of the International and rendered it great services, but he would not join it. It was

[1] F. Harrison to J. Morley, 11 January 1872.
[2] R. Congreve, Notes on Education for Geo. Howell, MSS in Congreve Papers (Wadham, C.).

only with reluctance that he and Harrison went into the Reform League and they never tried to secure leading positions for themselves. They accepted official advisory positions for the miners, but regretted it, and even found their honorary membership of the Amalgamated Society of Carpenters and Joiners an embarrassment.[1] They were frequently invited to take over the editorship of the Labour papers to which they contributed, but they shrank from the task.

Late in 1863 and early in 1864, Harrison was advising Beesly not to waste words on 'that animal Troupe', the Confederate sympathiser who had been the first editor of the *Bee-Hive*. He also advised him to curb his francophilia since it was possible that the paper would pass into his hands.[2] About this time he did actually encourage his friend to think in terms of starting a journal of his own to be called the *Republican*, but he warned him against a 'full paper'! The *Bee-Hive* had cost not less than £500 to £1,000 in its first two years. The labour, the responsibility, the 'varied vexations' of editorship ought not to be incurred. 'You would be worked to death in order to get up the facts and find the truth about a dozen topics of public interest . . . I know the *Bee-Hive* now does with less. But then because it is done in a mere catch-penny way.'[3]

Characteristically, Harrison was prepared to consider the possibilities of editorship, if not for himself then for Beesly, in a conjectural way or at a theoretical level, but when it came to the crunch he found reasons for withdrawing.

Connolly has been here inveighing against Hartwell and on being invited to express himself distinctly came out with a plan for getting rid of Hartwell, i.e. making him a penny-a-liner again and finding a *new editor* (the principal point) at 2 gns. a week. I told

[1] 'Consider if we ought not to take our names off the Miners' Council over the violent strike of which we know nothing . . . We are in a false position' (F. Harrison to E. S. Beesly, 1864). When Cremer tried to remove Applegarth from office in the Amalgamated Society of Carpenters and Joiners, Beesly suggested that the Positivists should transfer their honorary membership from a London to a Manchester branch. 'I have not heard the anti-Applegarth side, but my conviction is that Cremer is one of the dirtiest scoundrels that the working class has turned up lately' (E. S. Beesly to H. Crompton, 21 September 1871. BUC).

[2] F. Harrison to E. S. Beesly, '1863' and March 1864.

[3] Ibid., 1864, but not one of letters cited earlier.

him at once that neither of us intended to be a means of turning Hartwell out and we should take care not to fall into any such scheme . . . I tell you what it is—the whole thing is so rotten and disgusting I shall cut it all together. They are a bad lot and it is hardly likely that we can go on smoothly or do any good to them.[1]

But a year later when the whole question of the American Civil War had been virtually left behind, Harrison reported that Connolly

> talked to me about Potter and himself looking after the business, and you and I being responsible for all the articles. I said if the paper were to become a *bona fide* trade organ we might possibly. If you think this scheme plausible, I am ready to go in. Godfrey Lushington would join in. We should practically have all the advantages of having the paper to ourselves, at least we could try. I am quite prepared to make it the systematic organ of the true faith on industrial matters . . . I can't see that any use has been made of the *Bee-Hive* to make it the organ of any body of thought or rules of life. What do you say to trying with Bridges' help perhaps?[2]

However, he declined, telling Beesly that he would 'talk it over'.

At the end of 1865 the Potter/Junta antagonism was attaining its full force and Howell and the middle-class nonconformist Miall came to ask Harrison if he would consent to edit the *Workingmen's Advocate* which was soon to become the *Commonwealth*.

> I told them [wrote Harrison] that it was a serious and costly affair. They say they have the money (T. B. Potter to a large amount). I said 'who are the shareholders?' because those who have the shares and own the property will be masters of the Paper and not you and it will become a middle-class organ directly and the Editor will be *their* Servant. They said 'no' . . . They assert that T. B. Potter and some enthusiastic friends will put the money in on that footing (votes by number of shareholders, not the num-

---

[1] F. Harrison to E. S. Beesly, 19 January 1864.

[2] Ibid., 15 January 1865?. ('1865' is the date added by Harrison subsequently, but the possibility must be allowed for that it belongs in the same year as the last letter cited. Harrison could blow hot and cold with startling suddenness.)

ber of shares held). I said, what, sink a large sum in a concern over which they have no control! They said 'yes'—well T.B.P. must be an open-souled enthusiast!

Harrison's doubts on this score proved to be well founded and he was soon in as much hurry as Marx to avoid the disgrace of being associated with the paper, but it was in the next paragraph of his letter that he came to the class of reasons for declining, which had the greatest weight with him:

> I see the great opportunity and the terrible power which it is giving up. As editor one would have the means and the right of getting to the bottom of these trade questions and be able to influence industry in a way it never yet has heard of. 'By God, Sir,' as Clive said, 'I wonder at my own moderation.' Just conceive how one could work or suppress strikes as would be just. But it is a responsibility which I decline. Unless one's whole efforts were given to it and even then perhaps . . . Is it not a responsibility which no one but a working man can rightly assume? And suppose we thought right to recommend reduction of hours with loss of wages, could we do so freely? Then on political and social things, can we go in for less than Comte pure and simple?[1]

While the refusal to assume final responsibility was always there, concern with the welfare of the workers' press was real and active. A year after declining to edit the *Commonwealth*, Harrison asked Applegarth, Cremer and Odger to come to tea with Beesly and himself. 'I want the *Bee-Hive* and the C.W., not to agree, but to buy up one another. If they could pay Potter enough—the thing could be managed. I mean make it Potter's interest to give in.'[2] This concern with the future of the *Bee-Hive* lasted right into the 'seventies. In 1873 Mill and Fox Bourne wanted to make the *Examiner* into a working-man's organ. Mill was ready to spend £500 and to write continuously for it, if Harrison and others would help. The Positivist noted that the Utilitarian was 'shy of Beesly'; that Fox Bourne was a dull dog; and questioned whether he (Harrison) was sufficiently at one with Mill to do it. What decided him against it was that they would never make it a workers' paper unless they bought the

---

[1] F. Harrison to E. S. Beesly, 8 December 1865.
[2] Clearly, this refers to George, rather than to T. B., Potter. Ibid., n.d. (1866?).

Bee-Hive,[1] and Mill's friend Maxse had explored this project and abandoned it a year earlier.[2]

If the Positivists never edited the *Bee-Hive*, the *Commonwealth* or the *Fortnightly Review*, their contributions filled a large percentage of the columns of these journals and those who did serve as editors refused to be embarrassed by the charge that they were running Comtist organs. Harrison was the most prolific writer for the *Fortnightly* and he or his fellow Positivists contributed approximately 300 substantial articles to the *Bee-Hive* as well as being prominent contributors to the *Commonwealth*, the *Birmingham Weekly Post*, the *Eastern Post*, the *Labour Standard*, the *Industrial Review*, the *English Labourers' Chronicle* and other papers.[3] It is astonishing that they found time for their own professional work. Indeed, they sometimes came close to the limit of possibility.

> Tyrant [wrote Harrison to John Morley], take your pound of flesh. Your copy has gone this morning to the printer. It was finished at 2.00 a.m. this morning—with many a groan for my task-master. Go! I feel like Antonio having made his last speech— like the beaver who has just bitten off his own .....s and flung them at the hunter, like Caliban before Prospero—ugh! curses, toads, newts; ah! I feel my bones ache. You are the best of masters and yet the hatred I feel for you at these moments enables me to realise the enmity between workmen and employer all over the world.[4]

With the intellectuals' sense of the impurity and inadequacy of office went a belief that it was pleasanter, more practicable, more in accordance with Positivism, to work upon opinion and to influence events from behind the scenes. 'Let us,' they said, 'return to our own diggings. These platforms and committees are beastly.'[5] Their self-denying ordinances with respect to assuming editorships or leading roles in Leagues or Associations did not prevent them from feeling—from about 1867 onwards—

[1] F. Harrison to J. Morley, 19 April 1873.

[2] J. Morley to F. Harrison, 1 December 1872 and 4 December 1872. FHC.

[3] See the select critical bibliography to my thesis: 'The English Positivists and Labour Movements' (D.Phil. Oxford), 1955.

[4] F. Harrison to J. Morley, 24 April 1871.

[5] F. Harrison to E. S. Beesly, 1865 or 66, but placed with letters written in 1868.

that they were making their mark. In that year, Beesly looking at the attention being given to Positivism, the prominence which he and his friends had achieved as a result of their unpopular defences of Fenians and Trade Unionists, could observe: 'When I think there are (only?) half a dozen of us that make all this stir, I must say we manage wonderfully well. We run here, and peep in there, and tread on this man's toes and stick a pin in that man and blow up the next so they are all hitting about wildly as if they were assailed by a legion.'[1] Two years later (when Beesley and Crompton were directing the Trade Union Labour lobby from outside, while Harrison was working with great effect within the Royal Commission, and Godfrey Lushington was ensconced in the Home Office drafting what was to become the Government Trade Union Act of 1871) Harrison remarked:

> For the first and perhaps the last time in my life I wish I were in the House for the debate (on the Trade Union Bill) only. But perhaps we can frighten 'em more outside. Isn't it like the Punch and Judy man pulling his puppets about behind the green baize and the children below half afraid when he speaks through his nose . . . Did I tell you Gladstone is converted? He is as soft as my grandmother.[2]

In 1871 when the Positivists were being denounced as the most dangerous revolutionaries of any age or nation, in consequence of their defence of the Paris Commune,[3] Harrison reflected feverishly on the nature and potentialities of the sort of power which he felt that he and his friends had come to possess.

> It is true that we have done almost nothing with the workmen. But yet we are not wholly without result. We modify them without being their leaders—perhaps more than if we were their leaders. They come back every now and then after a while and always find us *there* . . . Beesly and I are at bottom (and he in no bad sense) conspirators . . . Beesly is a mute inglorious Hampden—a party leader in an age when there can be no party leader. I am a conspirator in a time when conspiracy would be an idle crime . . . But for all that we are potentially dangerous men. I admit that . . . And if ever occasion came (which is most improbable—in fact

[1] E. S. Beesly to H. Crompton, 5 October 1867. BUC.
[2] F. Harrison to E. S. Beesly, 16 April 1869.
[3] 'Our Own Reds', *Pall Mall Gazette*, 15 April 1871.

impossible) and people asked us to advise them I do believe Respectability would have to open its eyes. Then you would see Congreve come out of his rags like Ulysses, and I think see something of which we have had few examples, that is a knot of revolutionists who have a social future far more perfectly meditated and realised than any revolutionists in church or state ever yet lived. And at the same time, and this is the principal point, who have all their lives studied the Present and the Past with a view to transform them into the Future. We are thus the true Constructive Revolutionists and therefore I think the most formidable.

We belong by education, habit and even sympathy to the old thing, from our compromising creed we have patience to study it inside and out. We understand its weak and strong points just as well as those who have to work it; we are on the very edge of the official world and socially and politically (perfectly?) behind the scenes. They admit we understand it and actually use our help in pushing the old machine along. And yet we would turn the old thing inside out as completely as Rousseau—though more tentatively and cautiously. We know that you cannot get rid of the Present (in the Past) but must act at its organs. The Revolutionists who have operated on its old carcase have hacked away blindly at its limbs and yet it is still alive and kicking. Now we are anatomists. We have studied the organs, and once let us get it down on our dissecting table, leave us only 24 hours, and as much as a pen knife, and you will see us cut straight down up its liver and lights, and what will you bet we don't hit his vitals to a point. We understand the old brute's constitution just as well as Gladstone or Lowe, a deal better I think since the Budget. And yet we have the kind of feeling for him that St. Paul had for the Corinthian men of pleasure . . . I do feel dangerous. I hope and trust my dangerous propensities may get no call. In the meantime I am quite satisfied with forming and expressing my mind.[1]

How was it that the young men who looked to Bright in the 'fifties and early 'sixties became so closely identified with the proletariat and so close to social revolution by the late 'sixties and early 'seventies? They were conscious of no dramatic change of opinion. They believed that they had throughout displayed a fidelity—perhaps a growing fidelity—to the essentials of Positivism. When Harrison called upon Beesly to lead the way in collaborating with Bright he remarked:

[1] F. Harrison to J. Morley, 4 May 1871.

English revolutionaries, yourself among them—at bottom rest on continental principles—Who showed you how a new society could arise out of feudalism? Who gave the first example of a democratic republic? As a Mirabeau, as a destroyer of feudalism, follow Bright, but not to let him found a middle-class constitution.[1]

Beesly 'followed' Bright to the point of passing over to join forces with Marx,[2] but this was not something which could properly be described as accidental or merely personal or apart from Positivism. Marx would like to have construed it as such. He expressed a limitless contempt for Comte, and tried to single Beesly out from his co-religionists as a particularly brave and courageous man who had an insight into crises and turning points, not shared by his colleagues. But Marx was essentially mistaken in trying to do this. Beesly was the most truculent of the Positivists; the one most committed to the cause of Labour; the one most persuaded of the great distance which capitalists would have to travel before they were 'moralised'; but he differed from the others in degree rather than in kind.

The association of Positivists and Marxists in general, and of Beesly and Marx in particular, was based upon certain affinities between Positivism and Marxism although these were not adequately recognised on either side. Comte's law of the three stages—which taught that the human mind inevitably proceeded from theological interpretations of experience to metaphysical ones and from these finally to positive or scientific ones—had exactly the same set of jobs to do as Marx' historical materialism. It was at once an epistemology, a philosophy of history and a programme of social reconstruction. Both Positivism and Marxism were fashioned out of much the same materials and put to the solution of broadly similar problems.

Comte, like Marx, drew heavily upon classical German philosophy, French Socialism (especially Saint Simon), and upon Adam Smith, if not upon English Political Economy as a whole. Out of these materials both men attempted to fashion a new science of society which was considered the *sine qua non* of a

[1] F. Harrison to E. S. Beesly, 1859.
[2] See my 'E. S. Beesly and Karl Marx', *Int. Rev. Soc. Hist.* (Amsterdam), Pts. 1 and 2 (1959), pp. 22–58 and pp. 208–38. This deals in considerable detail with the relationship described in outline in the next few pages.

new world. Neither of them could conceive of this science except in terms of history and historical laws. Just as Marx argued that philosophers had hitherto only interpreted the world, whereas the task was to change it: so Comte made his guiding principle, '*Science, d'où prévoyance; prévoyance, d'où action*'.

Admittedly Marx was much more modest than Comte. Indeed, he went so far as to deny that his socialism was 'scientific' except to distinguish it from that of the Utopians. He made this point in his attempt to rebut Bakunin's charge that scientific socialism would end by producing the same kind of authoritarianism as Comte's Positive priesthood.[1] But in the absence of any clear statement by Marx about the logical status of moral judgements (and in the face of the kind of employment to which he put his sociology of morals), it was reasonable to suggest that he saw himself, like Comte, putting an end to the divorce between science and the affirmations of our moral experience by giving point to facts and ground to values. (He imagined that he had achieved an organic unity of analysis and ideals.[2])

[1] Karl Marx's marginal notes to Bakunin's 'God and the State', first published in English *Études de Marxologie* (Paris, 1959), No. 2, pp. 91–115, by H. Meyer, 'Marx on Bakunin: A neglected text.'

[2] Thus in the *Communist Manifesto*, Marx argued as if he believed that he was rebutting objections to Communism, when all he was doing was disclosing the class basis of these objections. Similarly, he wrote as if he supposed that a demonstration of the inevitability of socialism was all one with its justification. A modern Marxist philosopher has expressed the point with disarming candour. He asserts, 'the ethics employed in the Manifesto is simply the expression of the needs, hopes and desires of the modern working class . . . this ethic alone accords with the necessary and desirable (in the sense of being desired) [*sic*] direction of social evolution . . . It is no exaggeration to say that this is the first document in history to achieve any such organic unity of scientific social analysis with ethical ideals . . . The success of Marx and Engels was due to the fact that they derived their values from their scientific study of capitalist society itself . . .' (H. Selsam, 'The Ethics of the Communist Manifesto', *Science and Society* (New York), Vol. XII, No. I, 1948, pp. 22–32).

The secular-religious possibilities of Marxism were swiftly recognized. Joseph Dietzgen was probably the first to exploit them and to cast near-Marxian socialism into an avowedly religious form. The result was astonishingly like the Religion of Humanity (J. Dietzgen, 'The Religion of Socialism', *Philosophical Essays* (Chicago, 1914), pp. 90–154). Beatrice Webb sensed the secular-religious quality of organised Marxism and expressly compared it with Positivism: 'It is the invention of the religious order, as the determin-

Marx and Comte were at one, as against the Utopian Social-ists, in viewing the proletariat not merely as the most suffering class, but as the one destined to play the decisive part in the transition to the new society. For Marx this transition would be marked by the dictatorship of the proletariat: for Comte merely

---

ing factor in the life of a great nation, that is the magnet that attracts me to Russia. Practically, that religion is Comteism—the Religion of Humanity. Auguste Comte comes to his own. Whether he would recognise this strange resurrection of his idea I very much doubt.' M. Cole (editor), *Beatrice Webb Diaries, 1924–1932*, 1956, p. 299.

The affinities between Positivism and Marxism have been discussed from a Marxist point of view by several writers, but notably by L. Prenant, Karl Marx and Auguste Comte, in: *A la lumière du Marxism*, 11 (Paris), 1937. Opponents of Marx have enjoyed the topic. In particular see K. R. Popper, *The Open Society and its Enemies*, 11, 1945: H. B. Acton, *The Illusion of the Epoch*, 1956: I. Berlin, *Historical Inevitability* being the Auguste Comte Memorial Trust Lecture, No. I, 1954. Popper, Acton and Berlin neglect the association of Positivism and Marxism as *movements*. T. B. Bottomore and M. Rubel have tried to turn this omission against them. They try and make out that Marx was hostile to the Positivists and that this hostility 'brings into relief his own repudiation of philosophical speculations upon the course of history, and his rejection of ideologies, even [*sic*] in the form of a new "positivist" religion' (*Karl Marx: Selected Writings in Sociology and Social Philosophy*, 1956, pp. 13–14). Even if the argument of Bottomore and Rubel was in a logically satisfactory form, the historical premise from which it proceeds is false: after the death of Ernest Jones there was no other English intellectual with whom Marx was on such friendly terms as he was with the Positivist, Beesly.

It is not only only the relations of Positivism and Marxism in England which tell against Bottomore and Rubel. It is a fact of singular interest and importance that both Marx and Comte expected their doctrines to triumph first of all in the advanced countries of the West, whereas they had the greatest impact in those lands which had not yet achieved their industrial revolutions. (In the case of Positivism: Portugal, Turkey, and—above all—Latin America. See L. Zea, *El Positivismo en Mexico* (Mexico, 1953), and his 'Positivism and Porforism in Latin America' in F. S. C. Northrop's *Ideological Differences and World Order* (U.S.A., 1949). Conceived by their founders as guides to the future of the most advanced lands of modern industry, Positivism and Marxism became important as means to the creation of modern industry in backward countries.

Those who wish to preserve the 'profane' Marx need (i) to recognise the pervasive ambiguity of much of his writing; (ii) the importance of distin-guishing between what Marx meant and the use to which he was put. If they renounce the organic unity of analysis and ideals, they will help to preserve Marx' scientific achievement but at the expense of severing the nerves of Marxism as an ideology.

by the dictatorship of a proletarian governor. Both saw the new society in terms of competition giving place to central planning and control. For Comte, this was seen as dependent upon the rise of a common intellectual authority which would end intellectual competition and moralise existing property relations. For Marx, it required putting an end to competition in the market, and the overthrow of existing property relations. Comte described the organisation of his new society in pedantic detail: where he was incautiously precise, Marx was studiously vague. Thus, when in 1848, Marx called for the organisation of the proletariat into class, and Comte summoned it into a new church, the resemblances between what they were doing were no less striking than the differences.

Comte held that the test to which any political or social action ought to be submitted was whether or not it was in conformity with the interests of the working class. Just as with Marx, this was held to be ultimately consistent with the interests of humanity and a truly human morality. On the other hand, for Comte, the working class was not, properly speaking, a class at all, but the whole body of society of which other classes were but special organs. This doctrine opened the door to 'class collaboration', but in the meantime Comte expected the division between workmen and non-workmen to become more and more marked and the antagonism between them more and more bitter. Like Marx, he believed that Capital was becoming concentrated in fewer and fewer hands. When great captains of industry emerged they would be more easily moralised by the workers in their Trade Unions in conjunction with the Positive philosophers. Before that stage was reached there lay the prospect of many a bitter class struggle and the dictatorship of a proletarian governor.

Provided the English Positivists interpreted their Master aright, there was evidently quite sufficient grounds here to allow them to collaborate with Marx as well as Bright. Their enthusiasm for the great Tribune of English Radicalism was always distinguished by certain reservations. They knew from the building strike that the great contractors bore no resemblance to Comte's captains of industry. Bridges taught Beesly and Harrison that the 'sturdy Northern Manufacturers' were very oppressive in their administration of relief during the cotton famine. With a heavy heart Beesly gave up the delusion that the millowners of Lancashire, stimulated by the crisis, were inaugurating new and wholesome relations between master and man. They were further from Comte's 'normal state' than he had thought. Probably he would not live to see it.[1] Evidently, Bright had to be regarded as the exemplar of his class rather than as its most characteristic representative. Besides, noble as Bright was, Cromwellian as they hoped he would become, he was backward on social questions. They always chided him for his mistaken views on Trade Unions and strikes. During the Reform Agitation his leadership seemed indispensable, but the Positivists never ceased to warn workmen that there was an even deeper cleavage between the interests of working- and middle-class reformers than there was between reformers as a whole and the ruling oligarchy. They tried to persuade workmen that the Reform Agitation was only a preliminary trifling before the grand collision between workmen and non-workmen dwarfed all else.[2] When the question of a secure legal status for the Unions took the place of America and Reform as the leading issue in working-class politics, Beesly's whole purpose was to split the workmen off from the middle-class radicals. He tried to encourage the formation of a Labour Party, observing to Congreve 'there will be little harmony between Bright and us henceforth, I fear'.[3]

Before 1867 Beesly had already been in association with Marx. He and Congreve had helped to establish ties between English and French workmen and Beesly was the obvious choice as chairman at the inaugural meeting of the I.W.M.A. In so far as Beesly's Positivism led him to regard the Anglo-French alliance as the proper keystone of the International and inclined him to resist anti-Bonapartism, he annoyed Marx. On the other hand, they were united in their attitude towards the working-class press. Both were dissatisfied with George Potter and the *Bee-Hive* and were associated with the establishment of the rival journal, the *Commonwealth*. They were equally determined to

[1] E. S. Beesly, 'Lancashire Discontent', *Bee-Hive*, 28 February 1863.

[2] E. S. Beesly, 'The Middle Class and Reform', *Commonwealth*, 12 May 1866. J. H. Bridges, 'The Reply to the Middle-Class Radical', *Commonwealth*, 19 May 1866.

[3] E. S. Beesly to R. Congreve, 28 August 1867 (pos. A. B.M.).

dissociate themselves from this new venture when it appeared to be falling into the hands of middle-class manufacturers.

Beesly and Harrison were impressed by Eccarius' statement of Marxist economics in the pages of the paper; at the same time, Marx gave a rather condescending approval to their contributions to the *Fortnightly Review*. It was at Marx' suggestion and with his direct assistance that Beesly subsequently published in the *Fortnightly* the first detailed account of the origins and history of the I.W.M.A. He there introduced Marx to the British public as the man most responsible for the success of the Association and declared him to be the greatest authority upon the history and statistics of the Labour Movement in all Europe. It must have been particularly satisfying to Marx to have this praise lavished upon him by a man who was not a member of the International, but was entitled to great respect in view of the fearless way in which he stood up for the rights of Trade Unionists and Fenian prisoners.

Beesly married Henry Crompton's sister in 1869. He assured Marx that his wife was 'heartily sympathetic with my political and social views and there is no fear that I shall have to become respectable'.[1] He soon proved that he was as good as his word. In September 1870 Marx implored him to use his influence among the workmen to demand that the English Government recognise the French Republic. Beesly and his fellow-Positivists were already at work. Indeed, Beesly had produced a pamphlet which, as Marx acknowledged, coincided almost literally with his own Address to the Central Council.[2] Although Marx disapproved of the way in which the Positivists pushed the demand for Recognition into one that England should take to arms on behalf of France, he admitted that the Positivists had the main credit for rousing opinion during the last months of 1870.[3]

The friendship of Marx and Beesly was finally sealed in the defence of the Commune and then in the work which they did together on behalf of the Communard refugees. For this they were both pilloried mercilessly, and if a respectable English

[1] E. S. Beesly to K. Marx, 21 May 1869. MELI.
[2] E. S. Beesly, *A Word for France*, 1870.
[3] Minutes of General Council I.W.M.A., 3 January 1871 (I.I.S.H., Amsterdam).

FREDERIC HARRISON

HENRY CROMPTON

gentleman had been asked which of them was the worst, he would have had to reply as Dr. Johnson did, when it was enquired whether he thought Rousseau as bad a man as Voltaire: 'Sir, 'tis a nice matter to proportion the degree of iniquity between 'em.'

Frederick Greenwood, soon to become notorious for his part in the Suez Canal deal, attacked them both with particular violence. Marx hinted that he would have challenged his calumniator to a duel had they been living on the continent.[1] Beesly asked Marx for the Christian name of their adversary. Marx replied:

> My dear Sir, Enclosed the photograph for Mrs. Beesly. The Christian name of the illustrious Greenwood is Frederick. Ce n'est pas Frederic le Grand. Vous savez que Voltaire dans sa retraite suisse, avait auprès de lui un jésuite, nommé Adam, qu'il était accoutumé a représenter à ses visiteurs en disant: ce n'est pas le premier des hommes! Jenny will give herself the pleasure to call on Mrs. Beesly on Wednesday next about 1 o'clock. Yours most sincerely, Karl Marx.[2]

Marx' personal friendship with Beesly did not extend to the other Positivists. As has been suggested already, this was because Beesly was more actively committed to the Labour Movement and to the International than they were and because he was more deeply impressed by the reality of the class struggle. Beesly was a fighter and rebel by nature. Harrison did not like Marx. He told some odd stories about him and ultimately condemned him in the most unmeasured terms.[3] Yet Beesly was essentially correct when he told the German Socialist:

> You are quite wrong in supposing that my attitude differs in any respect from that of my co-religionists. Harrison at bottom agrees with me, though in writing he is inclined to be too diplomatic, in my opinion, and to spare the susceptibilities of the middle class. But Congreve (our director) and Bridges have warmly approved

---

[1] K. Marx to the editor of the *Pall Mall Gazette*, 30 June 1871, published in *Eastern Post*, 8 July 1871. (See Marx' explanation in his letter to Kugelmann, 27 July 1871.)

[2] K. Marx to E. S. Beesly, 19 October 1871. (Letter seen when in the possession of the late Alfred Beesly.)

[3] A. Harrison, op. cit., p. 150.

all that I have written . . . Our members in Paris though hostile to Communism, have frankly served it and risked their lives for it. All the English Positivists have been ardent supporters of it from 18th March. No doubt whenever it becomes a practical question whether private property is to be abolished, you will find us opposed to you firmly. But it is likely that long before then we and you shall have been crushed side by side by our common foe.[1]

It was as a Positivist that Beesly exposed the way in which talk about individual liberty could be used as a pretext for middle-class oppression. It was in the same connection that he taught that parliaments were popular institutions only in a formal and spurious sense and that in reality they left power to the irresponsible exercise of the bourgeoisie. While Beesly was still an undergraduate at Oxford, Positivists had been arguing that the Parisian workmen,

> not having received a metaphysical education, have fewest prejudices; belonging to the most numerous class, their views have the greatest generality; having the interests which are least implicated in local affairs, they display the greatest disinterestedness; finally, being the hardest pressed by the need for social reconstruction, they are the most revolutionary section. On all these counts, it is just that political power in France should belong to Paris; and on all these counts also, power comes to the proletariat.[2]

It is not to father such a series of *non sequiturs* on Marx that one draws attention in this way to the ideological conclusions which he shared with Beesly.

Positivism produced differences as well as an identity of view—for example, in inclining Beesly to treat the Anglo-French alliance as the core of the International. But the very differences between Positivism and Marxism sometimes contributed in an indirect way to the harmony between Beesly and Marx. It led Beesly to steer clear of position-seeking within the International and caused him to repeatedly insist on the distinction between Positivism and Communism. This suited Marx very well since he had no desire to have his position confused with Comte's 'Crotchets', nor to have to battle with yet another alien tendency within the I.W.M.A. From his point of

---

[1] E. S. Beesly to K. Marx, 13 June 1871. MELI.

[2] E. Sémérie, *La République et le Peuple Souverain: Memoire lu au Club Positiviste de Paris*, 3 April 1871.

view it was all to the good that the Positivists thought in terms of a church when they should have been creating a party.

An attempt has been made to provide some insight into the general theoretical position of the English Positivists in relation to the Labour Movement of their day. Perhaps something has been done to dispel the quite extraordinary confusion which has characterised earlier accounts of their ideological position.[1] It is to be hoped that the attraction of Positivism to a number of young intellectuals living in a period in which the professions were rapidly increasing in numbers and self-consciousness[2] has been made clear. It remains to consider what the Positivists can be said to have accomplished in the course of their association with Labour.

II

Between 1861 and 1881 the English disciples of Comte may be credited with one major and several minor achievements in relation to the Labour Movement. First, they played a decisive part in securing a satisfactory legal basis for Trade Unionism. They formulated the Unionists demands and—in the end— the Government's own measures. They played a vital part in shaping the strategy which workmen followed in pressing their case home, and they made an important contribution towards changing public attitudes towards that case.

Most of their other achievements can best be considered in relation to this master activity. It was largely in the course of it

[1] Max Beer thought them 'a very conservative body' (*History of British Socialism*, 1921, II, p. 233). Raymond Postgate, following the Webbs, referred to them as 'strong Liberals' (*The Builders' History*, 1923, p. 204). J. Morrison Davidson discussed them under the heading of 'Neo-Socialist "Origins"' (*The Annals of Toil*, 1899, pp. 420–5). Theodore Rothstein pointed to them as 'links between the labour world and bourgeois society' and charged them with part responsibility for 'the political demoralisation of the leaders of the English working class' (*From Chartism to Labourism*, 1929, p. 192). Selig Perlman singled them out for praise as demonstrating 'how intellectuals in their relationship to labour may combine a light and modest touch with a truly remarkable usefulness' (*A Theory of the Labour Movement* (New York, 1949), p. 285). He would have been appalled had he realised how much the Positivists resembled other intellectual groups against which he was so anxious to warn.

[2] G. D. H. Cole, *Studies in Class Structure*, 1955, p. 34.

that they helped to make Trade Unionism conscious of itself as a movement and encouraged it—with but indifferent success it is true—to concern itself with foreign and imperial policy and to engage in independent political action.

At the very moment when the Reform Act appeared to be inaugurating a new relationship between the working class and the State, the legal status of the most cherished of working-class institutions was called in question. In the Courts, Trade Unions were declared to be illegal associations, and those of their leaders and members who organised peaceful picketing were sent to prison under the law of conspiracy. Terrorism and 'rattening' by the Sheffield saw-grinders was used to inflame middle-class opinion against the entire Trade Union movement. In the celebrated case of Hornby v. Close, the Court of the Queen's Bench found that the Boilermakers' Society was so far in restraint of trade as to make it an illegal association having no power of redress under the Friendly Societies (Amendment) Act of 1855 against defaulting officers. A few months later Baron Bramwell was sending the London tailors to prison for conspiracy.[1]

Auguste Comte regarded the free operation of Trade Unions as of far higher importance than the suffrage. Accordingly the Positivists threw themselves into the new struggle with far more zest and determination than they had shown earlier. It was

[1] The Webbs' *History of Trade Unionism* gives an admirable short summary of the labour laws agitation. As they state, it would be difficult to exaggerate, the zeal, devotion and service rendered by the Positivists (p. 247). However, they are inclined to dwell on the soundness and the ingenuity of the legal advice which the Trade Union leaders received from Frederic Harrison and to take too little account of the contributions of the other Positivists and the importance of their political proposals.

R. Y. Hedges and A. Winterbottom, *Legal History of Trade Unionism*, 1930, is the standard guide to the intricacies of the law, although it seems to devote too little attention to the law of conspiracy.

H. W. McCready, 'British Labour and the Royal Commission on Trade Unions, 1867–69', *University of Toronto Quarterly*, XXIV (1955), and 'The British Labour Lobby, 1867–75', *Canadian, J. of Econ. and Pol. Sci.*, XXII (1956), 141–60 is good on the detailed work done by Harrison on the Royal Commission, but misses the importance of Comte in interpreting the English Positivists and finds them scarcely distinguishable from the middle-class radicals. The following account concentrates attention on those aspects of the Labour Laws agitation which appear to have received insufficient attention.

Beesly who was first to make a stand against the tide of opinion which was rising against Unionism. Public opinion was ready for him, for only a few weeks earlier he had joined with the other Positivists in a petition on behalf of the Fenian prisoners which had led to a great storm in the House of Commons when Bright introduced it.[1] Even the Positivists' friends remarked on their bloody-mindedness. 'Whatever way average opinion tends,' wrote one observer, 'the influence of the Positivists is sure to tend the other way.'[2] If the middle class treated poverty with clinical detachment, Beesly and his friends rounded on it and denounced it for its callous and selfish attitudes. On the other hand if the middle class was in a state of righteous indignation over Irish terrorists, it had to listen to the Positivists calling the honour of the British Army into question and suggesting that it was the British Government which was responsible for the conditions under which terrorism arose.

On 2 July 1867 the Trade Unionists of London held a public meeting in the Exeter Hall with the object of dissociating themselves from the crimes of Broadhead, the ringleader of those who had committed the trade outrages in Sheffield. Beesly's first reaction to the crimes had been one of near-despair. He told Harrison that they would have to redouble their efforts to spread Positivism among the workmen 'for without it Unionism can become a frightfully immoral power. I have felt quite miserable all day about it. It is the merest chance that Broadhead is not an acquaintance of ours . . .'[3] Privately he advised Applegarth 'to take active steps to put the law in motion against every perpetrator of any act of violence'.[4] But on the platform at Exeter Hall he had to sit and listen to Trade Union leaders delivering one penitent and guilt-ridden speech after another. At length, the chairman announced 'a special treat', an address from Professor Beesly.

Beesly announced that they need not expect to hear any expressions of remorse from him since he belonged to a class from

---

[1] *The Times*, 4 May 1867.

[2] J. McCarthy, 'The English Positivists', *Galaxy* (New York), March 1869.

[3] E. S. Beesly to F. Harrison, 21 June 1867 (BC. UCL).

[4] Letter by Beesly in *Daily News*, 10 July 1867. Applegarth told *The Times* that he had received this advice from Beesly before the Exeter Hall meeting. *The Times* did not publish his letter.

which penitence and remorse was not expected. They should remember that a defensive attitude was a weak attitude and guard against assuming a guilt which was not properly theirs. They did right to pledge themselves to root out terrorism from the Trade Union Movement, but they ought to remember that a Trade Union murder was neither better nor worse than any other murder. Broadhead was a thief, but did the middle class not encourage thieves and swindlers to steal the Trade Union funds which they were afraid to lay their hands on themselves? Broadhead committed outrages; but who would say that he committed as many as the Bow Street magistrate when he was dealing with tailors out on strike? Here were workmen expressing horror at the crimes which Broadhead had committed in the interests of their class, but did the middle class do likewise when Governor Eyre murdered hundreds of natives in the interests of property?[1]

Some years before he made this speech Harrison had warned Beesly:

> You must see you might any day get into an affair which might place you in the position (in the eyes of respectable people) of Mr. Holyoake or Ernest Jones. With those who really know you and with those whom care to be friends with you, you will be just yourself, do what you will—but I take it if you were ever drawn into a notorious religious or political fracas (and what is to prevent it?) it would avail you little in the world being a scholar and a gentleman.[2]

After he read the reports of Beesly's speech Harrison knew that the time had come. 'I need not tell you that your speech has stung people up more than anything I can remember and is the most dangerous word which they have heard for many a year. On the whole I think it will do good—like our Petition it opens the gulf beneath their feet.' But he went on to explain that he would have addressed the men differently. He found 'very much that is cruel, selfish and secret in Unionism'. The final line in his letter must have cut Beesly to the quick: 'I cannot find a spare hour to see you or a spare evening.'[3]

To appreciate the force of those last words it must be under-

[1] J. Jeffreys (editor), *Labour's Formative Years*, 1948, pp. 101–4.
[2] F. Harrison to E. S. Beesly, 1864.   [3] Ibid., 5 July 1867.

stood that Beesly found himself in the midst of uproar the like of which has probably never been heard since. *The Times* found his speech to be as 'astounding and disgraceful as the Sheffield outrages themselves'. It declared that Beesly had insinuated that 'a dastardly murderer was as good as a lawful magistrate'. It decided that 'a more scandalous and unpardonable statement was never made'.[1]

Other papers described him as a 'perfectly unique specimen of the human race'—longing to set class against class. Longing to excite among the poor an inextinguishable hatred of the rich. Did he want to be the Marat of an English Revolution?[2] He deserved to have his statue placed beside Broadhead's in Madame Tussauds and should have his name changed to Bees*tly*.[3] Moves were set afoot to deprive him of the chair of History at University College and to expel him from the Reform Club. He told Congreve:

> I am afraid it is all up with me. I am faced with the loss of my Professorship and consequently of the post (as Principal of University College Hall) and expulsion from the (Reform) Club. I have a clear conscience and I hope to go through all with dignity. If I knew you approved of my action I should feel firmer.[4]

Beesly's friends did rally round him. Goldwin Smith, Marx and others wrote in a kindly sense. Positivists and Trade Unionists were lavish with testimonials as to his honour and integrity. Despite the best efforts of powerful men in the University and elsewhere he weathered the storm. He explained to Marx:

> I have had a great deal to bear both in public and private, but I have the satisfaction of not having retracted anything, and I believe I shall have the further satisfaction of seeing those who tried to visit me with penalties fail. The Council of the College decided yesterday to do nothing and I think other attempts will fail in the same way. But it has been a near thing and, after all, the combat is only adjourned. In some shape it must sooner or later be renewed, for when duty calls I hope I shall never be silent.[5]

[1] *The Times*, 4 July 1867.
[2] *Globe*, 3 July 1867.
[3] *Punch*, 13 and 20 July 1867.
[4] E. S. Beesly to R. Congreve, 5 July 1867. PABM.
[5] E. S. Beesly to K. Marx, 24 July 1867. MELI.

To Henry Crompton he confided: 'I was rather depressed for two or three days, but I have quite recovered my elasticity and I really think I shall miss the excitement when it is over.'[1]

The speech in the Exeter Hall was not only memorable as an act of courage, it was the first great turning point in the Labour Laws question. It was a serious blow to the enemies of Unionism. They had hoped to tar the Allans and Applegarths with Broadhead's brush. As the *Spectator* explained à propos of Beesly's action: 'A single word coming from a man whom artisans admire and respect, of a kind which *they* could take for *extenuation*, will do more to deaden their sense of guilt of what has been done, than all the denunciations of the middle-class press can do to deepen that sense of guilt.'[2] By October 1867 even *The Times* admitted that Trade Unionists had some case regarding the unsatisfactory legal status of their organisations. Beesly was quite entitled to argue that if nothing had been done to stop workmen being humble and despondent in July, then they should not have found *The Times* confessing to the injustice of middle-class laws three months later.[3]

Within a few weeks of his Exeter Hall Speech, Beesly was in Bradford trying to organise support behind his proposals for a Trade Unionist party to fight the workmen's battles in the next election. Bradford was a regular lion's den of 'new model employers'. Bridges and he patiently explained that not only had the old Tory Radicalism come to put the Altar and the Throne ahead of the Cottage, but that middle-class Radicalism had also outlived its usefulness. It had an excessive dread of government interference. The new Radicalism made freedom of labour and the control of capital its watchwords. It placed at the head of the Labour programme, not such rotten tests of Radicalism as the ballot, but laws to protect Trade Union funds; to secure them against the law of conspiracy and to ensure the popular character of juries in cases involving trade offences.[4]

---

[1] E. S. Beesly to H. Crompton, 14 July 1867. BUC.

[2] Cited in *Globe*, 6 July 1867.

[3] E. S. Beesly, 'The Policy of Trade Unions', *Bee-Hive*, 19 October 1867.

[4] 'The General Election of 1869: Programme for Trade Unions' (in Beesly's hand, 'written by E. S. Beesly') Webb, WTUC, Section B, Vol. CXX, Item 41). See the *Bradford Review* for 14 September, 9 November, 7 December and 21 December 1867 for four letters by J. H. Bridges in support of this programme.

Beesly was delighted with his success in Bradford, for despite the Kells and the Illingworths, this place was to become the home of the I.L.P. He persuaded himself that 'in all the large towns the Unionists would come gladly to consult with me and listen with respect to my opinion'.[1] But when Applegarth's Conference of Amalgamated Trades, which had been established to protect the interests of the larger Unions, asked for his advice and he sent them his programme, they decided that they had better confine themselves to trade questions. They thought it unwise to commit themselves to a programme which espoused the cause of workmen as a whole and called for the extension of the Factory Acts; reduced military expenditure, a property tax in place of indirect taxation, and a system of national, secular and compulsory primary education.[2]

When Beesly learnt of this decision of the Amalgamated Trades, he did not go off in a huff. He called on Applegarth and told him that he would, with his permission, attend the next meeting of his 'Conference' and that he would have in his pocket a Bill which would provide a complete settlement of the Unions legal difficulties.[3] He began to rouse Henry Crompton's interest, explaining: 'It is a serious crisis and as all views of workmen are floating at present it lies in our hands to give them shape. In six months it may be too late.'[4] He insisted that no one else but Crompton could help. Harrison was a Chancery lawyer and busy. Hughes was tainted with House of Commons diplomacy. Ludlow was crotchety and impractical. Godfrey Lushington was haunted with the scruffles.

We should meet the Unionist leaders with our plan of action prepared and they will be sure to agree to it. This is really the most important thing of the day and you have the opportunity of doing an invaluable service to the Cause. Now don't make any excuses but just undertake to do it . . . Leave your mark on the Statute Book.[5]

---

[1] E. S. Beesly to R. Congreve, 28 August 1867. PABM.
[2] Minutes of Conference of Amalgamated Trades, 30 September 1867 (Webb T.U. Coll.).
[3] Ibid., 3 October 1867.
[4] E. S. Beesly to H. Crompton, 12 September 1867 (B.C. UCL).
[5] Ibid., 14 September 1867.

A few days later he reported:

> I had a long talk with Applegarth today. His friends are in a most
> muddled and unsatisfactory state—not at all up to the proper
> mark. We must silently take the management into our own hands.
> After long beating about the bush, I found that mortal funk and
> jealousy of Potter is at the bottom of it. They were actually going
> to send round a circular of their own (of a most useless kind) lest
> Potter should ... I persuaded Applegarth to drop that for the
> present and undertook that the four societies should be the first
> body to have the Bill laid before them and that it should be
> published with their approval.[1]

The Bill which Beesly and Crompton presented to the Conference of Amalgamated Trades was entitled the Trade Societies Act 1868 and was debated by the Conference on the nights
of 7 and 10 October 1867. The Bill provided that a mere combination for trade purposes should not be deemed a conspiracy.
It provided penalties of three months imprisonment for violence
or threats of violence committed in the course of a trade dispute. But the clauses around which opinion divided were those
which stipulated that all cases involving trade offences should be
tried before superior judges and before juries drawn from the
electoral register. Allan, of the engineers, opposed this clause
declaring that he would rather be tried by a middle-class jury
than a working-class one. Harrison and Godfrey Lushington
also resisted the clause on the grounds that it was too great an
innovation and might jeopardise the Bill. Beesly and Crompton
eventually carried the day, thanks to the support of Applegarth,
Odger, Guile and Howell.[2]

Unfortunately divisions persisted after the Conference had
endorsed the Bill. There was sharp disagreement between
Applegarth and Odger as to whether the newly founded Conference or the London Trades Council should take charge of
it,[3] Beesly made a diplomatic approach to George Potter to lend
his support to the measure, but met with a sharp rebuff.[4]
Workmen went into the General Election of 1868 with one hand

[1] E. S. Beesly to H. Crompton, 3 October 1867 (B.C. UCL).
[2] G. Howell's rough notes on proof of Beesly's Trade Societies Act 1868
(H.C.B.I. 331. 88. 34c). This gives a fuller—and slightly different version—
from the one in the Minutes of the Conference of Amalgamated Trades.
[3] Ibid.   [4] *Bee-Hive*, 16 and 30 November 1867.

tied behind their backs as a result of Howell's compact with Glyn,[1] and the other rendered useless as a result of the division among Unionists themselves as to what sort of measures they required. It was not until Frederic Harrison produced the Minority Report of the Royal Commission of Trade Unions in 1869 that something like unity and clarity was secured behind a Trade Unionists's charter.

It was a measure of the failure of Applegarth and his friends to act with sufficient speed and determination that Harrison actually owed his place on the Royal Commission to the pressure of Potter's London Working Men's Association. Harrison was very unhappy about this for he disliked Potter intensely. He was firmly persuaded that the manager of the *Bee-Hive* was unscrupulous and his friends 'thieving scoundrels', but he could not publicly dissociate himself from them for fear that he would appear to be turning his back on the Cause for which they presumed to speak.[2] His discomfort was increased by the way the evidence went during the early meetings of the Commission. 'I am greatly grieved, but not astonished at this Sheffield business . . . What I feel to be worse, not quite outrages, but a sort of general selfishness, had previously come out before our enquiry. I feel the position is very difficult. But I am quite clear. I am not going to cave in now.'[3]

The testimony of the representative of the Master Builders was particularly impressive. Harrison wrote to Beesly: 'My God! Think if I were to publish a formal recantation. But I keep my counsel as yet . . . Mault is an exceedingly clever fellow who has got up his case perfectly, if they can't beat him the game is up.'[4]

Harrison would dearly have liked to have had Beesly alongside him in the Commission. As it was he kept him fully informed and consulted him about tactics. Through Beesly, Harrison kept in touch with Applegarth. The Master Builders had to exonerate Applegarth and his Society as far as charges of violence and petty tyranny were concerned. Harrison now succeeded in preventing Potter from dominating the proceedings by subduing him under a mass of theoretical questions while he kept Applegarth before the Commission. Gradually the

---

[1] See Chapter IV.   [2] F. Harrison to E. S. Beesly, 27 September 1867.
[3] Ibid., 24 June 1867.   [4] Ibid., 1867.

enquiry was led away from the violence of the old, local societies into an examination of the actuarial soundness of the Friendly Society functions of the great Amalgamations. Roebuck remarked that Harrison had not liked the Commission at first, but he seemed quite happy now.[1] Mundella's evidence re-enforced the impressions left by Allan and Applegarth. Harrison was delighted. Mundella's testimony was 'first rate'. He was 'a regular Unionist by nature'.[2]

By October 1868 Harrison was becoming confident that he could break up the opposition within the Commission. By the end of the year the Report was being drafted and he had already prepared the Bill which was to legalise Unionism and confer a privileged status upon it. He wrote to Beesly:

I send you a copy of my Bill. Mundella evidently funks.

We are getting on first rate at the Commission. I am regularly breaking down the Report . . . Yesterday and today we took 'Proposed Legislation' which is 12 pages. Of this 12 pages only 2 or 3 sentences survived yesterday and not a single line today. The two fundamental clauses as to Combination were prepared by me and carried. In fact Roebuck and Booth are muttering that nothing is left. Roebuck says he can't sign it in its meagre form and Booth will have to decline to sign his own Report! Meridale is very good and Lord Litchfield first rate—whenever there has been a decision against us it is only carried by Erle's own vote and then his casting vote . . . But we fight every line, sentence and word and whittle it down to nothing and then we shall consider if we can sign after all. It is very hard work. I have been . . . protesting all day—I am quite tired. They are all very fair and respectful I must say, and old Roebuck is very fair and civil to me though he groans and curses over the way we are going on. God, I wish we were both in together. We would sweep a hole in the Bill I think . . . We go at it every day and all day.[3]

Having helped to change the direction of the enquiry and having greatly reduced the effectiveness of the anti-Unionist forces within the Commission, Harrison went on to produce his own Minority Report together with the legislative proposals that have since 1871 served as the basis of Trade Union law in Britain. It was his ingenious suggestion that Unions should

[1] R. Leader, *Life of Roebuck.*
[2] F. Harrison to E. S. Beesly, 25 July 1868.
[3] Ibid., 15 December 1868.

enjoy the protection of the Friendly Societies Acts while ac-
quiring the privilege of being incapable of being sued or proceeded against as a corporate entity. The Positivists had to work
hard to explain to Trade Unionists that mere legalisation
would expose them to endless litigation, and end in crippling
them. It was no easy matter to persuade Potter and others that
the workmen's needs would not be met by simply demanding
'no exceptional legislation for Labour'.

As soon as the Reports of the Commissioners had been published, the Positivists set to work to secure the unity behind the
Minority Report which had been lacking in relation to the
earlier Bill drafted by Beesly and Crompton. In the spring of
1869 Harrison reported:

> I am going in for agitation for the Bill. Potter's conference is to
> meet on Wednesday next ... and I am going to expound it to
> them at Odger's on the Wednesday following. I have proposed
> both sides should act in concert, and hold a *bona fide* joint and
> aggregate meeting at Exeter Hall, and both sides agree in Whitsun
> week in support of the Bill. I have asked Mill to take the chair and
> Hughes and Mundella and you and others are to attend and
> speak. As the Government hesitate, and as we are the only party
> before the House we shall carry it in time. Only they must make
> row enough ...[1]

The meeting was duly held, but it was not Mill but the ubiquitous Samuel Morley who was in the chair. Beesly called for
a vigorous class struggle on behalf of the Bill and in the course
of his remarks recalled the 'Days of June'. Harrison told him:

> Your speech was excellent—Something quite startling—How Karl
> Marx grinned a ghastly grin—and S. Morley a sickly smile—I had
> intended to take just that line had I spoken ... But what is the
> good of such a meeting if they don't report it or of such a speech
> as that if no one knows anything about it? I thought Morley did
> promise to do this. But he is just a play-thing in their hands.[2]

With Unionists at last united behind an agreed measure, the
Positivists sought to combine presure from without with bur-
rowing from within. While Harrison briefed Applegarth for

[1] F. Harrison to E. S. Beesley, 16 April 1869.
[2] Ibid., 24 June 1869.

private interviews with the Home Secretary, Godfrey Lushington went into the Home Office itself in the capacity of permanent Counsel to advise on all Bills and to sketch legislation. 'Really capital work,' declared Harrison who moved into Lushington's old job as Secretary to the Digest Commission. He pointed out that they were all falling into the 'bottomless pit of Office'. He told Beesly: 'You only are left alone the Prophet of the Land! They will be offering you the Board of Trade or Foreign Affairs next.'[1]

Mundella had originally been shaky about associating himself with Harrison's Bill, but the meeting at the Exeter Hall helped to persuade him that Trade Unionists were united, and determined to see the measure on the Statute Book. Hughes and he introduced it into the House, but their Liberal colleagues were not easily baffled. When the Bill was brought forward on 7 July 1869, they knew that no further progress could be made with it so late in the Session. Sitting in the Public Gallery, Beesly watched as the farce was played out to its conclusion. Only one of all the manufacturers and opponents of the Bill in the House, Edmund Potter, had the courage to say that he disapproved of it. It passed the Second Reading only to be shelved. Beesly warned workmen that this 'success' did not mean that Home Secretary Bruce was bound to introduce a satisfactory measure on behalf of the Government. He explained that pressure of business was a perennial excuse with slippery parliament men.[2] From 'personal observation', the Positivists knew that 'a regular process of ear-wigging of social and political pressure' was going on. Henry Crompton noticed that 'even the opinions which Mr. Harrison and I held about Positivism were used to malign this simple demand for justice. It was whispered that the Trade Union Bill meant Red Republicanism, Communism, Atheism. . . .'[3]

It was not until 1871 that the Government came forward with a measure. It had been drafted by Godfrey Lushington. It incorporated many of the most important proposals of the Minor-

[1] F. Harrison to E. S. Beesly, 16 November 1869.

[2] E. S. Beesly, 'The Trade Union Bill', *Birmingham Weekly Post*, 12 February 1870.

[3] H. Crompton, 'The Defeat of the Workmen', *Bee-Hive*, 2 September 1871.

ity Report, but the blessings which it conferred with one hand it withdrew with the other. It legalised Unions in the required fashion, but it effectively outlawed peaceful picketing. As Counsel to the Home Office, Lushington's powers were obviously limited. Besides he was both the most respectable and the most latitudianarian of Positivists. He had written usefully on the Master and Servant Acts, but he sinned in the Positivist book by standing for Parliament in 1868 and engaging in anonymous journalism. In fact, he was an occasional leader-writer for *The Times*. 'It seems', said Walter, 'that his "hobby" is Trade Unionism.'[1] If Godfrey had influence in the Home Office, the Home Office had influence over Godfrey. Even before 1871 Harrison wrote: 'I am extremely disgusted with Godfrey Lushington.' Bruce had planned to appoint a commission to investigate some aspects of the truck system. He had intended to appoint Henry Crompton as one of the Commissioners. 'There could be no man in England fitter,' said Harrison. 'Would you believe it G.L. protests against him as not impartial, a most unfit man, and read me a lecture on the necessity of conciliatory people in posts of responsibility. He said he should as soon think of recommending me. And this is Godfrey, who drew the Trade Union Bill!'[2]

The mixed character of the Government's Bill spread the greatest confusion among Unionists. Sections of the press recognised that its most important feature was its incorporation of Harrison's proposals for conferring a unique legal status on the Unions and argued (quite correctly) that this mischievous arrangement would never have been accepted by workmen if he and his friends had not sponsored it.[3] A number of Trade Unionists, such as T. J. Dunning, were by now so impressed by the Positivists' arguments that they saw this one aspect of the Bill as all important, and proposed not to take any action against the objectionable clauses for fear of imperilling the whole measure.

There is [wrote Dunning] in respect to this Bill, a most unwise cry against exceptional legislation. This Bill, it is said, does not deal with working men as citizens, but as Trade Unionists. Granted.

[1] *History of The Times*, 11.
[2] F. Harrison to E. S. Beesly, 25 July 1870.
[3] *Examiner*, 4 March 1871.

But neither in the Factory Acts, which have been so beneficial, are the millowners treated as citizens, but as employers of labour, which employment is liable to be abused to the injury of those employed. It was upon the grounds of it being exceptional legislation that Mr. Bright opposed every one of the Factory Acts.[1]

J. M. Ludlow, who had been aggrieved that Harrison rather than himself had been placed on the Royal Commission, went to the other extreme and argued that quite aside from the obnoxious third section on picketing, the new Bill would place Unionists in a worse position than they had been in before. He did not like the title of the Bill nor the manner in which it severed unions from Friendly Societies to which, in his opinion, they essentially belonged.[2]

Beesly, Harrison, Henry and Albert Crompton, together with Ludlow, served on a Committee which was charged with reporting on the Government's measure to the Trades Union Congress meeting in London. The Committee was unanimous in recommending Congress to reject the whole Bill rather than to accept its third section.[3] Congress endorsed this view, but the Government could be induced to do no more than separate the clauses that workmen took exception to from the rest of the Bill. These clauses were then passed into law as the Criminal Law Amendment Act.

The second phase of the Labour Laws agitation began with the struggle against this measure. The leadership passed from Robert Applegarth's conference of Amalgamated Trades into the hands of the Parliamentary Committee of the T.U.C. of which George Howell was the Secretary. The friendship and mutual confidence which had distinguished the relationship between Beesly and Harrison on the one side and Applegarth on the other was not to be repeated in the case of Howell. While Howell was supplicating before a middle-class Parliament for a satisfactory Trade Union Bill, Harrison and Beesly were applauding the Communards for finishing with Parliaments altogether. They were going out of their way to relate events in London and Paris. Beesly insisted that 'the Party of Blood' was to be found in England as well as France. He deplored the fact that

---

[1] *Bee-Hive*, 4 March 1871.

[2] J. M. Ludlow to G. Howell, letter published in *Bee-Hive*, 12 August 1871.

[3] *Bee-Hive*, 11 March 1871.

English Trade Unionists were so preoccupied with narrow and petty issues. It was their profane indifference to the fate of the Paris Commune which explained, so he said, the Criminal Law Amendment Act. The defeat of the Communards had convinced the middle and upper classes that, whether tested at the barricades or at the polling booths, the power of the workers was a delusion.[1]

To make matters worse Beesly supplemented this explanation of the British Trade Unionists difficulties with another one. He stated bluntly and publicly that workmen had been sold at the election of 1868. Certain secretaries and officials of Unions, he named no names, had got 'money or money's worth' by serving wealthy politicians instead of looking after the interests of their members and pushing the Trade Union Bill.[2] This charge aroused the indignation of honest men, such as Daniel Guile,[3] as well as infuriating the real culprit. Howell denounced Beesly for his 'dastardly' and 'unmanly' attack.[4]

During 1871–72 Harrison and Beesly were excluded from the deliberations of the Parliamentary Committee. Their place was taken by Henry Crompton. He had made no public pronouncements on the Commune. Crompton was a friendly and gentle soul and he made Beesly and Harrison appear formal, stern and unbending by comparison. He endeared himself to almost all the Trade Union leaders by what one of them described as his 'eminently sympathetic and winning manner'.[5] He was also a most devoted and energetic worker whose experience as a Clerk of Assize gave him great knowledge of the interpretation of the law, and peculiarly qualified him as an adviser now that the struggle had reached a new stage. He was, however, in poor health and he found it necessary to leave London for Farnham, and to take frequent trips abroad. In consequence, he gave much of his advice to Howell and Alexander

[1] E. S. Beesly, 'The Division on the Trade Union Bill', *Bee-Hive*, 29 July 1871.

[2] Ibid.

[3] D. Guile, 'Professor Beesly and the Trade Society Secretaries', *Bee-Hive*, 5 August 1871.

[4] G. Howell, 'Professor Beesly and the Pall Mall Gazette', *Bee-Hive*, 4 November 1871.

[5] E. S. Beesly, 'Henry Crompton', *Positivist Review*, May 1904, quoting T. Burt, M.P.

MacDonald, the President of the Parliamentary Committee, by letter.

Formally, the Parliamentary Committee was far more representative than the Conference of Amalgamated Trades had been, but in practice it was completely controlled by Howell and MacDonald. From the Nottingham Congress of the T.U.C. until June 1872 the average attendance at its sittings was three out of ten and on no occasion were more than four members present at any one time. Allan was often away through illness and Halliday out of town on Union business. The provincial members were told that they would be summoned when 'thought necessary' and sharp rebukes were administered to provincial Trades Councils which dared to show any initiative. Crompton had called for joint Trade Union Committees in every large constituency to bring pressure to bear on M.P.s and report every prosecution which occurred under the Criminal Law Amendment Act, but Howell did nothing to encourage this. His personal ascendancy was reflected in the way in which he kept the Minutes. The scrupulously neat and correct record which he had kept as Secretary of the Reform League was replaced by careless and rough jottings to which MacDonald added his signature. These Minutes were the work of a man who had no one to call him to account.[1] The oligarchical spirit in which the officers performed their work is revealed in Howell's discussion with MacDonald as to how to organise the next T.U.C. 'so as to keep as much work in our hands as possible'.[2]

In certain respects the two principal officers of the Parliamentary Committee made a startling contrast. It was Howell's constant study to be correct and respectable; whereas MacDonald would spit on the floor and turn his heel in 'the sputa thus evolved'. Howell's vanity took the form of striking airs about his intellectual accomplishments. MacDonald, for all his time at Glasgow University, never affected to be an economist or a jurist, but in the manner of some 'prosperous pastry-cook or luxurious linen draper' he would simmer with satisfaction at 'holding easy converse with a live Lord'.[3] What they had in

---

[1] Minutes of the Parliamentary Committee T.U.C., 15 February–14 June 1872. HC.   [2] G. Howell to A. MacDonald, 24 August 1872. HC.

[3] R. J. Hinton, *English Radical Leaders* (New York, 1875). Chapter on Alexander MacDonald.

common was a preference for what Howell termed 'legislation not agitation'. and a number of highly compromising ties with supporters of the Government or other Members of Parliament. MacDonald, probably as a matter of principle as well as for reasons of social prestige, cultivated the great mine-owner and old Adullamite, Lord Elcho. In consequence he became known as 'Elcho's Limited'.[1] Howell had been in the pay of Glyn and the arrangement which he had made with Morley when the Electoral and Registration Agency was wound up involved permanently compromising his independence.[2] As if this was not enough, even while he was Secretary of the Parliamentary Committee, he was asking Edmond Beales to sound the Government about finding him an official position. Beales conducted the overture on his behalf but without result. Howell wrote to Beales:

> I sincerely thank you for your kindness and hope that Mr. Glyn will bear the matter in mind for there are plenty of chances wherein he may, if he so pleases ... Mr. Glyn should remember not merely good offices rendered but the abstention of adverse criticism upon many points of the Government promise and performance. I, of course, could not do anything which would run the risk of a Liberal defeat, but upon some questions they have really invited it, and if we had been hasty in taking up the cudgels I think considerable dissatisfaction would have been the result. I wonder if Mr. Stansfeld ever remembers how some of us worked for him, now that he is reconstructing his office. Surely there would be a chance of some good appointment where my qualifications would be a fair test.[3]

The T.U.C. assembled at Nottingham early in 1872. It was upon this occasion that Morley and Mundella breakfasted the delegates, and the latter told them that the good intentions of the Government had been frustrated by amendments introduced by the Tories and the Lords. Beesly branded Mundella as an apologist for the Ministry as a result of this speech. 'No one,' he wrote, 'knows better than Mr. Mundella that the objectionable law of the last session was the work of the Liberals just as much as the Conservatives.' Beesly admitted that the Lords had made the clause about 'watching and besetting', i.e.

---

[1] A. J. Mundella to R. Leader, 4 July 1872 (Sheffield U.Lib.).
[2] See pp. 200-1. [3] G. Howell to E. Beales, 23 August 1871. HC.

picketing more stringent, but that should not be allowed to divert indignation from the man and the party who had introduced a clause about besetting in the first place.[1] Mundella had his enjoyment of the Nottingham meeting diminished by playing host to Henry Crompton whom he described as a 'red' and a 'half cracked academic radical'.[2] The Congress went on record for the total repeal of the Criminal Law Amendment Act.

Within one month of this decision by Congress the Parliamentary Committee decided that the demand for repeal would never be met by the existing Government. Consequently its officers began to enter into private negotiations with Harcourt, James, Mundella, Rathbone and other advanced and well disposed Liberals with the object of preparing an amending Bill. In March 1872 the Parliamentary Committee presented a Memorial to Bruce. This was drafted by Crompton and called for the repeal of the Act,[3] but MacDonald in speaking to it indicated his readiness to settle for an amendment.[4] In vain did Crompton try to impress upon Howell the importance of promoting a measure which would divide the House upon a clear issue, and that the Bill drafted by Wright was only a measure to erase the Lord's amendments. In vain he advised him to consult Harrison and to distrust 'big-wigs'.[5] He told Howell that Vernon Harcourt and Henry James were men to keep a close eye upon, but Howell was in no mood to pay attention to any of this advice.

> The Criminal Law Amendment Act [*sic*] is in my opinion a really good bill. It has been drawn with very great care, every word has been weighed by us most carefully. And I find that I win respect from such men as Vernon Harcourt and Henry James by the way which I meet them even in the discussion of law and discuss some of its abstract principles. This is not boastful, but what I have seen and felt from very close contact with both the men.[6]

[1] E. S. Beesly, 'The Criminal Law Amendment Act', *Bee-Hive*, 13 January 1872.

[2] A. J. Mundella to R. Leader, 10 January 1872 (Sheffield U.Lib.).

[3] H. Crompton to G. Howell, 19 March 1872. HC.

[4] G. Howell to J. Kane, 6 April 1872. HC. Kane had evidently protested against Macdonald's action.

[5] H. Crompton to G. Howell, 1 May 1872.

[6] G. Howell to C. Bartlett, 18 May 1872. HC.

There were other Trade Unionists who may not have been able to discuss the law and its abstract principles, but who were far from happy about the Amending Bill which Howell was suspected of preparing. 'I have had no end of letters to reply to as to our Bill,' said Howell to MacDonald, 'And I told Guile, if they are not satisfied with our work let them call on us to resign and let other and better men be elected—the London Trades Council to wit.'[1] A day or two later he had something more formidable to deal with than this muted criticism: he found himself subjected to a fierce attack by both Harrison and Beesly in the *Bee-Hive*.

The Positivists argued that the proposed amending Bill was an ineffectual measure which would not prevent workmen from being prosecuted for peaceful persuasion in trade disputes. It contained a new clause against threats or acts calculated to intimidate, which would allow of the widest and most dangerous interpretations by justices. By simply removing the Lords' amendments and re-enacting the rest of the Act it placed workmen in a thoroughly false position. If Unionists made this their Bill they would allow the Liberals to pass it into law and pretend that they had kept their pledges to Labour. Had the Government introduced the Bill itself, Unionists might have been well advised to accept it as a concession, however inadequate, to the demands of justice. But instead of this, the Parliamentary Committee had been tricked into sponsoring a measure which re-enacted almost all the clauses in the Act which it had been instructed to get repealed.

Howell replied by complaining that he had not been trusted. Why had the Positivists gone to the London Trades Council and appealed to the shoemakers inciting them against the Parliamentary Committee? They ought to have come quietly to him with their complaints. The new clause to which they directed attention was only in the proof copy and had been cut out of the final version. All the prosecutions which had so far occurred had taken place under the clause which was going to be repealed. There had been no spontaneous criticisms of the Parliamentary Committee's conduct until Beesly and Harrison had started stirring it up. Their behaviour was not becoming in sincere friends of Trade Unionism however much it was to

[1] G. Howell to A. Macdonald, 25 May 1872. HC.

be expected in those who had pretensions to be the Positivist high priests of the Labour Movement.[1]

Howell's rejoinder was a tissue of lies and half-truths. Nevertheless, he managed to get other members of the Parliamentary Committee to rally to his defence and even to vote him a rise in salary.[2] However, the Positivists had achieved their object. The Home Secretary declared that the articles by Beesly and Harrison showed that workmen were uncertain as to what they wanted, and that under these circumstances the Government could not endorse the Bill.[3] It took little time for the House to bury it.

Not content with pursuing Howell, Beesly next set about MacDonald. He disclosed that during the interval between the Second Reading and the Committee stages of the Mines Regulation Bill, MacDonald had engaged in negotiations with the employers and had agreed not to oppose two amendments which they wished to introduce. These amendments had the effect of rendering useless clauses in the Bill relating to ventilation and the employment of juveniles. Lord Elcho had got up in the Commons and said that these amendments were supported by the Miners' delegation and in consequence one of them was carried against the Government.

Howell advised MacDonald to give Beesly three paragraphs and 'finish him off'.[4] The miners' leader was incapable of brevity, but the gist of his case was that he had thought that the Government was going to give way on some clauses and he wanted above all to secure the one in which payment for weight was to be substituted for payment by measure. He compromised on the other issues to make sure that this went through. Unfortunately for MacDonald, Beesly knew that Godfrey Lushington had met MacDonald just before the Committee stage of the Bill and given him a most solemn assurance that the Government intended to defend every clause in the measure. As soon as Beesly reported this fact, the controversy came to an abrupt end.[5] The Miners' leader had hacked his sword and said

[1] For the entire controversy see *Bee-Hive*, 31 May–28 June 1872.
[2] Minutes P.C. (T.U.C.) 13 and 14 June 1872. HC.
[3] According to G. Howell to D. Guile, 16 July 1872. HC.
[4] G. Howell to A. MacDonald, 24 August 1872 HC.
[5] See *Bee-Hive* from 6 July to 24 August for four articles by Beesly and three rejoinders by Macdonald.

it was in fight. 'What trick, what device, what startling hole canst thou now find out to hide thee from this open and apparent shame?' MacDonald went to the Home Secretary and implored him to help him make peace with his furious membership. Bruce was soon expressing grim satisfaction at having 'MacDonald and the other delegates on their knees'.[1]

Although Howell managed to weather the storm, the system of personal government and the tactic of private negotiations in the lobby of the House were finally discredited. After the Positivists' attack in the summer of 1872 there was never any further doubt that the Trade Union Movement was committed to the goal of total repeal of the Act, and to securing it by mass pressure from without. What put this shift of policy beyond doubt was the prosecution at the end of the year of the Gas Stokers on a series of charges under the Criminal Law Amendment Act, the Master and Servant Act and the law of conspiracy. This case made it abundantly clear that the Parliamentary Committee had made too slight an estimate of the task with which it was confronted. At the Leeds T.U.C. held at the beginning of 1873 Howell was severely criticised for exceeding his powers by entering into a compromise. Delegate after delegate called upon him for an explanation, until at one stage nearly everyone was on his feet. Howell replied that passing a Bill through the House of Commons was not child's play and called into question the honesty of some of his critics when it came to money matters. Other prominent leaders tried to tone down the criticism. Odger explained that the Parliamentary Committee had 'done its best but its best was of a dilettante character'.[2]

At the Leeds Congress and at many subsequent ones it was Henry Crompton who provided the wanted leadership. In a series of papers which he read to Congress he set out in the clearest terms the precise nature of the legal disabilities under which the movement was labouring. In 1873 he directly drew up the Programme which Congress endorsed, and he inspired it on other occasions.[3]

[1] H. A. Bruce, *Letters of Lord Aberdare* I (printed for Private Circulation).
[2] *Bee-Hive*, 18 January 1873.
[3] Ibid., and see Programme of Parliamentary Action for the year 1874 to be submitted to the Congress of Trade Unions at Sheffield drafted by H. Crompton and enclosed with his letter to Howell of 28 December 1873. HC.

In his paper at Leeds Crompton summed up the legal position as he saw it at that date. Reviewing the cases that had occurred under the Criminal Law Amendment Act he observed that 'men have been convicted for simply standing still in the street . . . The cases show, as I pointed out last year, that if there is a strike, the magistrates will infer coercion from any facts, or even from the strike.' As far as this Act was concerned matters had 'passed beyond the stage of argument'. On the other hand, the prosecution of the Gas Stokers had shown that Lord Elcho's Master and Servant Act was most oppressive. 'The iniquity of it is, that it makes fine the punishment for the rich, imprisonment for the poor. Whereas, if there is to be a difference it should be inverted, because a fine is a real punishment to a poor man, and not to a rich man.' Pointing to the growth of the summary jurisdiction of magistrates, Crompton denounced it as a systematic encroachment upon the right of trial by jury.

> The moral is that if you do not stir yourselves, and that in a different way to what you have hitherto done, you will feel the smart of the Criminal Law more and more . . . What is to be done? I declare, and I do so under a feeling of the deepest responsibility, that you ought to use all lawful means to stop these proceedings by raising an excitement and agitation throughout the land.[1]

Since raising an 'excitement and agitation' did not appear to be too congenial a task to the Parliamentary Committee, Crompton together with Harrison, Beesly and others attempted to get the Gas Stokers Committee transformed into an organisation, which would not only look after the defence of the strikers and the welfare of their families, but which would be a headquarters for the kind of mass agitation they had been pressing for since 1871 or earlier.[2] Their efforts met with success. By the middle of the year Trade Unionists were bestirring themselves as never before: 100,000 men are said to have demonstrated against the Labour Laws in Hyde Park in June 1873. Two months later 15,000 were marching through Edinburgh while a letterpress printer mounted on a lorry ran off a cartoon of the Scottish Lion trampling the Criminal Law Amendment Act

[1] *Bee-Hive*, 18 January 1873.
[2] See Report, 'The Imprisoned Gas Stokers', *Bee-Hive*, 8 February 1873.

under foot. It was also in the Scottish capital that an event of exceptional good omen occurred. William Paterson leader of the carpenters and joiners and an ardent Liberal, successfully carried a vote of no confidence in his friend, the Senior Member for Edinburgh.[1]

A year earlier Hughes and Mundella had declared that there was not a man in Parliament who would vote for the repeal of the Criminal Law Amendment Act. Now Mundella himself undertook to introduce the appropriate Bill into the Commons. The time of the next General Election was drawing near. The season, as Crompton quietly observed, of the spring-time of the mind.[2]

At the beginning of 1873 all the Positivists were agreed that 'the great thing is to form a third party'. The time seemed ripe to try and re-float the proposals made by Beesly in 1867. Even the demand for Labour Representation was beginning to lose its narrow, merely careerist character and becoming associated with a distinctive working-class programme and the provision of financial independence for Labour candidates. At the Labour Representation League's Conference held in Birmingham in December 1872, Broadhurst proposed that the Unions should raise £15,000 through a political levy.[3] At the same time Beesly was advising the Gas Stokers' Committee to 'bring pressure to bear upon Gladstone and Bruce, and on Borough Members everywhere. If these will not do what is wanted, that is get the men released and the laws altered, you must have them all out at the next election.'[4] A month later Harrison was telling the T.U.C. that it would be suicidal for Unionists to back any established political party. If this meant the disintegration of the Great Liberal Party then there would be nothing for it but to let it break up.[5] Crompton used the *Bee-Hive* to propagate the view that the defeat of Gladstone and Bruce had become a 'religious duty'.[6] Workmen were advised to vote against every

[1] See Report, 'The Imprisoned Gas Stokers', *Bee-Hive*, 3 January 1874.
[2] H. Crompton, 'Sir Thomas Bazley's Conversion', *Bee-Hive*, 14 February 1874.
[3] *Bee-Hive*, 14 December 1872.   [4] Ibid., 28 December 1872.
[5] F. Harrison, 'Address to the Working Men's Congress at Leeds', *Bee-Hive*, 25 January 1873. It was this paper which Howell 'mislaid'. See p. 261, fn2.
[6] H. Crompton, 'The Government and the Working Classes', *Bee-Hive*, 5 July 1873.

Liberal who failed to give a clear pledge to vote for the repeal of the Criminal Law Amendment Act. In the middle of 1873 all the Positivists felt that it would be best to let in the Tory, whether or not he was prepared to meet the Trade Unionist demands, rather than return hostile or prevaricating Liberals. The ideal, of course, was that Labour candidates pledged to the Unionist programme should take the field whenever possible.

By August 1873 the intervention of such Labour candidates had cost the Liberals two seats at Greenwich and Dundee. Beesly congratulated workmen on these results.[1] However, he had no programme of his own which could begin to compete with Joseph Chamberlain's 'firmly drawn quadrilateral'—Free Church, Free Land, Free Schools, Free Labour. Harrison tried to get Chamberlain to sharpen up his section on Labour and then concluded: 'a mere working class, Trade Unionist platform is not enough; it is a little too classy still . . . Chamberlain's programme is wide enough and clear enough for all'.[2]

If the weakness of a mere Trade Unionist programme was that it would be 'too classy', Beesly saw that the trouble with Chamberlain's proposals was that they assumed that the Dissenters could come to terms with the Unionists. He demanded 'payment in advance'. 'The danger about any coalition to agitate about any number of points more than one, is that when some of them are carried the coalition dissolves and one section finds itself duped.' If the Dissenters' attitude towards Labour was questionable, no one but a 'goose' could doubt that workmen were not going to be satisfied with

the contemptible process which the parson, and his humble deputy, the national schoolmaster, are pleased to call education . . . They will demand that the vast funds now worse than wasted on teaching superstitious rubbish from pulpits shall be employed to meet the expense of providing first-rate instruction in real knowledge.[3]

[1] E. S. Beesly, 'The Greenwich Election', *Bee-Hive*, 9 August 1873.

[2] On his side Chamberlain tried to get Harrison to tone down the Trade Union demands so as to reassure the manufacturers. 'Is it not possible to make allowances for their weak digestions without sacrificing principles'? J. Chamberlain to F. Harrison, 17 September 1873. FHC.

[3] E. S. Beesly, 'The Middle and Working Classes', *Bee-Hive*, 13 September 1873.

Congreve was in entire agreement with Beesly, but he deplored the fact that workmen were so determined on land nationalisation.[1]

The *Daily News*, the organ of Samuel Morley and his friends, declared that the political organisation of labour, the promotion of Labour candidates, and talk about a future Labour Party, were not a true reflection of the temper of workmen. They were 'animated by the ideas set forth in the later writings of M. Comte'.[2] Other journals alleged that the Positivists were engaged in a deep-laid plot to overthrow the entire Constitution.

> Professor Beesly does not believe in Parliamentary institutions at all. He is, we believe, for plebiscites, with himself or some other Comtist for emperor or 'elect of the people' . . . The conjunction of such political philosophers with the Labour Representation League is surely one of the oddest that ever happened. Working men in the constituencies frequently ask its meaning and nobody can tell them. Is it that Mr. Beesly and his fellow believers see in an effort to promote class representation the possible dry rot of those Parliamentary institutions they dislike and are glad to join in hastening their decay.[3]

The truth of the matter was that the Positivists wavered between a conception of a third party organised *de novo* in the country and a reconstruction of the Liberal Party on the basis of Chamberlain's programme. Just as the Labour Representation League would talk one month of creating a Labour Party and in the next invite Thomas Brassey to be its President,[4] so the Positivists—particularly Harrison—blew hot and cold. In the middle of 1873 he was ready for the break-up of the Liberal Party, but the week before the election he was advising the readers of the *Bee-Hive* to vote Liberal. He even suggested that they should vote for the arch-individualist Henry Fawcett on the grounds that he was an honest man. At the first opportunity workmen should form a true Labour Party; in the meantime they should use the slogan of 'no class legislation!'[5]

[1] F. W. Hirst, *Early Life and Letters of John Morley*, 1927, (i), p. 291.
[2] *Daily News*, 5 January 1875.
[3] *Capital and Labour*, 13 January 1875.
[4] Minutes of the Lab. Rep. League, 23 July 1873 (Broadhurst Coll. LSE).
[5] F. Harrison, 'Workmen and the Elections', *Bee-Hive*, 31 January 1874.

Henry Crompton told George Howell that it would be desirable to invite Chamberlain to the T.U.C.—'it would end in his being pinned down to our programme'[1] but it was too late in the day to cement the alliance. Howell persuaded the Parliamentary Committee to throw out the 'Quadrilateral' which he described as 'Broadheadism'.[2]

It would be wrong to conclude that nothing came of all the talk and gestures in the direction of a third party. It helped to rouse the Labour Movement to serious political action. Many a Tory candidate—including Cross the future Home Secretary—was induced to swallow the entire Unionist dose.[3] Beesly was one of the few who recognised that despite the spread of Unionism to agricultural labourers and the infusion of capital into their ranks the Tories might be more inclined to repeal the offending laws than the Liberals.[4]

However, Disraeli's first move once he was back in office had all the appearance of one of his more disagreeable strategems. A Royal Commission, which looked like further stalling, was to be appointed. The Commissioners were recruited by hustling. They were called upon to take an immediate decision about a course of action which they had never heard contemplated before. The Positivists knew about this because Crompton was invited to serve on the Commission.[5] Hughes and MacDonald accepted seats on it and aroused intense indignation against themselves in consequence. MacDonald was forced to resign as Chairman of the Parliamentary Committee. Harrison told Howell: 'I shall myself make no public comment on the conduct of those who joined the Commission. Privately, I will not conceal from you that as to Mr. Hughes at least, I can never feel the slightest confidence in him again.'[6] The London Trades Council decided to give evidence to the Commission; the Parliamentary Committee declined to do so. The Positivists had to exert themselves to try and prevent Potter from turning on the Trades Council with all his old vehemence.

[1] H. Crompton to G. Howell, 30 December 1873. HC.
[2] G. Howell's Diary, 10 January 1874. HC.
[3] E. S. Beesly, 'The Workmen's New Friend', Bee-Hive, 21 March 1874.
[4] E. S. Beesly, 'Tories and Workmen', Bee-Hive, 28 February 1874.
[5] H. Crompton to G. Howell, 20 March 1874.
[6] F. Harrison to G. Howell, 26 April 1874. HC.

The real object of Disraeli's exercises was not, however, to divide and conquer; but to divide so that he could gracefully concede. One of his first decisions was to settle the Labour Laws question [1] and he needed the Commission so as to cover himself against the charge that he had yielded to popular clamour. He knew that, once the Government's Bills came before the House, nobody would pay the least attention to the fact that they owed next to nothing to the recommendations of the Commissioners. In the event, it proved quite useful to have Mac-Donald on the Commission because he appealed to Henry Crompton to help him to prepare a distinctive statement. Crompton was thus fully aware of what was going on in the Commission and was able to get out a statement on behalf of the Parliamentary Committee the moment the Commissioners' Report appeared. [2]

In the *Bee-Hive* Beesly growled that workmen would be making an end of Parliamentary government altogether before the Liberals and Tories had finished with their commissions and enquiries. He found that the Parliamentary Committee had acted with a promptness and unanimity worthy of the progress which Trade Union organisation had been making since 1872. 'The working class is no longer a blind giant groping with uncertain hands, and blundering in fitful efforts to grasp what he most sorely needs, making sport for his masters when he is not grinding in his prison house.' [3]

The strength of the Unionists' resolve to sweep the statute book clean of the oppressive laws reached its height a month or two before the Government introduced its labour legislation. Their anger had been rising steadily as one spectacular prosecution succeeded another. There had been the cases of the seventeen women of Chipping Norton, [4] and the case of the repeated prosecution and imprisonment of William Cutler for the same offence under the Master and Servant Acts. [5] The Positivists

[1] G. E. Buckle, *Life of Disraeli*, V (1920), p. 363.

[2] G. Howell, handwritten 'Memorandum' on his copy of *The Labour Laws Commission*.

[3] E. S. Beesly, 'Dangers Without and Within', *Bee-Hive*, 28 March 1874.

[4] F. Harrison, 'The Chipping Norton Case', *Bee-Hive*, 7 June 1873.

[5] See *Bee-Hive*, 27 June 1874, for the appeal by the P.C. of the T.U.C. together with Beesly, Harrison, Crompton, Maxse, Mundella and Hughes on behalf of Cutler.

had been able to use these cases to impress even *The Times* with the injustices of the existing laws. Then early in 1875 the firm of Jackson & Graham resolved to abolish the system of a fixed price for each piece of work done by the cabinet-makers in its employ and to adopt a system of free bargaining with each individual workman. The men went on strike and picketed the shop. There was no violence, no threat of violence, only what the Judge, Baron Cleasly, ruled to be a conspiracy for the 'coercion of the will of the employers'. This judgement established beyond all doubt that strictly moral pressure was a crime. Hitherto there had been no instance of a prosecution under the Criminal Law Amendment Act which had not been complicated by allegations of physical molestation or threats of violence. Before the cabinet-makers' trial the distinguished Mr. Justice Lush had declared, as against the Positivists' contention, that peaceful picketing was legal.

Five cabinet-makers were sentenced to one month's imprisonment each. When they were released more than five thousand people assembled to cheer at the prison gates. At Beesly's suggestion the London Trades Council gave a dinner in their honour.[1] He presided, and Congreve, Crompton and Bridges, all the members of the Parliamentary Committee and all the leaders of the Trades Council, attended. So did three Members of Parliament—Burt, MacDonald and Biggar. The press allowed that it was an impressive occasion and few journals attempted to defend the law. Criticism was reserved for the Positivists who were alleged to be popularity hunting. Beesly was singled out for attack because he refused to state that men ought always to obey the law even if it was unjust and inequitable.[2]

A month later it was all over. Cross introduced his Conspiracy and Protection of Property, and his Employer and Workmen Bills which, as usefully amended by Lowe, Mundella and others, finally restricted the application of the law of conspiracy in relation to trade disputes; explicitly legalised peaceful picketing and abolished imprisonment for breach of contract. Confidence in final victory had been growing since 1873, but so sudden and complete a triumph was unexpected. 'It still sur-

[1] *Bee-Hive*, 15 May 1875.
[2] E. S. Beesly, 'Positivists and Workmen', *Fortnightly Review*, September 1875.

prises me,' wrote Crompton, 'I cannot but think that we owe a good deal to a fortunate number of circumstances and that it would not have taken very much to have roused the House of Commons into a fierce opposition to us.'[1] The Positivists, in their disgust at the parliamentary game, were hardly prepared for it to have such a happy outcome. Disraeli explained to the Queen that his action would help 'to soften the feelings of the multitude'.[2] Given this anxiety, the familiar pattern of party-manoeuvring operated in favour of a useful measure. The Liberals could not allow themselves to be outbid by their opponents and they therefore carried through to a satisfactory conclusion the work which Cross had begun.

If it is true that 'No major political development can be attributed with certainty to Fabian influence',[3] the same cannot be said of the Positivists. In so far as a small society of intellectuals can ever be credited with great changes, the credit for the legal emancipation of British Trade Unionism belongs to them. They were the authors of the demands which were eventually carried, the drafters of Bills the substance of which became law and of memoranda which the Unionists submitted to successive Home Secretaries and sent to every member of Parliament. They were also in large measure the organisers of victory. They actively fought for Trade Unionism, and not merely in the Royal Commission or in the Home Office. They impressed their conception of political strategy on the Conference of Amalgamated Trades and eventually on the Parliamentary Committee. They helped to apply it through the Gas Stokers Committee and to win converts for it in the London Trades Council and in successive Trades Union Congresses. Tirelessly, week after week, they explained and fought for the Trade Unionists charter in the Labour Press and still found time to carry their arguments to the very different audiences in *The Times* or the *Fortnightly*. Their political strategy, with its curious blend of coercion and persuasion, its threat of third party and reconstruction of the Liberal Party, was a recognisable anticipation of the confusions of Fabian permeation. But, by the standards of the working-class

[1] H. Crompton to G. Howell, 24 August 1875.
[2] Disraeli to Queen Victoria, 29 June 1875.
[3] A. M. McBriar, *Fabian Socialism and English Politics* (Cambridge, 1962), p. 349.

political thought of their day, it was relatively more advanced than anything the Fabians managed. They went on pushing the idea of a Labour Party which would be independent of the Liberals, until this led in 1881 to their break with the T.U.C. and the rapid decline of their influence. Indeed, they were writing to this effect in the *Labour Standard* in 1881, just as Engels was encouraging the same development on a slightly different basis. They were represented at the foundation meetings of the Democratic Federation and by their presence established a direct link between those who attempted independent working-class politics in the 'sixties and 'seventies and the better-known pioneers of the 'eighties.[1] In the last chapter it was shown that the Republicans and Land Nationalisers prepared the ground for the triumphs of Henry George. In conjunction with these developments the Positivists' use of the experience of the Labour Laws agitation helped to accustom workmen to the idea of an independent political life for Labour.

It is evident that no great change in the law can be accomplished without changes in public and parliamentary opinion. It is not suggested that in the case of the Labour Laws these were effected by the Positivists single-handed. There were others, notably the Christian Socialists, who are entitled to some share of the credit, but they cannot be accorded anything approaching 'parity of esteem'. As has been shown, Ludlow misunderstood the legal requirements of Trade Unionism and would have conferred a status upon them which would have exposed them to endless litigation.[2] Hughes left the leading role on the Royal Commission to Harrison and became increasingly 'divorced' from Labour in the 'seventies.[3] The Christian Socialists had no consistent ideas on how to wage the struggle for Labour's demands. They were much more important in relation to the Co-operative Movement than they were with respect to Trade Union and political developments.[4]

[1] *Newcastle Weekly Chronicle*, 12 March 1881.

[2] See p. 290.

[3] E. C. Mack and W. H. G. Armytage, *Tom Hughes* (1952), p. 196 et seq.

[4] For a contrary view see P. M. Backstrom, Jr., 'The Practical Side of Christian Socialism in Victorian England', *Victorian Studies* (Indiana), Vol. VI, No. 4. But notice the neglect of the difference in the legal requirements of Friendly Societies and Trade Unions and the absence of any analysis of

III

The Positivists' achievement was not exhausted in their work for the legal emancipation of Trade Unionism and in their anti-cipations of a Labour Party. After the victory of 1875 Henry Crompton continued to serve as Attorney General to the Trades Union Congress and for many years he furnished it with its pro-gramme of law reform. Since it had virtually no other pro-gramme worth talking about, he became the effective leader of the T.U.C.

Apart from securing a few minor changes in the Trade Union legislation of 1875–76, Crompton believed that there was a whole series of legal reforms which ought to be regarded as complementary to the new legislation. He advised the T.U.C. to take up the Criminal Law generally; to press for its codi-fication, and above all to direct attention at how it was ad-ministered. 'We must,' he remarked to Howell, 'be ready to hit hard at the judges whom we have spared up to now.'[1] Con-gress had in fact already gone on record for a reform of the system of the summary jurisdiction of magistrates and a reform of the Jury Laws. At Crompton's instigation these demands were given a new prominence. After 1877 the scope of the whole programme was enlarged when a call for the codification of the Criminal Law was endorsed.

It would be a grave mistake to see in the T.U.C.'s pro-gramme no more than a lawyer harnessing the power of work-men to his personal and professional enthusiasms. Dissatisfaction with the way in which the law was being administered was both widespread and justified. Perhaps the Tichborne case had some bearing on this, but all over the country workmen were still smarting under the bias with which they were met in the Courts. The Royal Commission on the Master and Servant Acts, hostile as it had been to the claims of Labour, was forced to admit that magistrates not only misunderstood the law in many instances,

[1] H. Crompton to G. Howell, 6 September 1875.

---

the politics required to carry the measures under discussion. Despite his sympathy with Christian Socialism, N. C. Masterman (John Malcom Ludlow, Cambridge, 1963) comes much closer to my estimate. See particularly p. 187 and p. 224.

but upon occasion imposed sentences which were more savage than those permitted under the statutes.[1] In insisting that reform of the criminal law was not a 'class question', Crompton did not conceal the fact that workmen were the principal sufferers under the existing system. Capitalists were not debarred from sitting on juries and few bankers were sent to prison under the Small Penalties Act. He meant that his proposals aimed at no special class advantage, but represented a further step in the direction of the Positivist ideal of the 'incorporation' of the proletariat into English society.

Crompton was the most valued and popular friend of the Unionists in the second half of the 'seventies and, had he not urged these reforms, such items as the codification of the Criminal Law might not have figured in the T.U.C.'s programme. Odger and other Trade Unionists were not always clear on why he attached so much importance to these demands.[2] But the packed meetings which Crompton addressed on these subjects, the time which they were accorded in Congress debates year after year, the publication by the Parliamentary Committee of Papers, Bills and Memoranda relating to these topics, all goes to show that Crompton's prestige was not the only consideration involved.[3] However much later generations might come to despise so austere a programme—advocated in years of trade depression by an organisation adopting an attitude of complacency towards the pressing problems of the semi- and unskilled labourers—it represented a response to substantial grievances.

By the middle of the 'seventies more and more people were being sent to prison despite the fact that the police found that the criminal class was much diminished and the number of indictable offences had decreased. The Home Secretary himself

[1] H. Crompton, *The Reform of the Magistracy and of the Laws Relating to Summary Justice*, P.C. (T.U.C.), 1877.

[2] Letter by H. Crompton read by H. Broadhurst to T.U.C., 9th Congress, Newcastle.

[3] See Congress Reports, 1875–79, particularly Bristol, 1878, for summary jurisdiction and Edinburgh, 1879, for this together with codification. See also H. Crompton, *Reform of the Jury Laws*, being a report of meetings addressed by him in the Manchester Offices of the Carpenters and Joiners, under the auspices of the London Trades Council; and before Working Mens clubs: P.C. (T.U.C.), 1876.

admitted that one-third of those behind bars were merely people who were unable to pay fines imposed upon them in the magistrates' courts unless they were allowed some period of grace. More and more people were coming before these courts. Between 1860 and 1875 the number of summary convictions was doubled. But, while the summary jurisdiction of magistrates was being continually extended, nothing was being done to ensure that those who dealt out heavy sentences of whippings and imprisonment were sufficiently qualified to hold office. Before 1879 the poor wretches who were hauled before these magistrates had no option of trial by jury.[1]

At public meetings, in articles in the working-class press, at the T.U.C. and in the publications of the Parliamentary Committee Crompton urged that the system of summary jurisdiction should be the subject of a systematic reform. Magistrates should be appointed by the Home Office; the number of stipendaries should be increased, and various means of combining the work of paid and unpaid magistrates should be considered. Criminal and Civil procedures at Petty Sessions should be clearly distinguished, and anyone who was liable to be sentenced to any term of imprisonment should be allowed the option of trial by jury. The Small Penalties Act should be abolished and every facility afforded to allow the payment of fines and costs before anyone was sent to gaol.

The agitation on behalf of this programme was effective. Crompton drafted a Bill which was introduced into the Commons and which became the basis of the Summary Jurisdiction Act, 1879. In this measure the Government went some way to meet Crompton's principle of the option of trial by jury. The value of this concession plainly depended, to some extent, upon a reform of the jury laws. In 1876 the Parliamentary Committee embarked on a national campaign to secure such reform. There had been a number of attempts to do this already, but always the object had been to raise rather than lower the qualifications for jury service and, coupled with this, had been attempts to reduce the size of juries and to abolish the unanimity principle. Crompton drafted a Bill providing for all skilled artisans to be made liable for jury service—other respectable

[1] H. Crompton, *The Reform of the Magistracy*, op. cit.

workmen to be enabled to enroll themselves voluntarily on the jury list—and for a small payment to jurors.[1]

By far the most remarkable of Crompton's achievements during these years was his success in enlisting the support of Trade Unionists for codification of the criminal law. The Parliamentary Committee displayed an enthusiasm for this project that would have gladdened the heart of Jeremy Bentham. Even the question of employer's liability hardly aroused more enthusiasm. In 1877 the Trade Union leaders convened a great meeting on the subject which was presided over by Sir Alexander Cockcroft and addressed by Sir James Fitzjames Stephens. This meeting was the signal for an orgy of reconciliation. Frederic Harrison saluted Sir James whom he had recently been lashing for his *Religion of Inhumanity*. Broadhurst and Shipton exhausted their supply of superlatives in extolling Lord Bramwell, one of the most hidebound reactionaries in the country and the author of the famous judgement which had sent the tailors to prison in 1867.[2]

Mr. Cross, whom Crompton described as the best Home Secretary the country had ever had, could only bow to the wishes of such an improbable and imposing alliance. He prepared to introduce a Government Code Bill. But such remarkable compacts have a way of beginning better than they end. Cross was not ready to defer to Trade Unionist wishes and place Crompton on the Commission charged with drawing up the Code.[3] The Unionists soon discovered that it was one thing to agree with the Bramwells on matters of form, and another on questions of substance. At the Edinburgh T.U.C. of 1879 Crompton was obliged to tell the delegates that they ought not to give the slightest countenance to the Code Bill. He said that, under cover of an admirable principle, an attempt was being made to refurbish old laws against freedom of speech and association, and to introduce a species of inquisitorial enquiry into the magistrates' courts. Unless a whole host of detailed

[1] H. Crompton to S. and B. Webb (N.D.), Webb T.U. Coll., Section A., Vol. 11, folio 221–222 (LSE).

[2] Sir J. F. Stephens, Address on the Codification of the Criminal Law with the report of the proceedings and of speeches by Sir A. Cockburn, Lord Bramwell, Frederic Harrison, etc., P.C. (T.U.C.), May 1877.

[3] Memorial to the Lord High Chancellor on Codification, P.C. (T.U.C.).

provisions were removed, the Bill would have to be opposed by Congress with all possible energy.[1]

Crompton looked back on his activities in the late 'seventies without regret. 'The result of our action,' he told the Webbs, 'remains in the shape of a vast amount of work done simplifying our penal laws . . .'[2] Other Positivists could share with him a sense of satisfaction about important, if modest, legislative achievements. Thus J. H. Bridges did valuable and unobtrusive work in public health and in the Local Government Board, and helped to prepare the ground for improvements in sanitary and factory conditions. Indeed the Hammonds linked Bridges' name with those of Leonard Horner and Hugh Tremenheere as a man of courage, independence and ability, who was able to strike at grave abuses with more effect than politicians or journalists.[3]

Yet by 1880 the Positivists were sadly aware of how limited their success had been in lifting Trade Unionism above its narrow craft and party allegiances. Indeed Crompton reached the sad conclusion that Trade Unions had 'hindered rather than promoted political progress'. They were, he said,

> altogether indifferent in respect of the crimes committed by England against other nations. It is impossible to interest even their leaders upon such questions as England's wrongs upon the Chinese . . . They are easily deceived and led by a few rhetorical speeches: forgetting how they have been cheated and thrown on one side when used, they are ready to believe any specious vague platitudes about 'Liberals' and 'Liberal principles'. We shall see them trust again and again to the promises of the party politicians who have deceived them so often.[4]

Attempts to arouse the concern of workmen with foreign and imperial issues was one of the distinctive features of the Positivists' work in the Labour Movement. They were seen at their most effective during the American Civil War, and in encouraging the association of British and French workmen around the time of the formation of the International. They showed that

[1] T.U.C. Report of Edinburgh Congress, 1879.

[2] H. Crompton to S. and B. Webb, op. cit.

[3] J. L. and B. Hammond, *Life of Lord Shaftesbury*, 1923, p. 35, fn. and p. 149.

[4] H. Crompton, *Industrial Organisation in England*, Women's Protective and Provident League, n.d., 1878?.

they had an appreciable influence with them during the campaign on behalf of the French Republic in 1870, although it was woefully inadequate in relation to the object which they had in view. Crompton held that Beesly's work in exposing British plans for a war in Burma in 1875—he got up a petition with the help of some workers' clubs—helped to delay British penetration into Yunnan and the valley of the Yangtse.[1] However that may have been, most of their efforts to thwart imperialism met with an indifferent response. Governor Eyre escaped the clutches of the Jamaica Committee, and few hearkened to Frederic Harrison's denunciations of the bombardment of Kagoshima or the Abyssinian War.[2]

The Positivists taught that the expansion of Empire was exclusively in the interests of the commercial and trading classes and that workmen ought to oppose it by every means in their power. But by the late 'seventies the T.U.C. was ready to listen to a long paper by a Manchester Merchant, J. Bradshaw, entitled 'Africa, the Remedy for the Trade Depression of England'. Bradshaw claimed that he had the backing of the Duke of Manchester and Lord Shaftesbury, as well as of a group of capitalists in London who were good for £1,000,000. He wanted Trade Unionists to invest in an African trading corporation, and explained that 'the securing of Africa was the best way of paying off scores with America for her protective tariffs'. He was greeted with cheers as he drew a graphic picture of the fabulous commercial possibilities. He declared that 'centuries of commercial development could not exhaust the necessities of 350,000,000 of population'. The question, as he put it, was 'how could Africa best be utilised for the benefit of British industries?'

Crompton instantly made an impassioned attack on the whole project. 'He looked upon all schemes with the utmost horror, and regarded them as schemes for conquest involving England in crime and war as in the past.' He was supported by Shipton, Weiler and other delegates who asked: 'How could this scheme be accomplished except by the edge of the sword?' But the Empire builders had influential sympathisers within the

---

[1] H. Crompton, 'England and India', *Echo*, 9 May 1878.

[2] F. Harrison, 'The Massacre in Japan', *Bee-Hive*, 14 November 1863 and 'The Bombardment of Kagesima', 13 February 1864 and 'The Conquest of Abyssinia', *Bee-Hive*, 23 November 1867.

T.U.C. The very presence of Bradshaw was proof of that, for standing orders laid it down that outside speakers should only be invited under very exceptional circumstances. Prominent members of the Parliamentary Committee (Prior of the Carpenters and Joiners and Birtwhistle of the Factory Operatives) supported Bradshaw and affirmed 'in Africa there was a large field for British enterprise'. The episode closed with a non-committal resolution thanking Bradshaw for his able paper.[1]

This debate was a significant pointer to the events of the next few months. The Positivists were already at odds with most Trade Union leaders over the correct attitude to adopt towards the Eastern Question.[2] When Mr. Gladstone returned to power and introduced his policy of coercion in Ireland, it was condemned in the most vigorous language by Beesly and the other Positivists.[3] The London Trades Council supported them, but the Parliamentary Committee, under the leadership of Broadhurst, who was soon to take office under the Liberal leader, backed the Government.

Irish coercion dealt the Positivists a double blow. It separated them from the Trade Union leadership after an association that had lasted twenty years. It joined them to the new Radical leadership which was moving in the direction of Socialism, a direction which they could not follow. They rapidly lost all influence in the Trade Union Movement, while in the working-men's clubs their prestige as men of the Left was soon being challenged by the Socialists.

IV

The limits of Positivist influence and the causes of their decline can best be discussed in terms of the criteria for successful pressure group activity set out at the beginning of this chapter.[4]

---

[1] Report of Edinburgh Congress, 1879, T.U.C. (Standing Order No. 31).

[2] E. S. Beesly, 'Lord Beaconsfield at the Bar', *Bee-Hive*, 16 September 1876.

[3] E. S. Beesly: articles on the Irish question in the *Labour Standard*, 8 and 22 October, 3 December 1881 and 13 and 20 May 1882. Also by Congreve 5 November 1881. Crompton wrote seventeen articles mostly on the Irish Question and the need for a Labour Party in the *Labour Standard* between 7 May and 31 December 1881.

[4] The discussion does not follow the criteria in the exact order in which they have been listed.

English Positivism grew out of close personal friendship, but it was not the friendship of fundamentally creative and independent minds. They had neither a Bentham nor a Sidney Webb among them. Their leader did not emerge on account of his intellectual pre-eminence, but because of his seniority. His followers were accepted as such only to the extent that they were prepared to regard themselves as disciples unto a disciple —a disciple whose heart was set upon becoming a sort of 'backroom Pope'.

Lacking the benefit of a Bentham or a Webb, the Positivists were also in want of a Pease. It was not until 1867 that the London Positivist Committee was established; before that date there was no formal organisation. The members lived 'well nigh an hour's journey apart' and 'they lacked the first-rate secretarial organisation behind the scenes'.[1] However, instead of bothering themselves about these important but mundane matters, when they did turn to organisation it was not to remedy administrative short-comings but in the interests of Congreve's grandiose projects for religious regeneration. Thus, the Positivists came to attach an importance to organisation and proselytising which was quite foreign to the Utilitarians or Fabians.

As early as 1870, Harrison was complaining that Congreve, without consulting anyone, had fixed a tablet of white marble to the wall of the Positivist meeting-place or school, headed 'Religion of Humanity'.

> I don't know what your opinion is, but I consider that a distinct breach of faith with us, and a paltry attempt to start a ritualism which it is well known we do not accept . . . I suppose Congreve is a priest—and what is once in a man who had the bishop's hands on him can't come out. We shall have a woman and baby next and be expected to touch the three organs.[2]

(The reference is to Comte's Positivist Catechism which dealt with the devotional and liturgical forms appropriate to the new religion. Madame Clothilde de Vaux took the place of the Virgin Mother, although she was neither mother nor virgin. Positivists were expected to touch the three organs of love, order and progress. Comte was speaking phrenologically, of course.)

[1] P. Geddes, Introduction to S. Liveing, op. cit., p. 9.
[2] F. Harrison to E. S. Beesly, 25 July 1870.

From 1871 until 1878, when the Positivist society divided into two camps, the men who were the closest and most trusted advisers of Labour were locked in an increasingly bitter quarrel among themselves. It drained their energies and did much to discredit their cause. The trouble began when a Parisian Positivist named Pradeau arrived in England in 1871. He was taken to be a Communard refugee, but he was evidently equally anxious to make his escape from a friend whose wife he had seduced and with whom he was still living. All the Positivists except Congreve considered that he had 'committed a crime of no ordinary magnitude'.[1] They would appear to have had Comte's authority on their side, for the founder of Positivism insisted most strenuously upon the sacredness of marriage. Indeed he had delighted in devising stern improvements upon Christian doctrine. By the vow of eternal widowhood monogamy was to be made perfect, while during the lifetime of the spouse conjugal relations were to be regulated by a most austere code, the like of which is not to be found anywhere except among certain tribes of North American Indians.[2]

Congreve decided not to confront Pradeau with the choice of separating from his mistress or facing excommunication. Beesly and his friends were gravely disturbed and held that to sanction freedom in sexual matters would lead to Positivism being confounded with the 'purely destructive side of the present revolutionary movement'.[3] Congreve was equally aroused by this challenge to his authority. 'There are moments when I might well wish to be quit of this world,' he wrote. 'My

[1] E. S. Beesly to R. Congreve, 18 November 1872. PABM.
[2] M. Mead, *Male and Female*, 1950, p. 207.
[3] E. S. Beesly, F. Harrison, J. H. Bridges, Henry Crompton, V. and G. Lushington to R. Congreve, 18 November 1872. PABM. In the 'sixties, before his marriage, Frederic Harrison does not appear to have taken so solemn a view of sexual matters. Beesly was a success with the ladies and Harrison teased him about being ' "a fascinating William" '. He told Beesly the following anecdote: 'Poor Lucas I regret to say—can't you see it—has got either delirium tremens or softening of the brain. Poor devil! There is a story all over town how he came one night into the Garrick smoking-room and offered to bet that he had "the most symmetrical tool in Europe" which he offered to prove on the spot—his wife, he said, could never keep her fingers off it!' (to Beesly 'Thursday' 1865).

direction has become merely nominal as far as Messrs. Beesly, Bridges, Harrison and Crompton are concerned.'[1]

Congreve was grieved that the head of world Positivism, Pierre Lafitte, did not join forces with him against the rebels. He aspired to take Lafitte's place, and to this end he entered into a conspiracy with a French Positivist named Sémérie, who had taken an active part in the Commune and who was dissatisfied with Lafitte's leadership on the grounds that it was not political enough. According to Sémérie only the indolence of Pierre Lafitte stopped Positivism leading the way to a Dictatorship based on the union of the great towns under *the* leadership of Paris which would impose the Republic on the reactionary *peuple souverain*.[2] Thus an alliance was formed between those who wanted to make Positivism more of a Church with those who aspired to make it more of a Party against those who were content that it should remain a School.

While the conspiracy between Congreve and Sémérie was maturing, Pradeau was producing a number of illegitimate offspring. Congreve agreed to perform the Positivist sacrament of 'Presentation'[3] for these children, and great was the disapproval of Beesly and his associates in consequence. Crompton told him: 'Nothing in my life has given me more pain or distressed me more—nothing could—because there is no one else in your position—and it is to you that we owe all our teachings, all the practical efficacy of the Positivist Religion.'[4]

In 1877 the political crisis in France reached its height and Sémérie launched an open attack on Lafitte because of the latter's support for Gambetta. Congreve reproached Beesly with attempting to enlist the sympathies of the English Positivists for the Parisian Director. He told him: 'The time is come to say that I look upon all friendly relations as at an end between us.'[5] Beesly was shocked and astonished by this letter.

[1] R. Congreve to E. Sémérie, 7 July 1873 (M d'A.C.), Paris.
[2] E. Sémérie, 'L'Avenir du parti positiviste', *La Politique Positive*, 1872–1873 (Paris), p. 263 et seq.
[3] There were nine social sacraments in the Positivist Religion. Presentation, Initiation, Admission, Destination, Marriage, Maturity, Retirement, Transformation and Incorporation. Comte explained, 'In the first sacrament our religion, the final one, gives a systematic consecration to every birth.'
[4] H. Crompton to R. Congreve, 12 May 1876. PABM.
[5] R. Congreve to E. S. Beesly, 26 November 1877. PABM.

Our friendship [he replied] which has existed during the greater part of my life has been on my side singularly warm and deep—I venture to believe on yours also. If your renunciation of it had been motivated solely by the events of last week—(a letter of sympathy which he had addressed to his cher maitre, Lafitte, of which Congreve had first heard from Paris)—I might have remonstrated and asked you to reconsider your determination. But it has become a source of weariness to you and you have broken it off remorselessly and with a sense of relief . . . The advantage has been all on my side. You have done much for me, I nothing for you.[1]

The High Priest of English Positivism was to some degree reassured by this profession of affection and indebtedness, but during the following months he repeatedly returned to the discussion of their friendship. While requiring Beesly to tell him what he thought of its condition, Congreve went on foretelling its close. His mind was entirely occupied with plots and counter-plots. He studied how to make his *coup d'état* at the most judicious moment. 'The cauldron,' he remarked, 'is seething all round. For the present I am for as little action as possible, wait and watch events is my motto.'[2] In May 1878 he resigned the Presidency of the London Positivist Society and declared that it was dissolved. In the autumn he completed the break by announcing that he would no longer subscribe to the Sacerdotal Fund from which Pierre Lafitte derived part of his income. But Congreve and Sémérie were beaten in both London and Paris. The bizarre conspiracy between religious fanaticism and revolutionary intransigence, a conspiracy which aimed ultimately at nothing less than the spiritual and temporal direction of Humanity, was conducted with such ineptitude that it failed to displace the indulgent and professorial Lafitte from his quarters in Comte's house at 10 Rue de Monsieur le Prince. All the most eminent English Positivists, with the exception of Crompton, separated themselves from Congreve and established their own Positivist centre. Congreve was left with a few mediocrities who were ready to address him as 'My Dear Father', and he passed into an unwelcome, but well deserved, obscurity.[3]

[1] E. S. Beesly to R. Congreve, 28 November 1877. PABM.

[2] Congreve to an unnamed correspondent, 4 and 17 October 1877. PABM.

[3] Despite the attempt to destroy much of the correspondence relating to the Positivist split, enough of it has been preserved in the British Museum,

The dispute had begun as one about authority rather than about doctrine. The Congrevians, however, insisted that the division was between complete and incomplete, religious and merely philosophic, Positivism. The Harrisonians denied that they shared Mill's scorn for Positivist religious observances, but they insisted that there was 'no gain in the outward sign when it is not the expression of the inward life'.[1] Beesly never regarded Comte as infallible; never thought of him as a perfect moral type; and increasingly came to believe that a discreet veil ought to be drawn over the weaknesses of a great man.[2]

The split occasioned the most intense bitterness. One of the leading working-class Positivists changed sides. He first denounced that *sang froid* man Professor Beesly and then wrote to Congreve 'erase my name from the list of those who form your group. Please also to regard this communication as final, both as regards yourself, your family and the group.'[3] He sent a letter to Crompton, the gentle advocate of appeasement, which concluded with the words: 'I detest you.'[4] The spectacle of a few dozen men who were set on creating a new universal church and putting morality on a demonstrable basis, rebuking each other on their spiritual pride and pedantic arrogance was hardly likely to increase the confidence of workmen in Positivism. Those who had read Mill were likely to take this episode as confirmation of all he had said about the preposterous character of Comte's 'second career'.[5] Beesly might try to maintain a measure of co-operation with Congreve in political work and ask him: 'How, Sir, do you find workmen talking about the Zulu War,'[6] but when workmen talked about Positiv-

---

[1] J. H. Bridges, *Appeal to English Positivists*, 12 October 1878.

[2] E. S. Beesly, *Comte as a Moral Type*, Address of 5 September 1885 (1888).

[3] J. W. Overton to R. Congreve, 15 December 1878. PABM.

[4] Referred to by H. Crompton in his letter to R. Congreve, 25 Caesar 90 (The Positivists had their own Calendar!) May 1878.

[5] J. S. Mill, *Comte and Positivism*, 1865.

[6] E. S. Beesly to R. Congreve, 4 March 1879. PABM.

---

the Comte Museum and in University College to allow it to be reconstructed in great detail. It might be worth doing. In its absurd extravagance it throws light on the Soul of Man under Victoria. For those who enjoy this sort of thing it has everything, including murder in the Liverpool Church of Humanity.

ism it was to mock those of their number, such as Charles Rogers, the President of the London Coppersmiths, who had ventured to associate with such ridiculous people.[1]

How far did Positivism ever enjoy the support and confidence of workmen?

In the early 'fifties Harriet Martineau had expected that it would have a special appeal to them, provided it could be introduced to them in a popular form.[2] She expressed this view to G. J. Holyoake who joined with a number of moral-force Chartists in bringing out a journal called *The People's Review of Literature and Politics*. The editors, who all claimed to be workmen, styled themselves, 'Friends of Order and Progress' and expressed admiration for Comte.[3] They incurred the wrath of the *Northern Star* by arguing that the failure of Chartism and of the Revolutions of 1848 was due to a failure to see the need for reconciling Order and Progress. This gesture in the direction of Positivism was evidently made quite independently of Congreve. Holyoake, as a good bourgeois democrat, repeatedly attacked the Positivists as 'political cuckoos who laid their eggs in other people's nests'. Yet he told Harrison: 'In many respects I have always had the Comteian mind.'[4] He certainly stimulated interest in Comte, and the Liverpool Positivists looked upon the great champion of secularism and co-operation as one who had prepared them for Positivism.[5]

The early spontaneous approach to Positivism by English workmen was not destined to be followed by many others. Of the founder members of the London Positivist Society in 1867 only one, the old Owenite, Edward Truelove, had early ties with the Labour Movement. Truelove was a brave and charming man. A publisher in the tradition of Carlile and Hetherington he published Marx' *Civil War in France* and went to prison as a result of the Bradlaugh–Besant birth control case in the 'seventies. He did not stay with the Positivists because he could not suffer the restraint which they wished to impose on

[1] J. W. Overton to R. Congreve, 15 December 1878.
[2] H. Martineau to G. J. Holyoake, 6 October (1851?) and 9 April (1853?). BM. ADD MSS 42726.
[3] *People's Review of Literature and Politics*, No. 2, July 1851.
[4] G. J. Holyoake to F. Harrison, 25 November 1905. FHC.
[5] A. Crompton (Preface), *The Message of Humanity from the Pen of Edward Carson*, printed for private circulation (Liverpool), 1908.

criticisms of Napoleon III. His departure meant that Positivism lost a figure who enjoyed the confidence and affection of many working men.[1]

In the early 'seventies, the Positivists were disturbed by their failure to convert proletarians—although they never appear to have had more than two or three hundred members of any class. Albert Crompton suggested that

> our attitude has been too much inclined to be constrained by our middle-class prejudices—were we not labelled as 'well-meaning bourgeois' by some French communist?—this label has always seemed to me to have too much truth to be altogether pleasing.[2]

Congreve explained to his French co-religionists:

> Our great difficulty, the problem for us English disciples, is to get ourselves listened to, and above all, accepted by, our workmen. I don't believe they think badly of us. On the contrary they are favourably disposed towards us personally, but the long, traditional opposition which separates the various social groups presents us with an obstacle which we will have much difficulty in surmounting . . . It would be another matter if all our ideas were presented to workmen from a less suspect source, if he saw the Religion of Humanity at work in his own immediate surroundings, acknowledged and practised by men living his own life, having the same interests as he had, and exposed to the same social pressure.

Given a few intelligent workmen, rapid progress was sure to be made. Congreve actually toyed with the idea of a 'Narodniki-like' movement among Positivists in which some of the younger ones would voluntarily adopt proletarian status.[3]

No such dramatic expedient was ever resorted to. As a result of articles in the working-class press, lectures given at the Positivist School and in the Trades Guild of Learning, a small knot of workmen were converted to Positivism. Among them were some interesting personalities such as John W. Overton, copper-smith and forerunner of Tressall as a proletarian novelist. He

---

[1] Edward Truelove, *The Radical*, June 1887.

[2] A. Crompton to R. Congreve, 13 October 1878. PABM.

[3] R. Congreve, 'L'Union des Proletariats Anglais et Français', *Essays: Social Political and Religious*, 1, being a lecture delivered in Paris on 4 September 1872.

wrote two books. The first, *Harry Hartley* or *Social Science for the Workers*, was written in 1859, and reflected the influence of *Alton Locke*. The second, appeared twenty years later after his conversion to Positivism. Entitled *Saul of Mitre Court*, its main interest lay, perhaps, in its satire of middle-class wire-pullers, who appeared in the character of Mr. Long Canvass. 'We should try to work up a strong workmen's party,' declared Overton's hero, 'such a party exists and is being systematised. We are finding workmen leaders. Let us follow them and leave Long Canvass and Co. to the constituents.'[1] It was Overton who brought his Union's President, Charles Rogers, to Positivism. Beesly valued Overton, but testified to his bitter and rebellious spirit, his 'Rousseauesque' nature.[2]

Edmund Wallace Jones, a Liverpool basket-maker, came to Positivism after a lifetime's experience of working-class politics. He had been a prominent Chartist and had addressed many important workers' meetings before 1848, including one held at the bottom of a coal mine, at which the miners asked him to buy arms for them with £150 which they had collected for that purpose. He declined to do so and someone eventually absconded with the money.[3] Jones was the Liverpool delegate to the Chartist convention of 1848, and subsequently played a part in the agitation for the second Reform Bill in Liverpool. In the end he became persuaded that political remedies were of little use. At the end of the 1870s he joined the Positivists, declaring that what was needed was a concentration of power in hands which could be watched and taught.[4] Some of his old Chartist friends did not take kindly to these changed opinions, but the Coffee House which Jones opened in his old age remained a centre for the discussion of Socialism and advanced Radicalism in Liverpool. Before his death in 1881, Jones materially assisted the Positivists in their organisation of a great meeting against Irish coercion.[5]

Henry Ellis, a clerical worker who became a Positivist in the middle 'seventies, was more erudite than either Overton or

[1] Published for private circulation at Overton's own expense, 1879.

[2] E. S. Beesly, 'The Worship of the Dead', *Positivist Review*, 1893.

[3] T. Joff, *Coffee House Babble* (Liverpool, 1916?).

[4] A. Crompton (preface), op. cit.

[5] E. S. Beesly, 'Necrologie: Edmond Wallace Jones', *La Revue Occidentale* (Paris), Vol. IX, 1882.

Jones. As a boy, Ellis had joined Garibaldi's red-shirts in Italy and had been wounded in action. He became a frequent contributor to the working-class press, his writings appearing in the *Bee-Hive*, the *Industrial Review* and the *English Labourer's Chronicle*. He defended Positivism against Marxist criticism in the Socialist journal, *Today*.[1]

Overton, Rogers, Jones and Ellis were Positivists in the 'seventies. In the succeeding decade they were joined by other workmen such as S. A. Challis, an umbrella-maker who had once been a street-corner orator for the S.D.F.,[2] F. W. Bockett a compositor who became a most active propagandist,[3] and the extraordinary Malcolm Quinn, author of *Politics for the Proletariat* and *Memoirs of a Positivist*. Quinn was a foundation member of the I.L.P. and like Henry Tompkins, who was the first Labour member of the Hornsey Borough Council, tried to reconcile his Positivism with active membership of Socialist Organisations. The biographer of H. M. Hyndman was also a Positivist. He tried to synthesise Comte, Marx and Guild Socialism.[4]

The converts were interesting, but neither very numerous nor very important. It is more to the point to enquire how far the Positivists succeeded in impressing their principles upon the working-class leaders with whom they worked in the London Trades Council or the Conference of Amalgamated Trades. They made no headway with William Allan. The engineer was that rare bird among Trade Union leaders—an active member of the Established Church.[5] If he accepted Positivist advice it was because he had satisfied his own canny intelligence about the merits of the case. Any connection between this advice and some religious or philosophic system was of no interest or concern to him. Matters stood rather differently with Odger, Applegarth, Coulson and even Howell. In varying degrees and in rather different ways they recognised in Positivism a system with which they had a natural affinity, and which might be

[1] H. Ellis, 'Can the Capitalist be Moralised?', *Today*, August and September 1885, reprinted as a pamphlet 1896.

[2] *Positivist Review*, August 1903.

[3] 'British Pilgrimage to Paris', *La Revue Occidentale*, Vol. XVI, 1886.

[4] F. J. Gould, *Labour's Unrest and Labour's Future: Brief Notes on Comte, Marx, Orage, National Guilds and the Social Outlook, 1919*.

[5] J. M. L. (Ludlow), *The Ironworkers Journal*, December 1874.

used to supply them with some of the clothes of philosophy, if not of religion.

Beesly regarded George Odger as the noblest and most receptive of the British Trade Union leaders. Partly because he was free from some of the burdens of office work and administration, which lay so heavily upon his colleagues, Odger displayed an interest in political and foreign issues, which the Positivists admired and encouraged. Beesly put him in touch with the proletarian Positivist, Fabien Magnin, and Odger and he became life-long correspondents.[1] Magnin was greatly grieved by the shoemaker's death and organised a subscription among French workmen for the benefit of his widow.[2]

Odger was not only a frequent visitor to Positivist households —one interesting entry in Congreve's diary reads, 'Call from Odger. Not a democrat'[3]—but he became a regular attender at the Positivist School when this was opened early in 1870 in Chapel Street. A clergyman, who visited the place in order to hear Bridges lecture on how acquisitive society corrupted art, observed that most of the people around him were *bona fide* working men and women. George Odger was there with a group of his friends and supporters. He 'passed up to the chief seat in the synagogue as if he had been on the floor of St. Stephen's already'.[4] In the course of the year 1872–73, Odger attended a whole series of lectures by Beesly on the French Revolution, and one of his friends, William Chatterton of the A.S.E., formally joined the Positivist Society.[5]

Beesly and Harrison actively assisted Odger in his famous election campaign in Southwark. Most of the planks in his platform corresponded closely with Positivist teaching, and one of them—the demand for the abolition of anonymous journalism —was unmistakenly inspired by it. Beesly had the highest opinion of Odger's oratorical powers: his dexterous management of his points; his shrewd appreciation of the mood of the audience; his ability to be by turns humorous, passionate and

---

[1] See introduction to F. Magnin, *Etudes Sociales* (Paris), 1913.

[2] E. S. Beesly, 'George Odger and French Workmen', *Weekly Despatch*, 23 December 1877.

[3] R. Congreve's Diary, 22 September 1870. PABM.

[4] C. M. Davies, *Heterodox London*, Vol. 2, 1874, p. 242.

[5] W. Chatterton, *Positivist Review*, December 1909.

persuasive. He insisted that, when Odger dealt with a subject which he really understood, there was no speaker in the country to equal him except John Bright at his best.[1] However, oratory was not highly rated by Positivists, and Odger's talents on the platform do not explain the high regard which they had for him. His great merit in their eyes was his freedom from envy, jealousy and rancour. They believed that he was above the small-mindedness of some of his colleagues, and they found no vanity or affectation in him.[2] Appreciation for these qualities led Beesly and Harrison to join the immense procession that followed Odger's coffin to the churchyard where—standing upon a mound of earth—Beesly delivered his eulogy. The shoe-maker was not only a good citizen, but a great one; and he took that to be the highest title that could be accorded to any man, 'a title beyond the power of Kings or of Act of Parliament to bestow'.[3]

The extremely close personal relation, which the Positivists established with the Trade Union leaders of the 'sixties, is al-most equally well illustrated by the case of Robert Applegarth. Beesly publicly declared that he was proud to call Applegarth his friend,[4] while the Carpenters' Secretary said of Beesly, that to enjoy the confidence of that 'heroic soul' seemed the highest honour of his life.

> When in the grief of bereavement [said Applegarth] he was my comforter; when spite and envy were doing their worst, he it was that cheered me, that encouraged me to persevere, that reminded me that I ought still to work for my class and be useful to my fellow men.[5]

Beesly, Harrison and Crompton were all honorary members of the A.S.C.&J. Speaking in 1869, Applegarth declared: 'If the policy I pursued has been wise and beneficial it is not due to myself alone, but in the first place to Professor Beesly . . .'[6]

[1] E. S. Beesly, 'George Odger', *Weekly Dispatch*, 11 March 1877.

[2] Ibid.

[3] 'The Funeral of George Odger', *Weekly Dispatch*, 18 March 1877.

[4] E. S. Beesly, 'The Amalgamated Society of Carpenters and Joiners', *Fortnightly Review*, March 1867.

[5] 'Commemoration of Edward Spencer Beesly', *Positivist Review*, November 1915.

[6] Amal. Soc. Carpenters Joiners, *Monthly Report*, July 1869.

He informed the Webbs that his struggle for the New Model Unionism had been aided and inspired by Beesly and Harrison.[1]

Many attempts have been made to account for the enigmatic element in Applegarth's character and outlook; to reconcile his natural aggressiveness and determination with his conciliatory and peaceful policy; his association with Marx and the International—which lasted long after the other English notables had departed—with his friendship and collaboration with Mundella. How could a man of such intelligence and character remain on the General Council, and, at the same time, be party to a confidential arrangement whereby he worked for 'Glyn and the Government'?[2] He was faced, during the early 'seventies, with serious financial difficulties, but he was a man of much higher principle than Howell, and too much weight must not be given to this consideration. To understand Applegarth, one must penetrate through the empiricism and pragmatism of the Trade Union leaders to the odd assortment of theoretical assumptions about society, which they entertained. Some of these they certainly derived from the Positivists.

Beesly and Harrison were able to keep on reasonably friendly terms with both Mundella and Marx. The former was a 'good employer', capable of seeing beyond the immediate interests of his class and recognising the advantages of collective bargaining. His limitations arose from his attachment to a shallow parliamentary Radicalism and to 'certain old books';[3] but these did not stop the Positivists from regarding him as an approximation to Comte's 'Captain of Industry'. Marx was working to broaden the sympathies and opinions of workmen; his revolutionary and Socialist theories were limitations of secondary consequence which were, to some extent, allowable in a German. The Positivists, having no formal ties with either of these men, imagined that they knew how to fit them both into their own comprehensive, developing world-view. It is reasonable to conclude that Applegarth—who acknowledged that the Positivists were his teachers—was a loyal, but not altogether accomplished, pupil. Just as George Howell thought that the International stood for 'Order and Progress', so Applegarth worked with it

[1] Interview (n.d.), Webb T.U. Coll., Section A., folio 393 (LSE).
[2] See below, p. 202.
[3] F. Harrison to A. J. Mundella, 1 May 1880 (Sheffield U.L.).

expressly on Positivist grounds—he thought that it counter-
acted the narrow and exclusive tendencies of the Unions.
Unfortunately, the carpenter formalised his relations with both
Marx and Mundella and carried them to a point at which his
position became thoroughly compromised and ridiculous. His
conduct on the General Council shows that he had no real grasp
of the synthesis he required.

Thus, in 1871, Applegarth came to the I.W.M.A. with the
request that he be granted credentials so that he could, at the
invitation of an employer, act as arbitrator in a trades dispute
which was taking place on the Continent. Marx's impatience
with this ingenuous proposal may well be imagined. The International, he explained, had nothing whatsoever to do with
employers.[1] But if Applegarth once more received this repri-
mand with a 'diminished head', it did not cause him to revise
the view that Karl Marx was an honest man 'with no revolution
about him'. After all, the Positivists had been repeatedly
charged with being revolutionaries and friends of terrorism.
Applegarth knew that these charges were false, and he knew
that the events of 1871 had not caused the Positivists to de-
nounce the I.W.M.A. It is not an inadmissible conjecture that
Positivism made its contribution to those 'inner experiences'
and that 'generous sympathy' and—let it be confessed—to that
muddleheadedness, which enabled Applegarth to look 'beyond'
both Mundella and Marx.[2]

When Applegarth resigned office the Positivists lost their most
powerful friend in the Trade Union world. However, in the
struggle of 1881 they had a staunch, if far less effective ally, in
Applegarth's disciple, Edwin Coulson of the Bricklayers'.
Crompton observed that the London Trades Council was 'not
what it was when Allan, Odger and Applegarth used to be there
representing large Societies—but there are good men there,
like King and Coulson . . .'[3] Coulson certainly played an im-

---

[1] Minutes of General Council I.W.M.A., 26 September 1871. IISH.

[2] A. Briggs, 'Robert Applegarth and the Trade Unions', Victorian People,
1954.

[3] H. Crompton to G. Howell, 31 March 1881. Without a doubt the
death or departure of the leaders of the 'sixties contributed to the decline
of Positivist influence. A few workers' circles in Scotland conducted readings
from Comte (R. Congreve, The Religion of Humanity, an address on the
Festival of Humanity, 1 January 1871), but Positivist influence was heavily

portant part in helping the Positivists to line the Council up against the Parliamentary Committee on the question of Irish coercion. At the London T.U.C. of 1881 he was elected President, and his opening address deserves to be remembered as the most perfect expression of Positivist principles ever advanced by a workman at that assembly. Whether Coulson actually wrote the speech is another question. George Shipton had tried to persuade Frederick Engels to 'ghost' for Coulson, who was certainly not a man of many ideas or of easy speech on great occasions.[1] Engels apparently declined to do so, for it was certainly Positivism and not Marxism which came before the T.U.C. All the Positivist major themes found expression, and in just the sort of language which they used themselves. Thus, wars of Empire were declared to be 'demoralising crimes of the worst kind'; Irish coercion was denounced, and the demand was made for the total abolition of the law of conspiracy; delegates were told to guard themselves 'jealously against party influence of any kind, especially such as comes from the ruling classes; at the same time, the hard and fast line we attempted formerly to draw between trade questions and political questions cannot be maintained'. The depressed state of trade resulted from 'disastrous competition and over-production, from the fact that industry is not organised, and that industrial and commercial operations are not regulated by moral conditions . . .'[2]

But the most astonishing tribute to the prestige and pervasive

[1] G. Shipton to G. Howell, 2 December 1879. HC.
[2] Report T.U.C., London, 1881.

concentrated in London. The Northern Leaders who increasingly came into their own after 1875 thought of them as cranks who had, at one time, had a certain academic influence. (W. Owen to S. and B. Webb, T.U. Coll., Section A, folio 393.) These leaders were less emancipated in relation to theology than the Londoners. The Positivists tried to avoid stirring up religious prejudices, but in the case of Beesly his own private loathing for the priest and parson crept through. When his Mother was dying Beesly suffered from the knowledge that, as a good evangelical, she believed that he was destined for hell while she could take no comfort from him. 'When I dwell on this it makes me wish that all the priests had but one windpipe and that my thumb was upon it. It is at such moments that one realises what a curse theology has become to human society' (E. S. Beesly to H. Crompton, 18 September 1868, BUC). Harrison was continually having to restrain Beesly from savaging the Christian Socialists.

influence of Positivism upon the leading workmen of the 'sixties and 'seventies was that George Howell suggested that he was seriously interested in Comte and was considering becoming a Positivist. Understandably he made his approach to Henry Crompton rather than to Harrison and Beesly. 'I heartily rejoice that you are studying Comte,' wrote Crompton, 'if you become practically one of us, no one would welcome you more warmly than I should.'[1] Some days later he wrote again:

> Few letters have given me more pleasure than yours. I was always sure that if you had only leisure, your mind would, if you read Comte, converge with our minds, on the great questions and leading features of Positivism . . . I should value your adhesion—partly from personal motives—but chiefly because I think you would have the noblest career before you—and that you would be a most powerful help. Also because I think you would be able to help me in the unfortunate and unwise difference that has divided our body . . . I hope that you will come either to me, or to Harrison, Beesly and Bridges, because I am sure that by discussion we see things in a very much clearer light . . . I have worked so much with you in the past that I should like working with you upon that which I have always regarded as the principal work of my life.[2]

Crompton's trusting and uncritical nature can rarely have found purer expression. Within a year or two Howell was in the Commons as a Lib–Lab M.P. and was no longer expressing any interest in Positivism. Like the founders of the *People's Review*, Howell could find in Positivism a compromising creed, which was in tune with the mid-Victorian Labour Movement to the extent that it emphasised the primacy of social and moral over political remedies. Given his intellectual pretensions and his enormous appetite for factual knowledge, the encyclopaedic character of Comte's work had a special attraction. But it was exactly this encyclopaedic aspect which presented the most formidable obstacles to workmen becoming acquainted with Positivism.

However, the deficiencies of Positivism as compared with Utilitarianism or Fabianism became most apparent not in its want of creative originality, nor in its excessive and ill-directed concern with organisation, but in its want of those principles

[1] H. Crompton to G. Howell, 2 December 1879. HC.
[2] Ibid., 30 December 1879.

'which have such fecundity that they can supply and replenish legislative programmes'. So long as the Labour Movement's principal preoccupation was with the legal emancipation of Trade Unionism this weakness hardly revealed itself. Although they reiterated their faith in moral rather than political remedies, the Positivists were indeed far ahead of their contemporaries in their attitude towards State regulation of economic activity. They dissociated themselves from *laissez-faire* objections to it and were prepared to call for the extension of the Factory Acts and the nationalisation of the mines.[1] But collectivist measures were never at the forefront of their programme and their contribution to economic literature was critical rather than constructive.[2] Comte derided all 'futile' and 'tedious' enquiries into the origins of wealth. In the early 'seventies the Positivist Society had set up a sub-committee to report on pauperism, but it never produced its report. The onset of the Great Depression soon exposed the limitations of Positivist social and economic theory. A few illustrations of how this happened must suffice.

Henry Crompton was the author of what was to become known as the classic work on arbitration. The book excels in its description of the working of existing conciliation machinery across a number of industries. The author had a first-hand acquaintance with this side of the question, being himself an arbitrator in the Nottingham lace trade. It offers, however, no theory of wages, nor does it attempt to state the criteria by which a fair wage is to be determined.[3] With the onset of the

---

[1] E. S. Beesly, letter in *South Wales Press*, 7 July 1870, declared: 'If I do not call myself a Socialist it is not that I am ashamed of a name which imparts everything that is noble and good, but because it is too wide and vague . . . Mines are a property which ought to belong to the State.' When H. Crompton told workmen to make 'Socialism not Radicalism' their slogan and to organise an army to get it, he explained that revolution did not mean violence; that the army would be for peace; and that Socialism meant 'social objects and organisation to gain them'. H. Crompton, *Bee-Hive*, 23 September 1871. Still, as Mr. Noel Annan has pointed out, Frederic Harrison's *Order and Progress*, 1875, was one of the few books which took a positive view of collectivism written in this period.

[2] The most distinguished economist among the Positivists was J. K. Ingram: see in particular his *History of Political Economy* (Edinburgh, 1888). He addressed the T.U.C. in Dublin in 1880.

[3] H. Crompton, *Industrial Conciliation*, 1876.

Depression, Crompton was soon awarding wages cuts amounting to as much as 25% in one instance, and he was doing this on principles which were not clear to the operatives or anyone else.[1] Moreover, it soon became apparent that, where the employers could not get cuts of this type through the machinery, they were ready to dismantle it or ignore it. Many big employers adopted this policy in 1879 and there were some savage and prolonged struggles in consequence. Crompton could do nothing but deplore the employers' conduct: he had neither analysis to offer nor counsel to give.[2]

An episode which occurred in the following year (1880) provides a still better example of the confusion and helplessness of the Positivists in the face of the Depression. Crompton wrote a foreword to a pamphlet by Lord Bramwell. He suggested that Bramwell's argument deserved the careful consideration, if not necessarily the approval, of workmen. The pamphlet was little more than a statement of the *prima facie* case that for workers to restrict the production of wealth could not contribute to prosperity. Frederic Harrison then wrote a rejoinder which was published by the Parliamentary Committee: this was no more than a statement of the *prima facie* case that to maintain or increase the volume of production of goods or services for which the market was already satiated could only intensify the Depression. The Positivists could show workmen no way of extricating themselves from the horns of the dilemma presented by these two self-evident, but seemingly contrary, propositions. All that they could suggest was that consumers should be educated to be less fickle in their tastes. Apart from this one would simply have to wait until the growing concentration of capital led the anarchy of competition to be replaced by planned production.[3]

Unable to indicate a way out of the Depression, the Positivists did their best to console workmen with the thought that things could be a great deal worse than they were. The most striking instance of this complacency was provided by the paper which

[1] Lloyd Jones, 'The Dispute in the Nottingham Lace Trade', *Industrial Review*, 30 June 1877.

[2] *Liverpool Weekly Post*, 5 April 1879. (Report of meeting at the Chapter House of St. Paul's Cathedral on Conciliation and Arbitration.)

[3] Lord Justice Bramwell, *Diminished Production*, 1879. F. Harrison, 'Diminished Production: A notice on the paper recently published . . .' P.C. T.U.C., November 1879.

Harrison read to the T.U.C. in 1883. Reviewing the history of Trade Unionism since the building strike of 1859, he amassed an imposing array of figures which were intended to show how well the great amalgamated societies had weathered the storm. He dwelt upon the immense sums of money which they had spent on out-of-work benefit, and cheerfully pointed out what all this meant in terms of relief for the ratepayers. He gently admonished the stonemasons for appearing to regret that they could not spend more on strikes. He treated Unions, as T. J. Dunning had reproved him for doing in the past, as if they were mere Friendly Societies, and he traced their history and progress without a single reference to their influence on wage-rates. Daniel Guile had reported only a year or two earlier that 'various trade societies that were once in prosperity lie prostrate and mangled in the vortex of want and starvation . . . the victims of capitalists who are treating them as only relentless foes can treat their enemies',[1] Harrison could only make one practical proposal: in view of the increase in the amounts which Unions had to devote to superannuation benefits some of the older workmen might set an example by voluntarily renouncing all claim to them.[2]

Under these circumstances it was not surprising that even parsons contrived to be on the 'Left' of the Positivists. The *Christian Socialist* joyfully turned the tables on these reactionary infidels who preached pious cant about moralising the capitalist. 'Appeals to the morality of the rich have always been met with an answer very much in the sense of the reply of Vanderbilt when asked whether he would work some of his railway lines more in the interests of the people: "Damn the People" was the now historic answer.'[3]

By the middle 'eighties the Positivists had been completely outdistanced by the Socialists. The Nottingham T.U.C. of 1883 was the last which a Positivist addressed. Harrison wanted to intervene in a debate so as to oppose land nationalisation, but the delegates voted 61 to 46 against allowing him to speak. Two years later the Positivist performance at the Industrial Remuneration Conference put paid to their reputation as a

---

[1] D. Guile, *Industrial Review*, 12 January 1878.
[2] F. Harrison, *Trade Unions*, T.U.C., Nottingham 1883 Report.
[3] *Christian Socialist*, February 1884.

constructive and progressive group. George Bernard Shaw was able to commend Beesly's exposure of profit-sharing schemes,[1] but all the working-class delegates and the entire Socialist and Radical press were united in deploring the absence of any practical suggestions in the papers which Harrison and he read.[2]

Shortly before his death in August 1895 Frederick Engels discussed the relationship between the English Positivists and the Labour Movement. He asserted that some years after the Paris Commune they 'cooled off' towards the working class.

> The workers had become too powerful and it was now a question of maintaining a proper balance between capitalists and workers (both producers, after all, according to Saint-Simon) and to that end of once more supporting the former. Ever since then the Comtists have wrapped themselves in complete silence as regards the Labour question.[3]

There was an element of truth in this analysis. In 1873 Harrison had written: 'Every true Positivist is a real Conservative and I am thirsting for the time when, as Conservatives, our turn will come to defend the immortal institutions of man against sentimental sophists noble or ignorant.'[4] He became increasingly reactionary so that during the suffragette agitation he could rejoice in a letter from Curzon in which the noble Lord remarked: 'I can see no objection to allowing any of these she-devils, as you very properly call them, to starve herself in prison if she so desires.'[5] But Beesly cannot be said to have followed along the same road, although like all Positivists he thought that women were higher moral and lower political types than men. As editor of the *Positivist Review* Beesly was prepared to advise his readers to vote Social-Democrat, and he welcomed the arrival of the parliamentary Labour Party which he expected to make a stand against imperialism.[6]

[1] G. B. Shaw, 'The Industrial Remuneration Conference', *Commonwealth*, March 1885.

[2] Report of the Conference. See also the *Democrat* for 16 May and 31 October 1885.

[3] F. Engels to F. Tonnies, 24 January 1895.

[4] F. Harrison to J. Morley, 8 April 1873.

[5] Lord Curzon to F. Harrison, 17 March 1914. FHC.

[6] E. S. Beesly, 'Positivists and Social Democrats', *Positivist Review*, June 1900, and 'Liberals and Labour', *Positivist Review*, November 1906.

It was not so much that the Positivists wrapped themselves in silence after 1881 as that they had diminished opportunities for making themselves heard and what they had to say no longer sounded relevant, realistic or progressive.

> We know well enough [declared Beesly] that if we had chosen to dwell exclusively on what I may call the popular side of Positivism: its republicanism, its plans for the social elevation of the poor, its stern lessons for the rich, we might easily by this time have gathered the working class round us in masses, like many a socialist quackery which has lived and died in a generation.[1]

Following Comte, Beesly persisted in the view that Socialism would prepare men for Positivism. He presided at the founding of the International, took part in the formative meetings out of which the Democratic Federation arose and took the chair at Socialist meetings without ever bringing himself to see that the relationship was the very reverse of the one he expected.

V

Even more conspicuously than Republicanism and Land nationalisation, Positivism contributed to the Socialist revival of the 'eighties. It is exceedingly difficult to find a Socialist of this period who was quite uninfluenced by it. At the same time the depth and extent of that influence cannot be measured by simply following Positivist threads that lead to the Fabians, the S.D.F. or the Labour Church Movement. The importance of the Positivist bequest to British Socialism can only be assessed within the context of a prolonged discussion of all the sources of the Socialist revival. Only then would there be any chance of getting the scale and the proportions right. All that can be done here is to indicate that this is a fit subject for enquiry.

At the outset there are two propositions about the general bearing of Positivist to Socialist experience which may be affirmed with some confidence. First, in the association of the Positivists with the Labour Movement we meet for the first time the type of attitudes and relations between intellectuals and workmen which were to become characteristic of future developments. The intellectuals, conscious of themselves as such,

[1] E. S. Beesly, 'Positivists and Workmen', *Fortnightly Review*, July 1875.

turn to Labour as their natural ally. The man of ideas can triumph over the philistines, the wealthy wasters, the place-seeking politicians only with the aid of the proletariat. Once he enters the Labour Movement the faith of the intellectual in the historic destiny of the working class and its revolutionary capacity, has to be strong enough to withstand all the evidences of parochialism and careerism which he will find there. The alliance between the philosopher and the proletarian may well have its foundations in a common interest, but it is character-ised by impatience and irritability on both sides. In this respect, the Positivists anticipated the experience of the Socialist intellectuals.

Second, the issue around which these attitudes of attraction and repulsion formed themselves and found their clearest expression was the problem of an independent political life for Labour. This was as true for the Positivists as it was for their Socialist successors. When Engels was calling in the *Labour Standard* for an independent workers' party, the Positivists were writing to much the same effect in the same paper.[1] They had been thinking in these terms on and off since 1867. Long before Keir Hardie, they tried to encourage the formation of a Labour Party which would be based upon the Trade Unions and inde-pendent of the existing parties, without being Socialist. There is a tension, a contradiction, which lies at the heart of all such projects. A developed ideological basis may reduce you to a sect, while the absence of such a basis may continually lead you to compromise your independence. There is a tendency for the intellectuals to be drawn to one of these poles while the work-men are pulled towards the other. In the struggle around such issues as the Labour Laws the working class begins to see in terms of its immediate experience the need for political inde-pendence, but it draws back again and again from generalising from such particular experiences to conclusions about the ulti-mate relationship of its interests to those of other classes and parties. It draws close to the challenge of this theoretical prob-lem, only to withdraw from it complaining about the divisive effects of taking it up, and pointing to the need to concentrate on 'practical' issues. The intellectuals become more and more

[1] F. Engels, *The British Labour Movement*, 1936, pp. 46, reprints these articles. The key article is the one published on 23 July 1881.

impatient. They point to the 'aristocracy, in alliance with middle-class wealth, entrenched in the House of Commons, employing all the terms and methods of representative government and electioneering devices to blind the people to the true nature and source of the power ruling them'.[1] They tell the Trade Union leaders:

> The working classes must come sooner or later to see that their position is not that of ragtag or bobtail to a party; to be silenced and satisfied by judicious legislative sops thrown to the Congress (T.U.C.) from time to time; or even by half a dozen working-men Members of Parliament being courteously and generously treated and listened to.

The T.U.C. must be freed

> from any subordination to any other power, whether of wealth or political power—to make the working-class forces independent . . . forcing these quarrelsome, speechifying people (in the Government) either to deal with the real wants of the people or to stand aside.[2]

In the end, inflamed by the wrongs done by British imperialism in Asia or by Coercion in Ireland, the intellectuals throw discretion to the wind and declare that if the Trade Union leaders will not make the proletariat the dominant influence in the State then they will be failing in their duty and 'must be cast aside'.[3] When this point is reached it is generally the services of the intellectuals rather than those of the Trade Union leaders which are dispensed with.

In view of all that has been said before, it is perhaps not surprising that it was H. M. Hyndman among the Socialists who made the highest estimate of the Positivists' achievements and paid the warmest tributes to their work. He said of them: 'I question if, in modern times, a small band of highly educated men, who professed and vigorously preached an unpopular doctrine, ever had so great an influence.'[4] He described Beesly as his old friend and teacher.[5] He liked to repeat his facile judgement that 'the Positivists' theories are all wrong, but their

---

[1] H. Crompton, 'The Supremacy of Law', *Labour Standard*, 27 August 1881.

[2] H. Crompton, 'Liberty and the Workman', *Labour Standard*, 9 July 1881.

[3] Ibid.   [4] *Justice*, 15 July 1915.   [5] Ibid.

actions are all right.'[1] It was particularly with respect to the tradition of opposing imperialism that Hyndman and the Positivists shared common ground. It was the work of the Positivists James Geddes and Henry Cotton which first opened the eyes of the leader of the S.D.F. to the grave moral and political issues raised by the Empire.[2] It was the Positivists' reputation as courageous fighters which helped to secure them the respect of old veterans such as George Julian Harney, and revolutionary Socialists like Hyndman.[3]

Hyndman's fellow-Marxist, E. Belford Bax, was under a much greater obligation to the Positivists than Hyndman, but he was far less ready to acknowledge the debt. As a young man he had been attracted to Beesly and his friends by their defence fo the Commune.[4] During the 'seventies his name appeared regularly among those who attended the meetings of the Lon-

---

[1] H. M. Hyndman, *Record of an Adventurous Life*, 1911, p. 158.

[2] F. J. Gould, *H. M. Hyndman, Prophet of Socialism*, 1928, p. 51. (Sir H. Cotton, *Indian and Home Memories*, 1911, was the first English President of the Indian National Congress. He was a Congrevian at the time of the split and the only English Positivist ever to secure election to Parliament. Beesly and Harrison both stood twice without success during the Home Rule crisis of the mid-'eighties.)

[3] Harney admired Harrison's contribution to the *Fortnightly* on the Eastern Question and told the Positivist it was 'the very best and by far the most forcible and eloquent of any articles on the subject that I have read. But I must regret that such writing should be limited to the readers of the *Fortnightly*—It is a far wider circle you ought to address.

'We pay dear for that "untaxed knowledge" victory to which I, in my humble way, contributed (thrice behind the bolts and bars before I was 20). All the newspapers printed in London today contains not a tithe of the honest and vigorous writing of *Cobbett's Register*; and our unstamped papers, published "in defiance of law" overflowed with "thoughts that breathe and words that burn" utterly unknown to the puny exponents of the "Liberalism" of these times. You should have been—most sincerely I say so—the successor of Cobbett and Junius.

'I have noticed in the *Athenaeum* and other publications the issue of translations of Comte's works—translated by yourself and others. I am now too old to embark upon the labour of studying this extraordinary man's thoughts, visions, plans and aspirations, but I am glad for the sake of my juniors to find yourself and friends thus engaged. Amongst those who read through these may be many not made "disciples" even they must be made *thinkers* and that must be a great good achieved . . .' (G. J. Harney to F. Harrison, from Boston, 6 February 1877. FHC.)

[4] E. B. Bax, *Reminiscences of a Mid-, and Late-Victorian*, 1918, p. 30.

don Positivist Society. Bax, in his autobiography, certainly understated the influence which these discussions had upon him. The impression which they made upon him is evident from the manner in which he appraised continental Socialism in 1878— the last year in which he attended the Positivist Society. He found the meaning of Socialism to be:

> In politics the substitution of the international for the national idea, and the adoption of the Federal Republican solution through the splitting up of existing nationalities into independent sections; in Industry, co-operation under the immediate control of a democratic state; in Religion, the complete substitution of ethical for theological teaching.[1]

This was Socialism as seen through the spectacles of a well-disposed Positivist. The course of Bax's conversion to Socialism can be closely followed in his contributions to the journal *Modern Thought*. In May 1879 he asked: 'What is the highest form of consciousness of which we have any positive knowledge? The answer cannot fail to be *Humanity*, and the religion of the future must therefore be the Religion of Humanity.' In August of the same year he noticed that Socialism, like Positivism, was an attempt 'to render progress systematic'. By 1881 he was writing a tribute to Karl Marx in the course of which he remarked: 'We hear much sometimes from that excellent body of persons, the followers of M. Auguste Comte, of the moralisation of capital in the society of the future. I need scarcely say that to the Socialist this is much as though anyone should talk of the moralisation of brigandage.' By 1886 he could state that the

> religion of the Socialist differs from that of the Positivist. The Positivist seek to retain the forms, after the beliefs of which they are the expression have lost all meaning for him. The Socialist, whose social creed is his only religion, requires no travesty of Christian rites to aid him in keeping his ideal before him.[2]

To the end of his life Bax retained the most curious (to his colleagues) opinions respecting the unwisdom of conferring votes on women.

But it was not only, or perhaps even mainly, the doctrinaire

[1] *Echo*, 7 July 1878.
[2] E. B. Bax, *The Religion of Socialism* (4th edit.), 1908, p. 52.

Marxists who owed most to Positivism. At the end of the century Edward Bernstein, the leader of 'Revisionism', wrote to Beesly thanking him for sending a copy of a pamphlet by the working-class Positivist, Ellis, entitled: *The Capitalist as Ruler*. Bernstein asked for more copies and remarked: 'It deals with a subject I have much at heart, and if you had seen my writings in later years you would also know that from quite a different starting point I have come to views which, though not identical with yours, approach them in many respects.' He continued: 'In a recent book on the philosophical and sociological foundations of Marxism an Austrian Scholar, Professor Masryk of Prag [*sic*], has pointed out with much plausibility that Marx in this respect was much more indebted to Comte, and Comtism than is generally known.'[1]

After reporting that Positivism was growing in Germany, Bernstein went on to express his regret that he had only a secondhand acquaintance with Comte's writings. 'But there is one social principle in regard to which I am quite disposed to accept the Comtists' conception, and this is the acceptation(?) of social responsibility. The absolute neglect of this point is one of the main faults of Marxism, in economics as well as in politics.'[2]

If Bernstein's acquaintance with Comte was second-hand, the same cannot be said of his Fabian friends. The latest historian of the Fabian Society has recognised that Positivism was one of the tributaries of one of the two main streams from which Fabian thought emerged.[3] Indeed, in a vague way, the importance of Positivism in this connection has been recognised for a long time. Edward Pease recalled that the English followers of Comte were

> known to number amongst them some of the ablest thinkers of the day. It (Positivism) suggested a new heaven, of a sort, and it proposed a new earth, free from all the inequalities of wealth, the preventible suffering, the reckless waste of effort which we saw around us. At any rate, it was worth examination, and most of

[1] The suggestion that Marx drew on Comte is about as plausible as Professor Hayek's suggestion that all the important ideas in Saint Simon derive from Comte. See *The Counter Revolution of Science*.

[2] E. Bernstein to E. S. Beesly, 17 September 1899. BUC.

[3] A. M. McBriar, op. cit., p. 92.

the free-thinking men of that period read the *Positive Polity* and the other writings of the founder, and spent some Sunday mornings at the Little Conventicle in Lamb's Conduit Street (the Congrevian centre), or attended on Sunday evenings the Newton Hall lectures of Frederic Harrison.

Few could long endure [continued Pease] the absurdities of a made-up theology and a make-believe religion; and the Utopia designed by Comte was as impracticable and unattractive as Utopias generally are.[1]

When G. B. Shaw read this last passage he scribbled against it:

This last is a very rash sentence. All theologies are made up; all religions are make-believe; and most Utopias are attractive. I should say that the theology and religion, offered as new, were really both obsolete; and that the Utopia, unlike most Utopias, was so unattractive that one shuddered at its practicability.[2]

Shaw was an exception to the general rule among the major Fabians in being so unimpressed by Positivism. Annie Besant—who first came in touch with the National Secular Society while searching for Positivist literature—had a high regard for Comte. She even produced a short study of his life and work in which the French philosopher was acclaimed as the greatest thinker of the nineteenth century. She found the *Polity* to be 'noble in its scope, but childish in its details; grand in its aspirations, but puerile in its petty directives'. She concluded that despite his weakness and absurdities 'we may yet wisely learn from the mighty brain and loving heart of Auguste Comte much that will help us in our struggles towards a purer and more settled social state'.[3]

Besant's fellow Fabian Essayist, Sydney Olivier, was, for a time, even more deeply influenced by Comte, whom he judged to be 'very much the most comprehensive thinker we have had since Aristotle'.[4] In the early 'eighties he acted as Tutor to Henry Crompton's son and managed to let himself be persuaded that there was much in the Positivist Catechism—by far the

[1] E. R. Pease, *History of the Fabian Society*, 1916, pp. 18–19.

[2] G. B. Shaw's notes on Pease's MS. History (LSE).

[3] A. Besant, *Auguste Comte—His Philosophy, His Religion and His Sociology* (n.d.).

[4] M. Olivier, *Letters and Selected Writings of Sydney Olivier*, 1948, p. 62. Letter of 22 January 1884.

Webb

most bizarre of all Comte's productions. As he advanced towards Socialism he kept looking over his shoulder at Positivism. In 1884 he was still defending Comte and offering apologies for his omniscience and dogmatism. He read Hyndman's *Historical Basis of Socialism in England* and thought highly of it, but he took care to add a heavy Positivist rider: he charged the Marxist with 'ignoring the inevitable evils of a Socialist system, organised without as thorough a revolution in morality as would suffice to obviate the evils of the capitalist system, which if moralised, I am not *sure* is not economically superior'.[1] It is not surprising that Olivier's contribution to the famous volume of essays was on Socialism and Morals.

Like Bernstein and Olivier, Sydney Webb was ready to eke out his Socialism with some Positivist morality. After a paper which he read to the Society on 'The Economics of a Positivist Community' he was taken to task by Frank Podmore and others for being too sympathetic to Comte. 'He felt obliged to state I am not a Positivist, and I am by no means *sure* that the capitalist can be moralised, and I call myself a Socialist because I am desirous to remove from the capitalist the temptation to use his capital for his own exclusive ends. Still the capitalist may do good by accumulation.' When Podmore objected that Positivism could not stop violent fluctuations in the level of investment and employment, Webb simply trotted out the familiar Positivist answer about teaching consumers to be less fickle: 'so-called over-production is in reality the production of the wrong thing'. All that Webb added to the Positivist remedy for crises was a characteristic suggestion that they might be avoided 'to a great extent by an intelligent use of statistics'.[2]

Webb argued that: 'Positivists, so far as they have thought out their economic system, come clearly under the definition of Socialism.'[3] Perhaps this judgement made it easier for him to borrow from them when he had to meet objections urged against his own system. Thus, if it was suggested that the skilled worker might use full employment to force huge wages for himself, Webb's reply was that this worker must be reminded that 'other workers are helping him, and besides that; his brain and

[1] M. Olivier, *Letters and Selected Writings of Sydney Olivier*, 1948, p. 64. Letter of 22 January 1884.
[2] *The Practical Socialist*, February 1886. [3] Ibid., June 1886.

skill are not his alone; *it is the result of past ages*; a social and not an individual product'.[1]

One might cite many other instances of the impression Positivism made on the Fabians. It is amusing to recall that their treasured working man, W. L. Philips, was a Positivist and that he wrote the first tract, *Why are the Many Poor?*[2] But the two salient points to notice are probably first, that the Positivists were to some extent a model for the Fabians of how a small society of intellectuals might make the most (and the least) of its time and chances; second, that it was from the Positivists that some of them learnt the technique of social investigation. Beatrice Webb confessed that it was from Frederic Harrison that she first learnt the validity of Trade Unionism and factory legislation.[3] In his youth Harrison had projected a vast study of the working class and of labour institutions.[4] He and Beesly did write some pioneer articles in this field, but it was left to the Webbs to extend this work in their own incomparable fashion.

Philip Wicksteed had been a student under Beesly at University College Hall and had been immensely interested in Comte.[5] Did he, through his friendship with Trevor, impart something of the Positivist tradition to the Labour Church Movement? The Positivists sometimes described their own organisation as a 'Labour Church'.[6] How deeply was Fred Jowett impressed by Positivist critiques of parliamentarianism?[7] As has been said already, to evaluate all these bits and pieces of association would require a re-appraisal of the entire Socialist revival.

In words borrowed from George Eliot's Positivist prayer, the thoughts of the English Comtists may be credited with having shown that 'mild persistence' which urges man's search to

[1] *The Practical Socialist*, February 1886 (My emphasis).

[2] M. Cole, *The Story of Fabian Socialism* (1961), p. 6.

[3] B. Webb, *My Apprenticeship* (Pelican edition), p. 169.

[4] F. Harrison to E. S. Beesly, 8 December 1865. (Proposed a study of The Industry of the People: 'a full picture of the history and actual conditions of all the industrial occupations'. It was to cover social institutions, an estimate of the Poor Law, land laws and industrial legislation. It would begin with an examination of supposed economic laws.) The Webbs knew Beesly and Harrison's articles on Unions and on industrial relations in the *Fortnightly*.

[5] C. H. Herford, *P. H. Wicksteed* (1931), pp. 41–3. See also Wicksteed on Comte and Beesly in *Inquirer*, 22 May 1875 and July 1915.

[6] J. W. Overton, 'Labour Churches', *Industrial Review*, 29 September 1877.

[7] F. Brockway, *Socialism Over Sixty Years* (1946), p. 233.

'vaster issues'. The Positivists provide part of the evidence that in the 'sixties and 'seventies the dream of a new society to be ushered in by the supremacy of the working class was not abandoned but deferred. Perhaps that dream will always persist in a class society. Perhaps it will always be deferred in times when a rise in the real standard of life is such as to mask the perpetuation of inequality.

SOURCES
(UNPUBLISHED)

(A) Manuscripts

(These items have been arranged in an order which approximates to that of their relative usefulness in preparing the present volume.)

The George Howell Collection, Bishopsgate Institute, London (HC). (There is a good account of this collection in S. MacCoby, *English Radicalism, 1853–1886* (1938), pp. 409–10.)

The Frederic Harrison Papers, London School of Economics (FHC). (Thanks to the courtesy of the Librarian and his staff I was allowed to consult these papers very shortly after they had been acquired by the Library and before they had been fully catalogued. I concentrated on the Labour Movement side of Harrison's activities. This rich collection would allow anyone with sufficient talent to do with Harrison what Noel Annan has accomplished for *Leslie Stephen*.)

The Webb Trade Union Collection, London School of Economics (WTUC).

The E. S. Beesly Papers, University College London (BUC). (This is a small remnant of what must once have been one of the greatest sources for the study of Mid-Victorian Labour. One of the letters preserved here makes it almost certain that the vast majority of letters, including the ones which he received from Marx, were destroyed in the interests of Positivist unity.)

Positivist archives, Le Musée d'Auguste Comte, 10 rue de Monsieur Le Prince, Paris (MAC). (This remarkable Museum contains collections of letters from the English and other Positivists. When the Positivists' International discovers its historian, as it ought to do, this will be his major source.)

A Positivist Archive, The Richard Congreve Papers: The British Museum (PABM).

The Richard Congreve Papers, Wadham College, Oxford. (The residue of the Congreve collection.) Now in the Bodleian Library, Oxford.

343

E. S. Beesly to Karl Marx, some thirty letters sent on microfilm from the Institute of Marxism–Leninism, Moscow (MELI).

Archives of the International Institute of Social History, Amsterdam (IISH). (This is one of the world's most superb collections of materials relating to the history of Socialism and Labour Movements. I valued it mainly for its Minutes and other records of the International: material about Republicanism and the Land nationalisers: and a few scraps about the Positivists.)

The Home Office Papers, Public Record Office.

The Mill–Taylor Collection, London School of Economics.

In addition to the above I consulted the Gladstone, Bright, Dilke and Martineau Collections in the British Museum: the Henry Solly and the Broadhurst Collections in the London School of Economics: the T. H. Huxley Papers in Imperial College; the Mundella–Leader correspondence in the University of Sheffield: the Minutes of the London and the Bradford Trades Councils: the correspondence of the 9th Earl of Wemyss and March (by courtesy of the present Earl) and of the Thomas Larcom Collection in the National Library of Ireland (by courtesy of Chimen Abramsky who lent me his microfilm).

(B) Doctoral Theses

BELL, A. D., 'The Reform League from its origins to 1867' (Oxford, 1961). (Important for an understanding of the organisational character of the League.)

COLLINS, H., 'The British Sections of the First International' (Oxford, 1958).

COLTHAM, S., 'George Potter and the Bee-Hive Newspaper' (Oxford, 1956).

CROWLEY, D. W., 'Origins of the Revolt of the British Labour Movement from Liberalism, 1875–1906' (Brit. Lib. Pol. Sci., 1952). (As against Dr. Pelling's, *The Origins of the Labour Party*, this thesis places the main emphasis on a gradual shift in trade union attitudes.)

HARRISON, R., 'The English Positivists and Labour Movements' (Oxford 1955). (A few scholars may still find this thesis of some use in so far as it elaborates points of detail and contains an extensive bibliography.)

HOBSBAWM, E. J., 'Fabianism and the Fabians, 1884–1914' (Cambridge, 1950).

LAMB, W. K., 'British Labour and Parliament—1865 to 1893' (Brit. Lib. Pol. Sci., 1933).

McCREADY, H. W., 'Frederic Harrison and the British Working Class Movement, 1860–1875' (Harvard, 1952). (Professor Mc-Cready could find little evidence that Positivism touched the British working class in any way. He considered that the English Positivists were barely distinguishable from other middle-class radicals.)

PRESSWOOD, W. L., 'The Influence of Auguste Comte and the Rise of Positivism in England up to the formation of the English Positivist Society in 1867' (Sheffield, 1935).

(C) Books Printed for Private Circulation

(i) BRIDGES, M. A., *Recollections of J. H. Bridges, M.B.*, 1908. (Courtesy of the late Alfred Beesly.)

(ii) BRUCE, H. A., *Letters of Lord Aberdare*, Vol. 1, 1902. (British Museum.)

(iii) CROMPTON, A. (Preface), *The Message of Humanity—From the Pen of Thomas Carson*, 1908. (Courtesy of Dr. Baier, Hull.)

(iv) OVERTON, J. W., *Saul of Mitre Court*, 1879. (British Museum.)

(v) TORLESSE, F. H., *Some Account of John Henry Bridges and his Family*, 1912. (Courtesy of Mrs. D. Smith, London.)

(vi) WEMYSS AND MARCH, EARL OF, *Memories 1818–1912*, Vol. 1. (Courtesy of the 12th Earl.)

INDEX OF AUTHORS AND
WORKS CITED

INDEX OF NAMES AND
SUBJECTS